The American Historian

THE
AMERICAN HISTORIAN

A Social - Intellectual History of

the Writing of the American Past

HARVEY WISH
PROFESSOR OF HISTORY
WESTERN RESERVE UNIVERSITY

OXFORD UNIVERSITY PRESS
New York   1960

© 1960 BY OXFORD UNIVERSITY PRESS, INC.
LIBRARY OF CONGRESS CATALOGUE CARD NUMBER: 60-13202

Fourth printing, 1968

PRINTED IN THE UNITED STATES OF AMERICA

To

Merle Curti

A Leader in the Social Interpretation of Ideas

Preface

In recent years many historians both here and abroad have displayed keen interest in the underlying social and intellectual assumptions as well as the questions of craftsmanship in their discipline. The rise of intellectual history has stimulated historiography as a field, for it too is a study of ideas. As a result, numerous excellent books, articles, and dissertations have appeared dealing with currents of historiography, interpretive biographies of historians, and even with the long-neglected philosophies of history. By providing perspective upon the writing of history, the historiographer adds a much-needed dimension of depth and sophistication to man's efforts to discover his past. No apology is therefore required for a new survey of American historical writings treated largely, but not exclusively, from a social-intellectual point of view.

Since 1952, the author has made an intensive effort to read (or reread) the representative writers in American historiography with a primary view to determining their social conditioning. While the author is no relativist, but a believer in a reasonable idea of "objectivity," he finds that the social determinants are but too intrusive in the writings of so many of our leading historians and inspire caution on the part of serious readers. But the mid-twentieth century shows a more sophisticated historian, much more self-critical and therefore more fully aware of the subjective factors in the writing of history. He knows that it is very difficult indeed to escape the context of his world of social action.

During these years of research, the writer has tested his hypotheses in papers before our national historical societies and in graduate seminars in historiography that he has conducted at Western Reserve University, the University of Michigan, the University of Hawaii, and the Amerika Institut of the University of Munich.

The larger facets of American historiography are explored and illustrated by concrete examples of the great (and lesser) historians, although Prescott, Motley, and other American historians who have dealt primarily with non-American themes have been omitted. No effort has been made to be truly inclusive of all of the eminent historians of our day and no invidious distinction is intended when one is discussed and a score of perhaps abler scholars are not mentioned. While the writer has concentrated upon the actual books of the central figures, he has also taken into account the great volume of the critical secondary literature and suggested some of these in the footnotes. But since the text material itself offers a discussion of the chief books, gives their publication dates, and includes other relevant bibliographical data, these titles are omitted in the footnotes.

Many warm thanks are due to those with whom I discussed various aspects of this project, particularly to my colleagues, Dean Carl F. Wittke and Professor Mortimer R. Kadish, head of the Philosophy Department, both of whom read certain chapters, and to my graduate students in historiography. Credit is also due to my wife, Anne Wish, who assisted me at various stages of this laborious task.

HARVEY WISH

Western Reserve University
Cleveland, Ohio
June 1960

Contents

The American Historian

From Bradford to Mather:
The Puritan Mission in History

1

New Englanders read sympathetically the Old Testament epic of the Israelites wandering through the wilderness to a promised land under the guidance of God who transmitted the most minute directions to Moses. Calvinists felt that this story, but for a few alterations of names and places, was essentially their own. Since the Hebrews had forfeited their central role in history, the Puritans were now the Chosen People, the Choice Seed, the Elect, for they were guided, as Cotton Mather later declared in his history, by a new Moses, William Bradford, to Plymouth, and by another, John Winthrop, to the Massachusetts Bay Colony. God revealed his special providences in daily interventions that were now almost exclusively devoted to the Puritans—or so it seemed to New England historians. Only the captious might quibble that Massachusetts and Connecticut offered a small stage for this latter-day drama of redemption, but even they had to concede that the land of Canaan was much smaller.

These Protestant rebels had inherited the Christian interpretation of history and progress from the early church theologians, who saw God's design in the whole story of mankind, beginning with the Creation, on to the fall of Adam, an event which loosed tragic consequences for man; after that came the promised redemption by Christ, followed by the Second Coming and the Last Judgment, and the eventual triumph of heavenly purposes. It was less important to tell what actually happened than to discover the plan of God, whose nature could never be known save for the attributes inferred from His deeds. In somewhat modified form, this theory of history had been taken up and restated by St. Augustine in his *City of God.*

At a time when Alaric had sacked Rome, Augustine tried to answer those who saw in this event the logical consequence of the desertion of the pagan gods. He minimized the importance of the imperial capital by pointing out that only the City of God (the spiritual side) was everlasting, that the Earthly City (the flesh) was transitory. Between the two, there had been a long struggle since the fall of Adam. To him the great events of human history had emerged from a predestined divine plan. The rise and fall of man-made empires were therefore relatively unimportant in the higher scheme of things. He rejected the classical theory that history moved in endless cycles and dwelt on the idea of Christian progress on the road to final redemption. Despite the Renaissance revival of classical culture and ideas, including scientific techniques for rediscovering the past through textual criticism based on a secular philosophy, there remained much of this superstructure of the Christian interpretation of history for the Bradfords, the Winthrops, the Mathers, and the lesser historians of the seventeenth century in America.

To the Puritans, who followed the teachings of Geneva's theocrat, John Calvin, history had been deflected from its divine progress by Satan and the "inventions" of the Catholic hierarchy, which had displaced primitive apostolic Christianity of the first century by Rome's worldly power and pagan splendor. To keep to the right course, Puritans often resorted to unsparing self-examination, recorded faithfully in detailed, introspective diaries; and their leaders looked into contemporary history itself for proof that their policies reflected a divine purpose. Under these circumstances, history was no ordinary branch of literature intended to entertain or to satisfy those who enjoyed the past for its own sake; it ranked next to the Bible itself as a revelation of God's will. As Thomas Prince, a son of Puritans, once testified in his history, "Next to the sacred History, and that of the Reformation, I was from my early youth instructed in the History of this country." In 1682, the Massachusetts General Court voted fifty pounds to publish the Reverend William Hubbard's history of New England's Indian wars and began their preamble with these words: [1]

Whereas it hath binn thought necessary and a Duty incumbent upon us, to take notice of all Occurrences and Passages of God's Providence towards the People of this Jurisdiction since their first arrivall in these Parts, which may remayne to Posterity . . .

Such uses for history are suggested in the very title of Captain Edward Johnson's book, *The Wonder-Working Providence of Sion's Saviour in New England* (1654). Like other Puritan historians, he saw evidences of God's design in the events of everyday life rather than in the classical accounts of dominant personalities. To Calvinists, history served as functional a purpose as their utilitarian (though not artless) architecture. It is noteworthy that they were also indebted to St. Augustine for their emphasis on predestination, the idea of an inscrutable and arbitrary God, and the total dependence of man on God's gift of grace.

The writing of history with a religious motif was spurred on by the vogue for interpretive church histories since the Reformation. Few New England home libraries were without some of these controversial theological histories. The Catholic Counter-Reformation, led by the Jesuits who based their narratives upon the rich Vatican archives, put the Reformers on their mettle. Jesuit missionaries and explorers in the New World were to benefit future historians of the American and Canadian colonial period by the voluminous annual reports they sent home to France, known to historians as the *Jesuit Relations* (1610-1791). German Protestant princes had struck back at the earlier Catholic historians by sponsoring the monumental and authoritative *Magdeburg Centuries* (1559-74), the first general history of the Christian church written from a Reformer's standpoint. In Bradford's time, this served as a point of departure for Calvinist histories, since the *Magdeburg Centuries* ended its narrative with the year 1400. Thus the battle of the church historians raged alongside the bloody religious wars.[2]

In New England households, as in Old England, Protestants read and re-read a popular history of the bitter persecutions suffered by their co-religionists under "Bloody Queen Mary" as well as the story of earlier Christian martyrs. This was John Foxe's *Actes and Monuments of these latter and perillous Dayes,* better known as *The Book of Martyrs.* An Anglican priest who had become attached to Calvinist doctrines, he published his book in 1566, and it caught on so rapidly that an eighth English edition appeared in 1641. Unfortunately, accuracy was not Foxe's strong point, and his book served to embitter Protestants still more against Catholics. His history kept before the public the agonies of three hundred Protestant men and women who had perished in the fires of Smithfield and elsewhere. This detailed martyrology strengthened the Puritan idea that their sacrifices had rescued primitive Christianity from the Roman anti-Christ.

But the Puritans and other American settlers were heirs of the Renaissance as well as of the Reformation. The Puritans, as recent scholars have shown, were no mere cult of "enthusiasm" which used emotion to displace logic and classical rationality. They might dismiss Aristotle as too "papist" because of his authority among Catholic scholastics, but many, among them Increase Mather, read him reverently nevertheless. Puritan theology had been refined in the universities, particularly at Cambridge, whose Emanuel College served as the model for Harvard. The logical principles of the Calvinist scholar, Peter Ramus (or Ramée) had tightened the inner intellectual coherence of Puritan thought. Out of the Elizabethan Renaissance came a mighty intellectual ferment that influenced the middle class, so many of whom were Calvinists. The Reformation urge for enough literacy to read the Bible was supplemented by the Renaissance ideal of the educated man in search of truth about nature.

Puritan libraries reflected the rich cultural tradition of middle-class Calvinism. Governor William Bradford of Plymouth left a library of eighty volumes which included not only the popular church histories and theology reference works (including Foxe's indispensable *The Book of Martyrs*), but also such classics as Virgil, Ovid, Livy, Plutarch, and Thomas More's more contemporary *Utopia;* among the modern histories was the widely read Walter Raleigh's *History of the World.* John Harvard's large gift of books to the college named after him was heavily theological in content, but it included the leading Greek and Roman historians. At the end of the seventeenth century Cotton Mather possessed a library that showed his broad humanistic interest. In his writings he made frequent learned references to Thucydides, Xenophon, Tacitus, Sallust, Suetonius, and other ancient historians.[3]

Bradford, more than other Puritans, practiced the scientific ideal set down by Thucydides in narrating the Peloponnesian Wars, "It rests partly on my own experiences and things I have seen with my own eyes, partly on the witness of others, which I have verified by the severest and minutest tests possible." Few New Englanders were as meticulous as Bradford in treasuring letters and manuscripts to refresh their recollections of the facts; nor were they in as favorable a position to know the truth. Plymouth's governor echoed the phrases of Thucydides regarding historical research and thought of himself too as weighing causes, motives, and processes; he tried to write, as the Greek had put it, "exactly how things happened in the past."

While the supernatural bulked too large in Puritan histories to put them in the same class as the secular work of Thucydides and Dionysius, Calvinist historians had a sense of historical purpose and religious destiny that the rationalist Greeks lacked. It is true that many a classical writer lost his perspective in emphasizing the irrational intrusion of "fate" and chance in human affairs, but this tendency was largely minimized in Herodotus, "father of history," Thucydides, and Dionysius, among other noted historians; it was Dionysius of Halicarnassus who coined the famous adage that history was "philosophy teaching by examples" and minimized the role of accident in explaining events. Both Greeks and Puritans had in common the idea of a Golden Age from which men had fallen. For the Greeks, this meant a cyclic theory of history in which the rise and decline of civilizations marked the fortunes of men, and no true progress was possible, considering the nature of fate and human weakness. Christians, however, began with the fall in the garden of Eden, but they retained a religious notion of progress which would be fulfilled by the second coming of Christ, and, as Carl Becker has put it, "then the earthly city would be destroyed and all the faithful be gathered with God in the heavenly city, there to dwell in perfection forever." While the Greeks therefore minimized their own "ancient history" in favor of the more contemporary, the Puritans went back to "primitive Christianity" as a necessary point of departure in their cosmology.[4]

Sometimes the learned classical references of colonial writers were mere affectation intended to impress the reader. The astonishing historical erudition of the Puritan poet-historian, Anne Bradstreet, hailed widely as the Tenth Muse, has turned out upon inspection by a skeptical scholar to be almost completely second-hand. While New England libraries did contain copies of the histories of Berosus, the Babylonian annalist, and many more of Plutarch, both of whom she quoted too easily, Anne Bradstreet preferred to borrow these citations from Sir Walter Raleigh's well-known *History of the World* (1614). Raleigh had written it while he was imprisoned in the Tower of London on a false charge of treason. Like so many medieval chroniclers, Raleigh had begun his history with the Creation and treated the past as a moral lesson to be derived from his loose miscellany of topics ranging from politics and law to theology and magic. Anne Bradstreet's versified history of the ancient world, *The Exact Epitomie of the Four Monarchies,* was a superficial moralistic treatment of evil kings with haughty hearts, palace intrigues, feuds, personal incidents, and biblical digressions—always, of course, from the Puritan's Bible, the Geneva Version. Her facts and interpretations were frequently mere paraphrases of Raleigh's *History*.

The many Englishmen who liked to read history books were greatly stimulated by the Elizabethan vogue for translating the classics. Literate Puritans knew Plutarch largely through Sir Thomas North's rendering of the *Lives*, with its fascinating accounts of Pompey, Alexander, Caesar, Anthony, Cicero, and other great leaders of ancient times. Exciting geographic discoveries and adventurous voyages inspired many contemporary books on history and geography. New World historians leaned heavily upon the geographic and historical works of the Oxford scholar and colonization promoter, Richard Hakluyt. His accounts of discoveries by French, Spanish, and English seamen and explorers were widely circulated long after his death, as well as within his lifetime. In 1589, he had published *The Principall Navigations, Voiages, and Discoveries of the English Nation . . .* which was later praised as "the prose epic of the modern English nation" by James Anthony Froude, the historian. Many of Hakluyt's precious manuscripts, together with other original sources were later gathered and edited for publication by an uninspired, but very widely read Anglican priest, Samuel Purchas. This prolific compiler left voluminous data on sea voyages and land travel by Englishmen since earliest recorded times. Hakluyt's activity as an investor in the London and Virginia companies gave his unique geographic and historical knowledge a promotional aspect; but Purchas's work, which is so often coupled with that of Hakluyt, seemed innocent of any motivation save the collecting of antiquities. Finally, there were the numerous Elizabethan and Tudor plays which frequently referred to New World life and discoveries.

The chance of writing scientific history in that day was naturally restricted by the benumbing inheritance of magic, superstition, and fable, even among the most literate and sophisticated. Witches and mermaids were taken seriously, even by members of the Royal Society. While John Milton spoke of a new day of freedom of speech and liberal social institutions, he began his *History of Britain* with a reference to the giant Albion and the Trojan War. James Westfall Thompson, the historiographer, illustrates the lack of critical historical knowledge during the era of Elizabeth and the Stuarts by taking the case of Sir Edward Coke, England's greatest legal mind: [5]

Coke believed that Britain had been settled by Brut, the grandson of Aeneas, about 1000 B.C.; that the common law, much as it was in his own time, was established then; that England's system of land tenures and a government of kings, lords, and commons existed in Britain centuries before Rome was founded; and that Alfred the Great established Oxford University.

Thompson could have said much the same of the brilliant contemporary of Coke, John Selden, and of other eminent English leaders and scholars.

2

This mixture of fact and myth, of the critical classical spirit and Reformation zealotry, permeated seventeenth-century Puritan literature, of which history was a large part. William Bradford drew deeply of this compound in writing his odyssey of the Pilgrim Fathers, *Of Plymouth Plantation*. It was written in piecemeal fashion while he was governor of the colony (1630-46). Although the book circulated only in manuscript before 1856, colonial historians borrowed so slavishly from it that Bradford's version of the Pilgrim story became substantially the early American epic. For example, Nathaniel Morton, Bradford's nephew, in writing the first general history of the province, *New England's Memoriall* (1669), had little more to say about Plymouth— even down to the same phraseology—that had not already appeared in Bradford's work. Cotton Mather had obviously consulted *Of Plymouth Plantation* in preparing his own history of New England, *Magnalia Christi Americana*, published in 1702. This indebtedness to Bradford continued among many historians and chroniclers of the following century, notably in Thomas Prince's *Chronological History of New England* (1736), a work widely praised, and in Thomas Hutchinson's craftsmanlike *History of Massachusetts Bay*. Thereafter the Bradford manuscript disappeared from this hemisphere for several generations, turning up finally in London. Some historians have assumed that Hutchinson, the embittered Tory, carried off the manuscript in his flight to England, but New England's modern historian, Samuel E. Morison, has argued against this theory and suggests that perhaps some British soldier took it as a souvenir. Although the manuscript was not returned until 1897 after many appeals and delays, a copy of it served the American publishers for the two editions issued in 1856, one under the imprint of the Massachusetts Historical Society, the other (for the general market) by Little, Brown, and Company.

Bradford, like his fellow-Brownists or Separatists of Plymouth, enjoyed little formal schooling, although he did not share the contempt

for the intellectual life held by the English Brownists. The son of a
Yorkshire farmer in good circumstances, he had been converted in his
youth to Calvinist tenets and came under the influence of the erudite
and deeply devout William Brewster of Scrooby Village. He read the
Geneva English Bible so closely that many of its literary phrases stud
the pages of his history of Plymouth. Intensely interested in both
theology and the classics, he mastered Latin, Hebrew, and Greek.
Cotton Mather, himself the soul of erudition, wrote enthusiastically
of Bradford's linguistic talents and claimed that he knew theology
so well "that he was an irrefragable disputant against the errors, especially those of Anabaptism, which with trouble he saw rising in his
colony; wherefore he wrote some significant things for the confutation
of those errors." [6]

After fleeing with the Scrooby congregation to the Netherlands, he
set himself up successfully as a merchant and a weaver, and eventually
sailed on the *Mayflower* to the New World in 1620. On the death of
Governor John Carver, he assumed the post of head of the Plymouth
colony, holding it during repeated elections until 1656. At the same
time he prospered from his investments in fishing and fur trading, but
did not use his official post to become the great landowner that he
might easily have been.

Bradford's "plaine stile" reflected the Puritan ideal of simplicity and
asceticism, harking back to the example of Christ born in a humble
manger and also to primitive Christianity. The Calvinists, whose fear
of Romishness in England led them to remove church images, white-
wash their "meetinghouse" walls, expel choir singers and organs, and
avoid other relics of Catholicism, liked to pride themselves upon their
simple unadorned literary style. Yet literary unpretentiousness, like
honest Puritan functionalism in architecture and furniture, developed
its own aesthetic qualities, as Bradford's straightforward style reveals.
Those who have taken too literally Bradford's profession of a plain
style have been surprised by his mastery of many literary ornaments—
the balanced sentence, antithesis, alliteration, and a few Elizabethan
puns. Even in less gifted hands, the plain style among American Puritan historians usually escaped dullness or crudity and aimed for the
craftsmanship of the English Bible and *Pilgrim's Progress*.[7]

Plymouth's governor, as already noted, felt the same solicitude for
accuracy in history that Thucydides had professed. He evinced "a
singular regard unto the simple trueth in all things at least as near
as my slender judgmente can attaine the same." Where he was the
sole witness for major events, he incorporated many letters by his asso-

ciates. Certainly, he was in an ideal position to know the facts, for Plymouth started out with no more than a hundred people and rose to less than a thousand by 1650 when the history ended. Naturally the "trueth" was seen through the eyes of a thoroughgoing Puritan who sought in the pages of history God's purpose and the destiny of the Pilgrims. He began with the Puritan cosmology:

It is well knowne unto the godly and judicious, how ever since the first breaking out of the lighte of the gospell in our Honourable Nation of England (which was the first of nations whom the Lord adorned ther with, affter that grosse darknes of popery which had covered and overspred the Christian world), what warrs and oppossissions ever since, Satan hath raised, maintained and continued against the Saincts [the Puritans], from time to time, in one sorte or other.

He went on to recount briefly Satan's persecutions through the agency of Queen Mary of "worthy martyrs," documenting these facts with the authority of Foxe's *The Book of Martyrs*. The historic quarrel, as he saw it, was between those who sought the simplicity of the gospel without "the mixture of men's inventions" and the papist-minded who insisted on bishops and anti-Christian ceremonies.

His pious desire to reveal the "spetiall providence of God" led him to dwell upon the supernatural intervention of God in the voyage of the Pilgrims to the New World. There was, for example, the "proud and very profane yonge man" of the crew who cursed the sick during an Atlantic storm and was himself struck down by illness and thrown overboard. But Bradford seldom allowed his concern for supernatural causes to conceal natural reasons for surprising events; thus he spoke of the New England earthquake of 1638 as evidence of the arbitrary and inscrutable will of the Calvinist God, but he added some pertinent comments on the natural aspects of the earthquake. He expressed shock at the crime wave of 1642, which included several cases of sodomy and other sex cases as well as the more conventional types of sin, and speculated that "the Divell may carrie a greater spite against the churches of Christ and the gospell hear" because Satan had more power in heathen lands than in Christian ones. But he had more matter-of-fact explanations also:

Marvilous it may be to see and consider how some kind of wickednes did grow and breake forth here, in a land where the same was so much witnesed against and so narrowly looked into, & severly punished when it was knowne; as in no place more, or so much, that I have known or heard of, insomuch that they have been somewhat censured, even by moderate and good men, for their severitie in punishments. . . . An other reason may be, that it may be in this case as it is with waters when their streames are stopped or dammed up, when they gett passage they flow with more violence, and make more noys and disturbance, than when they are suffered to rune quietly in their owne chanels. So wickednes being here more stopped by strict laws, and the same more nerly looked unto, so as it cannot rune in a comone road of liberty as it would, and is inclined, it searches every wher and at last breaks out wher it getts vente.

However, he concluded that there were not necessarily more crimes here than elsewhere, but that discovery and punishment were swift and more thorough.

Bradford's Puritanism was tempered by his own native kindliness. Like others of his sect he shared the medieval view that there was no freedom to err on doctrinal matters, though one might be charitable in judging the misled. He could not go as far toward the ideal of modern toleration as did his onetime neighbor, Roger Williams, who had served briefly as a church teacher at Plymouth but had uttered and then practiced "strang oppinions" contrary to Calvinist doctrines. Of him Bradford said mildly that he was "a man godly & zealous, having many precious parts but very unsettled in judgmente." He could write as a partisan, however, when it came to some of the controversies which affected his administration of the colony.

Posterity has not quite forgiven Bradford for his savage condemnation of what seemed to be innocent fun at Merrymount when Thomas Morton, the "petiefogger," and his friends were "dancing and frisking together" with the Indian maidens around a Maypole. On this occasion, Bradford permitted himself one of his rare puns about the "idol" or "idle" that the merrymakers worshiped. His Puritan condemnation of idleness and paganism appears again in his unfriendly treatment of Christmas observance; besides, Puritans did not regard Christmas as the true date of the nativity. In the case of Merrymount, so Bradford's defenders have pointed out, the Puritans had a genuine grievance in the fact that Morton was arming the Indians.

In this case, however, Bradford was not the sole historian to give posterity his version of the facts and their interpretation. Morton himself, gifted with a ready wit and fluent style, left a history, *The New England Canaan*, which casts ridicule on "Captain Shrimpe" (Miles Standish) and the Pilgrim force which came to arrest him and destroy his habitation. Morton satirized the Puritans' bigotry (he was an Anglican) and their hatred of "revels and merriment after the old English custome." His book appeared in Amsterdam in 1637, being one of the earliest published histories dealing with the colony and written by a resident. As for the Indians, whom he befriended and whose company he genuinely enjoyed, he observed, "I have found the Massachusetts Indians more full of humanity than the Christians." Like many Englishmen, Morton had an earthy love of things and a sensualism that his ascetic Puritan neighbors were struggling against. The frank words of his verses in praise of Hymen's joys must have nettled the Pilgrims. Morton was among the first American historians to develop the theme of the blue-nosed Puritans; later, another Anglican, Samuel Peters, was to write a "lying history of Connecticut" (as New Englanders called it), which exaggerated the myth of the blue laws. Finally, Hawthorne and his generation created a stereotype of the Puritan in his worst aspects, and then in the days of H. L. Mencken the anti-Puritan interpretation became the norm.[8]

While Bradford was too much the medievalist to admire the tenets of laissez-faire, he showed considerable satisfaction when the first communal experiment in his colony broke down. Believing in the Puritan principle of "to each according to his work," he condemned the "conceite of Platos" which had sanctioned communism—although he said nothing about its religious sanction. He pointed out that this experiment had overlooked human nature, that men would not work for other men's wives, and that the able refused to be satisfied with the same returns as the shiftless and incompetent.

There seems little reason to doubt Bradford's favorable picture of Plymouth's relations with the Indians, for his frankness in regard to the shortcomings of his people is reassuring. It was under Governor Bradford, apparently, that the first case occurred of an Englishman being tried and executed for the murder of an Indian. He observed that "some of the rude and ignorant sort murmured that any English should be put to death for the Indians." However, he was frank enough to note the argument for expediency in thus dealing fairly with the Indians.

3

John Winthrop, the first governor of Massachusetts Bay, plays a very favorable role in Bradford's history of Plymouth, though his own writings show a more conservative, aristocratic flavor than is true of the other's work. Unlike Bradford, he was college-bred, having studied at Cambridge and at Gray's Inn before he became a successful attorney and justice of the peace. Unlike the impecunious Puritan émigrés, he had been a lord of a manor in Groton; his marriage to an heiress had definitely improved his worldly lot and perhaps affected his social outlook. After a Puritan quarrel with the crown, in which he had taken a leading role, Winthrop sponsored the colonization project of the Massachusetts Bay Company and arrived in 1630, helping to found the town of Boston.

For twelve years, Winthrop was re-elected annually as governor until his death in 1649. Like a true Puritan he found time to prepare a voluminous diary, the famous *Journal* which is often referred to as *The History of New England from 1630 to 1649*. He made no secret of his inflexible religious and political (and economic) orthodoxy and presided with complete lack of sympathy at the trial which forced the expulsion of Anne Hutchinson for her heretical opinions in the Antinomian controversy. Anne had leaned toward a kind of "inner-light" mysticism that made ministers superfluous and hence threatened the very basis of the Puritan theocracy. Defenders of the Puritan position, like Perry Miller, believe that Anne Hutchinson's "enthusiasms" played havoc with the intellectual foundation of Calvinism and would have reduced Puritanism to the level of so many pietistic cults which substituted emotionalism for reason and philosophy. In Winthrop was combined the Hebraic theocratic beliefs of Geneva and the medieval aristocratic views held by a man of substantial property.

Historians have often quoted Winthrop's dictum that "a Democratie is, among most civill nations accounted the meanest and worst of all formes of Government—it hath been allwayes of least continuance & fullest of trouble." This judgment was easily reached by classically trained officials who thought of democracy in terms of Cleon, the demagogic tanner, and of the dangers of the "proletariat" in ancient Rome. Like the other middle-class members of the Bay Colony's ruling class, he tried to carry over the medieval idea of wage-fixing to the New World; as an honest historian, he had to record that this idea failed to work in a wilderness offering free lands, diverse economic opportunities, and social mobility:

> The court having found by experience that it would not avail by any law to redress the excessive rates of laborers' and workmen's wages, etc. (for being restrained, they would either remove to other places where they might have more, or else being able to live by planting and other employments of their own, they would not be hired at all,) it was therefore referred to the several towns to set down rates among themselves. This took better effect, so that in a voluntary way . . . they were brought to more moderation than they could by compulsion. But it held not long.

Winthrop's *Journal*, like Bradford's work, is full of matters of colonial policy and is also concerned with contemporary customs and manners. However, his style lacks the grace of Bradford's, though he shares the introspective manner of the Plymouth governor and the Puritan belief that God revealed his purpose in the most trivial as well as in the most weighty everyday events. Winthrop saw a clear connection between the fact that a monster was born to the wife of a settler and the coincidence that she was "notoriously infected with Mrs. Hutchinson's errors." He even had the body of the still-born examined and thought he detected horns, claws, and scales; he recorded his suspicion that the midwife was a witch. In that era when science still permitted a belief in witches and the Old World killed thousands of suspects charged with practicing black magic (so contemporaries tell us), Winthrop was not unduly naïve. The reader must therefore not be surprised to read Winthrop's observation that the mice in his son's extensive library ate only the pages of the Romish Anglican prayer book, but significantly left all else untouched!

Winthrop also shared the Calvinist faith in the great Puritan epic of mankind that was told with such inspiration in John Milton's *Paradise Lost,* the story of the age-old struggle between God and Satan. As Winthrop explains in one passage, "Satan bestirred himself to hinder the progress of the gospel." He saw eye to eye with Bradford and his contemporaries in presenting the history of New England as revelatory of God's plan for the Protestant Reformation and the redemption of all mankind. Winthrop's *Journal,* though it was first printed only in part in 1790 and then appeared completely only in 1825-26, served historians and laymen while it circulated in manuscript. For all its drawbacks, it remained for many years the best history of the Massachusetts Bay Colony.

The Puritan traits of Bradford and Winthrop reappear in such lesser contemporaries as Captain Edward Johnson of Woburn, Massachusetts. This self-made colonial businessman, Indian trader, and official was scarcely a whit behind Winthrop in defending Puritan orthodoxy and blasting such heretics as Anne Hutchinson. In 1654, a London firm published his ultra-orthodox history, *The Wonder-Working Providence of Sion's Saviour in New England.* In his militant style, he found fresh illustrations for the fact that the Puritans were God's chosen people. He stated confidently,

. . . here thou shalt find, the time when, the manner how, the cause why, and the great successe which it hath pleased the Lord to give, to this handfull of his praying Saints in N. Engl.

Like Bradford he deals with social life and the affairs of trade. Always God protected His Saints, inflicted smallpox on the Indians while leaving the colonists untouched, and singled out evildoers for exemplary afflictions. The narrative, like the *History of Plymouth Colony,* is interlarded with poetry in the mode of Elizabethan times or after the model of Puritan psalms. Because Johnson's frequently inaccurate and biased account was the first published general account of that colony, his influence upon the historians of New England was far greater than his merits deserved.

4

Above all, pioneer Americans of this day and their descendants for many generations liked to read the histories of Indian wars and the captivities of white prisoners, especially those written by facile New England storytellers. Sheer intrinsic interest as well as skillful narrative gave some of these books a long lease on life. As in the case of the standard Hollywood version of the ruthless redskin in the American West, this era of historians rarely bothered to study the substance of the Indian's grievances. While New England had its saint-like defenders of the rights and humanity of the aborigines in John Eliot, "Apostle of the Indians," and in Roger Williams, beloved by the Narragansetts, the ethnocentric Puritan had difficulty in understanding other races save as lesser breeds without the Law. Besides, the bitter realities of frontier savagery, kidnapings of whites, and callous brutalities on both sides made the contemporary historian a hot partisan. Too few followed Bradford in recording the aid that the Indians gave to the early settlers, and even he could not avoid sounding an occasional note of superiority.

A notable exception to the rule of anti-Indian historians was Daniel Gookin, a Puritan *émigré* from Berkeley's intolerant Virginia, who served as a major-general of Massachusetts' militia and as superintendent of Indians in that colony. Gookin's two books on the Indians, which remained unpublished that century, showed a humanity akin to John Eliot's. He told of his efforts to save the more pacific tribes from the indiscriminate slaughter wreaked upon their race during the great Indian wars. Much more in the standard groove of Indian stories were the tales of the "perfidious cruel and hellish Monsters" told by the Reverend William Hubbard in *The History of the Indian Wars in New England;* this was printed in London in 1677 and covered the Indian wars up to that year. Hubbard was an erudite man and wealthy landowner who had been a judge and an acting president of Harvard during the absence of Increase Mather. His reputation was to rest largely on his *A General History of New England,* which did not go too far beyond the facts of Winthrop's *Journal.* Hubbard's impatience with the Indians was partly due to their annoying resistance to conversion, a fact that he attributed to Satan's envy of the prosperity of the church. He pictured inoffensive colonists pitted against sadistic savages and defended their firing inhabited wigwams in the cold of winter, even though this meant killing Indian women and children. However, Hubbard recognized that the Indians did have grievances against the white man, such as the land piracy practiced by colonial leaders. Another popular anti-redskin account left to posterity was *A History of the Pequot War* (1677) written by John Mason, who captained a mixed force of colonials and friendly Indians. His story of the victorious campaign had the virtue of being a thriller based on first-hand experiences.

Perhaps no colonial raconteur absorbed the interest of so many generations of readers devoted to Indian tales as the autobiographical writer of the *Narrative of the Captivity and Restauration of Mrs. Mary Rowlandson* (1682). During King Philip's War this daughter of a wealthy landowner and wife of a leading minister had been carried off, together with her three children, by Indians who burnt her village and wiped out most of its inhabitants. For eleven weeks she was held captive until released upon the payment of a ransom. During the Indian retreat she had to suffer many hardships, but she admitted receiving many kindnesses from her captors. This book, she said, was intended "to be to her a memorandum of God's dealings" and "to declare the Works of the Lord." Publishers in London and in Cambridge (Massachusetts) eagerly brought out repeated editions of this engrossing account; since then more than thirty editions and reprints have appeared. College anthologies of literature have brought Mrs. Rowlandson's woes to the attention of present-day youth.

The most prolific writer of the century was Cotton Mather (1663-1728), leader of the Old Guard Puritans and the pedantic son of Harvard's president, Increase, who had written a history of Indian wars. Cotton had entered Harvard as a child prodigy who had spoken Latin and Greek even as a youth; he was graduated at fifteen. No colonial writer could match even remotely his output of 468 titles (although some of these may be erroneously attributed to him). But his range of interests, though heavily theological as one might expect from a Puritan pastor, comprised modern science, history, and the classics. The darkest stain on the reputation of Cotton and his father is the fact that they contributed the weight of their authority to the witchcraft frenzy. Cotton's *Wonders of the Invisible World* (1693) was perhaps no worse than similarly credulous accounts by contemporaries, even by members of the Royal Society, but it furnished dangerous ammunition for the witchhunters of Salem and elsewhere; however, by 1700 he changed his mind on the subject.

As the eighteenth century began, Mather showed an increasing affinity for the most advanced positions taken by science and a growing tolerance for men of other churches. Together with his father he kept Harvard abreast of the new Copernican-Galileo science at a time when Europe's older universities hesitated to teach the heresy that the earth moved around the sun. To say that the earth was not the center of the universe seemed to deny the biblical account of Joshua praying to keep the sun stationary so that he might have more daylight to rout his enemies. Cotton Mather had courageously defended the new practice of inoculation for smallpox (it was a dangerous form of treatment) against the charge that the inoculators were murderers.

In the filio-pietistic vein of Puritan historians, Mather wrote the ponderous *Magnalia Christi Americana: or the Ecclesiastical History of New England,* which appeared in London in 1702 and was so popular as to be republished in Hartford in two volumes in 1820. This large volume of narrative, sermons, and biographies was intended to stem the tide of secularism that had come with the Enlightenment. The *Magnalia* continued the Puritan theme of the Chosen People endeavoring to build a New Jerusalem despite the snares of Satan. Readers learned about numerous divine providences by land and sea, the trials of witchcraft, the struggle of the upright magistrates against heretics, and the remarkable conversions among the Indians. Such an orthodox picture (one overlooks his claims to objectivity), reinforced by his pride in New England's leaders and institutions, explains his assertion that church history ranked above all other historical forms.

Though the author liked to quote Plutarch and other classical historians, he did not emulate their critical spirit, for he warmly endorsed the political and economic orthodoxies of the Puritan fathers as well as their religious dogmatism. Governor Winthrop's strictures on liberty seemed admirable. However, in discussing Anne Bradstreet, Mather revealed a most enlightened attitude toward the role of women in shaping civilization. "Reader, America justly admires the learned women of the other hemisphere," he said. On this side the oft-reprinted poems of Anne Bradstreet "have afforded a grateful entertainment unto the ingenious, and a monument for her memory beyond the stateliest marbles."

Mather professed to follow the Greek historian, Polybius, in eschewing "the vices and villanies" of men and in commemorating their virtues, but he did not apply this rule to those outside the orthodox field —the "most venomous" Quakers, heretics like Anne Hutchinson, "papists," and bloodthirsty or shiftless Indians. He closed with an appeal that religious backsliders cease their apostasies and that the country save itself from the current "degeneracy." The reader closes his work with the wish that Mather had not "seasoned" his work with so many Greek and Latin quotations, far-fetched classical allusions, and lengthy biblical digressions which confuse the narrative. Scholars have complained of unforgivable omissions and inaccuracies, but the *Magnalia* is still not without some value, even for the most discriminating present-day historian.

5

While New England Puritans gloried in their prolific historians, the other seventeenth-century colonies had relatively few to boast of, and these were more concerned with promoting colonies than in portraying the mind of a people. Most of them lagged behind the numerous Spanish and Portuguese historians of the discovery era in describing analytically the geography, institutions, customs, ethnography, and developments in the New World. Spain and Portugal, unlike England, gave material sponsorship to their colonial historians. Literate men in the American colonies were well informed regarding the exploits of Cabeza da Vaca, De Soto, Coronado, and others—not to mention many French explorers and colonizers like Champlain—through the English translations of Purchas or the writings of Richard Hakluyt.

Scholarly editors of colonial histories, like J. Franklin Jameson, have bewailed the dearth of genuine history-writing outside of New England. Diligent translators of the Dutch narratives of New Amsterdam find no Bradford or Winthrop, only a miscellany of mediocre accounts of Hudson's voyages, the climate, the Indians, wars, and local customs. The compiler of the *Journal of New Netherland* (1647) has this enlightening information about Indian beliefs: "They have no knowledge at all of God, no divine worship, no law, no justice; the strongest does what he pleases and the youths are master." Perhaps the best of the Dutch accounts are the *Journal of Jasper Danckaerts, 1679-1680,* which is actually a diary rather than a history, but it contains some valuable accounts of sects like the Labadists and tells of early Harvard—the latter a rather derogatory description. Danckaerts observed that the smoke-laden atmosphere of Harvard gave a peculiar impression to visitors. "It certainly must be also a tavern," he thought as he climbed the stairs to the study room.

The most notable exception to the rule of sterility in historical writing ouside of New England was John Smith, the noted founder of Virginia, global adventurer, and versatile historian. Bradford and other colonials kept Smith's books as valued parts of their libraries, especially his early description of New England's topography; and the Virginian's sympathetic attitude toward the Puritans must have endeared him to many New Englanders. The young soldier of fortune who became the president of the Virginia colony could recount exciting battles and hairbreadth escapes that he had known in France, Italy, and in Turkish domains before coming to Jamestown in 1607.

When Captain Smith replied to his London critics in 1608, he was instrumental in publishing English America's first book: *A True Relation of Such Occurrences and Accidents of Noate as Hath Hapned in Virginia since the First Planting of That Collony.* Much of this and other writings were edited together with some new material in 1624 as *The Generall Historie of Virginia, New England, and the Summer Isles.* Only in this amorphous later work does Smith first tell the story of how Pocahontas, daughter of Powhatan, saved his life while he was a prisoner:

After some six weeks fatting amongst those Salvage Courtiers, at the minute of my execution, she hazarded the beating out of her owne braines to save mine; and not onely that, but so prevailed with her father, that I was safely conducted to James towne: where I found about eight and thirtie miserable poore and sicke creatures, to keepe possession of all those large territories of Virginia; such was the weaknesse of this poore Commonwealth, as had the Salvages not fed us, we directly had starved.

A host of scholars, led by Henry Adams, have taken the belated record of the Pocahontas episode as proof of the untrustworthiness of Smith as a historian; otherwise, it has been reasoned, he would surely have included so fascinating a story in *A True Relation* or told it to some contemporary writer on Virginia. However, the charge is actually inconclusive. Other attacks on Smith's self-praise, especially his habit of dwelling at length on his victories, also do not affect any sound judgment of Smith as a historian. The vital role of John Smith is vouched for by the journals of contemporaries. Dr. Lyon G. Tyler, editor of Smith's writings, observes, "Smith was often inaccurate in his estimates as to time and place and often very prejudiced in his judgments of others, but that is far from saying that he could mistake plain objects of sense or deliberately concoct a story having no foundation." [9] Thus Smith undoubtedly exaggerated when he blamed the loss of 8000 lives upon the Virginia Company and certain administrators rather than upon the effect of climatic diseases and Indian massacres. In the fourth volume of Smith's *Generall Historie*, which consists largely of extracts from other men's writings, Smith subjects himself to criticism for not having consulted the journals of the Virginia Company and for selecting very partisan writers on a highly controversial issue. Friends of Smith have called attention to his precision in preparing maps and his realistic descriptions of both New England and Virginia backgrounds; this has been taken as further evidence in his favor. Had he been a mere land promoter, he would scarcely have written the unflattering descriptions he left of some phases of New World life and economic conditions. Thomas Jefferson, who wrote a brief colonial history in his *Notes on Virginia,* came to this conclusion regarding Smith, "He was honest, sensible, and well-informed; but his style is barbarous and uncouth. His history, however, is almost the only source from which we derive any knowledge of the infancy of our State."

While Smith was no Puritan in outlook, he shared much of the Christian interpretation of history, for he saw God's hand in the repeated interventions against the Indians and the expression of divine wrath seen in the inflictions of famine and disease. However, he did not dwell upon the Augustinian-Puritan theory of God's plan unfolding through the progress of history. But by the time the century ended, the Christian theory of history was to meet a serious rival in more secular ideas of human development.

The Enlightenment: Hutchinson and the Tory Emphasis

1

Jonathan Edwards and the traditionalists labored mightily to stem such Enlightenment ideas as deism, secular rationalism, and material progress. The rising middle class, acting through lawyers, journalists, and essayists, struck at the intellectual defenses of the large landowners, princes, and clerics by exalting the supremacy of science and by assailing the established churches. In the French Revolution and, to a lesser extent, the American Revolution, the middle class captured power and proceeded to remold society in its own image. To break the hold of absolutism in church and state, they separated the two completely and preached religious toleration and secularism while attacking the power of the clergy.

This onslaught tended to dissolve the organic unity of the traditional Christian state into atoms of self-sufficient, isolated individuals, each jealous of his private rights. The eighteenth-century ideal became free enterprise, freedom of contract for labor and capital, the abolition of serfdom, slavery, and the guild system, and the passage of humanitarian reforms, such as the scientific penal laws which replaced the axiom of an eye for an eye with the idea of rehabilitating the prisoner. Many a historian of the Enlightenment reflected this program in whole or in part.

Liberalism raised the notion of the individual's worth. Man, according to the traditionalists, had been created in the image of God, but he had fallen to so depraved a state as to be unworthy of God's gift of salvation; now man was raised by the devotees of Reason to the status of an intellectually self-sufficient individual guided by the sound instincts of self-interest. Such optimistic assumptions were encouraged by the triumphs of Newton and his fellow-scientists in solving some of the age-old mysteries of the universe and by the economic expansion of Europe derived from its new frontiers in America, Asia, and Africa.

In this new, mechanically predictable universe, historians were prepared to secularize every avenue of thought. They rejected both the Greek idea of the cyclic rise and decline of civilizations rooted in mystical ideas of fate and the medieval Christian belief in religious progress guided by God's inscrutable purpose to a distant heavenly goal. Condorcet and the *philosophes* glowingly pictured the secular stages of progress toward a heavenly city on earth. To them it seemed clear that scientific knowledge, unlike the speculative opinions of medieval schoolmen and Greek philosophers, was *cumulative* in nature and hence must speedily advance men toward well-being and the successful pursuit of happiness. By taking thought man could raise his stature, control his destiny, and assure progress. And when Darwin and the experimental scientists took the center of the stage in the nineteenth century, progress assumed the mantle of *inevitability*.

The faith in secular progress raised the prestige of the present and the future at the expense of the irrationalist past, and rationalist historians mirrored this change. Modern history or modern uses for ancient history absorbed the attention of Gibbon, Voltaire, Hume, and Robertson. The past did not cease to enthrall rationalist historians, but they usually chose to look at history for the "laws of nature" and for cosmic generalities at the expense of personalities, the particular, and the unique. More than ever the past was enlisted in the battles of the present and the future. Gibbon gave ammunition to fellow-deists and liberals in the *Decline and Fall of the Roman Empire* by trying to prove that "the triumphant banner of the Cross on the ruins of the Capitol" was a triumph for fanaticism more than a victory for superior doctrines and morality. When he reached the Middle Ages, he concluded his work with the damning comment, "I have described the triumph of barbarism and religion." Thus rationalist historians replaced the Christian interpretation of history by a wholly secular view of natural law operating behind the accidents of history; but like their predecessors, they proved only what they wished to prove. They felt akin to the rationalist Greeks and their classical culture, but the newly discovered laws of progress compelled them to believe that cumulative scientific knowledge would inevitably carry the modern world far beyond the achievements of the ancients.[1]

The educated middle class of provincial America was also deeply influenced by the doctrines of progress, liberalism, deism, and other rationalist ideas. Franklin, Madison, Hamilton, and Jefferson used the Enlightenment interpretation of history (in whole or in part) as a guide to statesmanship. Men were guided by self-interest, they believed, and moved in pressure groups. Franklin wrote in 1731 that "the great affairs of the world, the wars, revolutions, etc.," were carried on by parties which professed the general interest but were motivated by the particular interest of each man "whatever they may pretend." Franklin believed, however, that he could organize a "United Party for Virtue" to transcend self-interest and to govern for the common good.

James Madison, in the oft-quoted Tenth Number of the *Federalist Papers,* made self-interest a cardinal historical factor long before Karl Marx—although he eschewed the class struggle in the exact sense used by the German:

> But the most common and durable sources of factions have been the various and unequal distribution of property. Those who hold and those who are without property have ever formed distinct interests in society. . . . A landed interest, a manufacturing interest, a mercantile interest, a moneyed interest, with many lesser interests, grow up of necessity in civilized nations, and divide them into different classes, actuated by different sentiments and views.

Thomas Jefferson shared the rationalist view that history should serve the present, but he rejected emphatically the propagandist uses of the past. He blamed Hume's *History of England* because of this, for it was laden with Tory prejudices. While he believed that the rich experience of previous times enabled one to "judge of the future" and make wiser decisions, he argued that chance and circumstance made it impossible to use history as a tool to *predict* the future. In planning a program of popular education for Virginians, he insisted that most of the reading should be historical in nature. Finally, as a great liberal of his century, he held that historical truth could exist only where opinions were free and tolerance existed.

2

The shift from the Christian interpretation of history to the rationalist approach of the Enlightenment was reflected in the fact that the chief American historians of this era were successful businessmen, lawyers, or land speculators rather than ministers or theologically minded officials. Virginia's remarkably gifted ruling class of rich, English-educated country gentlemen and planters furnished two of the ablest historians of the early century. Robert Beverley and his brother-in-law William Byrd of Westover, planter-aristocrats, were secularized men who felt no compulsion to justify the ways of God to men. Anglican Virginians of the previous century had been close to New Englanders in their adherence to asceticism—at least their statute books bulged with puritanical punishments for sabbath-breakers—but the day of the hair-shirt had gone.

Both Beverley and Byrd, as intellectual spokesmen for Virginia's elite of tobacco planters and officials, had been educated in England and developed discriminating and voracious reading tastes that led them to accumulate vast libraries—Byrd's 4000 volumes established a record for all the private libraries of America in his time. Although these men never forgot their privileged social position, they realized that, for all its splendid plantation mansions, Virginia was still overwhelmingly a land of small farmers, and that most of the aristocratic planters who now studied Renaissance handbooks on the Compleat Gentleman were barely once or twice removed from their indentured servant ancestor.

Beverley was born in 1673, the son of a powerful planter who had supported the reactionary Governor Berkeley. Following his education in England, young Beverley returned to inherit a vast plantation in Gloucester County and even larger unimproved tracts along the frontier. He married a sister of William Byrd II and shared his interest in history and literature, but he was only mildly interested in politics, though for a time he represented Jamestown in the House of Burgesses. His decision to write a book (*The History and Present State of Virginia*) came, as it does to many writers, after reading a particularly atrocious one—in this case John Oldmixon's *The British Empire in America* (1708), which had a wholly inaccurate section devoted to Virginia. Beverley's brief history had much to offer, even if he had little to add to John Smith's account for the early years. Like Byrd, he condemned colonial racial prejudices toward the Indians and asserted that Virginians would have escaped many wars had they emulated John Rolfe, who married Pocahontas. He derided the current affectation for the Noble Savage, but he did recognize that Indian grievances were real.

Faithful to the ruling class, he rejected Cromwell as a usurper and portrayed the bigoted Governor Berkeley as an enlightened and even popular sponsor of industry, economic improvements, and explorations. Instead of attributing Bacon's Rebellion to Berkeley's policies, he blamed the low tobacco prices, heavy taxes, and imperial trade restrictions. His skillful circumstantial account, however, conveys high plausibility; even today, the interpretation of Bacon's Rebellion divides historians.

While modern historians note the severe exploitation of slaves and servants by the masters who also controlled the courts, Beverley said that these servile laborers worked no harder than freemen and always had recourse to the courts for redress against a cruel master. His picture of the gentry is naturally warm and sympathetic. Servants were ordered

. . . to entertain all Visitors, with everything the Plantation affords. And the poor Planters who have but one bed will very often sit up or lie upon a Form or Couch all Night to make room for a weary Traveller, to repose himself after his Journey. . . . If there happen to be a Churl, that either out of Covetousness, or Ill-nature, won't comply with this generous Custom, he has a mark of Infamy set upon him, and is abhorr'd by all.

Beverley has enough solid and reliable information and observations about Virginia's social history to attract readers today.[2] A contemporary critic, Jefferson, was less convinced of the merit of any work that began with Walter Raleigh and ended with the year 1700 by compressing the entire period within a very small volume.

William Byrd II eclipsed his kinsman in wealth and talent, for he managed to expand his father's estate of 26,000 acres to nearly 180,000 acres, reckoned to be the best land in Virginia, and his writings show greater acuteness and breadth than those of Beverley. He is honored as the founder of Richmond, and for his services of thirty-seven years as a member, later as president, of Virginia's powerful Royal Council. While his classical learning was broad and deep, his historical works actually resulted from the large commercial and speculative ventures in which he was engaged. Thus he wrote *A History of the Dividing Line* as the chief member of the official commission which surveyed a boundary line between Virginia and North Carolina through the Dismal Swamp, part of which he hoped to add to his holdings. His simi-

lar *Journey to the Land of Eden* and *Progress to the Mines* also were
by-products of his quest for new investments.

Byrd's books are journals rather than history in the usual sense, but
he treats perceptively the small farmers, the highlanders, and poor
whites whom he met in the backwoods of Virginia and North Carolina. But in his rollicking *History of the Dividing Line,* one must read
between the lines to find the true explanation for the lassitude of the
inhabitants of Lubberland, their very joy in shiftlessness, the perennial pregnancies of their wives, the looseness of their young women,
their suspicion of authority, and their indifference to formal religion.
As a solid businessman, Byrd ridiculed their reliance upon paper
money, thus ignoring the need that drove rural folk throughout American history to solve their problem as debtors by resorting to inflation.

A *History of the Dividing Line* begins with a delightfully humorous (but historically superfluous) account of early colonial development. Jamestown, it seems, was founded by Englishmen, "most of them
reprobates of good families" and "like true Englishmen, they built a
church that cost no more than fifty pounds, and a tavern that cost five
hundred." He belabored the colonists for their refusal to intermarry
with the Indians: "For, after all that can be said, a sprightly lover is
the most prevailing missionary that can be sent amongst these, or any
other infidels." Of the Pilgrims he had this to say:

These saints conceiving the same aversion to the copper complexion of
the natives, with that of the first adventurers to Virginia, would, on no
terms, contract alliances with them, afraid perhaps, like the Jews of old,
lest they might be drawn into idolatry by those strange women.
Whatever disgusted them I cannot say.

This was indeed advanced ground for a Southerner, and, for that matter, most contemporary colonials to take. Like Jefferson, Washington,
and Mason, he was a slaveowner, but hated human bondage and
wished to see its abolition. His enthusiasm for eighteenth-century doctrines of equality led him to make this striking comment:

All Nations of men have the same Natural Dignity, and we all know that
very bright Talents may be lodg'd under a very dark Skin. The principal
Differences between one People and another proceeds from the Different
Opportunities of Improvement.

Like so many other manuscripts written in the rural South, publication of this book was delayed. It first appeared in 1841, and has gone
through several editions since, the last in 1928, edited by Mark Van

Doren. A year later Professor William K. Boyd edited the hitherto unpublished and largely unknown companion manuscript, *The Secret
History of the Line,* which revealed the serious political factionalism
that existed in colonial ruling circles regarding the future of the property in the Dismal Swamp. Never intending to print this version, Byrd
allowed his unconventional humor and sensualism full sway, revealing literary tastes that he may have acquired from the bawdy plays
and diaries of the Restoration era. He is mischievously detailed regarding the sex exploits of his associates and of his own desires toward the women he met on his journeys.[3]

Beverley and Byrd loyally aided other Virginian historians, among
them the hard-working but uninspired Reverend William Stith, president of the College of William and Mary and a graduate of Oxford.
Stith in his *History of the First Discovery and Settlement of Virginia*
(1747) went beyond John Smith and Beverley in using official London
Company Records, which Byrd had generously made available to him.
But the result was a partisan account of the colonial struggle against
James I. Stith's uncritical use of the official records led him into serious
errors of fact and interpretation, and readers were repelled by his
monotonous style and the small print of the large octavo volume.
Jefferson, though a loyal alumnus of Stith's college, gave this unflattering opinion in his *Notes on Virginia:*

> He was a man of classical learning, and very exact, but of no taste in
> style. He is inelegant, therefore, and his details often too minute to be toler-
> able, even to a native of the country, whose history he writes.

3

The Puritan spirit was compelled to come to terms with the Enlightenment. Jonathan Edwards had made Calvinism palatable to a
new generation by indirectly transforming the doctrine of the Elect
and the absolute sovereignty of God through the induced conversion,
but he declared that Newton's theories were part of the divine plan.
One of New England's historians, the Reverend Thomas Prince, went
even farther than the others in mediating between Newtonian science
and theology. He drew a sharp distinction between the supernaturalism of God's immediate hand and the purely natural causes. In the
early years of the century, before colonial newspapers had been thoroughly established, ministers like the Mathers, Edwards, and Prince
played a large part in diffusing the latest findings of experimental

science from their pulpits. Yet this zeal for science did not prevent Prince from discussing such extraordinary topics as "Agency of God in causing Droughts and Rains" and "Earthquakes the Works of God and Tokens of His Just Displeasure." [4]

Thomas Prince, grandson of the governor of New Plymouth, was born in 1687, educated at Harvard, where he pleased Increase Mather as his "praying student," and soon developed an overpowering reputation for sheer erudition—scientific, philological, historical, and theological—which challenged even the pedantic Cotton Mather. It is difficult for moderns to understand the tributes paid by some contemporaries to his poorly conceived history, *A Chronological History of New England,* of which the first part appeared in 1730. Present-day historians still give too much importance to his long, pretentious dedication, preface, and introduction. In them he congratulates himself for making acute historical criticisms, for the painstaking way in which he had amassed a thousand manuscripts, pamphlets, and books on his subject, and for having an enlightened belief in freedom of worship. His chief contribution, he said frankly, "is the orderly Succession of these Transactions and Events, as they precisely fell out in time, too much neglected by our Historians." His book was not "in the specious form of a proper History, which admits of artificial Ornaments and Descriptions that raise the Imagination and Affections of the Reader; but of a closer and more naked Register, comprising only Facts in a Chronological Epitome, to enlighten the Understanding."

This was no mere argument for the "plaine stile" of Bradford but an effort to plunge back into the Middle Ages, when the barest of annals made up much of history-writing. He quoted and was apparently fascinated by the flair for annals and chronology shown a century before by Archbishop James Usher of Ireland, who had convinced his generation that the correct date of creation was 4004 B.C. Prince therefore began with the story of Creation and inserted endless chronological tables with an impressive show of acumen in discussing their accuracy. He carefully avoided any genuine historical judgments of his own. In fact he made a virtue out of quoting his authorities verbatim; actually, he compressed rather than reproduced original sources, save in the minority of cases. His exhausting efforts compelled him to stop when he reached the year 1633, although the indifference of the public may also have been a factor. The best that can be said for Prince is that he offered a great convenience, judging from contemporary testimony, to those historians who chose to draw upon his allegedly precise chronology and summary of events.[5]

First in craftsmanship and lasting merit among eighteenth-century historians of this country was Governor Thomas Hutchinson of Massachusetts, author of the three-volume *History of the Colony of Massachusetts Bay*. The tragic end of this distinguished descendant of Anne Hutchinson as a Tory exile in England, after escaping from Boston's mobs, has been marked by such cruel epitaphs as that of Vernon Parrington: "Thomas Hutchinson was marked for a reactionary. And unhappily in his conventional soul there was not the faintest spark of idealism." The truth was far more complex than this sweeping judgment indicates.

Hutchinson was born in 1711 of a long line of conscientious Massachusetts officials and prosperous merchants; such a background made it easy for him to accept a high tradition of public service as well as an inflexible type of economic conservatism. Like so many of the ruling class, he received an intensive classical education at Harvard, and went on to obtain an M.A. Later he wrote, "In the course of my education, I found no part of science a more pleasing study than history, and no part of the history of any country more useful than that of its government and laws." With this love for the governing process, he moved upward in the hierarchy of colonial officials, beginning as a relatively popular member of the colonial assembly; in 1758 he became lieutenant-governor, then chief justice, and finally governor in 1771, at a time when his unhappy fellow-countrymen were embarking upon a revolutionary path.

In his upward climb he had crossed swords with popular inflationists, such as the father of Samuel Adams, champion of the soft-money "land banks." His own fixed belief in hard money reflected an inability to see the need of farmers and small shopkeepers for a more flexible and adequate currency than was possible under England's mercantilistic policies. This attitude inevitably colored his historical treatment of the currency controversies. In 1809 ex-President John Adams, who was fundamentally conservative himself, paid a high compliment to Hutchinson's understanding of the currency problem:

If I was the witch of Endor, I would wake the ghost of Hutchinson, and give him absolute power over the currency of the United States . . . provided always that he should meddle with nothing but the currency. As little as I revere his memory, I will acknowledge that he understood the subject of coin and commerce better than any man I ever knew in this country.

Sam Adams, of course, had another judgment of Hutchinson's merits, "It has been his principle from a boy that mankind are to be governed by the discerning few, and it has been ever since his ambition to be the hero of the few."

Like the English conservative, Edmund Burke, who sought conciliation with America, Hutchinson was averse to any break in the seamless web of tradition. His reverence for the past, his family's unbroken record of governing in behalf of the Empire, and his great wealth undoubtedly influenced his decision to stand by Britain, even if its policies should take a turn for the worse. Like his Canadian neighbors, who welcomed so many thousands of Loyalists, he would have liked to see an imperial federation in which substantial home rule existed in each part. In fact, he believed that this situation already existed in practice.

The first volume of the *History of the Colony of Massachusetts Bay,* which ended with the year 1730, appeared in 1764 and was only lightly touched by the spirit of controversy. It was well received, and Hutchinson was encouraged to cover the years 1730 to 1750 in a second volume. This was not published until 1767; meanwhile, an event had taken place that may have affected his final decision to leave America. During the excitement over the Stamp Act of 1765, at a time when he was still lieutenant-governor, he incurred popular dislike by his emphatic stand to enforce the wishes of Parliament, even when he believed them unwise. One day, while seated at the table with his family, he was informed that a mob was approaching. He and his family fled, and the mob arrived and thoroughly ransacked his house. His precious historical manuscripts, including the yet unpublished second volume of the history, were dumped into the streets. The change in his attitude from the judicious historian to the polemic partisan is obvious in the third volume recounting the stirring events of 1750-74; this, however, did not appear until 1828, after his death.

In the first volume Hutchinson professed no more ambitious aim than to save the memory of his ancestors from oblivion; he noted proudly that "for four successive generations [they] had been principal actors in public affairs." But as the narrative unfolded, it showed an imaginative breadth and scholarly depth that made it not unworthy of the great European contemporaries—if not of Gibbon himself, then of Voltaire, Hume, and Robertson. Hutchinson referred to the large manuscript collections that he had inherited from his forebears, as well as to the earlier colonial accounts, since Bradford's time, that he had read. Most surprising for a descendant of Anne Hutchinson is his unflattering judgment of that learned lady, whose heretical opinions he attributed to her vanity:

Countenanced and encouraged by Mr. Vane and Mr. Cotton, she advanced doctrines and opinions which involved the colony in disputes and contentions; and being improved to civil as well as religious purposes, had like to have produced ruin to church and state.

As a confirmed law-and-order man he could say, "Her lectures made much noise." In the orthodox Puritan tradition, he condemned her as an "enthusiast," whose emotional views threatened the social and religious order. While he does not cite Winthrop's *Journal* for the Hutchinson trial, but relies on much fuller official records, his verdict was as unfavorable as Governor Winthrop's had been. But Hutchinson is not particularly concerned in upholding the theocracy against heresy, but stresses the beliefs of the Enlightenment in civil rights:

It is evident not only by Mrs. Hutchinson's trial, but by many other public proceedings, that inquisition was made into men's private judgments as well as into their declarations and practice. Toleration was preached against as a sin in rulers which would bring down the judgments of heaven upon the land.

But he reminded his readers that such was the temper of the time and then quoted, in a footnote, Governor Dudley's ditty on tolerance:

Let men of God in court and churches watch
O'er such as do a toleration hatch

He frankly condemned colonial bigotries, particularly the persecution of the Quakers, though he did not forget to upbraid them for their sins against public order. His critical conclusion is clear enough:

The most that can be said for our ancestors is that they tried gentler means at first, which they found utterly ineffectual, and that they followed the example of the authorities in most other states and in most ages of the world, who with the like absurdity have supposed every person could and ought to think as they did, and with the like cruelty have punished such as appeared to differ from them.

An enlightened twentieth-century historian could not have put it better.

He showed considerable sympathy for the Indians—the cynical may remark that the Massachusetts Indians were scarcely a menace in 1764. Like Bradford he deplored the tendency of colonial juries to discriminate between the guilt of killing an Indian and that of killing an Englishman, "as if God had not made of one blood all the nations of men upon the face of the earth." In defending the motives of the

Indian chief King Philip in provoking a bloody frontier war, he observed kindly, "We are too apt to consider the Indians as a race of beings by nature inferior to us, and born to servitude." His careful description of Indian customs and beliefs seems far more convincing than that of his predecessors; he contradicted the popular notions that the Indians worshiped the devil and that they were the lost ten tribes of Israel.

The last volume is so thoroughly Loyalist in tone that Americans have found it intolerable. No objective historian today on either side would explain James Otis's valiant fight against the Writs of Assistance as motivated solely by a family feud against the governor; or assert that John Hancock's principles merely concealed his love for applause; or say of John Adams, "His ambition was without bounds." Yet Hutchinson's interpretation of the Revolution has more adherents today than a century ago. His argument that the struggle was caused by the colonial fear of events to come rather than current British abuses has been upheld by recent historians. Colonists, he thought, began reasoning with the premise that "Interest [was] a governing principle with all mankind," and hence Britain would inevitably impose an unequal share of the tax burdens, while debarring them from an equal share in the benefits of government. He tried to show that this fear was groundless. He dwelt upon the unusual prosperity of Massachusetts, emphasized the security offered by remaining within the Empire, and stressed the military futility and costliness of resisting England.

Some of his defenses of British acts have already infected American textbook writing (a situation long lamented by the *Chicago Tribune* and the late Mayor William Hale Thompson of that city). He pictured the Boston Massacre as an affair in which an unruly mob attacked the soldiers, who fired in defense only after they had shown exemplary forbearance. His dislike of the new revolutionary vogue for tarring-and-feathering critics, hanging suspects, and boycotting or ostracizing Loyalists has been shared by innumerable readers of such modern historical novels as Kenneth Roberts's *Oliver Wiswell*. Recent historians might agree with his judgment that the propaganda of the Boston and New York newspapers played a substantial role in bringing about the Revolution.

Yet he attempted to convey in his narrative, albeit not too emphatically, his own impression that Parliament had misapplied its indubitable power in such legislation as the Sugar Act and the Stamp Act. He argued that no basic principle was actually involved in the resistance of the colonial merchants to the enforcement of the mer-

cantilistic system, and he said of the Sugar Act, "Had it been then reduced to a penny, or three-half pence, it would have been acquiesced
in by the merchants."

With the third volume Hutchinson made his last plea for conciliation;
thereafter he remained in London as an exile from the land that his
ancestors had called home for a century and a half. England pensioned
its loyal servant, and Oxford honored him as a scholar and statesman.
But his roots were still in Massachusetts. Symbolically, the manuscript
of his second volume shows even today the mud stains made during
the night that the papers lay in the streets, cast there by a mob of
erstwhile neighbors who had rejected Hutchinson and all his work.
Revolutionists seldom feel too kindly toward history and tradition;
they are too busy breaking with the tyranny of the past.[6]

4

New York City had its Hutchinson in a partisan Tory historian,
William Smith (1728-93), whose social background resembled that
of the Massachusetts governor in many ways. William Smith, like his
father, was a wealthy lawyer and colonial official. He had been given
a good classical education at Yale, where he took his B.A. and M.A.
and developed a genuine scholarly interest in history. As chief justice
of the province in 1763 and a member of the Royal Council beginning
in 1769 during the turbulent prerevolutionary period, he tried to avert
the colonial separation from England by proposing an intercolonial
legislature with members selected for life by the various assemblies;
this was a conservative version of Franklin's famous Plan of Union.
But Parliament was only slightly more interested in the Smith plan
than in Franklin's idea, and nothing happened. Before the crisis of
independence came, he had shifted from his onetime Whiggish beliefs
to the Loyalist side and was exiled to England. In 1786 he was appointed chief justice of Canada, a post he held until his death in 1793.

Smith had been an intimate friend of the popular Scottish historian,
William Robertson, who shifted his attention from European history
to this hemisphere when he published a *History of America* in 1777.
The New Yorker seems to have read many of the historians of the
Enlightenment. But his interest in history, as befitting a legal scholar,
was not in social or economic history, but in the laws and politics of
New York. He and a partner had been commissioned by the legislature to publish the first digest of the colony's statutes. Smith's important two-volume work, *The History of the Province of New York,*

which was the model for other regional histories, began with the earliest discoveries and ended with 1762.[7]

Too many of the chapters revealed the author's class bias against "persons of inferior station" and the headless "multitude." He showed nothing but contempt for the "demagogues" who led the popular party, treated Jacob Leisler as one of these self-seeking irresponsible wretches, and ridiculed John Peter Zenger, whose court victory is today considered a landmark in the history of the freedom of the press.

He dealt with the Zenger case at length, drawing upon the colonial records and local information that must have been easy for one in his position to obtain. Although he had nothing but scorn for the dishonest, landgrabbing royal governor William Cosby, he disliked those who fought him even more. After Cosby had been allegedly libeled by the faction who were using Zenger's paper anonymously as their organ, the Council ordered four numbers of the offending *New York Weekly Journal* to be burned publicly by the common hangman or whipper at the pillory in the city. The attorney general, however, managed to bring suit against Zenger even after a grand jury had failed to indict him. In the trial, the popular party used the press effectively, according to Smith, by inciting public opinion, and reached the jury itself by publicizing facts regarding the libel that were held to be inadmissible as evidence. As for the famous Andrew Hamilton, who came forward as the champion of free speech, Smith had this to say:

> He set out by asserting with a firmness unabashed, and which often goes far to persuade, that the matters charged as scandals were true, and therefore no libels; and indulged such a vein of ridicule against the law advanced by the Judges, that a libel was the more dangerous for its truth, that the ignorant audience . . . thought the refusal of the Judges to permit evidence of the truth of the publications added to the tyranny and oppression of the time.

And as for Zenger, "a low printer, dandled upon the knee of popular applause," fate punished him (said Smith) by making his indolence finally ruin his family. Naturally, there is no appreciation of the far-reaching importance of the Zenger case in establishing the liberal principle that "Truth is a Defense against libel."

Yet William Smith showed some of the Enlightenment virtues of tolerance. He decried the dishonest tactics of factionalists who raised an anti-Semitic issue regarding the qualification of Jews as electors in order to divert attention from genuine issues. His treatment of New

York's alleged slave insurrection of 1741—actually an arsonist case—
shows an unusually advanced pro-Negro position. Examining the evidence carefully, he pointed out how much of it hung upon the un-
trustworthy testimony of an irresponsible woman. As a result, seventeen Negroes were burned at the stake, eighteen hanged, and seventy
transported elsewhere. He condemned the panicky legislators who
hastened to tighten the restrictions upon Negroes and to make manu-
mission difficult in New York.

Among the ablest colonial historians, the man who won the greatest
prestige was another loyalist, Cadwallader Colden. This unusually
erudite man was born in Ireland of Scottish parents, attended the University of Edinburgh, and studied medicine in London. Upon arrival
in America, he engaged with some success in a variety of occupations
—doctor of medicine, botanist, philosopher, mathematician, historian,
New York legislator, and finally lieutenant-governor. His official rise
had something to do with the fact that he ranked as one of New
York's great landowners and remained a conservative, true to the imperial connection, up to his death in 1776. Like Hutchinson, he was
a colonial executive who had to face a revolutionary mob.

Colden angrily rejected William Smith's history of the province as
hopelessly biased (Colden figured unfavorably in some of the situations described), despite the fact that Smith had kindly referred
readers to Colden's two-volume work for information on the Iroquois.
This account, *The History of the Five Indian Nations* (1727), lacks
sufficient narrative continuity for the casual reader to discover Colden's
own bias. Colden declared in his dedication that he wished to awaken
the public to the danger of the French in the West, especially if they
should win over the Iroquois to their side against the English. His
references to these tribes were usually sympathetic. Their worst vices,
such as heavy drinking, were borrowed from the whites, he wrote.

While the narrative seemed loosely integrated, it did have the virtue of critical analysis, which earlier writers about the Indians rarely
showed. He pointed out, for example, that "it is not easy to distinguish
the Notions they had originally among themselves from those they
have learned of the Christians." His use of official records to supple-
ment the standard French authorities might have enhanced the value
of the books a great deal, had they not served largely to bog down
the narrative with lengthy documentary digressions. He began with
a careful detailed account of Iroquois customs, took up their wars and
treaties at too great length, and then interspersed (or else his publisher did) innumerable documents, such as Penn's Indian laws. While

it is said that Colden is still useful to anthropologists, the reader will suspect that this is due to a paucity of other sources.

Underlying his thinking was a philosophical materialism—rather rare in the colonies—which made him hostile to the idealistic theories of Jonathan Edwards. Like the French materialists of the Enlightenment, he believed that Newton had proved that the world was determined by mechanical forces and that all existence depended upon matter and motion. Unfortunately for his reputation as a philosopher, contemporaries found his speculative writings such as *The Principles of Action in Matter* (1751) to be unintelligible.[8]

The near-monopoly of expert history-writing, held by economic conservatives and Loyalists in particular, is further exemplified in the career of George Chalmers. Like Hutchinson, William Smith, and Colden, this English immigrant was a talented lawyer whose well-to-do family assured him of a thorough education—he studied at Aberdeen and Edinburgh—and undoubtedly shaped his class bias. In 1763, at the age of twenty-one, he arrived in Maryland with an uncle and soon developed a very profitable legal practice. As the revolutionary crisis developed, he worked behind the scenes in behalf of Loyalists among the official class, the merchant factors of British firms, and newcomers still strong in their loyalty to king and Parliament. However, when the mobs and the revolutionary acts of proscription struck at his friends and came dangerously close to him in 1775, he escaped to England.

The bitterness of Chalmers toward America matched that of Hutchinson, whom he may have met in London, and he, too, was compelled to fall back on the largess of the Crown for support. Within a few years, the British ministry secured him an executive post in the Board of Trade. Even before this time, the ministry had started him off on a career as a historian by giving him unrestricted access to the unpublished and hitherto rarely used American state papers. In 1780 there appeared the first volume of his *Political Annals of the Present United Colonies*, which ended with the Glorious Revolution of 1688. It was moderate in tone, except for a few obvious barbs against the religious intolerance of the Puritans. However, two years later, he completed a violently anti-American book, *An Introduction to the History of the Colonies*, which, strangely enough, was officially suppressed and was not published until 1845 in an American edition.[9]

A single theme dominated his books: Colonial leaders had been steadily maneuvering politics in the direction of independence from the very beginning, while England's statesmen had been too inept or

George Chalmers—Loyalist

indifferent to block this tendency. As a liberal economist, he agreed with Adam Smith in rejecting the entire mercantilist system, whose enforcement had precipitated the war; he felt that trade should be permitted to flow into its natural profitable channels. But as a staunch orthodox Whig, following the tradition of a party which had ousted a king in 1688, he did not admit that there were limits to the supremacy of Parliament. He denied that there was the slightest legal basis for the colonial argument against taxation without representation; to him Parliament stood for the entire British nation regardless of the locale of English subjects.

In some of his other thirty-odd publications, Chalmers severely attacked Edmund Burke and the pro-American faction of Whigs who called for conciliation with America. When the French Revolution broke out and Burke led the traditionalists against social revolution, Chalmers did not need to change his older views to condemn this new explosion of the hateful multitude.

Despite the granite-like, upper middle-class bias of Chalmers and his legalistic efforts to use history as a tool to win a case, his histories proved to be so rich in solid factual data and thoughtful literary organization that many patriots found his books indispensable. Timothy Pitkin, for example, frankly admitted that he had not thought it necessary to use other sources for the early colonial period, because Chalmers's work had made it superfluous. Jared Sparks, a nationalist second to none, admired the "candor and honesty," as well as informative qualities of Chalmers, sufficiently to bring out an American edition of the bellicose work, *An Introduction to the History of the Colonies.*

When the Revolution drove out the Loyalists, the young republic not only lost some of its ablest historians, but also gave free rein to the chauvinism of ardent nationalists. The liberal ideals of the Enlightenment, which had been espoused in varying degree by both patriots and Tories, continued to affect the writing of history for at least a century. But the eighteenth-century idea of cosmopolitanism was modified by the belief that a modern democratic nation, such as the United States or France, was the true missionary of the highest republican virtues. Nationalism gave a secular garb to the Puritan notion of a Chosen People whose principles would usher in the millennium.

Jared Sparks and the Dominance of the Federalist-Whig Historians

1

Although the Tories were silenced, the writing and publishing of history books proved too expensive for mere sans-culottes. The new patriotic generation of historians were usually well-to-do lawyers and writers, many of them ministers. Besides, publishing was handicapped in a new country by the lack of systematic marketing of books, inferior typesetting, unusual capital risks, and the conscienceless way in which works by successful authors were pirated on both sides of the ocean. For all his popularity David Ramsay of South Carolina actually sold only small quantities of his histories, and he plunged his savings into the gamble of publishing his books here. Since the new American copyright law of 1789 protected native writers only against infringements within this country, Ramsay judged it expedient to issue a British edition as well, in order to forestall literary piracy. But even eighteen years were barely enough time to dispose of an American edition of 1500 copies.

Under these circumstances, the writing of American history required not only leisure and some talent, but an upper middle-class status that usually went hand-in-hand with a conservative social outlook, despite fervent expressions of liberal nationalism. Only a few were able to forgive agrarian radicalism or to present the facts objectively regarding Shays's rebellion of 1786 and the background of currency deflation and farm foreclosures. The selection as to what was important amid the endless facts of history lay in the hands of a single social class.

Many of the radicals of 1776—John Hancock and Patrick Henry, for instance—had turned conservative in the first decade of independence. The cautious framers of the Constitution had carefully protected creditors from inflationist farmers by forbidding the states to issue bills of credit or to impair contract obligations. When the French Revolution broke out shortly afterwards, Jeffersonians rejoiced at the overthrow of aristocracy, but the Hamiltonian men of substance trembled at the threat to the social order. For Jeffersonian liberals it seemed that American nationalism was a blend of liberty, equality, and fraternity, but most of them preferred to write pamphlets, poems, and newspaper articles rather than history books. The conservatives who did not have to content themselves with the most ephemeral forms of literature had the leisure to attempt the writing of the nation's epic based upon a type of nationalism that was sterilized from the germs of economic radicalism. They could agree with the Jeffersonians in exalting the Chosen People, the latter-day Puritans, whose national destiny was enhanced by an unusually favorable physical environment.

An almost unfailing ingredient in the writing of American history for this era was the ghost-writing of Edmund Burke, Whig leader of the pro-American faction in Parliament. Burke edited the highly influential *Annual Register* during 1759-97 and almost certainly wrote the famous "Historical Article" every year up to 1766. Although Burke was a traditionalist and warred upon the French Revolution, he did not regard the American Revolution as a social revolution—nor have most American historians since—but as a revolt against unwise imperial legislation and administration. He showed similar sympathies to Irish rebels and to natives oppressed by Warren Hastings's rule in India. A thorough realist in policy, he refused to argue over dangerous abstractions such as the question of Parliament's competence to tax the colonies. As an ardent Whig, he had no doubts in his mind as to the supremacy of Parliament; but as a practical politician who believed that philosophical absolutes must be tempered to meet the frailties of human nature, he denied that it was expedient to tax the colonies under existing disturbed conditions. In the Opposition he attacked the Tories for pursuing a policy leading to war and called for compromise. Americans, he believed, were content to remain within the Empire as long as no reversal of *de facto* colonial relations was attempted.

Few Englishmen had so profound a knowledge of colonial affairs as did Burke. His *Annual Register* articles were copious, acutely observant, and warmly sympathetic. Little wonder that the postrevolutionary writers naturally gravitated to them. Unfortunately, in that age when literary property was so little respected, practically every major American writer dealing with the era plagiarized shamelessly from the *Annual Register*. So it was with the most respected names—David Ramsay, John Marshall, William Gordon, and many more. The less pretentious popular historians merely borrowed the *Annual Register* at second-hand, via Ramsay, Marshall, Gordon, et al. These plagiarisms were uncovered a half-century ago by Professor Orin G. Libby and others, but Marshall's derilection was found only in 1948.[1] Each historian usually began with a virtuous profession of having read the basic correspondence. Sometimes, it is true, they conceded that some of their volumes included certain verbatim materials from the *Annual Register*, and that they had dispensed with quotation marks. But this indebtedness usually involved so many lengthy paragraphs and pages that the saving remnant of original research has been difficult to discover. Libby, who studied practically all of the histories of the American Revolution, finally concluded in disgust:

> Will it not be profitable, now that the last of the contemporary American historians yields his place of authority, to compile from the *Annual Register*, a history of the American Revolution which shall be known for what it is under its true colors?

2

No patriotic cult proved so lasting as that of George Washington.[2] The revered father of his country had faced partisan attacks in his lifetime, but ranks were closed now as all joined to pay him homage as a flawless symbol of a united nation. Some of the anti-Federalists like Thomas Jefferson, whose memories of Washington were still fresh, conceded that the first president was "in every sense of the words, a wise, a good, and a great man," but added that his mind was not of the first order and that his lack of a formal education was too apparent.

So rapid was the apotheosis of Washington that during the first ten weeks following his death 440 printed mortuary sermons were issued. All classes hailed his integrity and courage; upper-class Federalists exalted his conservatism and classical patriotism. Artists like Gilbert Stuart chose him as a subject and capitalized upon the rising investment values of Washington pictures, especially those that attitudinized in the classical manner. The neoclassical sculptor Horatio Greenough later chiseled a totally uninspired twenty-ton figure of Washington wearing a Roman toga, which was intended for the Capitol, but was hastily pushed from place to place, and finally was lodged in the un-influential Smithsonian Institution.

So it happened that the material advantages of writing a biography of George Washington were well appreciated by David Ramsay, John Marshall, and Mason Weems, among a host of others. At least five hundred biographies of this illustrious subject were issued before the new century ended. But the caviar for the millions was Parson Weems's biography, especially beginning with the fifth edition, which has the immortal cherry tree story in it.

The amazing Mason Locke Weems (1759-1825) has aroused more curiosity than his biographers are able to satisfy. A Marylander by birth, he was ordained as an Anglican minister in 1784, and preached at least once in the Pohick Church where Washington formerly wor-shiped. This distinction was later duly magnified on the title page of his famous biography to read, "Formerly Rector of Mt. Vernon Par-ish." His rationalist views, his secular gospel of humanitarianism, and his outspoken admiration for Thomas Paine, the deist, estranged the local clergy and may have influenced his decision to forsake preaching for bookselling, a vocation which he intended to make uplifting. He helped French revolutionary refugees and almost bankrupted himself for those in distress, but Marylanders and Virginians were unen-thusiastic about the special services he conducted for Negroes. Un-doubtedly his habits were peculiar; as the eminent Bishop William Meade of Virginia put it, Weems was "one of nature's oddities."

His own adventures on the road between New England and Georgia are far more intriguing than his priggish biography of Washington. With a stock furnished by Mathew Carey, one of the leading book-sellers and publishers, he peddled only "improving" books from his wagon and aroused customers by fiddling and by patriotic discourses. His best-selling book was the nation's favorite (50,000 copies were sold in the United States), Mrs. Susanna Rowson's *Charlotte, A Tale of Truth, or Charlotte Temple* (1791). This adopted the moralist's style popularized by Richardson in a melodramatic account of the seduction of a girl who was deserted by an unfaithful, dissipating naval officer and then driven out by the unfeeling world into a New York blizzard.

Weems's *Life of George Washington* is not now regarded as history, but it was creative folklore, even if some of the anecdotes which he attributed to well-informed contemporaries originated solely in his own well-stocked mind. He combined the Puritan's fear of idleness with Franklin's ideals of thrift, self-reliance, ambition, and hard work. To this was sometimes added the conservative medieval idea of fixed classes: Society was a body of which each individual was a part and was intended by God to serve forever in a certain station. Some were born to direct, others to obey, and hence the lower classes should be content to fulfill their duty and to pay taxes. This harsh organic theory was tempered by Weems's habitual sympathies for the distressed; but it did not change his unalterable belief that great opportunities exist for those who work for them.

Youngsters, including Abraham Lincoln who read the biography by firelight in a log cabin, must have enjoyed the Weemsian George Washington, even if his virtues and strait-laced qualities depressed them occasionally. After all, George was a superb athlete, the fastest runner and jumper, and so resourceful that he rose to greatness easily by his own efforts:

See Washington, born of humble parents, and in humble circumstances— born in a narrow nook and obscure corner of the British plantations! Yet lo! What great things wonder-working industry can bring out of this un-promising Nazareth.

The cherry tree myth is of course the *pièce de résistance* of his in-spirational biography, faithfully perpetuated in school readers. After George's father had been tirelessly teaching him morality and warning him particularly against telling untruths, he reaped the full fruits with the boy's confession of guilt:

"I can't tell a lie, Pa; you know I can't tell a lie. I did cut it with my hatchet." —"Run to my arms, you dearest boy," cried his father in transports, "run to my arms; glad am I, George, that you killed my tree; for you have paid for it a thousand fold. Such an act of heroism in my son is more worth than a thousand trees, though blossomed with silver, and their fruits of purest gold."

So Weems concocted a historical whopper to teach American boys to tell the truth. In fact, Weems's own inability to satisfy himself with mere reality was thoroughly exemplified in another biography of his, *The Life of Francis Marion.* A surviving lieutenant of the famed Swamp Fox, who had loaded down Weems with authentic documents and letters in order to make the biography fairly truthful (he did give permission to add "a few embellishments"), read the book despairingly and wrote to the ebullient biographer, "Most certainly 'tis not my history, but your romance."

Weems's *Washington* taught chauvinism as well as morality. The Revolution, he said, grew out of the jealousy that British officials felt toward American prosperity. "We were not to be treated as *brothers,* but as slaves! over whom an unconditional right was claimed to tax and take our property at pleasure!!!" He struck the eighteenth-century ideal of America's example enlightening the world:

The eyes of long oppressed humanity are now looking up to you as to her last hope; the whole world are anxious spectators of your trial; and with your behaviour at this crisis [This edition appeared in 1809, during the naval conflict with Britain] not only your own, but the destiny of unborn millions is involved.

As pictorial illustrations to accompany such rhetoric, he chose to reproduce the most patriotic paintings, such as the impressive revolutionary scenes done by John Trumbull.

This biography of Washington eventually eclipsed even *Charlotte Temple* in popularity. Six editions were exhausted in five years—no contemporary American historian could approach this record—and by 1931 more than seventy-five editions had come out. The aura that he cast about his hero was not easily removed by later scientific historians. Good taste could more readily afford criticism of the Constitution than of George Washington.

While Weems sold his books on the road, he also became an agent for a more pretentious biographer of Washington, Chief Justice John Marshall, whose publisher was seeking advance subscriptions for what became a huge five-volume work. Although Marshall knew Washington well and should have been able to produce a meritorious if inevitably biased work, his pressing need for ready cash and his impatience with the painstaking techniques of historical research led him to turn out a third-rate, heavily-plagiarized biography. In the first volume, which came out in 1804, Washington is not permitted to make an entrance, because the author decided that the space was needed for background. Even in the later volumes, the hero is so completely buried in general history that the reader has to search for Washington with the aid of the index.

Marshall tried the stratagem of anticipating unpleasant criticism by admitting at the outset that he had so freely relied upon the *Annual Register* and the works of Gordon, Ramsay, and Chalmers that he had frequently used their very words without bothering about quotation marks. It was then regarded as disarming to say, "Mr Chalmers has furnished almost all the facts which the historian of the United States would require." A recent historian, William A. Foran, has mercilessly exposed the routine plagiarism practiced by Marshall. Entire paragraphs, chapters, and even books were abridged without being reworked. In dealing with the Battle of Camden, for example, he copied almost twelve pages from Gordon—who in his own turn was an archplagiarist heavily indebted to the *Annual Register*. Little wonder that the Chief Justice tried at first to issue his biography anonymously. Although his revised version of 1832 corrected many errors, it could not change the fact of bald plagiarism.

Nevertheless, there was ample evidence left of Marshall's conservatism in his own contributions to biography, especially in the last volume. While Weems had stressed Washington's humble birth and simple virtues, Marshall molded him into a lofty Federalist aristocrat. He evened scores with one of his critical readers, Thomas Jefferson, by explaining that this remote kinsman of his had lived too long in France to know America. He presented Washington as a strong nationalist, praised Hamilton highly, and derogated Jefferson's anti-Federalists as a party with "lax notions of honor," while the Federalists "protected the faith of a nation" on financial matters. He showed his dislike for debtors and inflation in many pages, and his judgments of the Sage of Monticello reflected the bitter atmosphere between the two created by the war on the judiciary. Jefferson, expecting the worst, wrote of the forthcoming biography, "It is intended to come out just in time to influence the next presidential election." His own reply was *The Anas,* a lengthy essay which betrayed his deep unqualified bias against Hamilton and the Federalists:

From the moment . . . of my retiring from the Administration, the federalists got unchecked hold of General Washington. His memory was already sensibly impaired by age, the firm tone of mind for which he had been remarkable, was beginning to relax, its energy was abated, a listlessness of labor, a desire for tranquility had crept on him, and a willingness to let others act and even think for him.

Yet this "five volumed libel," as Jefferson put it, won the praise of a generation of Federalist historians and such devotees of the Washington cult as Noah Webster. More detached critics complained of Marshall's deadliness of style, numerous inaccuracies, and flagrant bias. It was a tribute to the deep affection for Washington, rather than to the intrinsic worth of the biography, that Marshall enjoyed considerable sales and was able to put out an entirely revised edition before his death.

Among the few Jeffersonians of talent who joined the Washington cult was James K. Paulding of New York, a literary satirist who graced the circle of another cultist, Washington Irving. Paulding's father—a sea captain, a perennial debtor, and a patriotic militia man of the Revolution—had apparently taught his son to dislike Britain, to coin chauvinist phrases, and to sympathize with popular causes. A Jacksonian agrarian, Paulding rose to the post of Van Buren's Secretary of the Navy. His widely read life of Washington, which was written in 1835, the year Marshall died, actually had little of explicit Jeffersonian philosophy and still less of literary art. Essentially, he followed the Parson Weems formula (rediscovered by Horatio Alger) of youthful indoctrination for morality and ambition, though he aimed more consciously for the adult market. Here is a not untypical example of his high-flown style in a description of Washington:

> He becomes the great landmark of his country: the pillar on which is recorded her claim to an equality with the illustrious nations of the world . . . and there is no trait so strongly marks a degenerate race as an indifference to his fame and his virtues.

Elsewhere he said, "In no age or country has there ever arisen a man who, equally in private as in public life, presented so admirable a model to every class and condition of mankind."

Paulding matched the cherry tree tale with another moralizing story. When the active youth broke a favorite horse of his mother's, he naturally admitted it freely. "Young man," said she, "I forgive you because you have the courage to tell the truth at once; had you skulked away, I should have despised you." In his biography, Mrs. Washington, rather than her husband, is the preceptor teaching the son a love of virtue. The supreme heroics come at the hero's death when he says stoically to a slave, "Take me to bed, it is high time for me to die!"

The historian who expanded most the modest stock of facts used by Washington's numerous biographers was Jared Sparks of Harvard, the first professor of history (other than church history) in the United States and the first to make a full-time profession of the subject. He began his education under the guidance of a gifted mother who was well read and liked to write poetry. In school he was acclaimed the local genius and at Harvard, where he was graduated in 1815, his sociable nature and scholarly tastes opened the doors of the well-to-do literati.

Among his fellow college students were William Hickling Prescott, the future historian of Spain, Mexico, and Peru; George Ticknor, the literary historian; and Edward Everett, whose prolific pen later produced a mediocre life of George Washington. Another embryo historian, George Bancroft, was at Harvard when Sparks was graduated. At the same time another youth of mark, Richard Hildreth, was preparing to enter the college; there he would begin plans for a monumental history of the United States that would eventually compete with Bancroft's. Within the next decade of New England's golden age of historians, there appeared John Lothrop Motley, Francis Parkman, and other noted men who took their training at Sparks's college and graced the salons of Boston's well-to-do educated classes.

At Harvard Divinity School, Sparks put aside the remnants of his Calvinism for the fashionable Unitarianism which had recently captured that school, and thereafter he became an aggressive pastor of liberal Christianity in the pulpits of Baltimore and other churches of the South. In 1823, he decided to leave the ministry for a literary career and bought and edited the Brahministic *North American Review*. Its former editor, Edward Everett, had been under the spell of the new German learning and had stressed European themes. Sparks, however, an uncompromising nationalist, insisted upon more and more articles on American themes, especially in biography and economic developments, and even added to the distinction of the *Review* among its elite circulation. Another Harvard classmate and apprentice to history, John G. Palfrey, who later wrote the *History of New England*, succeeded him as editor.

Sparks wrote entire libraries of history books and biographies, but most of these are now forgotten. His reputation rests upon his prodigious labors in collecting, editing, and publishing valuable documents of the American Revolution, particularly the letters of Washington and Franklin and the diplomatic correspondence of the war. The first book of his twelve-volume *The Writings of George Washington* (1834-37) was actually a biography, but, except for its large reservoir of fresh details, it was undistinguished. His claim of utter objectivity was the conventional prefatory promise that could not be taken seriously. How critical could a biographer be who could say of his hero that he "cannot be charged with an indiscretion or a vice"? In later years, Theodore Roosevelt, who was himself not averse to taking liberties with historical facts spoke of Sparks as a "professional eulogist." The New Englander took Weems's biography quite seriously, believing that stylistic requirements made it necessary for the Parson

to add obvious fictions to an otherwise sound work. Like Weems, he
approached history in a moralistic frame of mind, giving only passing
attention to economic and environmental factors. Here is one of his
appraisals of the father of his country:

> His temperament was ardent, his passions strong, and, amidst the multi-
> plied scenes of temptation and excitement through which he passed, it
> was his constant effort and ultimate triumph to check the one and subdue
> the other.

Historical causation dissolved amid the accidents of temperament and
personality. Nevertheless, he was far more critical of facts and anecdotes than most earlier biographers. The Washington who emerged
was often believable—a meticulous businessman, an able supervisor
of a large tobacco plantation, and a wise, though not brilliant, general.

The great controversy of Sparks's life involved the issue of honest
editorial standards. It centered on a lengthy public exchange of articles and letters with the British historian, Lord Mahon, over "tam-
pering with the truth of history," as the latter put it, in editing Washington's letters. Sparks had undertaken the Gargantuan task of editing
Washington's manuscripts after persuading Justice Bushrod Washington, the owner, to move them from Mount Vernon to the convenience
of Cambridge. The latter shipped off about seventy volumes of manuscript, two-thirds of them dealing with the Revolution, together with
some 20,000 original letters and a large quantity of miscellaneous
papers. This ambitious historical enterprise put all subsequent colonial
and revolutionary chroniclers in his debt. Very appropriately, he chose
to work in Craigie House, where Washington himself had temporarily
resided during the Revolution.

In December 1851 Lord Mahon castigated Sparks for his lax editorial standards in an appendix to his sixth volume of *The History of
England*. Mahon compared certain Washington letters that had been
reproduced in a biography of the revolutionary hero, Joseph Reed,
with the same letters in Sparks's edition. He found that the historian
had bowdlerized Washington, replacing slang and inelegant words
by stilted speech. Thus he replaced "fleabite," used as a reference to
a small sum, by "totally inadequate to our demands" and struck out
"two of a kidney." Washington's grammar, spelling, and style were
made to conform with Harvard usage. Worse yet, said Mahon, he had
omitted sentences that put the hero in a less imposing position or
that reflected upon New England. Wherever omissions were made,
there was nothing to inform the reader of this fact.

These editorial failings have often been cited by historians, but too often they have not weighed these misdeeds by the loose editorial standards of that age. Sparks met every charge in detailed explanations printed by the New York *Evening Post*. "The alterations," he said, "are strictly verbal or grammatical; nor am I conscious that, in this process, an historical fact, the expression of an opinion, or the meaning of a sentence has on any occasion been prevented or modified." Some of the discrepancies between his letters and those printed in the biography of Joseph Reed were demonstrated to be due to errors in the latter.

Fundamentally, Sparks based his defense on the common-sense observation that he was forced to compress many thousands of letters within the relatively brief compass of eleven printed volumes. The alleged suppressions of facts were usually items repeated several times elsewhere. As for his changes of Washington's sentences, Sparks pointed out that he had to rely upon an imperfect letter-book, which did not correspond precisely with the actual letters sent out. In later years, Washington himself had done his own "stilting" by correcting his copies, sometimes revising them so drastically as to change their meaning. Sparks continued this process of correcting spelling and striking out inelegant phrases. He had to infer from the rough drafts exactly what the final letter said. All this is of course unforgivable by modern editorial standards, but it was not inferior to the prevailing practices of his day.

Mahon apparently conceded some points, but he was not convinced. It seems quite likely that Sparks omitted some of the harsher, critical letters that reflected on a deified Washington or threatened to revive sectional controversies. His prudishness, which is obvious in his editing of Benjamin Franklin's letters—by his omission of the sage's unconventional comments on sex, for example—could easily have dictated his principles of selection in the case of Washington. Later editors were to make amends for Sparks's shortcomings, but his had been the pioneer task.

Far less defensible, though not altogether novel either, was Sparks's peculiar generosity in tearing off pieces of Washington's papers to give them away to friends as souvenirs. He offered the extenuating circumstance that Judge Bushrod Washington did the same thing.

After a Boston merchant endowed a history chair at Harvard, Sparks became in 1839 the McLean Professor of Ancient and Modern History and introduced education by lecture, research, and special readings rather than by the textbook and recitation method. He selected as his first course the American Revolution, a subject that he vainly hoped to deal with in a definitive work. In 1849 he was chosen president of Harvard, but, after an undistinguished four years of service, he resigned. He lived to see his twelve-volume Washington sell well, even in obscure villages of the South and West. More than 600,000 copies of his books (about 70) were sold before his death in 1866. Besides his mammoth Washington volumes, he prepared a ten-volume collection of Franklin's papers, including a fairly realistic biographic volume, and a twelve-volume *Diplomatic Correspondence of the American Revolution;* most of his numerous biographies proved justly ephemeral, however.[3]

Sparks's *Washington* might be a stolid piece of work, but his service in collecting and editing the documents related to his subject paved the way for an imaginative and absorbing five-volume life written by Washington Irving. The gifted New York litterateur transmuted the documents into the best Washington biography up until that time. Since Sparks had issued largely official papers, Irving contented himself with these and concluded comfortably, "Washington in fact had very little private life, but was eminently a public character." Still he kept him in the foreground, not buried in the history of the Revolution. Although he hewed away some of the austerity that hemmed in the human being, Irving approached his subject with the reverence of the cultist, stressing idealistic and ignoring social and economic forces. Actually this anecdotal biography betrayed Irving's declining mental powers. But his prestige, literary facility, and the renown of his subject attracted an entire generation of readers, especially after the five volumes had been abridged for school children.

Washington Irving belonged to the eastern Whig elite of bright salon conservatives who shuddered at the mob unleashed by Jacksonian democracy. He was the friend of John Jacob Astor, New York's fabulous real-estate and fur magnate, and had even been appointed executor of the vast estate. When Irving dealt with the Pacific Northwest in *Astoria,* he did not permit his sentimentality for the Indians to divert him into showing the actual grievances of the redskins. At all times he identified himself with the successful businessman. As a consistent Hamiltonian Federalist and Whig, he used his clever satire to caricature Jefferson (as Stanley T. Williams has shown) in his *A History of New York* (1809). In it Governor William Kieft is pictured as a blundering charlatan affected by puerile ideas of pacifism and economy and prone to invent such useless things as weathercocks that turned against the wind.

Probably Irving's best historical work was his *Columbus* (1828), which rested largely on the recent researches of Navarrete and partly upon his own studies while a diplomat in Spain; but this, too, like his *Life of George Washington,* was sentimental and idealized, though more craftsmanlike. The liberties that he took with the facts and his perpetuation of such Columbus legends as the story of the egg made specialists wince at the "pure moonshine." Samuel Eliot Morison has written, "Washington Irving, scenting his opportunity for a picturesque and moving scene took a fictitious account of this nonexistent university council (of Salamanca) published 130 years after the event, elaborated on it, and let his imagination go completely." In this way, Irving made Columbus's "mere force of natural genius" refute the academic pedants who held that the earth was flat. But so great was Irving's appeal to his generation that his historical books alone earned for him a fortune of $118,000.[4]

3

In this period there are two indefatigable plagiarists whose books on the Revolution are still praised today by discriminating historians. They were Dr. David Ramsay of South Carolina and the English-born the Reverend William Gordon of Massachusetts. (Fortunately, they had other virtues as historians.) No one has yet discovered how much of what these men wrote originated in the *Annual Register* and kindred sources, but Orin Libby and Sidney G. Fisher leave a melancholy impression of slavish borrowing. Gordon took page after page from the *Annual Register,* including its Whiggish view that the patriots would have settled for a compromise short of independence if their commercial practices and *de facto* autonomy had been respected. Gordon had been a late arrival to the colonies, coming only in 1770, but his strong Whig beliefs made it possible for him to take a sympathetic view of colonial claims and a corresponding unfriendly view of the Tories in power. Contemporaries honored his presumably meticulous four-volume work, *The History of the Rise, Progress, and Establishment of the Independence of the United States of America.* Its sweeping claims of having consulted innumerable letters, documents, and other sources properly awed the readers until the end of the century, when Libby exposed Gordon's plagiarism.

The destruction of Ramsay's historical reputation is still far from complete, but the damaging inferences are almost irreparable. A medical doctor, state legislator, and a delegate to the Continental Con-

gress, he seemed credible when he, like Gordon, insisted that his researches had been unique in their extent. "Every letter written to Congress by General Washington, from the day he took command of the
American army till he resigned it, was carefully perused, and its con-
tents noted. The same was done with the letters of other general officers, ministers of Congress, and others in public stations." But to
save space, he explained, he was dispensing with documentation. His
very popular political and military biography of Washington, which
offered little that was new, went through several editions; its debt to
other historians of the Revolution, as well as to the indispensable
Annual Register, is now painfully clear. The same can be said of his
two-volume magnum opus, *The History of the American Revolution*
(1789).

Ramsay's judgments, at least, frequently differed from Burke's, and
his devotion to the tolerant ideals of the Enlightenment added a strong
personal quality. He showed a realistic appraisal of "the known self-
ishness of human nature" and made this evaluation of the Puritan
persecution of minorities: "Human nature is the same in all bodies
of men, and . . . those who are in, and those who are out of power,
insensibly exchange opinions with each other in a change of their
respective situations." He traced colonial self-government back to the
first settlements, which was only partly true, and pointed out the
wise early policy of England in refraining from enforcing the mercantilistic policy. One of the causes for the Revolution he saw in the over-
extension of the British Empire. "Power, like all things human, has its
limits, and there is a point beyond which the longest and sharpest
sword fails of doing execution."

English jealousy of American "opulence" was another factor, he
thought (a theme stressed by Parson Weems); and England's chief
error was in forgetting that the colonies were not originally established for the sake of revenue but on the principles of a commercial
monopoly. With the objectivity of an American who was making heavy
use of Burke's Whig arguments, he praised John Adams and the jury
for understanding that, in the Boston massacre, the British soldiers
had been goaded beyond endurance. As a good Whig, he blamed the
English gentry and the aristocratic ruling class for the war. The motives of the American Association in boycotting tea were not necessarily patriotic: "This proceeded as much from the spirit of gain as
of patriotism."

Ramsay's familiarity with medicine and the arts led him to enrich his
political and military history with a chapter or two of social, cultural,

and economic developments based on first-hand observations. His second volume of the history of the Revolution, devoted to military affairs, took up also the war-time role of the American Irish and Germans, the current spur to business, the battlefield gains for surgery, and the flourishing state of literature, music, and education. He displayed keen perception in depicting the revolutionary inspiration of excellent satiric verse, learned societies (especially in Pennsylvania), and free democratic institutions.

These volumes had not only to compete with Gordon's work on the same subject but ran into such British hostility that his publisher declined to get into trouble by distributing the books. Too many of the chief participants were still alive. From France, Jefferson supported the project vigorously: "I should be sorry," he wrote Ramsay, "that any circumstances should occasion the disguising those truths which it equally seems our honor and the just infamy of our enemies have handed down to posterity in their true light." He took the initiative of advertising the work as available in Paris, while his protégé Freneau even wrote a poem on Ramsay's quarrel with England. However, absolutely nothing, not even controversy, could improve foreign sales. Pirated editions in London and Dublin absorbed what overseas demand existed. The episode reveals how Jefferson's war against England's ruling classes included historiography as well as the effort to displace Georgian architecture by French classicism and the attempt to keep out the common law.

Still, Ramsay was actually a confirmed Federalist rather than a Jeffersonian in politics, for, despite many liberal views on slavery and the revolutionary tradition, he belonged to the tidewater conservatives who fought the small farmer in the legislature. While he was a state legislator, he opposed paper money and other measures for the relief of the debtor class.

Ramsay's disregard for literary property also injured his renowned two-volume *History of South Carolina* (1809), for the first volume was taken in part from Alexander Hewat's history of the state, although this was written from a Tory viewpoint. Happily, Ramsay's second volume—so far—is conceded to be a much more original work.[5]

Writing for a somewhat less popular audience, the scholarly Federalist, Timothy Pitkin of Connecticut, combined an anti-Jeffersonian career in Congress with a hobby of studying and collecting historical manuscripts and state papers. He was one of Connecticut's old guard, which kept that state among the last to separate church and state and to oust the Presbyterian theocrats. After 1816, the date his chief work,

A Statistical View of the Commerce of the United States, appeared, he gained a reputation as an accurate, if dull, economic historian whose statistics were indispensable for scholars, businessmen, and journalists. His more ambitious two-volume economic history which covered the years 1763 to 1797 gave the Federalist viewpoint further acceptance among the middle class. He drew largely from Chalmers for the facts and the interpretations of the colonial years, but there was little analysis added, save for occasional expressions of personal opinions. Yet he fully recognized the role of our democratic land system and of free schools in promoting the American's love of liberty.

Now and then a Jeffersonian who could afford the necessary leisure vied with the Federalists in writing history. Of necessity this resulted in quite a different selection of facts and interpretations. Mrs. Mercy Otis Warren, one of America's pioneer women of letters, was the sister of James Otis, brilliant opponent of the Writs of Assistance, and the wife of James Warren, noted Massachusetts patriot. Although her father was a well-to-do lawyer, she had actually had little formal schooling, but there were ample opportunities for a voracious reader like Mercy. Her residence in Thomas Hutchinson's former home apparently whetted her appetite for a liberty feud against the "Machiavellian" historian; in fact her writings contributed to his discomfiture and exile by making notorious his letter calling for "an abridgment of English liberties in colonial administration." Most of her prolific satires, plays, and verse had wide appeal, but her history tended to be dull.

Her three-volume *History of the Revolution* (1805) remained in manuscript for seventeen years; eventually it became clear that this work too belonged to the progeny of the *Annual Register,* at least as far as some of its chief sources were concerned. It assailed Thomas Hutchinson as "dark, intriguing, insinuating, haughty and ambitious, while the extreme of avarice marked each feature of his character." Her characterization of John Hancock stuck with later historians— fickle, fond of applause, and used by those who found his fortune useful. Sam Adams, unlike the usual Tory-Federalist portrait of him, was praised as quick of understanding, liberal, tranquil, and unruffled. But she had no use for the hereditary distinction of the Order of the Cincinnati and severely arraigned John Adams as too much the prejudiced admirer of the British monarchical idea to be reconciled to republicanism. When Adams vehemently protested, she reminded him of his former harsh comments about the necessity of governing the masses.

Mrs. Warren's liberalism derived from Locke's doctrine of natural rights. As a pioneer feminist, she argued the mental equality of both sexes and the right of women to full educational opportunities. On the other hand, she shared the conservatives' aversion to the radical agrarian program of paper money inflation. Nor did she permit her anti-Federalist liberalism to reconcile her to the religious skepticism of Gibbon, Hume, and Paine.[6]

4

Among a host of state histories, scarcely any eclipsed the craftsmanship of the patriot-historian, the Reverend Jeremy Belknap of New Hampshire. Born in 1744 of a well-to-do merchant, educated at Harvard, and valued as a popular pastor for twenty years at Dover, New Hampshire, he was intensely involved as a community leader who frequently used his pulpit to urge the cause of nationalism. Perhaps he learned to love history from Thomas Prince of Old South Church, where his family had worshiped. He was a moderate Calvinist, for he leaned toward humanitarian doctrines of practical ethics and tolerance rather than to dogmatic theology. A pioneer antislavery leader, he worked for the immediate abolition of the slave trade. But like the usual eighteenth-century liberal, he was far more interested in economic individualism than in legislative aid for rural debtors.

These Enlightenment beliefs underlay his three-volume work, *The History of New Hampshire,* begun in 1772 and printed in 1784-92; it was based without doubt upon numerous manuscripts, official documents, personal correspondence, and interviews. He tried to present the characteristics, the passions, interests, and traits of the persons discussed and to capture the most striking features of the times. In these books, as in later ones, he stressed social and economic history rather than political affairs. The sections on New Hampshire topography represented to a large extent his own first-hand explorations in the White Mountains and elsewhere. At the same time he also occupied himself with a two-volume *American Biography.* His treatment of William Penn, a rather full portrait, showed his enthusiasm for the Quaker traits of tolerance, humanitarianism, and even non-conformity. So popular were Belknap's histories that William Cullen Bryant paid him the compliment of asserting that he was "the first to make American history attractive."

Belknap's nationalist fervor grew with independence and the French Revolution. In his copious correspondence with Ebenezer Hazard and others, he followed Hamilton and the Federalists in calling for a strong

central government, a high tariff, industrialization, nationalist indoctrination in the schools, and a copyright to protect American writers.
The most concrete result of his nationalist propaganda was the organization in 1791 of the notable Massachusetts Historical Society, which
still continues actively to promote historical knowledge by collecting
sources and issuing publications on American history. One reason for
this step was the fact that fires had destroyed such invaluable collections as Dr. Prince's library in Old South Church. Also, a mob had
scattered and partly destroyed many of Hutchinson's precious manuscripts. Belknap's scholarly friend, Ebenezer Hazard, the postmaster-
general, earned the gratitude of historians by diligently collecting
masses of historical documents relating to New England, published as
Historical Collections (1792-94).[7]

5

Another Federalist historian and nationalist who did much for America's declaration of cultural independence was Noah Webster. Like
Jefferson, Belknap, Jedidiah Morse, the historian-geographer, and so
many of his contemporaries, he decried effete Europe and urged indoctrination in things American. The idea of unspoiled republican
America illuminating the world spurred him on to most effective propaganda. This "schoolmaster to America" earned a lasting reputation as
a maker of dictionaries, grammars, and school readers which emphasized native pronunciations, spelling, and background. Through his
widely distributed readers, a moralistic history made its way into the
curriculum of American schools. Instead of honoring the grand British
themes, schoolboys declaimed "Warren's Oration on the Boston Massacre," Washington's speeches, or Freneau's patriotic poems.

Noah Webster's full-length *History of the United States* first appeared in 1787 and expanded with each subsequent edition for many
years. It stressed the nationalist theme in a narrative which began with
"The Dispersion at Babel" of our English ancestors; in medieval style,
it even included some essential information on the biblical origin of
the world. His textbook questions, heavily laden with the American
point of view, made certain that the schoolboy knew only the patriot's version of the Revolution:

What jealousy did the English Court entertain respecting the American
colonies?
When was the first blood shed by the troops in Boston?

When and where did the British first fire on the Americans? How many men were killed?

Webster, like Belknap, Mercy Warren, and so many other contemporary historians, made no effort to be fair to Daniel Shays's cause; in fact, he was even less plausible than they in explaining the farmer's rebellion, declaring that "the habits of the people had become luxurious and licentious." Thus he ensured that the new generation escaped some of the "Jacobinical opinions" of the Revolution. Though he had broken away from the institutional Christianity of the Puritans, he still emphasized the hand of God in the unfolding of human events.[8]

Also in the forefront of the Federalist textbook writers was the Yale-educated preacher, Jedidiah Morse, "father of American geography." He was a Calvinist conservative who vigorously attacked the infiltration of Unitarianism into Harvard and other Congregational strongholds. His geography texts, which monopolized the schools, stressed American illustrations and encouraged regional pride in New England's past. He was the chief collaborator in the textbook, *A Compendious History of New England* (1804), which combined Calvinist morality and nationalism. "Idleness," he wrote, "even in those of independent fortunes, is universally disreputable." History, he thought, was essentially intended to improve morals:

[History] brings to view the exact fulfillment of scripture prophecies; she displays goodness in real life with all its felicities, vice with all its miseries. Examples of individuals, great and good, of communities distinguished for integrity and success, peacefully persuade to an imitation of their virtues.

Morse's histories, such as *Annals of the American Revolution* (1824), were usually patriotic compilations. All of his energies seemed concentrated upon the task of preserving Calvinist orthodoxy in New England and uncritical loyalty to the nation.[9]

The exile of Hutchinson, Chalmers, William Smith, and other talented loyalist historians during the Revolution left a vacuum for a generation that even Jared Sparks and Jeremy Belknap could not fill. Out of the new ruling class came only mediocre historians, Weemsian sentimentalists, and inept Washington cultists who offered a parochial interpretation of the nation's past. The impressive historical tradition from Bradford to Hutchinson was shattered. But this postrevolutionary record of futility in historiography was shortly to be redeemed by two gifted young men, Richard Hildreth and George Bancroft.

☆ 4 ☆

Richard Hildreth,
Utilitarian Philosopher

Among the historians who lent distinction to the New England Renaissance was the shy but versatile Richard Hildreth (1807-65), exponent of utilitarianism in his philosophy and in his theory of history. Unlike Prescott who sought exotic civilizations, or Bancroft and the elder Morse who gaily romanticized the American tradition, Hildreth applied to history the hard-headed tests of philosophic utility and shaped the result with his spirit of social protest. Then as if purposely to mystify biographers and historians, he engrafted upon his basically democratic outlook a Whig interpretation of history in which Jefferson and the Democratic-Republicans fared most cruelly.

The best key to Hildreth's theories lies in his adaptations of the novel English utilitarian philosophy of Jeremy Bentham and his followers. They expected that their ideas would replace the vague abstractions of metaphysics and morality with a kind of scientific empiricism that could be precisely measured. Their chief principle of social action lay in the idea that men seek pleasure (good) and avoid pain (evil). Thus they calculated the maximum of these pleasures and pains for a specific situation in order to determine "the greatest good of the greatest number."

The conclusions derived from this "principle of utility" are easily recognizable in Hildreth's histories and philosophical discussions: Society is ruled by interests and classes. Man by pursuing his "enlight-ened self-interest" is thereby serving all society. Utility in economics favored the doctrines of free trade, free competition, antimonopoly in business and finance, the removal of restraints on labor organiza-tions, and low taxes. In the field of penology it called for punishments that would seek mainly to deter crime and rehabilitate the criminal. Universal secular education and political democracy, not violent up-heavals like the French Revolution, should guide the individual. And religion must be rationalistic, devoid of superstition.[1] The emphasis on action, upon squaring experimental theories with radical practice, would justify what later historians called the New History—which was in large part the use of historical facts and theories to reform society.

Another key to Hildreth lies in his biography. Living on a farm in rural Massachusetts the Hildreths shared the pioneer tradition of many of their neighbors; they, too, could easily trace their ancestry to the area's seventeenth-century beginnings. Richard's father, the Rev-erend Hosea Hildreth, had emancipated himself from Puritan literal-ism by preaching liberal Congregational sermons, then turned to school teaching, and eventually becoming a professor of mathematics and natural philosophy at Phillips Exeter Academy. He also lectured upon American history and even wrote textbooks in geography and history.

Richard, born in 1807, was raised in Federalist Connecticut and studied under his father at the Academy. Later at Harvard, his inter-ests were strongly in history; he admired especially Gibbons, Hume, and the other leading rationalist historians of the Enlightenment. He tried school teaching and even practiced law for a few years, but his urge to write decided him upon the career of journalism and he joined the staff of the Boston *Atlas*. Later, in his own paper, the Boston *Spy*, he wrote prolifically in behalf of the Whig cause and even did a cam-paign biography for William Henry Harrison in the Log Cabin elec-tion of 1840. Like his father, as well as other Whig leaders, he propa-gandized for prohibition and against slavery.

He was no opportunistic Whig, for his lengthy attacks on slavery absorbed much of his energies. He pictured the slavocracy of the South as conspirators intent upon the annexation of Texas. Frankly considering himself as the exponent of a middle-class social outlook, he attacked the Democratic party as a coalition of reactionary plant-ers and demagogic working-class radicals. "The alliance of a rich and ambitious aristocracy with the corrupted and most degraded portion of the populace to oppress and trample upon the great middle-class is the natural course of things," he asserted.

Hildreth is credited with writing the first antislavery novel in the United States, *The Slave, or Memoirs of Archy Moore* (Boston, 1836), which may easily have furnished grist to the mill of Mrs. Stowe. But the book was premature, for no mass audience was ready for abolitionism. In 1840 he published another arraignment of slavery in *Despotism in America*, a title which revealed his intention to draw an unfavorable contrast with De Tocqueville's *Democracy in America*. He would solve the problem of slavery by offering compensated emancipation on the British West Indies model.

His ideas on finance showed how far he was from orthodox Whig doctrine on party essentials. In 1837, he published *The History of Banks* and insisted so uncompromisingly upon the utilitarian idea of free competition and anti-monopoly that he left no room for the fundamental Whig party banking program. He could not accept the Clay-Webster-Biddle idea of government-sponsored banking monopolies and went so far as to defend Jackson's war on the bank and his Specie Circular, which had the virtue of checking speculative inflation.

Bentham's philosophy of utilitarianism gave Hildreth's historical theory much of its clarity and consistency.[2] He absorbed this philosophy through his translation of the writings of French utilitarians, who were concerned with the reform of legislative practices. Unfortunately for Hildreth's style, he took too literally Bentham's advice to avoid literary art. Had not the great one declared flatly: "The partisan of the principle of utility is in a position by no means so favourable to eloquence. His means are as different as his object. He can neither dogmatize, dazzle, nor astonish. He is obliged to define all his terms, and always to employ the same word in the same sense." Although this formula actually permitted ample room for good writing, Hildreth often interpreted this in a strict sense, and the result was monotony for pages on end.

From Bentham, too, Hildreth borrowed readily the reformist slogan of the greatest good of the greatest number and the rationalist separation of ethics from formal religion and theology. Utility in action, not theological axioms, was the pragmatic test of right motives. He agreed with Bentham that property was the chief foundation of government, and he arrived at the distinctly non-Whig conclusion that a more equal distribution of property would actually enhance its security and the stability of society. Such beliefs and borrowed theories explain his unique mixture of Whiggism and what seemed at times to be outright Jeffersonian agrarianism, anticlericalism, and middle-class radicalism. But he felt confident that his brand of radicalism was as scientific as the mathematics table, whereas similar ideas to the left were mere demagogy. This, it will be recalled, was also an abiding belief of Karl Marx.

The book which put him in the forefront of American historians was his *History of the United States of America* (1849-52), a six-volume work for which he did the research mainly in the Boston Athenaeum library and used only printed sources. Hildreth's anti-literary approach guaranteed that his book would not reach the highly dramatic level of Bancroft. The advances made in philology in his time strongly influenced Hildreth's dedication to the scientific ideal. The European philologists and folklorists were teaching a painstaking method of internal and external criticism of documents which historians soon took up. Comte and the positivists had insisted that science required the search for facts which would be used later as the raw materials for scientists who were pioneer sociologists.

Like Thucydides (as well as Bentham), Hildreth made the unadorned style his vehicle of scientific history, but, fortunately for his readers, he frequently departed from his ascetic rule and created vivid pictures and made emphatic judgments. There was even humor in his work, though largely the mild "dead-pan" variety which easily escaped readers. It is not surprising that he made only small inroads into Bancroft's public, although, by the end of the century, when scientific history was in vogue, readers rediscovered the merits of Hildreth and showed dissatisfaction with the "spread-eagle-ism" of his competitor. By that time, Hildreth's volumes were winning warm praise from such discerning historians as Edward Channing, James Schouler, and G. P. Gooch. But during the first seven years, Hildreth's total royalties were less than $4500—scarcely comparable to Bancroft's earnings.

The advertisement of 1849, strangely enough, promised to present "living and breathing men"—a phrase which probably meant strict realism in contrast to dramatic picturization. The work was intended "to trace our institutions, religious, social, and political from their embryo state" up to the present. This suggested the author's adherence to the doctrine of historical development, if not organic historicism. He claimed—quite honestly—to have used recently published letters and memoirs, but renounced any "parade of references" which would increase the size and cost of the book. More promises were implied in his gibe at the chauvinistic historians of the Bancroft type:

Of centennial sermons and Fourth of July orations, whether professedly such or in the guise of history, there are more than enough. It is due to our fathers and ourselves, it is due to truth and philosophy to present for once, on the historic stage, the founders of our American nation unbedaubed with patriotic rouge, wrapped up in no finespun cloaks of excuses and apology, without stilts, buskins, tinsel, or bedizenment, in their own proper persons, often rude, hard, narrow, superstitious, and mistaken, but always earnest, downright, manly, and sincere.

New Englanders squirmed at his treatment of colonial times. "It was attempted," he wrote intolerantly, "to make the colony, as it were, a convent of Puritan devotees—except in the allowance of marriage and money-making." Furthermore, he said, the Catholics had far more reason to emigrate from England because of persecution than did the Puritans. His vigorous dislike of racialism was reflected in his sardonic comment on the Puritans' view of the Indians. Hildreth called it the mere rationalizing of bigots to justify the persecution of the redmen. He agreed heartily with William Byrd II that the refusal of the English to intermarry with the Indians despite the shortage of white women tended to widen the gap between the races and insure Indian wars. "But the idea of such an intermixture was abhorrent to the English, who despised the Indians as savages, and detested them as heathen."

It is not surprising that Hildreth frankly reported, in the 1853 edition of his work, "The undress portraits which I have presented of our colonial progenitors . . . have given very serious offense, especially in New England, region of set formality and hereditary grimace . . ." Defiantly, he said that he was "too proud to bask in the sunshine of national vanity," striking out apparently at the irritatingly successful Bancroft and his imitators. In case anyone missed this reference, the next words were clear enough: He felt only contempt for "all kinds of cant, especially the so fashionable cant of a spasmodic, wordy rhetoric and a transcendental philosophy."

His anticlericalism, which was strongly supported by the utilitarians, was reflected in his criticism of the Puritan theocracy. He spoke of "that everyday supernaturalism which formed so prominent a feature of the Puritan theology." Like a modern psychologist he probed the minds of the Mathers: "The secret consciousness of these doubts of their own was perhaps one source of their great impatience at the doubts of others." Yet, this time like present-day historians, he had only praise for Cotton Mather's courage and enlightenment in supporting smallpox inoculation against popular superstition, the violent threats of the mob, and the stubborn resistance of the doctors. When he came to the episode of the French Catholics exiled from Acadia by the British, he openly avowed his feelings, "Such is religious and national antipathy. May we not hope that hatreds so atrocious are fast dying out?" He showed similar sympathies for the persecuted when he came to the arrival of Jewish refugees to Georgia.

His rationalist outlook led him to denounce emphatically the sway of extreme emotionalism in religion, notably in the way he dealt with the Great Awakening. Caustically, he concluded, "As the necessity of education to qualify men to be teachers of religion and morals diminished in the popular view, reason and learning, not needed in the pulpit, found other avenues to the public mind." He theorized that politics became more secularized as the revivalists deserted it for the camp meeting. Triumphantly he argued that despite the undeniable success of the revivalists, religion had thenceforth declined in political and historical importance while religious freedom had gained. Naturally he showed only condemnation for the Puritan theocracy and their union of Church and State. To a good rationalist they represented only anachronistic survivals of medievalism.

Interestingly enough, he found a convenient explanation for discrediting Jefferson's type of anticlericalism. Jefferson, by opposing public aid to religious teaching, had thereby removed the check against the fanaticism of the shouting preachers provided by a well-educated clergy, strengthened by decent salaries. The result was the fanatical camp meeting of the South and the West. Ordinary rationalists, who had not been introduced to the utilitarian deviations from their faith, must have been surprised to read Hildreth's attack on the free-thinkers of the French Revolution: "Free-thinkers denounce prevailing opinions, and appeal to first principles, and religious enthusiasts do the same thing." Like the later pragmatists he rejected *a priori* arguments.

Along utilitarian lines he relied upon a basic economic interpretation of history to explain fundamental movements like the American Revolution. Britain's error, he thought, lay in her failure either to conciliate the colonists or to attach them by the ties of self-interest, since "mere authority" could not control them. The struggle, he felt, had taken on the aspect of inevitability since the victory of the commercial and manufacturing classes in the Glorious Revolution of 1688:

By strengthening the Parliament, and increasing the influence of the manufacturing class, it exposed the American plantations to increased danger of mercantile and parliamentary tyranny, of which, in the acts of trade, they already had a foretaste—a tyranny far more energetic, persevering, grasping, and more to be dreaded than any probable exercise of merely regal authority.

Hildreth's protracted military history of the Revolution was monotonous and did not have any guiding hypothesis. Nevertheless, his objectivity must have been annoying to a generation of Americans raised on "spread-eagle" history. Speaking of Bunker Hill, he remarked that all of the Americans engaged were not heroes. "The conduct of several officers on that day was investigated by court martial, and one, at least, was cashiered for cowardice." He was one of the few American historians to mention patriot atrocities against the Tories, particularly the "barbarous and disgraceful practice of tarring and feathering, and carting Tories." On the other hand, he did not permit the British to escape their share of the blame.

There is a striking similarity between Hildreth's explanation of the economic forces making for the Constitution and Charles Beard's *Economic Interpretation of the Constitution*. Beard, of course, shared Hildreth's pragmatic temper and distrust of *a priori* rationalism. For both men, concerned with the dominant drive of self-interest in history, the paramount theme was the conflict between creditor and debtor. Both stressed the pivotal significance of Shays's Rebellion as an indication of populist pressures, together with the role of other protest movements elsewhere at the time. Hildreth went as far as to say, "The democracy had no representatives" in the Convention. It was actually a conservative body which looked upon property "not so much as one right, to be secured like the rest, but as the great and chief right, of more importance than all others." In language that Beard might have used later, he said, "The public creditors, especially, demanded some authority able to make the people pay; and among a certain class, even monarchy began to be whispered of as a remedy for popular maladministration." Their victory was marked by the constitutional provision forbidding the states to emit bills of credit, thus reviving the anti-paper-money policy of Britain before the Revolution but in a more stringent form.

Beard must have read at some time Hildreth's observation that "it was exceedingly doubtful whether, upon a fair canvass, a majority of the people, even in the ratifying states, were in favor of the new constitution." In later years Beard and O. G. Libby were to document this statement. Like Hildreth, Beard, and Libby, modern historians tend to agree that the heart of the ratification vote lay in the commercial towns. Hildreth anticipated Beard's conclusion that the new Constitution worked because a solid core of self-interest held the new nation together. For Hildreth, with his fear of inflation and unsecured paper money, there was no alternative to the new Constitution. Similarity of interpretations makes it easy to understand why Beard so greatly admired Richard Hildreth.

Such opinions led him to write approvingly of Hamilton's program of funding the national debt and assuming the state debts: "By the restoration of confidence in the nation, confidence in the states, and confidence in individuals, the funding system actually added to the labor, land, and capital of the country a much greater value than the amount of the debt thereby charged upon them." Thus, as a good utilitarian, he calculated that the Hamiltonian system served the greatest good of the greatest number. Still, Hildreth was honestly disturbed by the crass bias underlying Hamilton's reforms; he conceded the justice of Madison's idea of keeping the speculator's gains down to the low market value of the government securities prevailing before the fiscal reform. He felt that Hamilton went too far in his desire "to attach the most wealthy and influential part of the community to (the Constitution) by the ties of personal and pecuniary advantage." While the Secretary was motivated by "an exalted sense of personal honor and patriotic duty," he tended "like many other men of the world, to ascribe to motives of pecuniary and personal interest a somewhat greater influence over the course of events than they actually possess." Having but little confidence either in the virtue or the judgment of the mass of mankind, he thought the administration of affairs most safe in the hands of the select few. But Hildreth as a utilitarian was not too far from the assumptions of Hamilton regarding the basic role of class and self-interest in history. Moreover, Hildreth's genuine reformist fervor on such issues as slavery kept him out of the camp of those who left human affairs to automatic self-correcting devices.

Hildreth was least plausible when he dealt with Jefferson. The Sage of Monticello appeared to him to be a bookish man, a rashly speculative bigot in politics, and a narrow politician who was always jealous of Hamilton. Even Jefferson's methodical habit of keeping a journal was taken by Hildreth as evidence of a desire to spy upon and censure his colleagues. He sneered at Jefferson's "affectation of indifference to office" and "ultra-Republican prudery."

On the impact of the French Revolution upon American affairs, he managed to combine the strong opposition that Benthamites felt for social changes by violence with a contempt for the alleged incompetence of the Jeffersonians, particularly for their toleration of the abuses practiced by the French revolutionaries. His evaluation of the French Revolution is characteristic: "The idea of a short cut to liberty and equality by killing off kings and aristocrats was quite too fascinating to be easily abandoned." As for Jacobinism, this he summed up as a new "horrible despotism, not to be paralleled except by the worst passages in the history of the worst times." It seemed to him justifiable, therefore, for the Federalists to look to England as champion of law, order, religion and property, against what seemed the "demoniac fury" of the French Revolutionists.

As a good civil rights man, he condemned the Alien and Sedition Acts, but he hastened to lighten the onus against Adams and the framers of these laws by saying, "It is sufficient to suggest here that the act was a temporary one, passed at a moment of threatened war, and while the government was assailed in print with a malice and ferocity scarcely paralleled before or since."

Critical historians have found Hildreth's explanation of parties to be downright partisan. He pictured the Federalists under Washington and Hamilton as representing "the experience, the prudence, the practical wisdom, the discipline, the conservative reason and instincts of the country." This left Jefferson's party with a monopoly of quixotic ideas and undisciplined individualism; it was the crude beneficiary of numerical majorities in the uncivilized West and the despotic slaveholders' South. He explained away the presence of the Southern tidewater aristocrats within the Federalist party as due to a combination of talent, English culture, and wealth.

Jefferson's commercial policies were also misinterpreted by Hildreth, who took literally some of the oft-quoted strictures on trade that appear in the Virginian's letters. The president, he thought, desired to destroy commerce and navigation, as befitted one who reflected the popular envy of the profits of merchants. On this matter of commerce, the Embargo, and the responsibility of the Jeffersonians in bringing about the War of 1812, Hildreth was a completely partisan New Englander. He held that the United States was heavily indebted to British trade and that the Embargo meant war. The War party of 1812, he thought, consisted of anti-British elements raised on the hatreds of the Revolution, Irish and French refugee editors and printers, Republican manufacturers in infant industries anxious to exclude British products, those affected by the current war spirit in Europe, and finally, the ambitious Clay and Calhoun, who wished to destroy the Federalists and to dominate the Madison administration.

Hildreth's sixth and last volume appeared in 1851 and ended the narrative with 1821, the mid year of Monroe's presidency and the completion of the Missouri Compromise struggle. The termination date, he said, marked a new era in American history, resulting from the new states carved from the Louisiana territory. The old party history was now fundamentally changed by the injection of the slavery issue. The old quarrels over the Embargo and the War of 1812 had been replaced by the bank controversy, the internal improvements issue, and the tariff question. With the Missouri issue, he concluded, "the slave interest, hitherto hardly recognized as a distinct element in the American social system, had started up portentous and dilated— disavowing the very fundamental principle of modern democracy, threatening the dissolution of the Union, unless allowed to dictate their own terms." [8]

Reading over some of his critical reviews, he was nettled by those who said that his history had "no philosophy" in it, so he proceeded to show that he had one. In his next book, *The Theory of Politics* (1854), which he claimed to have composed a dozen years before, he used the language of utilitarianism to explain that the nature of government was based on the "pleasure of superiority" enjoyed by the ruling class and the "pain of inferiority" which marked the ruled. Natural human equality was merely a fiction, anarchic when it was applied; men were kept down by fear, admiration of their rulers, and the assumed duty of obedience; but fraud and fear could be replaced by conviction and consent.

Like many writers of our day, he gave considerable attention to the role of power in politics and history and redefined it to include intellectual, psychological, and material ingredients. But he rejected all efforts to reduce social science to a simple monistic explanation:

The circumstance, indeed, that political power is so generally used as a means of accumulating wealth, so that wealth and power are almost always found in company, has led to the idea of a more intimate relation between them than actually exists . . .

Nor is there any more fruitful source of error, whether in philosophical inquiries or in the ordinary affairs of life, than the disposition to refer every effect to a single cause; whereas almost all the phenomena of human society result from a combination, and often a very complicated combination, of causes.

In typical utilitarian language, he illustrated the meaning of power, "He who possesses the means of conferring pleasures, or inflicting pain, upon others, possesses a power over them proportioned to the potency of those means."

As a true Benthamite, he put his reliance upon representative government, social reform, and the progress of knowledge and thought "to raise the mass of the people to a more equal participation in the goods of life." But he denounced clerical and mystical influences as most reprehensible from the utilitarian point of view: "The most diabolical actions recorded in history have originated in the influence of mystical ideas."

In his chapters devoted to the course of world history, he showed a clear understanding of social development and surprised those who assumed that he was merely an erratic Whig. Modern history, he thought, was already revealing brief glimpses of the rise of a new social phenomenon, the masses:

The clergy, the nobles, the kings, the burghers have all had their turn. Is there never to be an Age of the People—of the working classes?

Is the suggestion too extravagant, that the new period commencing with the middle of this current century is destined to be that age? Certain it is, that within the last three quarters of a century, advocates have appeared for the mass of the people, the mere workers, and that movements, even during this age of the deification of money, and of reaction against the theory of human equality, have been made in their behalf such as were never known before.

Then in language which convinced some readers that he was a socialist, he went on to suggest that more power be given to the masses; this meant more education, as well as wealth and the right to combine. He denied that he favored any redistribution of wealth, but only an increase of productivity amid conditions of peace and social order. In fact he asked for little more than a comprehensive and careful study of social relations. "This socialist question," he asserted, "is not to be blinked out of sight. . . . It is a question for philosophers." Therefore he ended with a plea for more deliberation and piecemeal reform, as any Benthamite might have done. Revolution was distasteful to the utilitarians.[4]

For all his drawbacks, Hildreth showed much more realism and intellectual sophistication than most American historians of his day. He was among the few to escape the New England chauvinism and Anglo-Saxonism of Bancroft, Palfrey, and Parkman, and he could treat controversial topics like the American Revolution with modern objectivity. Unlike middle-class writers who ignored the ordinary man, he showed a social consciousness that was novel. A half-century later, his pioneer economic interpretations were to impress men like Beard, who thought of history in terms of interest groups. He wrote too early to be afflicted by the vogue for biological analogies and evolutionism in history, and he was too critical to swallow the non-Darwinian "germ theory" of Bancroft that history developed from roots cultivated by a guiding Providence. Always ahead of his age, he was an ardent abolitionist, even before it became respectable in New England. If he did not fully appreciate the virtues of history as art, he managed indeed to reach the perceptive mind.

George Bancroft
and German Idealism

1

In the flowering of New England, historians played an important part. Their literary romanticism found a warm response from the readers of that day. The best-sellers of 1830-70 were the histories or biographies by Prescott, Bancroft, Motley, Parkman, and Washington Irving. Their works not only sold more than 5000 copies shortly after publication, but maintained a steady sale over the years. Romantics of all ages idealized George Washington and other great men of the young republic; or they sought to escape to Prescott's Aztec civilization or to the adventurous West of Parkman. Emerson published his lectures on history, great men, and kindred themes, and in his Transcendentalist variety of romanticism, portrayed history as an idealistic form of self-revelation, though he warned against imitating the past. Americans might not always understand the Platonist or Hindu mysticism that the Transcendentalists talked about, but they appreciated the idea of self-trust and self-help as indigenous to the American experience. Bancroft's heavily Teutonic ideas of history quite missed the mark for most readers, but his exciting romantic picture of American progress and his eulogy of the common man struck a favorite theme of his era. Even in the twentieth century, Bancroft's histories have frequently appeared on college reading lists for history.

In Bancroft's time, the rationalist history books of Gibbon and Hume were partly replaced by the basically mystical and intuitive works of the romantics. However, the eighteenth-century approach did not lose out completely, for the doctrine of progress remained, and the natural rights beliefs of the Enlightenment commanded almost a mass allegiance. The Jacksonian cult of the Common Man, as exemplified by manhood suffrage, public schools, abolitionism, and trade unions, went far beyond the narrow confines of eighteenth-century liberalism. Secularism was stronger than ever, although the bellicose anticlericalism of Voltaire had declined before a wave of millennialism and Utopianism, which was reflected in a profusion of sects—Shakers, Mormons, Millerites, and many more. The romantics did not have the prejudices against the past that the Enlightenment had, but they found that self-discovery was rendered possible by re-examining the distant, the exotic, and the unknown. It was also in keeping with the new times that the Puritan interpretation of history, as exemplified by Bradford, should be levied upon for its idea of a Divine Providence shaping the destiny of America as His Elect among all nations. This was the background for Bancroft's nationalist bias and the chauvinism of those like him who espoused the expansionist doctrine of Manifest Destiny.

While the eighteenth-century historians had sometimes neglected the notion of development in history, since they regarded the present as an abrupt break from an irrational past, the nineteenth-century romantics stressed the iron law of continuous development often to dubious extremes. They were much concerned with tradition, emotion, the irrational, and the ideal of humanity. American romanticists like Bancroft, as well as the next generation of "scientific historians" who studied in the Johns Hopkins seminar of Herbert Baxter Adams, were dominated by fresh historiographical impulses from Germany. Although Americans usually tended to look upon abstract "philosophies of history" with suspicion, few historians escaped the sweeping developmental hypotheses that came out of the German states, particularly from Kant, Fichte, Herder, Hegel, and Ranke. Prussia's rapid strides toward unification were spurred on by the nationalist feeling during the War of Liberation against Napoleon, by the work of folklorists such as the Grimm brothers, and finally, as Bismarck himself testified, by her historians. The French Revolution, with its ardent nationalistic slogans, awakened an interest among European peoples in their national origins and encouraged governments to sponsor archival collections. In Prussia, the historically minded statesman, Stein, who had organized the mighty struggle against Napoleon, patronized the publication of newly edited source materials dealing with the history of medieval Germany. Out of this vast co-operative effort was born the noted *Monumenta Germaniae Historica,* which became an indispensable quarry of data.[1]

2

Harvard College sent some of its most gifted graduates to acquire the new German learning in history, literature, theology, and pedagogy. Among the young men were George Ticknor, whose trips to Spain stimulated his interest in things Spanish and induced him to write an outstanding history of Spanish literature; Edward Everett, another of a long line of New Englanders to study at Göttingen, who eventually became president of Harvard and a United States Senator from Massachusetts; Joseph Cogswell, bibliographer and educator; Henry Wadsworth Longfellow; and, of course, George Bancroft.

Few took so readily to the speculative Teutonic ideas as Bancroft, a representative of the Boston Brahmin class but unlike them in his radical faith in the Common Man. Harvard was fast coming under the influence of liberal Christianity as the century began, but Bancroft had already imbibed from his father a nearly creedless form of Christianity. The Reverend Aaron Bancroft of Worcester, where George was born, had seceded from his orthodox Calvinist brethren and organized a liberal church; eventually he became a leader among American Unitarians. He had even written a very popular historical work, deeply tinged with the hero-worshiping mood of the day, entitled *The Life of Washington* (1807). His preface frankly stated that the book was intended for the "unlettered portion of the community."

Like many other Harvard graduates, George Bancroft studied in Göttingen's famed university, with a library that dwarfed those of American institutions and represented the center of educational efforts. The young scholar was transported by the current German enthusiasm not only for historical studies but also for other social studies and for classical and theological subjects: [2]

The darkest portions of history become almost transparent, when reason and acuteness are united with German perseverance. It is admirable to see with what calmness and patience every author is read, every manuscript collected, every work perused, which can be useful, be it dull or interesting, the work of genius or stupidity, to see how the most trifling coins and medals, the ruins of art and even the decay of nature is made to bear upon the investigated subject.

He also followed the current practice of attending lectures at other universities as well. At the University of Berlin, he may have listened very attentively to Hegel, the noted philosopher of history, despite his reputation for poor lecturing. However, the Hegelian ideas which seem to penetrate Bancroft's writings could very well have come from other lectures or writings to which Hegel himself was deeply indebted. One looks vainly in Bancroft's books for any discussion of Hegel, for the references seem mostly to be to the philosophies of history of Kant, Fichte, Heeren, and Herder.

Hegel had once admired the French Revolution and Napoleon, but he was shifting now to a type of state worship in which Prussia and the State incarnated the spirit of the Absolute moving through history. The newly orthodox philosopher of the University of Berlin went far beyond Kant in establishing a vogue for a "philosophy of history"— not merely a reflective attitude toward history (although Hegel accepted this definition also), but an integrated intellectual system. Bancroft was to quote Kant and his cosmopolitan ideas of erecting a "universal history" rather than the nationalistic Hegel. Kant hoped that such a universal history would show how the human race has advanced in rationality and hence increased its freedom; the history would unfold the development of the mind and spirit of man. From Herder, too, whom Bancroft acknowledged freely, he could have borrowed the idea of universal history and the theme of history as the record of the development of man's freedom, the moral reason of man.

In the Christian philosophy of history espoused by the followers of St. Augustine, divine purpose had been substituted for the classical notion of cyclic decline and fall. History was a revealing drama of Christ's redemption of man which followed in an inevitable process, culminating with the end of the world. Now the German proponents of a "philosophy of history" (Voltaire had originated the term), such as Herder, Heeren, and Hegel, offered a newer variety of "universal history" in which divine purpose would remain, but in a more secularized form, and be subordinated to "primordial ideas" and an underlying spirit of rationality which affected human events.

These Germans, whom Bancroft so extravagantly admired and followed, offered a schematic philosophy of history as a guide for mankind; for, as Hegel put it, the study of the mere facts of history might prove that vice is superior to virtue, since its triumph occurs so frequently. By making man a mere instrument of the evolving divine Idea, the German idealist historians and philosophers greatly reduced the importance of environmental factors as explanations of development. Bancroft's histories, too, showed this tendency. The American was also influenced by the notion of evolving "primordial ideas," the famous germ theory of historical growth which captured the American universities during the second half of the century.

Hegel's lectures on history, published later many times as *The Philosophy of History,* called for a universal history that was not merely the record of a single people or region but could reveal the logic and the principles of rational historical development, since Hegel believed that God ruled the world through reason. The goal of historical change was the "moral reign of freedom" attained through "the objective spirit of the State." He went on to say, "The history of the world is none other than the progress of the consciousness of Freedom; a progress whose development according to the necessity of its nature it is our business to investigate." Hegel's celebrated "dialectic" apparently came from Fichte, who explained progress and change by the struggle of conflicting ideas and their reconciliation into an ever-changing "thesis" which in turn disintegrates into new conflicts. Thus the conflict of absolutism and democracy, a central theme, was logically and historically resolved into constitutional monarchy. This kind of thinking, without the explicit technical Fichtean-Hegelian apparatus, affected Bancroft, Motley, and Parkman, among many others. Hegel expressed it thus:

> . . . it may be said of Universal History, that it is the exhibition of Spirit in the process of working out the knowledge of that which it is potentially. And as the germ bears in itself the whole nature of the tree, and the taste and form of its fruits, so do the first traces of Spirit virtually contain the whole of that History. The Orientals have not attained the knowledge that Spirit—Man as *such*—is free; and because they do not know this, they are not free.

At the University of Göttingen, Bancroft absorbed much from the distinguished historian, Arnold Heeren. In fact, while Bancroft was running the Round Hill School a few years later, he found time to translate Heeren's writings. In the *History of the Political System of Europe and Its Colonies* (1829), Heeren made a number of suggestions regarding the relation of the New World to the old which Bancroft found usable. The German's emphasis upon the need for a philosophic "universal history" brought praise from the translator. But, while critics praised Heeren's pioneer leadership in the economic interpretation of history, this left no impression upon the American whatever. Actually Heeren (like Ranke) was a rebel against the excesses in Germany of "our speculative historians," who regarded the European political system only as a link in a mystic chain of events and tried to measure the progress of humanity. Master and disciple differed also upon another fundamental: Heeren distrusted the potential despotism of the masses even more than he did the tyranny of monarchs, while Bancroft repeated over and over that the voice of the people was the voice of God; and the German rejected the idea of inevitable progress.

Perhaps Bancroft's debt to Herder (1744-1803) was more substantial, judging from his essays on this German poet and philosopher, who had published a monumental four-volume work upon the philosophy of history during 1784-91; there are also clear-cut similarities of ideas. Herder felt that history developed organically. He saw history as a process in which an entire folk matured with the inevitability of a flower. The notion of an evolving "folk spirit" affecting all facets of culture can also be found in Bancroft's work.

Bancroft's histories reflected many of these romantic tendencies associated with the German historians: the germ theory that made American institutions the flowering of ancient Teutonic folkways, the idealistic course of progress, and the teleological Divine plan of history which encompassed much more than the human will. But he was too imbued with the Christian interpretation of history—even if his Deity no longer acted as capriciously as the God of William Bradford and Cotton Mather—to believe that historical events should be judged solely by the morals and circumstances of their time. He was not a relativist, as were the late nineteenth-century "historicists," so many of whom (wrongly perhaps) hailed Ranke as their master. Unlike Ranke, Bancroft liked to make strong moral judgments, for he was perhaps constitutionally unable to take Ranke's passive attitude toward the victories of right or wrong in the pageant of history. The American was certain that justice lay with Jacksonian Democracy and the Common Man. However, like so many of the romantics, he often engulfed the personality of the individual within a blurred nation-group whose fate was already determined long ago in the "germ" of remote folkways and superior racial characteristics.[3]

3

After five years abroad, Bancroft came back to Boston in 1823, tutored Harvard boys briefly and unenthusiastically in Greek, and turned for a short time to the pulpit. His German enthusiasms irritated students, who groaned beneath his demands for thoroughness, and his sermons seemed too pagan even for reconstructed Puritans. He joined his talented friend Joseph Cogswell in introducing the new German-Swiss pedagogy through their preparatory school, Round Hill, a German "gymnasium" at Northampton, Massachusetts. A century before John Dewey, their school had foreign language tables, supervised play, individualized instruction, and pleasant varied assignments, as well as the classics, which were advertised as the school's outstanding feature. Unfortunately, this type of school proved too expensive and, besides, Bancroft became restless for literary work. He translated Heeren, wrote articles on German literature, and in 1831 severed his connection with Round Hill. He married a girl from a rich Whig family, which helped him financially, especially in securing assistants to transcribe documents.

Boston's Brahmins felt scandalized to observe Bancroft's upward march in radical politics and to read his populistic speeches delivered before Democrats and artisans of the Workingmen's party. Soon he became Collector of Customs in Boston, and the resulting patronage power gave him leadership in the state Democratic party. He told Orestes Brownson, "It is now for the yeomanry and the mechanics to march at the head of civilization. The day for the multitude has arrived." He held the radical Jacksonian anti-Bank views and even wrote a eulogistic campaign biography for Martin Van Buren. He helped to maneuver Polk into the Democratic nomination for President and was rewarded with the post of Secretary of the Navy. In office, he fought the flogging of sailors, made promotion contingent on merit rather than seniority, and successfully sponsored the building of a Naval Academy to train and indoctrinate an officer class. Few were more fervent than he in demanding the annexation of California in the name of Manifest Destiny. As Acting Secretary of War under Polk, he set the armed forces in readiness for action the moment war began. One of his major tasks was the planning of John Frémont's expedition into California, which was to be ready to strike in behalf of the American rebels in that Mexican province should war break out.

After the war, Bancroft became our minister to England, and he used that time to gather historical sources as well as to conduct diplomacy. After returning for a time to the writing of history, he emerged again in politics as the ghost writer for Andrew Johnson's message to Congress, a secret well-kept until revealed much later by William A. Dunning. Johnson rewarded him with the post of minister to Prussia, which he held during 1867-74. There he was able to meet Ranke and other great historians, as well as Moltke and Bismarck, the latter admired by him as a liberal conservative with a great love of liberty.[4]

Those years in Prussia were the stirring ones of the Franco-Prussian War and German unification. The patriotic historians came to the fore and repudiated Rankean objectivity for the idea that history must be interpreted in the light of present needs, which meant to the advantage of the German Empire. Johann Droysen, who had many American students at his lectures and seminars, had been deeply influenced by Hegelian idealism and by the scientific method and archival techniques of Ranke, but he led the attempt of Prussian historians to advance their nation's cause by interpreting the past in a favorable historical light. Heinrich von Treitschke, then at Heidelberg and Berlin, had also studied with Ranke but repudiated his principles of objective history. His colonial imperialism, which mixed Machiavellian ethics, racialism, and a Darwinian struggle for power made non-German historians apprehensive. His reward came as Ranke's successor to the post of historiographer of Prussia. Much more restrained than Treitschke was Heinrich von Sybel of the University of Bonn, a student and onetime colleague of Ranke, but he, too, stressed nationalist ideas in politics and religion. Bancroft, also, was a nationalist, but he never gave up his democratic, cosmopolitan sympathies.

Over in France, Bancroft's spiritual counterpart, Jules Michelet, had been dismissed from his history position at the College of France, presumably for offending Louis Bonaparte's regime by his advocacy of democratic movements. Like Bancroft, he was an enthusiast for the masses, romantic in his assumptions, and gifted with a lyrical style. His popular seven-volume history of the French Revolution taught the same lesson that Bancroft's history did; that the genius of a great historical movement was the common man.[5] His death in 1874 marked the end of a romantic era, though George Bancroft was to live on into another epoch, for he died in 1891.

4

For forty years, Bancroft's histories appeared regularly; they came to be regarded as national events. In 1834, he issued the first of his ten-volume (it was twelve volumes, if one includes his constitutional history) *History of the United States from the Discovery of the American Continent (1492-1660)*. He began with the founding of the colonies and intended to come up to the mid-nineteenth century at least, but he stopped short seven years of the time that the United States became a nation. The last volume appeared only in 1874 and together with the previous work aggregated no less than 1,700,000 words, which made it even longer than that of his prolific competitor, Richard Hildreth.

With the aid of research assistants, Bancroft examined mountains of original materials and copied many of the documents. He perused the documents in the British Record Office, manuscripts in the British Museum, public collections, and family letters. To the present-day historian, however, his sources for the later volumes seem inadequate, for he did not make sufficient use of newspapers and magazines. As a result, he emphasized political history at the expense of social developments. However, in Bancroft's own day, "scientific" historians like Freeman and Ranke were making politics the central, if not the total content of history.

In later volumes, he expanded his sources considerably, aided by his political contacts with the heads of foreign governments as well as those in Washington, by his mounting reputation, which opened the doors of the owners of large private collections, and by his private means, which allowed him to find the sources he needed (in his day there were very few major collections located in easily accessible places). While his research energies exceeded those of his predecessors, his emphatic claims to objectivity could not be taken seriously, for there were glaring examples of where he failed to be objective. He was not above suppressing unpleasant facts. Something of a snob, despite his encomiums to the masses, he was hypercritical of manners and dress and even wanted a frontispiece changed in order to remove the homely warts on Franklin's face.

Bancroft's Teutonic myth was dressed up in the attractive optimistic guise the mid-century Americans expected. He was willing to give the Prussians their due share of credit for the emergence of modern liberty, providing that it was understood that they came as John the Baptist for an even greater personage—the American—whose destiny to enlighten the world seemed above dispute. Among his numerous digressions—and he was apt to go off for a dozen pages or so on the Reformation or even less relevant themes—were thirty pages of volume ten devoted to German history pure and simple. Here Frederick the Great received credit for being the outstanding champion of colonial independence because of some very roundabout contribution he made to America. Here was a typical compliment to the Teutons: "Of the nations of the European world, the chief emigration was from that

Germanic race most famed for the love of personal independence."
He portrayed most sympathetically the mission of the Anglo-Saxon
people in early Virginia to achieve the final goal of spiritual freedom:

> The Anglo-Saxon mind, in its serenest nationality, neither distorted by
> fanaticism, nor subdued by superstition, nor wounded by persecution, nor
> excited by new ideas, but fondly cherishing the active instinct for personal
> freedom, secure possession, and legislative power, such as belonged to it
> before the Reformation, and existed independently of the Reformation, had
> made its dwelling place in the empire of Powhatan.

Bancroft frequently reiterated the idea of an all-determining Divine
Providence. He began his first volume with these words:

> It is the object of the present work to explain how the change in the con-
> dition of our land has been accomplished; and, as the fortunes of a nation
> are not under the control of blind destiny, to follow the steps by which a
> favoring Providence, calling our institutions into being, has conducted the
> country to its present happiness and glory.

God whispers to Columbus that the world is one and, at once, Columbus's purpose becomes not merely to open new paths to islands
or to continents "but to bring together the ends of the earth, and join
all nations in commerce and spiritual life." Thus he projects the unfolding of God's mind from its idealistic inception to its modern ma-
terialization.

Although he quoted approvingly Kant's views on history, particularly
the emphasis on the creation of a "universal history," in which certain
favored nations hold the stage for a time, he could not escape obvious
ethnocentrism. To him, as to so many Jeffersonians, the United States
was the agent of Providence in promoting universal freedom:

> The authors of the American Revolution avowed for their object the
> welfare of mankind and believed that they were in the service of their own
> and of all future generations. Their faith was just; for the world of mankind
> does not exist in fragments, nor can a country have an insulated existence.
> All men are brothers; and all are bondsmen for one another. All nations,
> too, are brothers, and each is responsible for that federative humanity which
> puts the ban of exclusion on none. New principles of government could not
> assert themselves in one hemisphere without affecting the other. The very
> idea of the progress of an individual people, in its relation to universal
> history, springs from the acknowledged unity of the race.

The cosmopolitan façade for his nationalism drops away somewhat
in a later discussion of the Revolution, "These British American colo-

nies were the best trophy of modern civilization; on them for the next forty years rests the chief interest in the history of man." Apparently Europe with its Enlightenment could not hope to share in the limelight of eighteenth-century history. His idea is even more emphatically stated elsewhere: "America knew that it involved for the world all hope of establishing the power of the people."

It is not surprising, therefore, that Bancroft will take an incident, the "germ," and make it the initial point for developments of world consequences. For example, in dealing with the preliminaries of the French and Indian War, he made young Washington's skirmish with the French the "signal for the first great war of revolution," marking the end of the Middle Ages here and in Europe. Unlike other historians of the subject, Bancroft argued that Britain was thus dragged into war by her colonies in what became a basic conflict between the Reformation and medievalism. "The successes of the Seven Years War," he held, "were the triumphs of Protestantism." He considered the Protestant right of private judgment to be "a principle of all-pervading energy."

His loyalty to New England involved him in a clash between the Calvinist intolerance, which he had perforce to portray, and the eighteenth-century virtues of reason and tolerance, to which he was strongly committed. He solved the conflict, as Harvard's historians have since done, by extolling the high intellectuality of the early Massachusetts ruling class. "Calvinism invoked intelligence against Satan, the great enemy of the human race; and the farmers and seamen of Massachusetts nourished the college with corn and strings of wampum, and in every village built the free school." Ignoring the role of economic interests in the colonizing of New England, he flatly declared, "Purity of religion and civil liberty were the objects nearest the wishes of the emigrant."

Bancroft's idealistic interpretation of history led him to minimize all economic causes and to insist that civil liberty was the goal of mankind's progressive development. For example, although he devoted quite a few pages to the workings of Britain's navigation laws, he made their effects wholly incidental by explaining the Revolution as primarily a conflict between tyranny and freedom. Into the warp and woof of his narrative went the Hegelian dialectic. The progress of truth and freedom emerged from successive struggles between tyranny and liberty, with each battle fought on a higher level than the previous one. There was, however, no echo of his populistic Fourth of July orations or his Jacksonian radicalism in the passages in which he justified the creditor class against the debtors in colonial America.

Even in 1882, when he issued his two final volumes, *History of the Formation of the Constitution of the United States of America,* he gave little attention to economic pressures and dealt almost wholly with abstract constitutional doctrines operating in a social vacuum and responding to the divinely ordered love of Union. In discussing slavery and the slave trade, he said emphatically that they were immoral and hostile to the inevitable goal of civil liberty, but he added nothing more.

Bancroft's idealistic view of history appears in passages such as this:

But the eternal flow of existence never rests, bearing the human race onwards through continuous change. Principles grow into life by informing the public mind, and in their maturity gain the mastery over events; following each other as they are bidden, and ruling without a pause. No sooner do the agitated waves begin to subside, than, amidst the formless tossing of the billows, a new messenger from the Infinite Spirit moves over the waters. . . .

Inspired by Kant's conception of universal history, he explained its purpose as the recording of the progress of the human mind:

While the world of mankind is accomplishing its nearer connection, it is also advancing in the power of its intelligence. . . . The faculties of each individual mind are limited in their development; the reason of the whole strives for perfection, has been restlessly forming itself from the first moment of human existence, and has never met bounds to its capacity for improvement.

His notion of "reason," it must be pointed out, was the Kantian or "transcendental" view of what he called "an internal sense which places us in connexion with the world of intelligence and the decrees of God."

Those of Bancroft's generation who were enthusiastically committed to the democratic dogma in its Jacksonian sense could appreciate his emphatic dictum that the voice of the people was indubitably the voice of God. His argument, which made the ultimate victory of truth comfortingly certain, began with the constitution of the human mind and the inevitable tendency of reasonable men to agree finally. In an age when universal manhood suffrage was an exciting and inspiring democratic novelty, Bancroft could find a wholly sympathetic audience for such assertions:

If reason is a universal faculty, the universal decision is the nearest criterion of truth. The common mind winnows opinions; it is the sieve which separates error from certainty. . . . Thus there can be no continuing universal judgment but a right one. Men cannot agree in an absurdity; neither can they agree on a falsehood. . . .

To put the case even more emphatically for "the sagacity of the many," he went on to say, "The common mind is infinite in its experience; individuals are languid and blind; the many are ever wakeful. . . . The decrees of the universal conscience are the nearest approach to the presence of God in the soul of man."

It is not surprising therefore that his histories should ring with the certainty that the common man was destined to ultimate victory:

> The great result of modern civilization is the diffusion of intelligence among the masses, and a consequent increase of their political consideration. The result is observable every where. In the field, the fate of battles depends on infantry, and no longer on the cavalry. Influence has passed away from walled towns and fortresses to the busy scenes of commercial industry, and to the abodes of rustic independence; an active press has increased, and is steadily increasing, the number of reflecting minds that demand a reason for conduct, and exercise themselves in efforts to solve the problem of existence and human destiny. . . . Every where the power of the people has increased. . . .

One of his early expressions of this idealistic faith appears in an oration of 1835 on "The Office of the People in Art, Government, and Religion." He said that "the best government rests on the people and not on the few, on persons and not on property, on the free development of public opinion and not on authority. . . . A government of equal rights must therefore rest upon mind, not wealth, not brute force, the sum of the moral intelligence should rule the State." [6] Above all, Bancroft usually practiced what he preached. In his eulogistic campaign biography of Van Buren, he presented a thoroughly pro-Jackson interpretation. He denounced Biddle's United States Bank, upheld Jackson's eviction of the civilized Indian tribes from the Southeast, and praised Van Buren's device of the Independent Treasury.

Among the few environmental forces in American history that Bancroft was willing to recognize was the influence of the frontier, a fact which gives him distinction among the contemporary historians, who tended to identify the Eastern seaboard with America. In discussing the colonial Virginians he declared that his countrymen were "children of the woods, nurtured in the freedom of the wilderness," struggling against isolation, unlike the peasants in Europe's compact farm villages. "The boundless West became the poor man's City of Refuge, where the wilderness guarded his cabin as inviolably as the cliff or the cedar-top holds the eagle's eyrie." Here was a suggestion of Frederick Jackson Turner's idea of the West as a safety valve for labor. He dwelt warmly and at length upon the virtues of the pioneers in the Mississippi Valley. His treatment of the Indians, however, varied from volume to volume. Sometimes he was cognizant of their rights; at other times, he dismissed them as ignorant savages.

It was not enough for Bancroft to present history as a mystical continuity; he also had to show by means of moral judgments what direction Providence was taking in history. He dismissed France's right to share in the New World by asserting that "a government which could devise the massacre of St. Bartholomew was neither worthy nor able to found new states." He spoke of Virginia's first colonists as dissolute gallants, broken tradesmen, rakes, and libertines, but he added, with the prescience of hindsight and the wisdom derived from his philosophy of history, "It was not the will of God that the new state should be formed of these materials; that such men should be the fathers of a progeny born on the American soil, who were one day to assert American liberty by their eloquence, and defend it by their valor."

Inevitably Bancroft's tendency to put his facts within an idealistic formula nullified much of the interpretive worth of his monumental histories. Critics like the acute New Englander, Thomas W. Higginson, found that Bancroft also fictionized history instead of adhering to his professed scientific standards. He charged that Bancroft emulated Jared Sparks in his utter disregard for the sanctity of quotation marks in order to enhance dramatic effect. In one notorious instance, when Bancroft wished to dramatize the protest of New York's colonists against the arbitrary action of a royal commission, he went even further than usual. "Bancroft," said Higginson, "has simply taken phrases and sentences here and there from a long document and rearranged, combined, and in some cases, actually paraphrased them in his own way. Logically and rhetorically, the work is his own. Like Thucydides he composed speeches for his heroes, but unlike the Greek historian he did not have the privilege of participating in the events described."

Bancroft's tireless search for epic values in history, which was in keeping with the effort of New England literary historians to stress drama and pageantry, did not always jibe with scientific trustworthiness. His florid style may have been vastly popular in this age of Carlyle and romanticism, but it did not properly lend itself to making exact distinctions or balanced judgments. His style made much use of literary devices which were fashionable then: the balanced **sentence,** the poetic phrase, the use of the present tense to enhance dramatic effect, and the crescendo-effect of mounting emphasis. Although these stylistic ornaments irritated conservative tastes—John Quincy Adams's, for instance—and are nearly intolerable to modern readers, they undoubtedly contributed to his books' popularity in his own day. The reasons for his popularity were best expressed by his famous fellow-historian, John Lothrop Motley, who had learned history from Bancroft himself at the Round Hill School:

> The secret of Bancroft's success is that by aid of a vigorous imagination and a crisp, nervous style, he has been enabled, by a few sudden strokes, to reveal startling and brilliant pictures, over which the dust had collected and hardened, as it seemed, forever. It is a work rather of genius than of laborious detail.

But a great modern master of style, Carl Becker, while willing to concede Bancroft's sound scholarship, made this apt criticism: "Still, one wonders a little why a Harvard man with sufficient independence to become a Jacksonian democrat, should not have realized that a 'style' suitable for telling the story of the Trojan War or the Fall of Lucifer is not the best for relating the history of the United States."

Becker, writing in 1917, could praise Bancroft's research as distinct from his style almost as warmly as Prescott and Parkman did. The great Arnold Heeren himself had already praised the first volume profusely for its meticulous care, extensive sources, and warmth. On the other hand, Bancroft was not sure that he liked Ranke's odd compliment (for a conservative) when they met in Berlin:

> I tell my hearers that your history is the best book ever written from the democratic point of view. You are thoroughly consistent; adhere strictly to your method, carry it out in many directions but in all with fidelity, and are always true to it.

Privately Bancroft fumed: "I deny the charge; if there is democracy in the history it is not subjective, but objective as they say here, and so has necessarily its place in history." Actually, the disciples of Ranke had introduced a form of scientific history which went far to break the grip of the philosophers over history. Ranke had been critical of those who so loved generalizations that they forgot that these could emerge only from a grouping of concrete facts.

Fortunately for Bancroft's reputation, he lived long enough to revise the style of his first edition and also to shear away many of the superfluous mystical interpretations. His revision of 1883-85 was therefore much closer to modern ideas of objectivity than the original edition. However, he denied that he had surrendered "the right of history to pronounce its opinion," but he had now taken care "never unduly to forestall the judgment of the reader, but to leave events as they sweep onward to speak their own condemnation." Bancroft had decided to recognize the newer historical trends, at least in part. Thus his works managed to survive into the new century. A younger historian, James Ford Rhodes, leaned heavily on Bancroft for the background to his own monumental series. He knew that Bancroft was not the man to incorporate the *Annual Register* into his work in order to tell the story of the American Revolution. There was no humbug about his claim to having used extensive original sources.[7]

In recent years high praise has been given Bancroft for his work on the Revolution. Professor Edmund S. Morgan declared that Bancroft knew the sources better than any historian has since that day. Despite Bancroft's naïve idealism, Morgan said in *The Birth of the Republic, 1763-1789* (1956), the New Englander was the greatest historian of the revolutionary period. Few historians had dealt so directly and successfully with the central question of how the United States came into being as a nation dedicated to principles of liberty and equality. By the mid-twentieth century when a new idealistic emphasis upon principles and ideas in history had begun to replace the old economic interpretation of the Great Depression years, the revolutionary synthesis of Bancroft had regained some of its vitality.

5

Bancroft was the first major historian to act as a bridge between the creative world of German historiography and American historians. This came at a time when the idealistic philosophers and their Hegelian or post-Hegelian formulas dominated German history-writing. Only Herbert Baxter Adams and his famous Johns Hopkins seminar of the 'eighties and 'nineties could vie with Bancroft as a carrier of the germ theory which dominated German historical thinking. Overemphasis on the unique mission of the Anglo-Saxon peoples was to affect many American historians, among them Woodrow Wilson. Bancroft's philosophy of history stands out favorably when compared with the timidity and extreme restraint of later historians afraid to make value judgments on the facts they had assembled.

Bancroft's social ideas are easily gleaned from his histories. The Jacksonianism of his political life has its verbal counterpart in his long digressions about the common man. Although his speeches often dealt with economic opportunity for all and the primacy of human rights over property rights, his politics were usually much more circumspect; his historical writings, in keeping with his idealistic philosophy, refused to consider the role of economic interests as a motivating force in the development of civilization. Always, ideas came first as a transforming agent in society. His unfriendly treatment of the debtor class in describing Shays's Rebellion was no different from what one would find among Whig historians. The conflict of classes is therefore lost amid the exposition of a hypothetical mass-man driven to act because of cumulative knowledge and a transcendental "reason." Too often, then, the common man is an abstraction rather than a person of flesh and blood.

In that optimistic nineteenth-century atmosphere, he found it easy to accept the doctrine of perfectibility and progress. A consistent son of a confirmed Unitarian, he showed more than ordinary tolerance to unorthodox believers. Quakers enjoyed the most friendly, even enthusiastic, treatment in his pages. His hatred of slavery, though held in abeyance during certain of the years in which his volumes appeared, was genuine indeed.

While the mid-twentieth century can appreciate his fervent emphasis upon the Kantian goal of individual freedom and cosmopolitan values, few will deny his strong ethnocentrism of word and deed. He regarded the history of the United States as the decisive part in modern times of that "universal history" of all mankind in which events flowed continuously in a single process toward human freedom; the pattern and direction had been determined by the germinal origins of human institutions created by a beneficent Providence. What happened in America changed the entire world—at least in modern times. The Americans were destined to take over the reins of history among the favored Teutonic or Anglo-Saxon peoples and so bring freedom and morality to the world. Both as politician and as historian he reflected the strong force of Manifest Destiny. As Polk's Secretary of the Navy and Acting Secretary of War on the eve of the War with Mexico, he felt he was applying his underlying principles when he took energetic steps to fulfill America's destiny to absorb California.

Quite a few American historians educated in Germany felt grateful for the guidance of George Bancroft. In 1870 the aging Minister to Prussia urged young John W. Burgess, subsequently a noted historian and political theorist at Columbia, to come at once to study in the German universities. Burgess was the son of a pro-Union Tennessee slaveholder and himself a Union veteran; his philosophic training at Amherst College had led him to Hegel and a Teutonized Bancroft type of history marked by the progressive unfolding of civilization under Anglo-Saxon dominance. Bancroft had planned Burgess's program to include Ranke, Droysen, and Mommsen as his professors. From these able mentors Burgess carried away the German seminar method and the new scientific history, with its emphasis upon the critical handling of first-hand documents and empirical research, although he was to turn increasingly to political theory. Like Bancroft, he too was to send talented young historians to earn their apprenticeship in the German universities, as he had done at Göttingen, Leipzig, and Berlin.[8]

☆ 6 ☆

Francis Parkman and the Pageant of the Wilderness

1

Francis Parkman blended the charm of the literary historians with an upper-class unawareness of the personality of the common man. Like the Whigs of 1840 and 1848 who glamorized conservatism and the strenuous life by offering a military hero for the presidency, Parkman substituted the excitement of marching men, Jesuit explorers, and aristocratic leaders for the bare annals of farmers, hunters, workmen, and petty tradesmen. After the Civil War, few Republican presidential aspirants lacked the appeal of a military record. From General Grant to Major McKinley, economic stand-pattism and the soldierly virtues usually went hand in hand.

Francis Parkman, born in Boston on September 16, 1823, conformed to the pattern of the Brahmin historians, for he was the son of a Unitarian minister, the descendant of English immigrants of Winthrop's day, and, on his mother's side, the descendant of the theocrat, John Cotton himself. Like so many other Brahmins, he reacted to this heritage by developing marked anticlericalism. The paternal grandfather, Samuel Parkman, had risen from rural poverty to mercantile riches and been able to endow a professorship of theology at Harvard, where Francis's father was an overseer. Inevitably, the youth went to Harvard College, where he concentrated upon rhetoric and history, became a member of Phi Beta Kappa, and made an early resolve to be a historian of the Old French War. After all, Harvard's sons such as Prescott (whose partial blindness paralleled that of Parkman), Motley, Hildreth, Palfrey, Bancroft, and other noted men had also made brilliant careers of history. Francis was greatly influenced by Jared Sparks, the first to occupy a chair of history in any American college. Sparks had recently finished the first series of his *American Biography* and had expressed a deepening interest in the early French explorations of the Great West.

With "Injuns on his brain," as Parkman later said of himself, he embarked upon a thorough preparation for a career in history. Already his penchant for the strenuous life had set a mark that even Theodore Roosevelt could not eclipse. As a child he spent five years on his grandfather's farm. At Harvard he practiced energetically the physical education ideas newly imported from Germany. He became an excellent shot and rode a horse skillfully. During the summers he hiked at a grueling pace and observed the historic invasion routes of French Canada and New England. To understand the European background of international diplomacy and institutional Catholicism, he kept a journal of his Grand Tour to Europe and closely observed the Church in Italy, where he was most impressed by a powerful hierarchy and an ignorant laity—a situation which later he thought he saw duplicated in Canada.

The pinnacle of his self-development was the trip that he took along the Oregon Trail in 1846. Accompanied by his cousin, Quincy Shaw, who expected quite a lark, and a skillful French guide, he observed the Sioux and Pawnees and kept detailed notes on their customs and behavior. He even met old Pierre Chouteau, founder of St. Louis and an acquaintance of Pontiac, the Indian leader of the Conspiracy of 1763, about whom Parkman decided to write a full account. With a fixed belief that all life was a struggle, it is not surprising that he eventually made his lifework not merely a study of Indian character, as he had intended, but an epic of the titanic struggle between England and France for the mastery of the continent. Even his volume, *The History of the Conspiracy of Pontiac* (1851), is no biography of an Indian, but offers, in its early chapters at least, a résumé of the entire Anglo-French conflict, the core of his other seven historical titles. And his efforts to discover objective reality, romanticist though he was in certain respects, led him to depart from the pattern of the eighteenth-century Noble Savage, even if he did admire extravagantly the novels of James Fenimore Cooper.

The Oregon adventure set him back physically. Parkman's health had been failing for some time and while studying law at Harvard his eyesight showed alarming symptoms of weakness, which led him increasingly to employ a reader. Determined to try a kill-or-cure remedy, he had embarked upon this trip where the primitive life had already laid low many an emigrant. But his eyesight became worse, dysentery enervated him, and chronic complications ensued—insomnia, rheumatism, arthritis, and worst of all, a painful nervous condition which took the form of a viselike pressure around his head and also produced semi-blindness. As the years went by, he hired more readers and assistants to take dictation. He even constructed an ingenious writing tablet which was guided by horizontal wires a half-inch apart. This made it possible for him to ease his eye strain and to do some of his writing while in a darkened room. He never knew the exact nature of his ailment, for the mystified specialists predicted insanity, impending death, and other frightening prognoses.

The tragedies which befell him could have terminated the career of a man of less iron. In 1850, he married his secretary, Catherine Bigelow, the daughter of a prominent physician, but their son died in infancy, and she did not survive the second child. He lived with the everyday realities of long periods of forced inaction, loneliness, and discomfort—he, the apostle of struggle and the vigorous life. But he made marvelous adjustments, and he was able to call upon a rich imagination to re-create long-forgotten scenes of the first wilderness in his great historical works. Every effective moment counted, and he occasionally was able to take a trip to some historical spot. Even out-of-doors, where his vision had to be carefully shielded from the glare of the sun, he found an absorbing vocation in horticulture. He produced new plant varieties and wrote scientific articles that won him praise and honors internationally. The wealth of his family and the increasing returns from his publications made it possible for him to escape the painful complications that poverty would have brought.[1]

2

Above all, encouragement came from the immediate popularity of his early books. *The Oregon Trail* (1849) was no history but a penetrating autobiographical sketch of his experiences along that route. Its focus was upon Indian life and habits among the Sioux and their tribal neighbors and on the rugged white hunters and trappers, but there was very little upon the parties of emigrants, whom he looked down upon as low, ignorant, and dirty. Eastern readers were captivated by the keen descriptions of the primitive frontier, the Plains Indians, and the thundering herds of buffalo.

The History of the Conspiracy of Pontiac was dedicated to Jared Sparks and began with a preface in which the author explained that he had chosen the subject because it afforded better opportunities than any other portion of American history to portray forest life and Indian character. He succeeded very well in capturing the atmosphere of the forest primeval, but his view of the Indian was prejudiced and reflected the racial errors of the day. Too much was said of Indian treachery and savagery in the manner of the embittered Puritan historians. To him the Indian owned no other authority than his "own capricious will." The Indian seemed to be hewn of rock and was unable to learn the arts of civilization, because he was bound by ancient usages and a veneration for the sages and chiefs of his tribe. Parkman conceded that the Indian was generous, ready to lay down his life for a comrade, and true to his own sense of honor. He went so far as to extenuate in part the Indian brutalities of the Seven Years' War by pointing out the provocations to which they had been subjected.

Parkman developed the central theme that Bancroft and the disciples of the German historians had emphasized: History reveals the progressive advance of civil liberties by peoples, such as the Anglo-Saxons, who were prepared to win them. Contemporary Protestants looked upon their own history as exemplifying the great modern victory of individual freedom over Catholic authoritarianism. This was the basic struggle that Parkman saw in the long drawn-out duel for empire between Catholic France and Protestant England. Almost every volume in the Parkman series repeated the theme of the Pontiac book:

Feudalism stood arrayed against Democracy; Popery against Protestantism; the sword against the ploughshare. The priest, the soldier, and the noble, ruled in Canada. The ignorant, light-hearted Canadian peasant knew nothing and cared nothing about popular rights and civil liberties. Born to obey, he lived in contented submission, without the wish or the capacity for self-rule. Power, centered in the heart of the system, left the masses inert.

He portrayed the French-Canadian as buoyant and gay, happy in the midst of poverty, lying side by side with his Indian mistress and his hybrid offspring, and forgetting his wife in France. The fur trade lent color and ferment to life in the wilderness. Behind this happy-go-lucky appearance, however, was an insecure economy due to arbitrary state meddling, a ruinous system of monopoly, and feudal exactions. The seemingly virile expansion of New France was due to the zeal of priests and soldiers who spread missions and forts, but these settlements lacked real roots and eventually declined.

Contrasting with the paternalistic French-Canadian state was Puritan New England, "where the spirit of non-conformity was sublimed to a fiery essence, and where the love of liberty and the hatred of power burned with a sevenfold heat." The Englishman called no man master, yet bowed reverently to the law which he himself had made. While the French Jesuit was often a martyr for the faith and a staunch ally of the imperial power, he was superficial in his contact with the Indian, because he was content with a few drops of water sprinkled in hasty baptism, while the English Protestant missionary like John Eliot sought to wean the Indian "from his barbarism and penetrate his savage heart with the truths of Christianity." Here one sees clearly the Protestant and Anglo-Saxon bias of Parkman.

Parkman's activism made him intolerant of the quietism of the Quakers. In this volume and in later ones, he criticized the Friends for failing to lend aid to the harassed Germans and Scotch-Irish along the exposed frontier. He argued that the Quaker policy of paying for Indian lands was inspired by opportunism and that they had little to fear from the disarmed Delawares who had been crushed by the Iroquois.

When the Indian allies of the French attacked the English colonists in the usual "treacherous" onslaught, Parkman made it clear where his sympathies lay amid the burning of houses and scalpings and "children snatched from their mothers' arms to be immured in convents and trained up in the abominations of Popery." Still he admitted that one source of French strength was not merely centralized religious-political power, but greater tolerance of Indian customs. Indian communities under French control usually enjoyed protection. Parkman, even in revising his later editions, continued to make a virtue of Anglo-Saxon racial exclusiveness. He blamed racial intermixture upon "the renegade of civilization," the *coureur de bois*.

Parkman dealt with the exploits of outstanding men rather than with social forces, although it is true that Pontiac does not even appear in one edition before page 165, and then only briefly. In fact the tremendous story of imperial conflict which occupied the next seven volumes (some were two-volume works) was summarized here to such an extent as to steal nearly all the chief scenes. Yet the most recent scholarly criticism of this volume, that of Howard H. Peckham, argues that Parkman has made too much of Pontiac and that the Indian chief was no more than the commander of three villages surrounding Fort Detroit and later on only a consulting chief of the Chippewas and Potawatomies. Peckham believes that in default of written evidence Parkman relied upon unsubstantiated Indian tradition. In doing this the New Englander followed a contemporary view of William Smith the historian and others that Pontiac was behind the entire series of frontier attacks of 1763.[2]

If one recalls that many of Parkman's prejudices are those of his time, nationality, and class, the favorable present-day estimate of his Pontiac may still be fully justified. Even Peckham has some praise for the book as surpassing everything previously written on Pontiac's War in wealth of detail and readable style. "It is Parkman's incomplete and not altogether accurate picture of Pontiac that has fascinated later writers on Indian topics." Critics of that day showed enthusiasm and the book enjoyed popularity from the beginning. Jared Sparks, to whom the book was dedicated, was naturally pleased, but complained that some moral judgments upon the brutality of the Paxton Boys had to be made:

Although you relate events in the true spirit of calmness and justice, yet I am not sure but a word or two of indignation now and then, at such unnatural and inhuman developments, would be expected from a historian who enters deeply into the merits of his subjects.

Such was the judgment of the dean of American historians in 1850: Parkman was not going far enough in making moral judgments!

On the other hand, the acute reformer and disciple of Emerson and Channing, Theodore Parker, who had been a companion of Parkman on his European travels, took advantage of the overwhelmingly favorable press to make a few honestly critical comments. He complained that Parkman had unjustly stigmatized the Indians as "treacherous" by taking the facts out of context, especially the context of Indian custom and the depravities of such white cutthroats as the Paxton Boys, whose deeds are mitigated by the author. Some mention should have been made of the white practice of intoxicating the Indians, taking their women and then deserting them, and finally betraying the Indians. Reference to the Quakers was also unjust. He suggested that in a future edition Parkman might point out that the various Teutonic peoples are exclusivist in race relations while the Celts, Greeks, and Italians tend to assimilate with others. (This suggestion was never carried out.) Furthermore, he complained that the central conspiracy was buried beneath extraneous facts and that the narrative suffered from poor organization. Finally, he called for a general summary that would contain more philosophical reflections.

John Fiske, the historian and philosopher, who became a great admirer of Parkman, praised the realistic portrait of Pontiac. He was indeed no Noble Savage. Unlike Prescott's Indians, Pontiac and his fellow-Indians appeared almost in the flesh, quite different from the pale image of the Aztecs that the historian of Mexico re-created from his Spanish sources. After all, Parkman had interviewed an acquaintance or two of Pontiac himself, and he had observed the tribes across the Mississippi who had but recently emigrated from the Eastern frontier.

Parkman's virtues as a historian are monumental even when his serious defects are kept in balance. Historians who have gone over the ground appreciate his gargantuan appetite for original sources and do not question that his Pontiac alone required over 3400 manuscript pages of sources taken from European as well as American public and private sources; to this was added many contemporary newspapers, magazines, and pamphlets. Little wonder that the particular subjects that he stressed have been retold with a major reliance upon his pioneer work. As the years progressed he was to show a greater awareness of the multiple factors which determined the Anglo-French imperial rivalry and a keener critical sense in handling social factors.

In 1856, the historian wrote a semi-autobiographical novel, *Vassall Morton*, which proved a failure in the world of fiction, but revealed much to his biographers regarding his social ideas and philosophy. Vassall Morton is a wealthy Boston youth whose imprisonment and escape suggests the trials of Parkman with his health. The triumph of will over fate is emphasized in his philosophy of life as an eternal struggle for the spirit of man. "Whatever new disaster meets me, I will confront it with some new audacity of hope. I will nail my flag to the mast, and there shall it fly till all go down, or till flag, mast, and hulk rot together." Later, he wrote, "Action, action, action!—all in all! What is life without it?" When the Civil War came, it was not the abolitionist cause that struck him particularly, but the fact that his hand was left "holding the pen that should have grasped the sword." The novel also revealed his dislike of the coonskin democracy that had taken over the party of gentlemen—the Whigs. He disliked the *nouveau riche*, too: the ultra-fashionable set at Saratoga, the ruthless financial oligarchy, and the parvenu industrialists. Too much an admirer of the eighteenth-century New England commercial aristocracy, he clung to outmoded chivalric concepts and condemned the new trend toward women's rights and utilitarianism.

3

The first of Parkman's seven absorbing volumes on the Anglo-French conflict appeared in 1865 as *Pioneers of France in the New World*. It began with the story of the Huguenot settlers in Florida and the Spanish attack on the Protestant French; the rest of the work dealt with Champlain and New France. Despite the copious and reliable sources, Parkman was far from objective in judgment, for he revealed his social values throughout. The story of Spanish atrocities against the Protestant French in Florida lost nothing in the telling. He struck at Catholic Spain for the brutalities of Menendez, the mutilation of the Huguenots, and the barbaric despotism of the Spanish empire:

> Gloomy and portentous, she chilled the world with her baneful shadow. . . . A tyranny of monks and inquisitors, with their swarms of spies and informers, their racks, their dungeons, and their fagots, crushed all freedom of thought and speech. . . . Commercial despotism was joined to political and religious despotism.

The theme of free New England and absolutist New France that had been initiated in his book on Pontiac was elaborated—the former was a "vanguard of the Reform," the latter "an unflinching champion of the Roman Catholic reaction." This time he added an evolutionary interpretation: "Each followed its natural laws of growth and each came to its natural result. Vitalized by the principles of its foundation, the Puritan commonwealth grew apace." But even in praising New England, he slyly poked fun at its acquisitiveness:

> New England was preeminently the land of material progress. Here the prize was within every man's reach; patient industry need never doubt its reward; nay, in defiance of the four Gospels, assiduity in pursuit of gain was promoted to the rank of a duty, and thrift and godliness were linked in equivocal wedlock.

While New England was free politically, she suffered from the tyranny of an intolerant public opinion. Besides, said the adventurous-minded writer, she was hopelessly prosaic. Despite the expansive energy of her people, who attracted the attention of the entire world, she lacked the striking forms of character which often gave a dramatic life to far less prosperous nations. New England had grown out of the aggregate efforts of "a busy multitude, each in his narrow circle toiling for himself to gather competence or wealth." On the other hand, New France grew out of "a gigantic ambition to grasp a continent."

He so loved antithesis that he took some liberties with history to show how completely different New France was from New England:

> Here was a bold attempt to crush under the exactions of a grasping hierarchy, to stifle under the curbs and trappings of a feudal monarchy, a people compassed by influences of the wildest freedom,—whose schools were the forest and the sea, whose trade was an armed barter with savages, and whose daily life a lesson of lawless independence.

But this fierce spirit had its vent in war, struggles with savage tribes, an untamed forest, heretics, and the British. The "brave, unthinking people" developed soldierly virtues and soldierly faults. Their leaders displayed the energies and passions of those entrusted with absolute power. However, he could not help feeling intensely fascinated by the romantic setting of New France: lords and vassals, black-robed priests, savage Indian warriors, impenetrable forests, and heroic explorers. Yet Parkman resisted the tendency to fictionize, for no one knew the objective facts and events of the Anglo-French duel as well as he did. In his mind's eye, he re-created a sound picture which did not conflict with the documents. To him Champlain is an adventurous leader with all of the virtues and the faults of the ruling class, ever a courageous explorer, an intrepid warrior, and an indefatigable builder of magic Quebec towering over the cliff. Parkman felt convinced, though, that Champlain had meddled fatally in the war feuds of the Algonquins and the Iroquois and hence was solely responsible for the Iroquois feud against France—a somewhat oversimplified interpretation of a famous fact in history. The primitive forest setting of Champlain's adventures allowed Parkman excellent chances to use his own Indian and wilderness background to give a realistic setting to the story.

Two years later he issued *The Jesuits in North America in the Seventeenth Century* (1867) and profited greatly from his imaginative use of the rich sources, *The Jesuit Relations*, which contained numerous letters and reports written by Jesuit missionaries in the field. Parkman's attitude toward Catholicism was ambivalent. No higher compliment to the bravery and dedication of the Jesuits appears even in Catholic histories. Once, during his visit of 1843 to a Benedictine church in Messina, he observed:

> This church and others not unlike it have impressed me with new ideas of the Catholic religion. Not exactly; for I reverenced it before as the religion of generations of brave and great men—but now I honor it for itself.

They are mistaken who sneer at its ceremonies as a mere mechanical farce. They have a powerful and salutary effect on the mind.

Yet, almost at the same time, his journal lapsed into unflattering references to Italian churchmen, particularly to a "fat hog of a priest" he had seen in Florence. His anticlericalism led him to draw a sharp line between Catholic dogma, which he apparently respected, and institutional religion.

He believed that the best side of the Jesuits was in the founding of New France; here there was no "end justifies the means jesuitry." His story-telling ability went to good purpose when he unfolded the many episodes of martyrdom by the Jesuit missionaries. Naturally, the Indians had to provide the villainous foil for all this goodness. Of the Hurons, he said, "In regard to these atrocious scenes, which formed the favorite Huron recreation of a summer night . . ." Elsewhere, thinking better of his shabby treatment of the Indians, he threw in a few instances of Indian kindness: 'The principle of honor was not extinct in their wild hearts." But ever a moralist, he paused frequently to complain of the immodest sex life of the Indian women and of the nakedness of their men.

Parkman was very alert to the role of dramatic accident in history. "It was an evil day for new-born Protestantism when a French artilleryman fired the shot that struck down Ignatius Loyola in the breach of Pamplona." He referred of course to Loyola's subsequent conversion to the religious life and his organization of the militant Society of Jesus.

Fundamentally he was hostile to the mission of the Church, "now a virgin, now a harlot." He put it strongly several times:

Holy Mother Church, linked in sordid wedlock to government and thrones, numbered among her servants a host of the worldly and the proud, whose service of God was but the service of themselves,—and many too, who in the sophistry of the human heart, thought themselves true soldiers of Heaven, while earthly pride, interest, and passion were the lifesprings of their zeal.

He saw the missionary as the ally of the fur trader:

The zeal of propagandism and the fur-trade were, as we have seen, the vital forces of New France. Of her feeble population, the best part was bound to perpetual chastity. While the fur-traders and those in their service rarely brought their wives to the wilderness.

The fur trader, he thought, was opposed to any real settlements in the forest because it opposed the interests of the fur business.

Essentially, the Jesuit missionary was to him a tool in the service of the wrong side in the contest between liberty and absolutism. While the triumph of liberty was never in doubt, it could have been dearly bought because of the Jesuit efforts. "Populations formed in the ideas and habits of a feudal monarchy, and controlled by a hierarchy profoundly hostile to freedom of thought, would have remained a hindrance and a stumbling-block in the way of that majestic experiment of which America is the field." The defeat of the missionary was due to the Iroquois resistance. Had they been converted or curbed, the French and their rich commerce would have blocked the expansion of the English colonies.[3]

Two years after the book on the Jesuits was published, Parkman issued the equally adventurous *La Salle and the Discovery of the Great West* (1869). The numerous French and American sources for this work were augmented by Jared Sparks's own collection. Sparks had once written a biography of La Salle and his quest for materials had gone on since. The book is largely a wilderness narrative with a minimum of those large generalizations which reveal Parkman's social ideas. The personality of La Salle and the detailed narrative of his explorations leave little else upon the historical canvas. The man stands out in clear relief, striving against the Jesuits as well as a hostile environment to win control of the Mississippi Valley.

After a somewhat greater interval, he finally brought out the lengthy institutional history, *The Old Regime in Canada* (1874). Although this contained plenty of adventurous episodes in the life of Canada's three settlements "gasping under the Iroquois tomahawk," he concentrated in part upon the paternalistic system of old Canada, focusing attention upon the powerful intendant Jean Talon and the transplantation of French feudalism. The extreme centralization that beset the French empire simplified the historian's task also. "The king and the minister demanded to know everything; and officials of high and low degree, soldiers and civilians, friends and foes, poured letters and memorials, on both sides of every question, into the lap of the government," he declared in a preface. In addition there were the voluminous records of the Superior Council of Quebec and many more preserved in the civil and ecclesiastical depositaries of Canada. Within the American state archives, particularly those of Massachusetts and New York, were many copied documents; and Parkman read fresh documents from France, copying these into his classified note system.

He described the minute administrative regulations that covered markets and inns, marriages, family quarrels, Sabbath observance, the kind of flour to be used in bread, the pay of chimney sweeps, and the handling of mad dogs. It must have pleased him to quote a letter of the intendant in 1685: "It is of very great consequence that the people should not be left at liberty to speak their minds." The priests also preached against parties and card games, much to the distress of the mighty as well as the simple *habitant*. Pillories existed for the stubborn offenders. Actually, as Parkman might have learned from colonial New England statute books, life on the American side was not too different, and many of the same restraints on daily life existed on both sides of the border. He was eager to establish a flawless picture of utter subservience and illiteracy on the French side in contrast to free Anglo-Saxon institutions.

This work gives many clues to Parkman's theories of history. "Not institutions alone," he wrote, "but geographical position, climate, and many other conditions unite to form the educational influences that, acting through successive generations, shape the character of nations and communities." Much more significant was his pioneer effort to develop a theory of the influence of the West upon civilization. The Canadians became much more than a docile people trained to subjection and despotism and planted in the wilderness by authority. Once the young man left his family to live as a fur trapper and hunter in the West, he was transformed into a savage *coureur de bois*. Church and state were not always able to control him. Unfortunately, while Parkman frequently made reference to the transforming effects of the frontier, he usually stopped with the same observation regarding the transformation of the tame *habitant* into an adventurous individual. He drew no inference here as to the possible democratic effects of this experience. The frontier theories of Frederick Jackson Turner were yet unpublished and the predecessors of Turner were apparently unknown to Parkman.

Like the contemporary American historians who had studied in Germany, Parkman was fertile in racial explanations of history. He wrote:

The Germanic race, and especially the Anglo-Saxon branch of it, is peculiarly masculine, and, therefore, peculiarly fitted for self-government. It submits its action to the guidance of reason, and has the judicial faculty of seeing both sides of a question.

The French, he thought, were excitable, went to extremes, tended to embrace abstractions, and to look upon life romantically. They, unlike the English, were unfit for freedom, and hence the free institutions of New England were inapplicable to New France. Parkman, however, made it clear that he was no admirer of the Puritans either:

Children are taught that the Puritans came to New England in search of religious liberty. The liberty that they sought was for themselves alone. . . . Their mission was to build up a western Canaan, ruled by the law of God; to keep it pure from error, and, if need were, purge it of heresy by persecution,—to which ends they set up one of the most detestable theocracies on record. Church and State were joined in one. . . . There was no choice but to remain politically a cipher, or embrace, or pretend to embrace, the extremest dogmas of Calvin. Never was such a premium offered to cant and hypocrisy.

Still, they were apparently much further along the path of freedom than the French Canadians.

Parkman's tendency to identify masculinity with the capacity for self-government is but the counterpart of his entire philosophy of action and virility. It helps explain why he considered women suffrage particularly debased. Elsewhere he had written that war was very important in civilization and in the development of individual and national character. His journal shows him as a Stoic in endurance and his early life displays him as a thoroughgoing Spartan. In a newspaper article, he asserted:

In every well-balanced development of nations as of individuals, the warlike instinct and the military point of honor are not repressed and extinguished, but only refined and civilized. It belongs to the pedagogue, not to the philosopher, to declaim against them as relics of barbarism.

In back of his mind were undoubtedly Montcalm, La Salle, and Champlain, refined agents of the chivalric military point of view, though representative of a lost cause.

Parkman's final books rounded out the pattern of the imperial conflict between England and France. *Count Frontenac and New France under Louis XIV* (1877) continues the tragedy of France's collapse in the New World as reflected in the politics of the homeland and the decisions of a powerful leader. Of the entire series, *Montcalm and Wolfe* (1884) pleased the critics most, partly because it had the dramatic advantage of reaching a great climax in the siege and fall of Quebec and the death of two heroic leaders. Parkman was at his best when he unfolded the complicated turns of action in an epochal struggle—and here his accuracy was on a far higher plane than were his dubious social interpretations.

Long before one comes to the last volume, *A Half Century of Con-*

flict (1892), it dawns upon the reader that few of the plain French Canadian folk are to be resurrected from the dim pages of the manuscripts. Parkman speaks disparagingly of the Acadian peasants, "Not one of their number stands out prominently from among the rest." To him history was a private affair of the elite; there was little room for supernumeries in a good dramatic tale. As for the humble Acadians, he kept the hostile Anglophile interpretation that he had already used in *Montcalm and Wolfe.* Apparently, he was unimpressed by the popular sentimental efforts of his fellow-New Englander, Longfellow, to depict in *Evangeline* (1847) personality as well as tragedy in the wholesale forced emigration of the Acadians. Parkman chose documents that were probably bowdlerized by the English editor, which suggested that the Acadians were disloyal. Much later, the historian yielded in part at least to evidence to the contrary that had long been urged upon him.[4]

From the craftsman's standpoint, *A Half Century of Conflict* had the virtue of placing the American aspect of the Anglo-French wars in its proper position within the complex of power politics. The author forged a tight chain of historical consequences which began with the ambitious schemes of Louis XIV, his exhausting wars, his revocation of the Edict of Nantes, the bankruptcy of the middle classes, the French Revolution, and the current revolutions of the nineteenth century. Each event precipitated the next. *Post hoc, ergo propter hoc* was the obvious fallacy of this line of thought. History was an organic process.

Parkman clarified his Whiggish idea of a democratic elite in history when he wrote "The Tale of a Ripe Scholar," published in the *Nation* in 1869. He pointed out that the need for exceptional men in democracies had nothing in common with the rising plutocrats or the political demagogues. While he praised the evolution of American scholarship since the futile days of the colonial clerical monopoly over learning, he feared that the new popular education actually depreciated sound scholarship and leadership. Like Emerson and Carlyle, he urged democracy to bring forth its men of thought:

In a country where the ruling power is public opinion, it is above all things necessary that the best and maturest thought should have a fair share in forming it. Such thought cannot exist in any force in the community without propagating its own image, and a class of strong thinkers is the palladium of democracy. They are the natural enemies of ignorant, ostentatious, and aggressive wealth, and the natural friends of all that is best in the popular heart.

There was no substitute for brains in the mere aggregate of average intelligence. Without a natural elite, our civilization would remain "a creature with a small and feeble head, a large muscular and active body, and a tail growing at such a rate that it threatens to become unmanageable and shake the balance of the vital powers." A similar theme is argued in "The Failure of Universal Suffrage," which appeared fittingly in the Brahminist *North American Review* in 1878. "The history of the progress of mankind," he asserted, "is the history of its leading minds." The masses, left to themselves, were incapable of progress; only the beneficent vitality of a few gifted men in history could do this.

Parkman disavowed any intention to weaken existing democratic institutions, though he questioned the value of the current panaceas. He was no aristocrat, for he shared the American faith in social mobility and he asked for a free society "where all men have equal opportunities of development according to their several qualities." So far universal suffrage had failed to elevate men, but this did not mean that oligarchy, autocracy, or aristocracy could do better. He had Carlyle's contempt for a nose-counting democracy of mediocre men, "a barren average," and "a weary conformity." In practice, as a citizen, Parkman went along with the antislavery movement, joined the Union Republicans during the Civil War, and later expressed his contempt for Grantism by voting with the reformist, middle-class Mugwumps whose appeal for a civil service merit system strongly attracted a man who believed in a democratic elite.

Although Parkman's elitism made a true history of the people impossible, he escaped the naïve enthronement of King Mob suggested in the later social historians. He was no Bancroft to equate the voice of the people as the voice of God. Like the Emersonians, he attacked "the ascendancy of material interests" among the people. He loved the forest primeval, but he disliked the individualistic frontier spirit which made clearing lands and building railroads the sum and substance of civilization. This materialistic spirit would "improve" our colleges into schools of technology. Already, public schools were interfering with the free development of the highest intelligence by emphasizing the trivial, the sensational, and the ephemeral. They did not inculcate a sense of moral and political duty or promote the feeling that the voter's interests were connected with those of the community. Education must cease cramming and develop instead the individual's powers of comparison, analysis, and observation. "The other remedy," he said, "consists in a powerful reinforcement of the higher education and the consequent development of a class of persons, whether rich or poor, so well instructed and so numerous as to hold their ground against charlatanry and propagate sound and healthy thought through the community.[5]

Another apostle of the strenuous life, elitism, and the Whig ideal of civic duty was Parkman's historical disciple, Theodore Roosevelt. On July 13, 1889, the enthusiastic aspiring historian wrote to his hero: [6]

I have always had a special admiration for you as the only one—and I may very sincerely say, the greatest—of our two or three first class historians who devoted himself to American history; and made a classic work—not merely an excellent book of references like Bancroft or Hildreth.

Roosevelt's review of Parkman's works in *The Independent* expressed a current and even lasting judgment: [7]

Mr. Parkman has done a great work which there is no need of any one trying to do again. He has shown all the qualities of the historian, capacity for wide and deep research, accuracy in details combined with power to subordinate the details to the general effect, a keen perception of the essential underlying causes and results, and the mastery of a singularly clear, pure and strong style.

Henry Adams praised *Montcalm and Wolfe* highly: "The book puts you in the front rank of living English historians. . . . The book is a model of thorough and impartial study and clear statement.[8] The same book drew the praise of literary leaders like Henry James and James Russell Lowell. The highest tribute was the fact that so many writers drew heavily from Parkman's pages for their narratives. Herbert L. Osgood, leading colonial historian, referred his readers to *Montcalm and Wolfe* for the entire story as to "what happened among the French" during Braddock's defeat and again for the full story of "the wild and lawless life of the forest." The Canadian authority, Professor George Wrong, said in 1938 of the lasting value of Parkman's writings: [9]

Though he wrote half a century ago, his account of the Jesuit martyrs, of Frontenac, of La Salle and other explorers, of British Wolfe and French Montcalm in the last struggle for Canada, remains the standard narrative.

A. L. Burt, author of books on Canadian history, wrote in 1942 that "For the period since the British conquest, there is no historian comparable to Parkman." [10] Even Catholic writers, quite deeply offended by Parkman's anticlericalism, found much that was good in his histories. Laval University came close to offering him an honorary degree; as it turned out, Protestant McGill University gave it to him instead. So the reputation of Parkman, for all his sins of omission and commission, has continued to stand high, and his works have been made available in new handsome editions.

The fact that Parkman has survived while the "literary historians" of his day are quite dead suggests that his histories retain elements of universal appeal, particularly his reportorial skill, despite a dramatic rhetoric almost as obsolete as that of Bancroft and Carlyle. He lacked, as C. W. Alvord, the historian of the West, and others have pointed out, an awareness of the significance of economics in history, and his social science framework is wholly untenable, but his accuracy and intensity of original research, put at the service of his masterly creative imagination, brought the past alive vividly for the reader. He had not traversed the battlements of Quebec and the course of Braddock's march for nothing; he had lived among the Indians and had tramped over many historic French and English imperial paths. In his later semi-blindness and invalidism these impressions had clung most tenaciously. For in these reportorial facts, as distinct from social synthesis, he had an overwhelming advantage over other historians. Even the best of his scientific successors were not as gifted as he in transmuting the moldy records into live impressions: marching men, Wolfe approaching Quebec, Jesuit martyrs facing Indian tomahawks, and Pontiac plotting to overthrow the Anglo-American forts.

4

The admiration of Theodore Roosevelt (1858-1919) for Parkman was no casual compliment, for he dreamed in 1888 of becoming a second Parkman able to capture the adventurous spirit of the West. What the New Englander did for the colonial Northeast, the New Yorker hoped to do for the Old Southwest and perhaps the lands beyond the Mississippi up to the period of the war with Mexico. He, too, loved the out-of-doors, the atmosphere of the primitive, the psychology of action and heroes; the company of wild animals thrilled him and the tales of Indian wars fascinated him. He admired virility, loathed weakness, and even as President was concerned that country life might lose its ruggedness and attractiveness for Americans. He overcame a frail childhood by sheer will power, cultivated the lore of the naturalist, and gave up for several years the comfortable New York City environment for a cattle ranch in western Dakota.

His upper-class family background sent him to Harvard, where he earned good grades and became a lifelong friend of Henry Cabot

Lodge, the scholar in politics who taught and wrote in the field of American history with a strong jingoist emphasis. Thereafter the young man studied law at Columbia but quickly decided to make a career out of a combination of politics and history-writing. He rose quickly to party leadership not only in New York state politics but on the national scene as well. After his wife and his mother died in 1884, he spent three years on his ranch and helped organize a battle against cattle rustlers. His apparently inexhaustible energies made it possible for him to turn out several biographies, usually in essay style not too steeped in adequate sources. For a short time he was even a publisher, having acquired a silent partnership in the firm of G. P. Putnam, whom he expected to issue the many books he was planning.

As early as 1882, he completed a workmanlike and readable book, *The Naval War of 1812* (1882), based on excellent sources, and showed such technical knowledge as well as dramatic skill in depicting sea battles that an English firm specializing on British naval history even invited him to write the 1812 section of a projected series on the British Navy. Reviewers praised Roosevelt's accuracy and objectivity. Throughout his life (as was to be true of his kinsman, Franklin D. Roosevelt), he believed in the primacy of seapower in history and almost worshiped the noted strategist and apostle of big navies, Alfred Thayer Mahan, whose highly influential books on the role of seapower appeared during the nineties.

In 1889, Roosevelt issued the first two volumes of his best-known work, *The Winning of the West,* and he managed to get the final and fourth volume out in 1896 while he was busy fighting against the menace of Bryanism and "that anarchist" Governor John P. Altgeld. In a year or two he became so involved in making history that he had little time to write it. Naturally, the dedication was to Parkman, "to whom Americans who feel pride in the pioneer history of their country are so greatly indebted." Like Parkman, he was no academic historian but a self-trained industrious researcher, one of the "literary historians." He probably did not exaggerate when he claimed to have journeyed through the entire country in order to consult manuscript and printed collections.

Roosevelt was not a social scientist like Frederick Jackson Turner, and his plain but highly readable style could not compare with Parkman's. However, he had the ability to identify himself with such dramatic situations in frontier history as the conquests of George Rogers Clark; as a result, his history is still very much worth the attention of present-day high-school and college students. Hamlin Garland enjoyed the literary quality and novelty of the material and what he regarded as the fair-mindedness and understanding of the author. The Middle Western novelist thought that Roosevelt expressed himself too clearly and realistically to be called a romantic, and he saw no evidence of tall writing. This is probably too generous, for Roosevelt's emphasis on dramatic incidents, the atmosphere of action and conflict, and the role of heroic personalities among frontier leaders and Indian chiefs put him very much in the tradition of Parkman and the other romantic historians.

Roosevelt shared the Anglo-Saxon Protestant interpretation of Parkman and the prevalent theory that Teutonic forest roots were fundamental in the evolution of Anglo-American democracy. The rise of the United States was the latest stage in this development, and among the great frontier creators of this civilization were Daniel Boone and George Rogers Clark. Roosevelt always stressed the importance of heroes and personalities in history. "They were doing their share of a work that began with the conquest of Britain, that entered on its second and wider period after the defeat of the Spanish Armada, that culminated in the marvellous growth of the United States." Bancroft, too, had stressed the idea that all world history had providentially moved toward the present high point of Anglo-Saxon civilization in America.

The author pictured the French *habitants* very much as Parkman did: "Hospitable, but bigoted to their old customs, ignorant, indolent, and given to drunkenness, they spoke a corrupt jargon of the French tongue." Though he feared that some of the poor-white characteristics came from the American frontiersmen, he gave his gratifying approval on the whole to the superior American contribution:

The Spaniards, the Portuguese, and the French, not to speak of the Russians in Siberia, have all enjoyed and yet have failed to make good use of, the same advantages which we have turned to good account . . . None but heroes can succeed in the work. . . . Looked at relatively, it must also be said that we have done better than any other nation or race working under our conditions.

The four volumes were well constructed and laid especial stress on the story of the West during the Revolution, the development of the Northwest Territory, the wars in the Northwest during 1787-90, and the rise of new western states. Roosevelt thought that the frontiersmen had played a large part in winning the Revolution, especially in the mountain campaigns, but he felt no great animus against the British.

Only later did he take them to task for inciting the Indians. "The ordinary American histories, often so absurdly unjust to England, are right in their treatment of the British actions on the frontier in 1793-94." Like the staunch moralist that he was, he sifted the villains from the heroes and flayed the traitor, James Wilkinson; but he had only admiration for the conquests of George Rogers Clark, who seemed so neglected by his state and nation. Much as he tried he could not altogether conceal a privately expressed dislike of the Indians. He admitted that the whites might have been at fault at times in violating their agreements, but he felt that the Indians would certainly have been even more unjust and brutal, had they only been in a position to strike back. Although he paid little attention to economic matters, he went beyond other writers in recognizing the significance of land speculation in western history. Naturally he preferred tales of combat such as border-fighting, and he told them with dramatic skill, just as he was at home in relating famous sea battles in his earlier work.

The Winning of the West was certainly successful in bringing history to the layman, and the newspaper and magazine critics recognized the history's worth. Even Professor Albert Bushnell Hart of Harvard, who reckoned himself to be of the scientific history school, praised it as a work of careful research, and he wrote a friendly introduction for the handsome 1924 edition of Roosevelt's writings. The work did not seem to show the haste that characterized T.R.'s biographies.[11]

The man who did most to divert frontier history into scientific channels, Frederick Jackson Turner, thought that Roosevelt deserved more credit than to be labeled as a mere adventure writer. Turner's comments were critical and guarded but far from unfavorable, even if he believed that Roosevelt was really a romantic who neglected such vital themes as government land policies. He wrote appreciatively in the *Nation* after three volumes had appeared:

Mr. Roosevelt had the historical insight and good fortune to make use of a vast amount of original material. These abundant materials he has used with the skill of a practiced historian, writing with appreciation of the fact that he is describing a phase in the general movement of civilization.

Roosevelt did not altogether deny his flare for the romantic, even though he once criticized Carlyle for this defect while still adopting the pose of hero-worship. In fact, he was rather proud to single out his popular book, *Hero Tales of American History*, which he wrote with

Henry Cabot Lodge to depict the virile military man and Indian fighter. But because of the mounting influence of Turner and his disciples, the Parkman-Roosevelt literary tradition of narrative frontier history sustained a severe blow. Roosevelt complained to his friends that the younger scientific historians demanded such things as that a historian must not take sides, or decide what was right or wrong, or permit literature to interfere with objectivity. It seemed that drama and the pulsations of life had become suspect.

Parkman and Roosevelt reflect certain tendencies also evident in the widely read books of Thomas Carlyle (1795-1881), whose best-known work, *The French Revolution,* appeared in 1837. These literary historians rebelled against the mediocrity, conformity, and impersonal qualities attributed to the democratic leveling process and found an antidote in hero-worship, dramatic deeds of warriors, and a gospel of action. The Americans also reflected some of the elitist philosophy and aristocratic radicalism so vigorously upheld by Carlyle. Together with the noted Scot, they attacked the materialistic tendencies of their day and disassociated themselves in varying degree from the alleged coldness of "the cause-and-effect" historians whom Carlyle loathed.

While they flatly rejected Carlyle's dictum that "History is the essence of innumerable biographies," the Scot himself also greatly qualified this view in an essay, "On History," by insisting upon the primacy of philosophy in history-writing and the need for a broad concept of social history that would recognize creative energies among all classes. The three men were stern moralists in appraising the men of the past (and the present), and none took the trouble to conceal their social prejudices. While Carlyle is too complex, inconsistent, and controversial a personality to fit within an actual equation, the many similarities between him and the American literary historians are indeed significant. The romantic hero-worshiping attitude in varying degrees seemed to be a natural reaction to the growing impersonal quality of urban, commercial-industrial life. Europeans, too, reacted somewhat in the same way as Americans to the dehumanizing threat of science and technology.

From Fiske to Gipson: The Rise
of Colonial Institutional History

1

When John Fiske began writing American colonial history in the
1880s and 1890s, he found that the social interpretation of the period
had been firmly set by previous historians. The orthodox view, expressed in the best-selling histories of Bancroft and Parkman and by
lesser men, was patriotic, liberal, and Protestant, based on native Puritan roots. It celebrated the providential emergence of free English
colonial institutions after a mortal combat with French and Spanish
feudal paternalism. The American historians, like their contemporary
British colleagues, took for granted the superiority of the alleged Teutonic origins of Anglo-American democracy and commonly regarded
American history as the ultimate stage of universal history.

The story of the American Revolution was still patterned after
Edmund Burke's Annual Register, whose Whig point of view condemned George III and his Tory cronies. Burke had not regarded the
Revolution as a social movement but as a political revolt against unwise Tory policies; his ideas and even language had been plagiarized
by David Ramsay, John Marshall, William Gordon, and others. A few
independent-minded historians such as Richard Hildreth had made a
class analysis of the Revolution and had seen economic pressures behind the movement for the Constitution; but John Fiske ignored this
approach.

One of Fiske's older contemporaries, John Gorham Palfrey (1796-1881) of Boston, was then writing popular filio-pietistic books on New England; they had the merit of thorough research—indeed, much more than Fiske cared to do in his histories. Palfrey, too, came of early seventeenth-century New England stock. He was graduated from Harvard, succeeded Jared Sparks as editor of the conservative *North American Review,* held a post as a Unitarian minister, and then served as Harvard's Dexter Professor of Sacred Literature. During his long life, he worked with Horace Mann in advancing public education in Massachusetts, was elected as an antislavery Whig to Congress (and even freed a few slaves that he had inherited), and then rather late in life turned to a noteworthy career as a historian. His magnum opus was a traditionalistic five-volume *History of New England,* the first four volumes of which appeared between 1858-75 and the last posthumously in 1890.[1]

The footnotes indicated he had done considerable research both in colonial and British records, and his facts tended to be relatively accurate. However, he put together his research mechanically; the only synthesis it reflected was that of a proud son of New England. Fiske too was to bear down upon the geographic setting, the aboriginal customs, and the Anglo-Saxon virtues, but he avoided Palfrey's tedious organization, which treated successive colonial administrations and concentrated on local and imperial politics. As a good traditionalist, Palfrey saw no flaws in the Puritan theocracy and even sided with the entrenched clericals against such foes as Anne Hutchinson. He admired the land of his ancestors for its pure English stock, struck an optimistic tone in his outlook, and told the story of the coming of the Revolution from the patriotic point of view.

Ever sensitive to middle-class views, Fiske shared the new Brahmin mood of hands-across-the-sea that called for conciliation with England, now that the Alabama Claims and the Venezuela Boundary Crisis had been settled. Like Bancroft, Parkman, Palfrey, and Roosevelt, he felt that the future belonged to the superior English-speaking peoples. He shared the British emphasis (also popular among Brahmins) on free trade, civil service reform, and hard or sound money.

The new hereditary societies like the Sons of the American Revolution (1889) and the Daughters of the American Revolution (1890) were not particularly exercised over the Red Coats, but many such members felt, as Fiske did, that the real danger lay in the immigrant tide of Italians, Slavs, and foreign radicals that threatened to engulf Boston and outvote the descendants of the Puritans. Fiske voiced these fears in his histories and on the lecture platform, and in 1894 he even accepted the honorary presidency of the Immigration Restriction League, whose persistent agitation finally led to the Literacy Test law of 1917, despite the vetoes of two presidents. He and his fellow-Brahmins admired the pursuit of genealogy, read Dugdale's startling book on the Jukes family, which implied the biological inheritance of criminal and asocial traits, and expressed concern over the alleged inferior stock arriving with the New Immigration after 1880 from southern and eastern Europe—though Fiske seems to have escaped the burgeoning anti-Semitism of so many other Brahmins.

Like the literary historians, Fiske hoped to write history for the educated layman without the ponderousness of the German-style monographs. However, unlike Parkman, Bancroft, or Roosevelt, he lacked funds for archival copyists and became so deeply involved in popular lectures as a mode of earning a living that he could not spare the time, even if he had the inclination, to peruse large quantities of original sources patiently. Too often his books were mere arrangements of lectures that he delivered in Boston, New York, Chicago, New Orleans, and sometimes to collegiate audiences at Washington University and Harvard. The rising vogue for women's clubs, headed by well-to-do dowagers, affected the style and content of his lectures. Yet his books did not sell as well as those of the famed and more substantial literary historians. Even his best-known book, *The Critical Period of American History*, took ten years to dispose of 34,000 copies, though it had a sustained sale thereafter. This was not too impressive for a man who was devoting himself to popularized history. The ovations to Fiske the historian did not quite equal the enthusiasm for Fiske the popular lecturer, who spoke to his elite audiences fluently and informally, scarcely looking at his notes. Yet he tried to please his readers as well as his auditors, for he avoided difficult concepts and even toned down his adverse opinions on slavery and the Civil War in deference to the South and his publishers.

The early education of John Fiske gave every promise of a great career. Born Edmund Fisk Green in 1842 in Hartford, Connecticut, of Puritan descent, he was a child prodigy who read Shakespeare and the English classics before his ninth year. By the time he was seventeen, he knew the Latin and Greek classics in the original as well as considerable literature in Portuguese, French, Italian, German, and even some Hebrew and Sanskrit. His reading led him to reject the Calvinist orthodoxy of his home and to drop the idea that the Bible was of divine authority.

At Harvard his heterodoxy was fed by Comte's positivism and the evolutionary ideas of Spencer and Darwin. Linguistic subjects fascinated him, law attracted him sufficiently so that he earned a law degree, philosophy absorbed him, but history finally became his favorite field. Perhaps he might have become a solid academic historian had not an outraged Harvard Board of Overseers canceled his appointment as history instructor on the ground that he held objectionable positivist and presumably atheist views. During the 1870's, he held a librarianship at Harvard, wrote a severe critique of Buckle's theory of civilization, and attracted attention for his four-volume *Outlines of Cosmic Philosophy with Criticisms on the Positive Philosophy*. In this and in other writings, he espoused the view, then popular, of the progressive evolution of society; and in his very popular lectures he expressed the spirit of liberal Protestantism as he tried to show the harmony of religion and science. Professor George Louis Beer, the colonial historian, thought that this championship of Darwinism in the 'seventies required courage. "What Huxley did for the doctrine of evolution in England, Fiske did for America." Besides, he made science comprehensible for the layman.

Philosophy could not support Fiske and his family, however, and so, with the example of the successful literary historians in mind, he turned to writing history. He scrutinized the praiseworthy and popular model of John Richard Green's *A Short History of the English People*, but he made no great effort to follow Green in emphasizing social history; instead, he continued down the familiar road of political history. He published no less than eleven books on colonial history and still others on the later periods.[2]

One of Fiske's most original histories was *The Discovery of America* (1892), dedicated to Edward A. Freeman, the English "scientific historian" who regarded history as past politics. As a confirmed social evolutionist who believed that human development moved along fixed stages, Fiske stressed the evolution of primitive society in aboriginal America—it took him 147 pages to furnish an instructive example of ethnic evolution operating in isolation from the Old World for more than 50,000 years. "'It was the study of prehistoric Europe and of early Aryan institutions that led me by a natural sequence to the study of aboriginal America." He stressed the comparative point of view: "The house-communities of the southern Slavs are full of interest for the student of the early phases of social evolution, but the Mandan roundhouse and the Zuni pueblo carry us much deeper into the past." He hoped that his book would bring an awareness of how archaeology could help explain the evolution of early American society. This preoccupation with genesis required over a hundred pages on pre-Columbian voyages of discovery and over two hundred on the conquest of Mexico and Peru. While Fiske claimed to draw heavily from original sources, the total product did not seem as novel as this suggests. Like Parkman, Bancroft, and Roosevelt, he stressed the superiority of the individualistic and buoyant English over the French and the Spanish, so the outcome of the race for colonization could be easily foreseen: "Wherever, in any of the regions open to colonization, this race [the English] has come into competition with other European races, it has either vanquished or absorbed them, always proving its superior capacity."

Fiske's two-volume *Old Virginia and Her Neighbors* (1897) seems to have been taken largely from his lectures at Washington University, where he had a visiting professorial status. His reliance on secondary sources deprived the narrative of freshness, and his political emphasis meant the neglect of essential social and economic history. He saw the Cavaliers as a dominant superior factor in Virginia's history, thus ignoring the fact that relatively few Cavaliers came to that colony. He paused to praise genealogy as a tool for the historian:

> By no possible ingenuity of constitution-making or of legislation can a society made up of ruffians and boors be raised to the intellectual and moral level of a society made up of well-bred merchants and yeomen, parsons and lawyers. . . . Without genealogy the study of history is lifeless.

Thus, the president of the Immigration Restriction League argued that those who migrated to Virginia and New England were indeed picked men and women. To leaven his political history, he inserted a large chapter on "Society in the Old Dominian," a topical review of crime and punishment, indentured servants, slaves, planters, antislavery feeling, the country store, roads, architecture, home furnishings, schools, and libraries. The dramatic tale of how Pocahontas saved John Smith was accepted in toto by Fiske, despite the doubts of contemporary historians such as Henry Adams. (Recent writers tend to credit the story, but for better reasons.) As for the Cavalier legend, it had been bolstered by proslavery propagandists; it remained for T. J. Wertenbaker and other younger historians to demolish it completely.

The two-volume history, *The Dutch and Quaker Colonies in America* (1899), is of minor importance. Since Fiske regarded the Dutch as a part of the Teutonic world, he hastened to claim kinship between the Dutch and the Anglo-American peoples. *New France and New England* (1902) had little to say that Parkman had not said better. The most informative section dealt with the Salem witchcraft craze. Despite his religious liberalism, he praised some of the results of the Great Awakening, and spoke of Jonathan Edwards as "one of the wonders of the world, probably the greatest intelligence that the western hemisphere has yet seen." Here and elsewhere, he tried to offset the theocratic intolerance of the Puritans by emphasizing their ethical and intellectual contributions. Like Perry Miller and other present-day cultural historians, he singled out their essential emphasis upon reason and distrust of fanatical interpretations of the Bible. But his sources seemed few indeed.

The American Revolution (1891) is informal and superficial military history almost devoid of documentation, though studded with maps, illustrations of weapons, and caricatures. It showed tolerance for the Tories and a good deal of pity for the Loyalist Governor Thomas Hutchinson: "None has been more grossly misrepresented by historians." He held the Burke view that the Revolution was not social but political and devoid of radical doctrines; and of course he placed the chief guilt upon George III. Like the institutionalist historians who succeeded him, Fiske closed with a hope for lasting understanding between the English-speaking peoples. Unlike them, however, he denounced the mercantilist system that had divided mother country and colonies as "barbarous superstitions about trade." After all, he was an ardent free trader who liked to inject present-day economic doctrines into the past.

His most influential book was *The Critical Period of American History, 1783-1789* (1888), which was to remain popular even after World War I. It grew out of lectures but had considerable substance, for there was convincing material on the breakdown and weakness of the newly independent states under the Articles of Confederation. The implication was that the Constitution saved the nation and that it was a popular reaction to chronic anarchy. The phrase "critical period" was inspired by Tom Paine's remark in 1783 that the crisis was over, but, said Fiske, "so far from the crisis being over in 1783, the next five years were to be the most critical time of all." He stressed such themes as the "unparalleled grandeur" of Washington, the long-term influence of technology on unification, the germs of national sovereignty within the setting up of the Northwest Territory, and the pettiness of the states. He even outdid Gladstone's famous praise of the Constitution

Fiske — The Crit. Per. of Amer. Hist., 1783-1789 (1888)

as "the most wonderful work ever struck off at a given time by the brain of man." Fiske called it "this Iliad, or Parthenon, or Fifth Symphony of statesmanship."

Charles Beard, among others, was to disintegrate the "critical era" thesis in his *An Economic Interpretation of the Constitution,* for he found these postwar years neither critical nor chaotic; furthermore he (and O. G. Libby) showed that the Constitution was the product of minority pressures. In 1940, in *The Articles of Confederation* Merrill Jensen condemned the Fiske theory as a tradition established by the Federalists whose interests were blocked by the Articles. But even by the 1950s, there were historical specialists who rejected the Beard and Jensen views in favor of an interpretation not far from that of John Fiske.

Professional reviewers usually pointed out that Fiske was a popularizer rather than a researcher, but they liked his ability to reach the masses, who were ignored by the academicians. James Schouler wrote in 1901 that this popularization should not be minimized: [3]

> For an easy and captivating style, for philosophical insight into the relation of events and rare skillfulness in bringing a wealth of general learning and general historical study to bear upon the . . . topic in hand, I consider John Fiske the chief of our native historians, living or dead. Others may have excelled him in original research, in continuity of effort prolonged in a single direction, . . . but few ever equalled him in the power to generalize or elucidate from materials already gathered.

That same year as Fiske's death—1901—George Louis Beer, the noted colonial historian, also discovered virtues as well as weaknesses in him, in fact he even compared Fiske with Lecky and John Morley. Fiske was not a great philosopher or a great historian, but a great educative force for the people. Unfortunately, thought Beer, Fiske had paid too little attention to social forces and too much to drama; political and military themes were overemphasized.[4] Such a judgment was largely reiterated in 1931 when Professor Jennings B. Sanders wrote a full-length essay on Fiske.[5] By that time, the New Englander's reputation had declined further among professionals, and the layman had found other interesting interpreters of colonial America. The ethnocentric and class prejudices of Fiske and his generation were no longer respectable, at least not in so overt a form. Fiske, it was generally agreed, was not a model for scientific historians, but he had exercised considerable influence upon the mind of his own generation.

2

From John Fiske to Herbert L. Osgood is a long step in colonial historiography. Each lacked what the other enjoyed in abundance: Fiske
was unable temperamentally to match Osgood's meticulous historical
scholarship, but Osgood did not possess even remotely Fiske's talents
for communication, unless one thinks of him, as his admirers did, as "a
historian's historian." Fiske also lacked the stabilizing influence of a
permanent academic post, which made it possible for Osgood to train
able disciples about him and to escape the money pinching that came
with irregular public lecture contracts; too often Fiske was forced to
turn literary hack to meet expenses. Whatever the reasons, Fiske
dabbled in the original sources while Osgood sought them out at great
expense and trouble to himself. Osgood, who was often given to writing critical reviews, did not spare epithets when reviewing Fiske's
books. Committed to a systematic institutional point of view which
looked upon the colonies as an organic part of an evolving British imperial administration, Osgood had little patience with historians like
Fiske who confined their view to the narrow limits of the colonies and
to dramatic events alone. He assailed *The American Revolution* because he felt that Fiske did not even try to explain the British colonial
system up to 1776 and had no understanding of England's aristocratic
society or the maturing American democracy:

> We learn nothing in this work of the efforts which the home government
> had long made to establish a tolerable administrative system here, or of the
> opposition with which it had met. The objects aimed at by the British
> ministers are not supposed to have been even relatively justifiable.

He thought that Fiske had even gone beyond Bancroft in his partisanship and quarreled with the former's justification of the slogan,
"no taxation without representation," and his insistence that Britain
should have admitted that the taxing power lay only in the colonial
legislatures. Actually, he said, these were completely revolutionary
doctrines which no British government could accept. Osgood rejected
much of the Burke thesis, and also did not think that George III was
a war criminal. His own interpretation was what has been called the
view of the "imperial school":

> Through a long course of development toward independence a crisis had
> been reached in the relations between the colonies and the mother country
> from which there was no issue except through war, and when the gauntlet

was thrown down by Massachusetts, the King was bound by the most sacred obligations to suppress the revolt if possible.

Herbert Osgood was born in 1855, the son of a hard-working Maine farmer in modest circumstances and the descendant of seventeenth-century English emigrants. At Amherst College, his instructor John W. Burgess persuaded him to follow his example by studying in Germany. At the University of Berlin, Osgood listened to Adolf Wagner's socialistic theories and Schmoller's historical approach to economic institutions, and even wrote a dissertation—an adverse interpretation—upon scientific socialism and Proudhon's anarchism. There is little of this influence apparent in his lifelong work on colonial history except for his central emphasis on institutional studies—very popular in the Germany of the 1880s.

Germans of the "Historical School" like Wagner, Schmoller, and Sombart had rebelled against the inadequacy of abstract economic theory such as laissez-faire and sought to further social reform by studying the history of actual social institutions—guilds, municipalities, mercantilism, capitalism, and imperialism. Schmoller, like Osgood, used a political and administrative analysis of economic institutions. There was prevalent an "historicist" assumption which—in one of its many meanings—implied that the truth of anything was to be found in its history. Usually, these institutionalists leaned heavily upon social evolution to guide them to the various "stages" of development. (So did Osgood.) The young American scholar was also attracted to and apparently influenced by the archival science and seminar method which German scholars such as Von Sybel and the disciples of Ranke were emphasizing. The "scientific historians" learned from philologists how to determine the authenticity and meaning of documents. If Osgood did not learn these methods directly from the Germans, he could have learned them from American scholars who had acquired this approach in German universities.

Columbia University, then developing its graduate program, invited him to become a faculty colleague of Burgess, Dunning, and E. R. A. Seligman. For a time he taught general European history, but soon he took charge of an ambitious graduate program in colonial studies. Students found that his thorough, original lectures required careful note-taking. It must have aroused the patriotic ire of some to hear objectivity go so far as a defense of the ministers of George III:

There was nothing that can be called tyrannical or unconstitutional in the plans of Grenville, Townshend or Lord North. Severe measures were not resorted to till they were provoked by colonial resistance. The most that we can say of the policy is that it was blundering and vacillating.

Liberty and progress were not the issue, but independence, and he conceded the legal rightness of the British position. The break arose because English traditional policy came into conflict with Puritan ideas and frontier conditions in America.

Osgood prepared for his magnum opus by examining at length the British and American local archives neglected by Hildreth, Palfrey, Bancroft, and Fiske. Even his inadequate professorial salary did not deter him from making first-hand intensive researches into the sources in London and those scattered around the United States. Fortunately, by this time, the British government (and also the American) aided such efforts through manuscript guides and published sources.[6]

The first volume of his major work appeared in 1904 as *The American Colonies in the Seventeenth Century,* which ultimately comprised three volumes; then came the four volumes of *The American Colonies in the Eighteenth Century.* Osgood's history was quite unlike the usual narratives, for it omitted much human-interest material in order to focus upon English colonial institutions in America, particularly their political and administrative aspects. Although he said that he would interpret colonial history in terms of public law, he was well aware of the dynamic social origins of political institutions, for he held that "political events and forms of government are very largely the product of social causes, while institutions are the avenues through which social forces act."

He dwelt upon the forms of colonial government as they grew out of English and colonial experience, the relations between the church and the civil power, the legal relations between the colonies and the mother country, and similar questions. The volumes on the seventeenth century were specially concerned with the dominance of the proprietary provinces, while the others dealt with the development of the royal provinces—presumably to furnish the thread of colonial institutional history. By the time he reached the eighteenth century, monograph literature was so limited on institutional themes that he had to rely largely upon original sources.

One major Osgood theme in his early volumes was the importance of private initiative as against state-directed colonial enterprise:

The voyages of discovery, the commercial enterprises, the single experiment in colonization of the reign of Elizabeth, were the results of private enterprise. Individuals, associations, and companies furnished the means, the state giving the requisite authority and verbal encouragement or guidance.

But the bulk of the work centered on the history of colonial administrations, beginning with that of Sir Thomas Smith. While his work was leavened by many acute observations, including the notion that the colonies were founded for profit and managed by absentees, Osgood avoided value judgments whenever possible. Unlike Adolf Wagner, Schmoller, or Sombart, he did not think that institutional history should be subordinated to the theme of social reform.

Had Osgood allowed himself a freer hand in dealing with social history, the burdensome synthesis might have been more tolerable for readers. He appreciated—even if he passed over these matters hurriedly—the influence of social factors in frontier life, the isolation of the colonists, and the role of Calvinist ideas—which he even exaggerated. Massachusetts was a theocracy, although democratic in form, and the clergy reincarnated the biblical Jewish theocracy and gathered strength from the support of the civil power. He made a shrewd analysis of heresy as a social factor, particularly in the cases of Roger Williams and Anne Hutchinson, and dwelt upon the intellectuality of Puritan culture.

The manuscript volumes on the eighteenth century were almost done when Osgood died in 1918—only a chapter on slavery was missing—but his friends and heirs discovered that the publishers were unwilling to take a chance upon a project that could attract relatively few readers. Only after one of Osgood's most affluent students, Dwight W. Morrow, a Morgan partner and Coolidge's Ambassador to Mexico, offered to underwrite publication did the Columbia University Press go ahead with publication (1924).

On the whole, as the author pointed out, the treatment and interpretation were the same as in the earlier volumes, except that such worn topics as the land system, the judiciary, finance, and the defense systems were dropped. He discussed the intercolonial aspects of the wars, immigration, Indian affairs, and church relations. Like Fiske, he was especially interested in the Great Awakening and had a high opinion of its leader: "The name of Jonathan Edwards came to stand for what was highest and most enduring in the great revival of 1740."

For all his stylistic drawbacks and woodenness of organization, Osgood had a creative influence among the rising generation of colonial historians, particularly George Louis Beer, Charles Andrews, and Lawrence H. Gipson through his emphasis on scientific interpretation and on the basic imperial context of colonial history. Under his guidance, Columbia University became a productive center for systematic studies of the colonies and the ideal of exact and objective scholarship. As for his style, some felt as *The Nation* did: "He was not interested in making learning attractive to those who needed to be persuaded." In 1933, a very competent critic in the *Mississippi Valley Historical Review* was still able to offer high praise: "It is safe to assert that no other period of American history has yet been treated in so detailed and scientific a manner. Osgood stands today, in these particulars, the American historical scholar without a peer." However, the same admiring critic said that Osgood's vaunted emphasis on manuscript sources was offset by the fact that perhaps 90 per cent of the seven volumes was actually based on printed sources. He was indifferent to newspaper sources (except in writing on the Zenger Case), but then he needed them less for legislative and administrative history.

Osgood minimized personality, seeming to care little for either the great man or the common man, although he did on occasion depart sufficiently from the objectivity of the scientific historian to make moral judgments and to display undue severity toward the Quakers. The same *Mississippi Valley Historical Review* critic complained of tiresome detail and of a lack of unity which left the burden of assimilation on the reader. But he concluded with a favorable estimate: [7]

> Osgood was ever the stern Puritan, holding himself and those under his direction tenaciously to the task. . . . He may be compared . . . to a consecrated monk, shutting out other interests (for he was aware of the world around him) in order to accomplish a great and high purpose. He mapped out for himself a pathway of difficult but worthwhile service and held courageously to it to the end. . . .

3

Osgood had a most distinguished doctoral student in George Louis Beer, who even outdid his master in defending British imperial policy and in elaborating upon the commercial rather than the purely administrative aspects of the Empire's record in North America. Yet Beer could claim no British ancestors, for he was the son of a Jewish merchant in Hamburg and identified himself with the leadership of Jewish welfare groups. Like James Ford Rhodes, he earned enough as a businessman, particularly in tobacco imports, to enable him to retire early and devote his life to historical research and public service. Academically, he was content to serve as a part-time lecturer in history at Columbia.[8]

In 1887, the year before Beer began his studies at the university, Osgood published his seminal article, "England and the Colonies," which attacked the patriotic school and argued that the colonies must be studied as an organic part of an integrated imperial administrative system that aimed at over-all efficiency. This point of view consequently dominated Beer's brief doctoral thesis, published in 1893 as *The Commercial Policy of England Toward the American Colonies.* His own lifelong thesis was emphasized in a prefatory quotation from William E. Lecky, an English historian of the Revolution:

> How often have the English commercial restrictions on the American colonies been treated as if they were instances of extreme and exceptional tyranny, while a more extended knowledge would show that they were simply the expression of ideas about the relation of dependencies to the mother country which then almost universally prevailed.

Beer and Osgood and their followers thought that a study of the colonies in a total imperial context would necessarily exonerate the government of George III of major responsibility for the Revolution. To Beer (and to the others as well) the Fiske-Bancroft patriotic school assumed that England consciously pursued an egotistic, tyrannical policy and then made the facts conform to their preconception.

Like so many scientific historians, Beer used the concepts of social evolution. Thus, he spoke of progressive advances and occasional retrogression in the evolution of mercantilism, which he regarded as a system superior to its predecessors. Only in the light of modern laissez-faire and free trade could this be condemned, and, he implied, it was unfair to use the standards of the present as an index of the past. Yet, it was obvious that his admiration for Victorian England influenced his admiration for Stuart and Restoration England. The worst that he thought could be said about mercantilistic abuses was that it was a policy of unconscious ignorance, not of conscious malice. In its everyday workings it was understandable and even desirable. Furthermore, it seemed quite natural and reasonable in 1763 for England to expect the colonies to pay for the defensive costs and sacrifices of the homeland. Mercantilism itself seemed to offer many positive benefits, such as the stimulation of colonial shipbuilding and the carrying trade.

Going far beyond Osgood, Beer became practically a historian of the British Empire with a focus as much on London as on the seaboard colonies. In 1908, he published *The Origins of the British Colonial System, 1578-1660* and defined his subject as "that complex system of regulations by means of which, though to a different extent, the economic structures of both metropolis and colony were moulded to conform to the prevailing ideal of a self-sufficient empire." He began with an explanation of English overpopulation and emigration, though he attributed the dislocation of population to political and religious conflicts rather than to economic causes. Throughout he showed a high opinion of British purpose and administrative wisdom and asserted that the cardinal doctrine of mercantilism was that private interest should unquestionably yield to public welfare. As a confirmed evolutionist, he saw everywhere an organic process of imperial growth: "In all of its phases this elaborate system implied an adjustment of the economic life both of the metropolis and of the colony to the gradually developing ideal of a self-sufficient empire."

In 1912 he published a detailed two-volume work, *The Old Colonial System, 1660-1688*, which continued his emphasis on the development of administrative machinery. Beer prided himself on a total objectivity in dealing with foreign trade that avoided the assumptions of free traders or protectionists—a rather difficult feat. In practice this forced his narrative into narrow descriptive channels. His broad canvas included the workings of mercantilism in the British West Indies and Newfoundland as well as the main American colonies.

Colonial historians usually prefer his book on *British Colonial Policy, 1754-1765* (1907), which was drawn from a mass of British state papers and deals exhaustively with the problem of imperial defense. Beer's viewpoint did not change. The American colonies were pictured as tending toward virtual autonomy, but they could not be relied upon to provide their due proportion of the armed forces and the imperial costs. Besides, they injured the war effort against France by persistently trading with the enemy. Although he never quite came up to the Revolution, he made it clear that he believed that it was a war for independence, not a struggle for civil liberty. He even believed that it was anachronistic in view of the evolution of the western world into ever larger political entities. He must have startled many readers (except those familiar with Osgood) with this conclusion:

It is easily conceivable, and not at all improbable, that the political evolution of the next centuries may take such a course that the American Revolution will lose the great significance that is now attached to it, and will appear merely as the temporary separation of two kindred peoples whose inherent similarity was obscured by superficial differences, resulting from dissimilar economic and social conditions.

Despite the changes wrought by younger revisionists and better writers, Beer had greatly extended Osgood's idea of the influence of English imperialism on American history. Actually, he opposed the oppressions of imperialism, but believed that the English colonial system of the seventeenth and eighteenth centuries worked on the whole for the welfare of the people. His Anglophilism grew. At the outbreak of World War I, he sympathized with Britain rather than his father's Germany and wrote *The English Speaking Peoples* to urge a lasting union against aggression. However, he had little to say about the Irish question and other restive areas in the Empire.

After the war, he accompanied Colonel House and Wilson to Paris and served as an expert on colonial questions. His basic belief in the progressive evolution of colonial peoples to freedom under international supervision is reflected in his coinage of the term "mandate" and his recommendation that the United States share some of this world responsibility in behalf of undeveloped areas. But his heavy public services and advancing ills made it impossible for him to bring his history of the old colonial system to 1776.

4

Charles McLean Andrews did not study under Osgood and Beer at Columbia but under Herbert B. Adams at the Johns Hopkins University. However, his approach was almost identical with the Columbia historians. He, too, perused thousands of manuscripts and printed documents both here and abroad in preparing his vast institutional and political history of the colonies. Like the Columbia leaders, he attacked the Bancroft-Fiske patriotic school, though he was more apt to recognize the shortcomings of British imperial policy. He was no less determined than the Columbia men to focus his long—and sometimes dreary—narrative on London and on the manipulations of colonial affairs by the bureaucrats and statesmen of Westminster and Whitehall. But he did not accept the Osgood-Beer thesis that London had steadily evolved an increasingly efficient administrative system.

Critics were to complain that all these three colonial historians were conservatives at heart, so lost in the minutiae of patents, charters, regulations of trade, and formalities of settlement that they forgot to deal with ordinary men and their everyday concerns, and the large issues of wages, prices, frontier life, Indians, and everyday customs. All tried vainly to forestall such critics by insisting that they had chosen so vast a subject that it was necessary to impose rigid limitations on the theme.

By the 1950s, another generation of historians complained that this thoroughly Teutonized school of "scientific historians" had ignored social ideas and seemed unwilling to recognize the fact that every historian deals with a past through the colored spectacles of the present. Osgood, Beer, and Andrews, proud of their English and German historiographical roots, believed that they were indeed objective and insisted that they did not permit the present to intrude on their image of the past. They perpetuated the Rankean tradition of emphasizing archival science and the techniques of textual criticism. And like so many social scientists at the end of the nineteenth century, they thought that their science was steeped in the solid foundations of Darwinism and that historians should try to solve real problems and not be overly concerned with narration. Style was a minor consideration. As for the controversies of the day, they were left untouched by the Populist and Progressive movements, though they showed interest in Anglo-American plans of international amity.

As a scientific historian, Charles Andrews echoed the prejudices against philosophy held by so many of his school. In 1924, in a presidential address before the American Historical Association, he expressed doubt whether there was such a thing as a philosophy of history, since so many of these systems had failed. He was unaware of the underlying philosophical assumptions that lay behind evolutionism, but drew freely, nevertheless, on the ideas of historical progress and evolutionary adjustments.

Andrews believed that he had escaped his social conditioning, for he dealt no undeserved favors to his Puritan ancestors. After all, he was the son of a Congregational father and had been born in 1863 in a Calvinist household in Wethersfield, Connecticut. His graduate work was completed at the Johns Hopkins University, the citadel of scientific history, where Herbert Baxter Adams and his pioneer, German-inspired seminar inculcated the idea that democratic institutions evolved from Anglo-Saxon and Teutonic roots. Institutional history dominated the dissertations. Andrews, like so many graduate classmates, concentrated upon village institutions and wrote a dissertation upon *The River Towns of Connecticut,* but after a year he dropped the notion of Teutonic origins and criticized the prejudice that "Anglo-Saxons were the salt of the earth and heralds of freedom." Still, he never gave up the Osgood-Beer hope that the future belonged to the unified English-speaking peoples and a democratic commonwealth of nations.

After teaching at Bryn Mawr and the Johns Hopkins University, he began in 1910 his noteworthy career at Yale, where he remained until 1931 training able researchers to continue the history of the Anglo-American past, writing textbooks in European and English history, and publishing essays. Andrews did have some talent for writing social history, had he chosen to take this seriously, as can be seen from one of his short volumes for Yale's *Chronicles of America* series entitled *Colonial Folkways* (1921). Here he dealt interestingly with topics that he neglected in his later institutional studies: ethnic groups, colonial architecture, libraries, schools, recreations, labor, clothes, and travel. He appreciated the impact of the frontier: "Where hundreds sought for freedom of worship and release from political oppression, thousands saw in the great unoccupied lands of the New World a chance to make a living and to escape from the landlords at home." [9]

Always consistent, he anticipated the main tenets of his subsequent books of the next few decades in *The Colonial Background of the American Revolution* (1924). Much more critical than Beer of British statesmanship, he pointed out the elements of accident, planlessness, improvisation, and inflexibility in the management and control of the Empire:

With characteristic opportunism, and with an eye only to the needs and obligations of the kingdom itself, her statesmen faced the problem of what to do with a colony and how to adjust its interests to those of the mother country without higher aim than that of business profit.

The authorities seemed to him generally better in intention than in achievement:

Except in a few instances, second-rate men conducted the government of England during these years, while the part that civilians took in the management of the army and navy was characterized not only by incompetence but also by peculation and bribery, often on an enormous scale. Such were the leading features of British colonial policy and conduct down to the year 1763.

The Revolution, as Beer had also suggested, grew out of two contrasting and apparently inevitable developments. The colonies were moving toward increased self-government, while the mother country went in the other direction aimed at empire; hence the conflict.

Andrews lived long enough to publish his main research work, the four-volume *The Colonial Period of American History* (1934-38). It approached the subject, as he said, "from the English end" and concentrated on a legal and historical unit which comprised all of England's colonial possessions in the West that had been founded in the seventeenth century. Thus, he examined thirty rather than thirteen colonies and maintained that they held in common a similar colonial experience. The standing of these settlements as colonies rather than as independent states seemed to Andrews to be the fact of greatest significance and the key to the whole colonial situation.

Three of the volumes were labeled "Settlements" and dwelt upon trade, constitutional questions, and legal matters with a minimum of personalities and continuous narrative. He pictured the era before 1660 as a period of a highly decentralized relationship between colonies and mother country which made possible American self-sufficiency. British statesmanship appeared to better advantage than in his earlier books, for he found that by 1700 there was a more clear-cut purpose at Westminster and Whitehall; however, time brought defects and weaknesses of policy. Volume four, "England's Commercial and Colonial Policy," stressed the fulfillment of British directives in the various colonies, Anglo-Dutch rivalry, England's system defined, the Enumerated Commodities, the Methods of Enforcement, the Customs Service, the Vice-Admiralty Courts, the Board of Trade, and related topics. This strong emphasis on formal colonial institutions appeared "fascinating," to Andrews, as well as relatively little-known.

He concluded with a dozen or more suggestions as to the contributing causes for the Revolution: England's determination to centralize her imperial authority, to keep her colonies subordinate politically and commercially, to refuse privileges asked for or to deny many that had been enjoyed, to put her own prosperity and security before that of her dependencies, and to belittle protests from America as the work of agitators. This was certainly not the thinking of a Tory.

In a lengthy and final footnote he paid his respects to the "economic determinists" as he called them—people like Beard, Hacker, Nettels, and similar writers who objected to his neglect of economic forces. He took specific issue with Louis Hacker of Columbia, who had argued that the Revolution was an attempt of American merchant and planter capitalism to win release from the fetters of the English mercantile system. He defended his lifelong emphasis upon institutional and structural history and attributed the new economic interpretations to Marxist class conflict ideas and the tendency to interpret the past in the light of the present.

A résumé of Andrews's shortcomings by a younger generation inevitably misses his solid contributions to colonial historiography. His brilliant disciple, Lawrence H. Gipson, thought that the master had not only attained a unique knowledge of vast sources of colonial history but had brought about a gradual reorientation of the study of early American history from the imperial standpoint which made America the transatlantic frontier for England.[10] Of course, Osgood and Beer had opened the door for this development. In many respects, Andrews clearly anticipated the contributions of later scholars. For example, his own study of the colonial merchants and the Revolution contains some of the elements in the fuller and analytical account of the subject by Arthur M. Schlesinger. On numerous technical problems he corrected or amplified earlier presentations. Unfortunately, his weakness in expository writing—though he was superior to Osgood or Beer—dimmed some of the glory that rightfully belonged to him.

5

In 1905, one year after Osgood had published the first volume of his major work, Edward Channing (1856-1931) of Harvard attracted wide attention with his own first volume of a six-volume series *A History of the United States* (1905-25). The author had intended to carry this study from the era of discovery to the end of the nineteenth century, but his death prevented him from going beyond the Civil War. He proposed to continue the London emphasis, the institutional treatment, and the evolutionary outlook of Osgood, Beer, and Andrews. To this he added his favorite theme: that "the most important single fact in our development has been the victory of the forces of union over those of particularism."

He, too, was a "scientific historian" who stressed original sources, social Darwinism, and objectivity; however, he admitted that "the time and place of one's birth and breeding affect the judgment, and the opportunity for error is frequent." This qualification was needed, for any reader could note that his world revolved around New England, although he was more generous than his Brahmin neighbors to the Middle Colonies (or states) and to the South, albeit from an antislavery point of view. After all, the Channings had been busily making New England history since they arrived in 1720 from England, and the Harvard-trained, Dorchester-born man could hardly escape notice of this fact.

Again, as a scientific historian, he agreed completely with Osgood,

Beer, Andrews, and many of their followers that historical events must be judged by the standards of their time. "To estimate them by the conditions and ideas of the present day is to give a false picture to the reader and the student." In his evolutionist theory he was teleological in his optimism: "I have tried to see in the annals of the past the story of living forces, struggling onward and upward toward that which is better and higher in human conception." Fortunately he did not permit his "scientism" to handicap his style, which, if not distinguished, was eminently readable and worthy of the successive editions that found readers even in the 1950s.

Channing attended the lectures of Henry Adams and of Henry Cabot Lodge, but did not share their anti-Jeffersonian bias. He also disregarded Lodge's jingoism and admired the early evolutionary emphasis of Adams. After a grand tour of Europe and a few minor appointments at Harvard, Channing received a professorial appointment in 1897 and earned a reputation as a sound though not popular teacher, an inspirer of research, and a very productive scholar. Eventually he learned to be less impatient with undergraduates, lectured informally, and came to class with fresh discoveries taken from his most recent research. His teaching in Tudor and Stuart England gave him an excellent background for American colonial history. One of his early one-volume American histories, covering the years 1765-1865 in the Cambridge Historical Series, was so well received that it was even translated into Russian. The novelist Maxim Gorki once told the author that the revolutionary foes of the Czar discussed the book at their meetings. It would be surprising if this intelligentsia discovered any radical flavor in the book, though it was democratic in outlook.

Channing's main work reflected a vigorous personalized style, tinctured by humor or irony, and a varied subject matter which rounded out institutional history with social developments. For a scientific historian he had more than the usual small quota of moral judgments, but he kept to a descriptive narrative. Though he noted the narrow class basis of the Puritan oligarchy, he thought that the Bay Colony marked a definite rise in the tide of human aspirations toward something better than the world had yet known. His facts were drawn from a variety of sources (except newspapers)—American manuscripts, transcripts from British archives, and a good number of dissertations and monographs.

Channing was not content with using a narrowly institutional approach to explain the coming of the Revolution, for he took notice of the new economic interpretation. He referred to class conflicts,

British oppressions, and economic forces. While Osgood and Beer recognized that the colonies existed for imperial profit, they would not say as Channing did, "The governing classes of the old country wished to exploit the American colonists for their own use," and that Parliament taxed the colonists in order to enrich the West Indian sugar planters. These facts were usually explained away in the books of the Columbia men. They were not concerned, as Channing was, over the alleged despotic power of unreformed parliamentarians and "an unreformable king."

Channing's approach to social history reflected his personal beliefs and prejudices. Speaking of the era after 1789, he was nostalgic for the simple and natural existence of men and women of that day. He could have strengthened the novelty of his social history by using newspaper sources, as McMaster did, although, as it was, he injected far too much trivia into his narrative. When he came to the War of 1812, he spoke as a New Englander, indignant at our quasi-alliance with Napoleon and "the blindfolded policy of the [Madison] administration as to commerce and impressment, and the undue truckling to France." Indifferent to the West, he thought of Jackson as primarily a Southerner and skipped the early sectional struggles.

Despite these defects, however, Channing was able to illuminate this vast period and to reach both the scholar and the general reader. Historians have continued to praise his work and to note that even his footnotes often were valuable starting points for other men's research. One of his gifted students, Samuel Eliot Morison, who mastered the art of writing cultural history, appreciated his literary skill and also respected his diligence as a well-equipped researcher.[11] Carl R. Fish, a political historian writing in the early thirties, was more unqualified in his praise, for he admired the objectivity, acumen, vigor, dry humor, personality, rich background, and synthesis of the man.[12] Claude Van Tyne, historian of the Revolution, also admired many of these traits and wrote of the second volume that "it stands in the forefront of scholarly efforts to tell the history of this country"; but Van Tyne complained that the third volume lacked evaluation and an awareness of social forces. In general, the series was acclaimed. Charles Beard, for instance, recognized Channing's unusual industry, penetrating judgments, and mental powers. This reputation had not disappeared by 1952, despite an accumulation of criticisms, for John A. De Novo, in an essay on the series twenty years after, spoke of Channing as one of the giants of American historiography. However, he criticized the author's Anglo-Saxon prejudices and said Channing seemed

to have a mystical faith in England's world mission—this justified the
elimination of French and Spanish power, for instance.[13] But this had
been an extremely common interpretation by American historians
since the middle of the nineteenth century. Channing shared the view
of such men regarding the importance of chance, providence, and
free will in history despite the impact of social Darwinism. Newer
intellectual interests and social theories did not make Channing obsolete, although the next generation gave much more attention to non-
political forces and made more frequent use of social interpretation.

6

By the mid-twentieth century, the Whig interpretation of the Revolution, which made George III and his Tory associates the chief villains, was having trouble even in the elementary and secondary schools.
English and American historians had found common ground in under-
mining this point of view. Foremost among the scholarly revisionists
was Sir Lewis B. Namier, a professor of Modern History at the University of Manchester and an active Zionist leader whose parents
lived in Austrian Galicia. Apparently congenial to the task of rehabilitating the Tories, he described himself as a conservative by
instinct and demonstrated how little George III had actually altered
British constitutional practices in behalf of personal power. Party
distinctions between Whigs and Tories were nebulous on the eve of
the Revolution. So the trouble apparently did not begin with the
famous maternal injunction, "George, be a king!" Other distinguished
British historians developed similar themes.

The imperial perspective upon pre-revolutionary America had a
most industrious and plausible scholarly proponent in Professor Lawrence Henry Gipson (1880–), who studied with Andrews at Yale. He
wrote at least eight volumes on the British Empire during the eighteenth century and sought to bring the narrative close to the opening
of the Revolution. He shared Namier's skepticism regarding George
III's alleged usurpation of power, but decided that a true perspective
upon such problems required a comparative study of imperial policy
in Africa and the Caribbean as well as in the mainland American
colonies. The subtitle of his series, "Provincial Characteristics and Sectional Tendencies in the Era Preceding the American Crisis," suggests
his painstaking survey section by section, beginning with Great Britain
and Ireland. His treatment of social history showed perceptive analysis
and genuine over-all synthesis; yet he took up such varied facets as

the farms, towns, schools, sports, arts, religion, and social welfare. The second and third volumes dealt similarly with the southern and northern colonies. Trade and the workings of the mercantile system were major themes.

He defended mercantilism by saying that its basic good points became clear only after a study of the objectives and the achievements of the British Empire and after an assessment of the total benefits derived by all its members. Mercantilism was no system of tribute but an effort to provide imperial protection "for all those great interests that were sources of material wealth and power." He conceded its inconveniences and occasional gross injustice, but such results were inherent in even the most modern legislative system that imposed national or imperial restrictions. For each restraint he saw a reciprocal benefit either direct or indirect.

Viewed in a large perspective, Britain's wars against France in the New World were not motivated by a lust for empire but by a natural desire to save her American colonies from seizure by France. The beneficiaries had to pay the bill. Thus the Americans, it was cogently argued, enjoyed a far lower tax burden and per capita public debt than the English and could easily have afforded the new taxes of Parliament to meet the imperial emergency after 1763.

While many reviewers were enthusiastic about Gipson's prodigious researches, others criticized his sweeping pro-British interpretations. For example, Professor Edmund S. Morgan, a colonial specialist, charged that the reasoning often showed bias and that some of these pro-British conclusions were based on a misinterpretation of documents. He questioned the author's belief that at the time of the Stamp Act the colonists claimed an exemption from internal taxes only. Too little was said about the repeated abuses by British customs officers and other imperial agents. However, he conceded the magnitude of the work and admired the graceful style. Scholarly committees gave Gipson at least four national historical awards, and he was appointed Harmsworth Professor of American History at Oxford.[14]

By mid-century, colonial historiography had its tourist symbol in Colonial Williamsburg, Inc., which reproduced (with decided improvements) the streets, houses, and costumes of seventeenth-century Virginia's capital. Specialists in colonial history came together through the Institute of Early American History and published sources, articles, and books in this field. Various official and academic agencies undertook the publication of the innumerable Jefferson and Franklin letters as well as those of earlier American figures. Microprinting

made possible such a source duplication project as that of the Readex
Microprint Corporation. Co-operating groups intend to make available
ultimately the texts of every existent book, pamphlet, and broadside
printed in this country from 1639 through 1800. Among the active
presses increasingly concerned with ethnic groups or minorities, the
Jewish Publication Society of America issued many original studies
of Jewish colonial communities and personalities.[15] Outstanding among
a host of books on colonial life was Columbia professor Richard B.
Morris's *Government and Labor in Early America* (1946), which drew
upon local legislative and judicial records to depict the actual wage
and price policies of the colonists and the effort of various classes to
control supply and demand in those days before laissez-faire. Louis
B. Wright examined the social structure erected by "the first gentlemen of Virginia" and showed how the favored 5 per cent of the people
dominated a society of yeoman farmers. Aided by increased source
materials and more sophisticated social science understanding, historians sharpened realistically their portrait of colonial life.

Colonial historiography had traveled far since the days of John
Fiske and George Bancroft. The standard Whig interpretation of the
Revolution held by Burke and his imitators had almost disappeared
among scholars. It is true that the Anglo-Saxon ethnocentrism of Fiske
and Bancroft was not so quickly dissipated but held on to some extent
even in the mid-century work of Gipson. The imperial perspective of
Osgood and his successors continued to stand even in 1960, despite
certain persuasive dissidents who believed that mercantilism had injured colonial interests.

These "scientific historians"—and the definition of this term varied
with time and place—had been trained directly or indirectly in the
Rankean seminar and archival techniques. They passed on to their
disciples a respect for arduous industry in uncovering manuscript
sources, in testing their reliability, in making every effort humanly
possible to reduce the intrusive human equation, and in treating history as institutional development rather than as a static enterprise
of remotely related topics. Their social evolutionism had become obsolete, their ideas of "objectivity" had met the attack of philosophers
(especially relativists) and social scientists, and their Anglo-Saxon
bias seemed out of place in an age when internationalism commanded
new prestige. But they had labored too well in erecting a vast historical structure and techniques of craftsmanship to forfeit quickly
the respect and emulation of the maturing younger generation of
historians.

☆ 8 ☆

John Bach McMaster and the Rise of Social History

1

In 1883, during the optimistic times of Chester Alan Arthur and Queen Victoria, there appeared the first volume of an engrossing eight-volume work by Professor John Bach McMaster entitled *A History of the People of the United States from the Revolution to the Civil War.* It awakened a vogue for social history that added a new dimension to the writing of man's past. McMaster ran full tilt against the dictum of Oxford's chief historian of the "scientific school," Edward A. Freeman, who had stated "history is past politics, and politics is present history." Germany's leader in scientific history, Leopold von Ranke, was saying much the same thing to his disciples.

McMaster, of course, had not invented the idea that the historian must tell the story of society and not merely of its leaders. However, modern historians tend to credit Voltaire with being the pioneer of social-cultural history, notably in *The Age of Louis XIV* (1752) and in the *Essay on the Manners and Customs of Nations* (1757). In the first, he assigned only one chapter to the private life of Louis XIV, about four to administrative matters, and half a dozen to the history of the arts and the sciences. "In this history," he asserted in an introduction, "only that which merits the attention of the ages will be dealt with—that which depicts the genius and manners of men, or which serves to instruct and inculcate the love of country, of virtue and of art." McMaster never went beyond the simple descriptive "manners and morals" type of social history, for he lacked the integrative approach that Voltaire used. However, he agreed that history should teach useful lessons and seek to foster national loyalty.

Even before Voltaire, William Bradford in his classic, *Of Plimoth Plantation,* had made the daily life of the people—not merely the culture of the elite—the staple of his history. Most important in the tradition was Edward Eggleston, the author of *The Hoosier School Master,* who was a journalist and a Methodist circuit rider. He had written to his brother just three years before McMaster's first volume appeared and told of his plan for a comprehensive social history:

> I am going to write a series of volumes which together shall constitute a History of Life in the United States—not a history of the United States, bear in mind, but a history of life there, the life of the people, the sources of their ideas and habits, the course of their development from beginnings.

Only two volumes of this project were completed before Eggleston's death in 1902, but they showed far more synthesis and reflective analysis in their portrayal of colonial life than McMaster possessed. In 1900, when Eggleston gave his presidential address before the American Historical Association, "The New History,"—a pioneer statement of an American *kulturgeschichte*—he called for a cultural history that would be "the real history of men and women."

McMaster, Eggleston, and their disciples drew upon the enthusiasm of the romantic movement which had deified the Common Man in Europe and America. The German folklorists, like the Grimms, had discovered the national roots of their people in the primitive Teutonic forest. Jacksonian democracy thrived on the frontier myth of the Common Man. During his lifetime, McMaster was fascinated by the ferment of religious communities and urban crowds, by the successes of abolitionism, feminism, pacifism, mass education, millennialism, and other panaceas based on the faith that the innate goodness of man could be reclaimed by reforming evil institutions based on force or outworn traditions.

The rise of the Common Man was reflected in the kingly position of the Fourth Estate, especially the sensational penny press which ministered to the needs of the newly literate and enfranchised masses. As an instrument of power, the press had proved its might during the European revolutions of 1830 and 1848 and in the upward struggle of workmen and farmers for enfranchisement and reform. McMaster was one of the first American historians to pursue the logic of this situation by making considerable use of the newspaper as a prime source in social history. Historians complained that it was impossible to apply all the tests of external criticism that were customary for the use of such official documents as treaties, laws, and court decisions. But if this were a nation of newspaper readers, as contemporary observers agreed, then some historical rules must be devised for the use of newspapers as sources. Social historians learned to appreciate the value of advertisements as mirrors of custom, as economic indices, and for other purposes. Libel laws kept rash editors in check to a certain extent, and the reporting of speeches as well as the letters to the editor often had as high a degree of authenticity as the traditional manuscript sources.[1]

Among those who made a hero of the people, none eclipsed the English historian, John Richard Green, who had published his *Short History of the English People* in 1874 and, following a tremendous international wave of popularity, completed by 1880 a four-volume *History of the English People.* It was a novel experience to find a history book which gave more space to Chaucer than to the Battle of Crécy. Strangely enough, McMaster knew little of Green's work in these years, although John Fiske, among others, was inspired to plan a similar work in the American field.

If the direct link between Green and McMaster seemed almost nonexistent, the indebtedness to Thomas Babington Macaulay was most embarrassingly evident, even to the extent of entire plagiarized paragraphs in the first volume. Macaulay's *History of England,* a five-volume work covering the years 1685-1702, had appeared during the mid-century and captured the enthusiasm of many thousands for its artistic style, its narrative qualities, and its generally high critical standards. Although Macaulay was no demagogue, but a middle-class conservative who lacked sociological synthesis, he could depict an entire generation in superb prose. His famous third chapter on the condition of England in 1685 so impressed McMaster that the American determined to concentrate upon social history. McMaster, unfortunately, lacked the literary craftsmanship of Macaulay and too fully shared the latter's indifference toward philosophical generalizations.[2]

The powerful hold that natural science exercised upon historians and other literati did not leave McMaster untouched. In fact, his training as an engineer and his interest in the advance of technology are reflected in his books. The dogma of progress which he shared with his generation was reinforced by the triumphs of the New Physics and the New Biology. He felt a strong sympathy for the Baconian ideal of inductive science and experiment, and greatly admired the English historian, Henry Thomas Buckle, author of the two-volume *History of Civilization in England* (1857-61), who felt he had discovered scientific physical, moral, and intellectual laws. While McMaster was indifferent to philosophical history, he was as greatly interested in the impact of soil and climate upon material wealth as Buckle was; the Englishman had furthered social history by emphasizing large groups rather than exceptional individuals. Both men were believers in the idea of progress.

2

The facts of McMaster's own life give the surest clue to his particular brand of history. He was born in 1852 in Brooklyn, attended New York's public schools, and received his degree at what is today the City College of New York. His lifelong residence in the middle states was reflected in the shift in emphasis that he gave the nation's history from the traditional New England focus to an unusual amount of attention to New York state, Pennsylvania, and their neighbors. His father, whose background was Scotch-Irish, had been a trader in Mexico, a banker in New Orleans, and a sugar planter in Louisiana. Although the son was an ardent anti-slavery man, he reflected this Southern background in his treatment of the South and the West. He went far beyond the hurried treatment, given in stereotypes, that previous general historians had applied to these regions. Also his middle-class background was reflected in his Whiggish sympathies for Hamilton, Webster, and Lincoln.

McMaster served in the Army Engineer Corps and then went to Princeton as an instructor in civil engineering. However, almost immediately after the publication of the first volume of his *History*, he became professor of history at the University of Pennsylvania. His undergraduate teaching was undistinguished, but his seminar became noted for the scholars who later attained national stature. He continued an active life of teaching, public lecturing, and writing almost up to his death in 1932.

The point of view and general pattern of the series is clear in the first volume. He promised that his history of America would show "how the ingenuity of her people became fruitful of wonders far more astonishing than any of which the alchemists had ever dreamed." Furthermore, he pointed out that our ancestors had been a highly favored people: "They were descended from the most persevering, the most energetic, the most thrifty of races. They enjoyed the highest form of civilization. . . . The consequence has been such a moral and social advancement as the world has never seen before." He mildly shared the contemporary interest in race and heredity, though he gave high praise to the Anglo-Saxon for the virtues of sobriety, dignity, and love of law and order that he showed, even in his national uprisings. Correspondingly, he had unfavorable judgments about the Irish, the Indians, and the newer immigrant peoples. Nevertheless, he showed sympathy for the Negro, both slave and free, and championed his rights eloquently.

More than anyone since William Bradford, he dealt with ordinary people, events of everyday interest and importance, and recreational activities. But such diverse themes were difficult to integrate, and McMaster failed to escape a rambling, topical approach. Here, for example, are the varied page labels for pages 17 to 29:

> Fruits and Vegetables Unknown in 1784
> Streets and Houses of Boston
> Books read in New England
> The New England Farmer
> The School-Master
> Money Units
> New Branches of Knowledge
> Lack of Scholarship in the South
> The Country Doctor

His narrative was too often static and was often held together only by chronology and geography, but he did make revealing observations. The facts buttressed his philosophy of inevitable progress. Much of this philosophy and method was obviously borrowed from Macaulay's optimistic *History of England*. Macaulay had shown the march of progress since 1685 by comparing the darker past with the glowing present—"then and now" as he put it. McMaster's treatment of society and times displayed his own "then-and-now" approach, which proved that the nation was advancing in every direction. Such contrasts with the backwardness of former times were comforting to the reader, even if the author was at times brashly critical of colonial and early national cultural achievements. For example, his evaluation of architecture in 1784 reads: "There did not then exist in the country a single piece of architecture which when even tried by the standard of that day, can be called respectable. . . . The houses which made up the

towns and cities were of the low-brow, hip-roofed order, strung along
the streets in disorderly array." In the same first volume, after critical
comments about social conditions, he goes on to cheer the reader:
"There can, however, be no doubt that a wonderful amelioration has
taken place since that day in the condition of the poor." As for the
literary judgments, written to suggest that things were getting better-
and-better, they can scarcely be taken seriously, even if one agreed
with this sweeping opinion: "There is indeed, no portion of our history which presents a spectacle of so much dreariness as our literary
annals during the two hundred years which followed the landing at
Jamestown. In all that time no one great work of the imagination was
produced."

The Buckle emphasis upon geography and climate in history is
clear enough in his writing, even when they stand as unspoken assumptions. Just a few years before, in 1876, he had published such
an article in the *National Quarterly Review* entitled "The Influence
of Geographic Position in the Civilization of Egypt and Greece." Professor Eric Goldman quotes a revealing letter that McMaster wrote
at the time that volume one appeared:

Nobody can deny that the Indians of the Six Nations, the Indians Cooper
knew, were much above the Indians of the South. They lived in a cold climate, they were human beings, and must therefore have been both physically
and mentally as much above the Natchez and Chickesaws [sic] as the
northern men of our time are above the southern. All the push, energy,
mechanical skill, business, wealth of the land lies north of the Potomac and
the Ohio.

This geographic determinism goes far to explain some of his severe
judgments on the South: its lethargy, frontier violence, wretched inns
and small unpaved roads, and the decayed Virginia churches. The
constant unfavorable contrast with life in the Northern states could
not escape the reader.

In 1898 (his eight volumes were not complete until 1913), he published an essay, "The Social Function of United States History" that
made this sectional contrast even more explicit than his *History* does.
He urged educators to teach students to study the westward movement to the Pacific so they could see the emergence of two different
peoples and institutions and hence understand the reasons for the
Civil War: [3]

He [the student] should see the northern stream engaged in a thousand
forms of diversified industry, and the southern stream ignoring commerce

and manufactures and devoting its energy to growing cotton and tobacco, and he should be made to see how from these two opposite economic conditions grew in time two separate and distinct people with utterly different ideas, institutions, customs, and purposes in life, and when this has been made clear to him he will understand the Civil War.

Whether he intended to say at this point that these basic economic differences sprang from climatic and geographic origins is not clear, but it is a fair inference. However, McMaster also used economic interpretation (or economic assumptions) so frequently throughout his work that the reader is not certain whether he actually believed that the source of economic differences was always geographic.

McMaster followed Francis Parkman, Theodore Roosevelt, and the other literary historians in emphasizing the West. His treatment of the Indians was far less friendly than that of Simms and Cooper and much closer to that of the literary historians. McMaster thought of the Indians as savages who had little reason to complain of their treatment at the hands of the government. Like Parkman, he greatly admired the explorers and the Jesuit missionaries. As an ardent nationalist, given to Manifest Destiny statements, he said that Northern expansionism was superior in motive to the South's narrow desire to acquire more slave territory. He had no difficulty in justifying the war with Mexico or the annexation of Texas, and he felt so enthusiastic about Jefferson's purchase of Louisiana that he departed from his rule of saying nothing favorable about that Virginian. He even wrote that wars had their beneficial aspects because they stimulated men to their utmost depths; and he speculated that eras of disorder and violence were usually followed by periods of intellectual activity. In public addresses, he showed his jingoism by vigorously supporting the aggressive Olney-Cleveland interpretation of the Monroe Doctrine in 1896 and used his lecture-room to exhort students to fight for Cuba; later he was impatient for immediate action after the sinking of the *Lusitania*.

These obvious evidences of partisanship did not loom large in the eight volumes of his history, though; indeed, it was often difficult to discover McMaster's actual opinions on certain major issues. To achieve objectivity, he would quote at length the contemporary opinion on both sides, leaving the reader caught between two highly plausible positions. Besides, he wrote social history as pageantry, and thus many pages could go by without any evaluation appearing in the narrative. It has been suggested that McMaster was so concerned

with depicting history from the standpoint of the generation that
lived it—and he tried to do it with the aid of newspapers—that he actually subordinated the present to the past, quite reversing the position of present-day historians. This judgment is misleading, for it is
clear that the author, in relying so frequently upon the then-and-now
comparisons to demonstrate progress, was anxious to teach the reader
lessons from the past and to inculcate admiration for the present social
order. In doing this, he would often select revealing controversial
issues, such as the perennial hard-money versus soft-money question.

As a good Republican in the Whig tradition, he was as concerned
as Hildreth had been that the currency be safeguarded against rural
inflationists and paper-money advocates. Therefore he did not try
to be impartial on incidents involving currency tinkering, whether
Shays's Rebellion, the struggle for the Constitution, the western attacks on sound banking, or the controversies connected with the Second United States Bank. On such issues he parted from "the multitude," as he termed the people. He could draw a fascinating picture
of the hatred between debtors and creditors in 1786:

The mere sight of a lawyer as he hurried along the street was enough to
call forth an oath or a muttered curse from the louts who hung around the
tavern. The reason is plain. During the war debts had increased to a frightful
extent. . . . The lawyers were overwhelmed with cases. The courts could
not try half that came before them. For every man who had an old debt, or
a mortgage, or a claim against a Tory or a refugee, hastened to have it adjusted. . . . Every young man became an attorney, and every attorney did
well. . . . They were denounced as banditti, as blood-suckers, as pick-
pockets, as windbags, as smooth-tongued rogues.

He described the popular newspapers as busily filling their columns
with inflammatory arguments and spoke of "Shays, with the spirit of
a craven." The inflationists of Rhode Island and New Hampshire fared
no better at his hands. He made no effort to understand the case for
the hard-pressed farmer, although he felt sympathy for his plight. In
the Whig reform tradition he was opposed to imprisonment for debt,
and, like many a middle-class citizen he held that poverty's main
cause was intemperance; against this evil, philanthropy was helpless.
In discussing the banking panic of 1818, he quoted approvingly from
one editorial which put the blame upon the people:

Let them not speculate; let them stop importing the needless trappings of
luxury from abroad; let rich men spend their surplus on home manufactures;

let the middling class live within its means; let young men live by labor, and not by their wits.

This was probably not far from McMaster's moralistic economic philosophy. Hard money, low tariffs, and prudence offered the best panaceas. In later years he called for more historians of ideas and customs like Lecky. They were to trace the history of public morality, the principle of full faith and credit, the sanctity of contracts, and the pernicious effect of cheap money on manners and morals.

Committed as he was to the triumph of hard money, McMaster proved to be completely Federalist on the issue of constitutional ratification. Here he dropped the objective façade and condemned the stupidity of the multitude for failing to appreciate the document:

Men who had neither the patience nor the wit to wade through the scholarly arguments of the Federalist, and who could see nothing but dry facts and barren statements in the pleasing letters of Tench Coxe, would read and re-read with increasing delight a piece of foolery by Francis Hopkinson, or a neatly turned allegory by John Mifflin.

He thought that the framers were "a most remarkable assemblage of men, to whom, under God, we cwe our liberty, our prosperity, our high place among the nations." With an emphasis upon economic motivations, he denied that the Constitution was, as Gladstone thought, a fortuitous product of a moment. "It grew out of business conditions; it was a business necessity; it was a product of the experience and daily life of a thoroughly practical people, and cannot be understood without a knowledge of that experience." This he asserted in an essay of 1898 on "The Social Function of United States History." (In his *History* the same idea appears differently phrased.)

In the quarrel between Hamilton and Jefferson, he was definitely for the former. He defended Hamilton's policy of invading Pennsylvania during the Whisky Rebellion, and at the same time neglected to explain the economic motives of the rebellious farmers but dwelt only on their heavy drinking, the tarring and feathering of excise collectors, and other abuses. As for Jefferson, said McMaster in an oft-quoted judgment, "He was saturated with democracy in its rankest form, and he remained to the last day of his life a servile worshipper of the people." His attack was personal rather than broadly based. He pictured Jefferson as a troublemaker who kept a journal of gossip to prove that his Republican enemies were actually monarchists and aristocrats. Jefferson's Kentucky and Virginia Resolutions were de-

clared to be "filled with foolish declamation." He gave this wholly
partisan picture of the opponents of the Alien and Sedition laws:

County politicians and liberty-pole orators, citizens who had once been
aliens, aliens who could not yet be citizens, good men who honestly believed that liberty was in danger, bad men enraged that licentiousness was
restrained, tricksters hungry for place, all joined in one renewed shout of
condemnation.

After denouncing the calumny and falsehood which these opponents
expressed, McMaster admitted that the laws were "most untimely and
unwise." Hamilton saw how it would hurt the Federalists and had
begged them to avoid any tyranny; and partly as a result of disregarding this advice the Federalist party began its march to ruin. But
the historian did not mince words in condemning the French Revolution, which he said "was fast reducing all men to an equality by
cutting off the head of each citizen who rose above the mass." French
democracy, as exemplified in the Democratic societies of the Jeffersonians, was, he explained, "mob tyranny joined to everything that
was immoral, indecent, profane." He blamed the violence and wan-
ton destruction of property by the Revolution on the racial character of the Celtic people. He defended John Jay, the Federalist
diplomat; censured Monroe and Madison, the friends of the French
Revolution; and branded the Jeffersonian, Joel Barlow, as "the author
of some of the most detestable verses in the English tongue."

He thought that after the War of 1812 American history consisted
largely of economic issues:

Henceforth, for many years to come, the questions of the day were to be the
state of the currency, the national bank, manufactures, the tariff, internal improvements, interstate commerce, the public lands, the astonishing growth
of the West, the rights of the States, the extension of slavery, and the true
place of the Supreme Court in our system of government.

Aside from some pet economic views, which do not intrude into the
narrative very often, he brought an excellent critical intelligence to
bear on complex economic problems.

McMaster retained his basic enthusiasm for the advance of the Common Man in history, despite his carping observations regarding the
prejudices and ignorance of the "multitude." He surveyed the social
progress in welfare institutions, prison reform, the abolition of slavery,
the growth of trade unions, women's rights, free schools, factory laws,
manhood suffrage, and the general level of economic betterment. Even

in his favorite domain of hard money, he could be charitable regarding populistic vagaries, as for instance in a lecture, "Is Sound Finance Possible under Popular Government?" While he tried to show that legislative panaceas had failed to change basic economic principles, he expressed faith in the "hard common sense of the people, who in their own good time and way have hitherto adjusted difficulties wisely." He could have been speaking of the Deity! He regarded the rise of trade unions and the right to strike as major gains, but expressed fears of contemporary "social agitators." For their edification he told the story of the early wage-earning class so that all might see how hard life was in early times. Yet he could express the most advanced democratic sympathies, as in his account of manhood suffrage in New England:

In 1820 the people of Massachusetts amended their constitution and there, too, in her convention was the same hostility to universal suffrage, the same distrust of the plain people, and the old struggle between the rights of property and the rights of man.

Such equalitarianism was worthy of Bancroft.[4]

His Whig beliefs led him to criticize government by a strong man or genius, but at times he expressed a Whiggism of the log cabin and hard cider type. The average man was good enough for President as long as he represented the popular will, but two terms in office were ample. The explanation that he gives for his faith in newspaper sources is that they are the truest index of the public mind, the pulse of democratic life. Apparently, he did not think that such opinions conflicted with his admiration of the conservative Daniel Webster or Alexander Hamilton or with his keen dislike of Jefferson. There was much here of the peculiar elements of Richard Hildreth's Whig-Radical views.

Eric Goldman, McMaster's able biographer, believed that his inconsistencies can be partly explained by the fact that the historian of the people used basically conservative assumptions beneath his oft-expressed enthusiasm for the growing social progress of people. "McMaster's new Federalism," he writes, "accepted political democracy and those economic and humanitarian changes which had long since been made, and it stopped there." To bolster this statement, he cites the historian's unfavorable comments on contemporary Bryan radicalism and the newer labor ideas; he was too ready to believe that the ten-hour day advocated by Van Buren ended the struggle for shorter hours forever. This analysis is borne out in McMaster's fatuous declara-

tion in "The Social Function of United States History": "There is no
land where the people are so prosperous, so happy, so intelligent, so
bent on doing what is just and right as the people of the United
States."

3

McMaster's craftsmanship has been carefully studied by William
Hutchinson [5] and Eric Goldman. An analysis of footnotes reveals serious shortcomings, despite a wide use of original sources—printed documents, pamphlets, and some manuscripts as well as numerous newspapers. Goldman writes, "The inaccuracies in the *History* are frequent
enough to suggest that no fact or quotation should be taken from
McMaster without independent corroboration." Yet he points out that
the historian was regarded as a model by such critics as Brooks Adams,
William Dean Howells, Barrett Wendell, and Walter Hines Page.
Many historians built their research upon McMaster's footnotes (Bancroft had warned him to be more chary of giving such generous aid).
Readers have complained that McMaster is so eager to dwell upon the
newsworthy side rather than the long-run significance of his subjects
that he often pours forth streams of trivia. He spent considerable time,
for example, on President Monroe's desire to delay his second term by
a day because of the Sabbath.

McMaster is vulnerable to the criticism that he acted improperly in
promoting his popular *School History of the United States* by request-
ing the text committee of the Grand Army of the Republic to tell him
what kind of history would be satisfactory to them and by submitting
this manuscript to them for comments and endorsement. Yet John
Fiske and other text writers of that day followed the same practice.
Readers have also complained that McMaster spends too much time
on military history. In volume four of his *History,* for example, which
seems to be devoted to social history, at least 279 pages actually deal
with army and navy affairs. Perhaps more serious is his tendency to
ignore parallel European social and economic trends, thus giving the
impression that American developments are wholly unique.

McMaster's contributions to his generation actually outweigh his
defects—and these weaknesses are usually shared with Bancroft, Parkman, and Schouler. He still holds a respected place on college reading
lists, although Allan Nevins and Edward Channing gained upon him
in social and political history.

4

McMaster's heir apparent and doctoral student at the University of Pennsylvania was the somewhat erratic Ellis P. Oberholtzer, who refused to heed the reviewers when they warned that the loosely descriptive social history formula was now obsolete—at least by the 1930s. He completed before his death in 1936 five large volumes, *History of the United States Since the Civil War,* with the first having appeared in 1917. While the last two volumes might be regarded as superior to Rhodes's treatment of the end of the nineteenth century, the work was scarcely of the calibre of McMaster's, and the author's social prejudices against Negroes, the new immigrant peoples, and the labor unions were much more intrusive.

Born in 1868 of a merchant family, of a mother who was a poet and novelist, Ellis Oberholtzer was well educated and had entrée to the upper-class circles of Philadelphia. Out of his tour of Germany came some articles on travel and a book on journalism. At various times, he edited a Philadelphia trade journal, the literary page of two city newspapers, and the popular *American Crisis* biographies dealing with Civil War leaders. His own biographies on Lincoln and Henry Clay added little to existing knowledge, and his life of Jay Cooke has now been replaced by Henrietta Larson's expert study based on extensive records and sound economic analysis. At one period, he served as an obviously heavy-handed motion picture censor, planned historical pageants, and took a leading part in the English-Speaking Union. But at the same time he worked industriously alongside of McMaster in the local historical society.[6]

His volumes begin with 1865 and end at a sharply accelerating pace with 1901. The McMaster formula was there: a history of the American people as a social entity told descriptively rather than analytically. But the proportion devoted to politics was far greater than the master permitted. Although he made very little acknowledgement to the parallel researches of Schouler, Rhodes, Dunning, and others, he did not alter the total picture of Reconstruction and its aftermath very much. There was the familiar Revisionist pattern of the vindictive Radicals using the Negroes as an instrument of power over the white South.

However, he knew how to select fascinating details about the social setting: the plight of the poor whites, the uneasy social contacts between Northern visitors and Southern whites, the boycott of the

Yankee schoolmarms, and the vindictive Southern belles. Drawing some details concerning the Negro from Southern newspapers, he pictured Loyal League meetings at midnight whereby freedmen yielded to the blandishments of the Radicals through incantation and African fetishism. The entire Negro race was savage and shiftless. The treatment of lynchings and other brutalities against the Negroes in later years was quite candid, but the context of explanation stressed not only bitter economic rivalry between the races but also Negro criminality.

Similarly he dealt fully with the rather numerous lynchings of Italians that he discovered, but he made apparent that Americans of British descent faced a serious problem of a "horde" of southern and eastern Europeans who descended upon them. These newcomers were unassimilable. As for labor and the unions, these usually appeared only in an explanatory context of violence and threats to property, although the severity of the great depressions was briefly mentioned. The Indians were by nature "stealthy, treacherous, and vengeful." Much better were the discussions of industrial growth, the mushrooming cities such as Chicago, and the oil booms.

While there were and remain admirers of Oberholtzer, and his publishers have reprinted his works, the scholarly reviewers in both the *American Historical Review* and the *Mississippi Valley Historical Review* were for the most part severely critical toward each volume. William A. Dunning of Columbia, whose anti-Radical interpretation had preceded the Oberholtzer work, began by praising the interesting style, judicial spirit, and sound judgment of the author, and the useful chapters on social conditions in the South, North, and West; but he greatly diluted this pleasant estimate by saying that the first volume was mostly political history written by a man who never saw more than one side of a controversy, belittled the motives of those on the other side, assassinated reputations, and used sensational vituperative epithets (like "Grant's low example").[7] The competent reviewer of the second volume disliked the exaggerated emphasis upon the scandalous tendencies of the time.[8] The third volume went to a disciple of Dunning, Walter L. Fleming, who politely conceded that numerous sources had been consulted, but that there was no evaluation of economic and social factors and there was besides a good deal of superficiality.[9] The fourth volume did no better, for the reviewer criticized the author's Victorian moralizing as well as his superficiality.[10] And the final volume went to Allan Nevins, then at work on a multivolume history of the coming of the Civil War in all its social, economic, political, diplomatic, and cultural phases. He found almost nothing to praise and a good deal to attack—undigested facts, upper-class bias, jingoism, failure to understand the farmer and the laborer, superficiality, and deep prejudices.[11]

By the time the last volume was out, scholars seemed agreed that the work was out of step with twentieth-century historiography. Some charitably suggested that there remained some reference use for it—although this implied a low opinion of works of reference. But Oberholtzer had already died, and no new McMaster was in sight.

5

The social history ideal of McMaster and Eggleston attracted an increasing number of historians, who were also influenced by a similar trend from abroad. Especially noteworthy were the ideas of Germany's leading cultural historian, Karl Lamprecht (1856-1915) of the University of Leipzig, and his brilliant disciples, such as the influential Belgian, Henri Pirenne. Lamprecht took issue with Ranke's overemphasis on national political history and demanded that politics be integrated with the facts of social, economic, and intellectual history. He borrowed some of his concepts regarding the central role of the history of classes, mass movements, and related intellectual trends from Marx. He helped to inspire the New History, particularly at Columbia University, where James Harvey Robinson wrote and lectured on this theme alongside colleagues in the social-intellectual history field such as Charles Beard, Carlton Hayes, and many more.

Robinson in his New History called for the same breadth of subject matter that Lamprecht did, "every trace and vestige of everything that man has done or thought." Critics disparaged this as "the past everything" which placed an impossible burden on the scholar. This comprehensiveness required, he said, the co-operation of the historian with new allies, the social scientists. Finally, Robinson held that the New History would guide men to social reform and a better world and that the interests of the present would provide a guide to the selection of what was relevant in the past. Here he reflected the current pragmatic spirit of the Progressive movement.

One of the New History circle, Arthur M. Schlesinger, Sr., was a chief editor of the thirteen-volume series, *A History of American Life,* which began to appear in 1928. Unlike Lamprecht, all contributors excluded political history save as an incident of social development. The titles usually revealed an effort to discover an integrating theme for the limited period covered: *The Revolutionary Generation, The Rise of the Common Man, The Irrepressible Conflict, The Emergence of Modern America, The Nationalizing of Industry, The Rise of the City, The Quest for Social Justice, The Great Crusade and After,* etc. As one critic put it, this was an achievement that went beyond the historian's usual effort to investigate a particular people living in a particular area at a particular time. The problem now was how to coordinate the bulk of facts regarding the diverse social and economic facets of society and still continue to emphasize flux and direction. Bernard De Voto, the literary historian, praised the series as far superior to previous histories. "They are the first history of America that the student of literature can count on to assist in his trade." Some historians complained that the series was too heavily descriptive, too little analytical or integrative, and lacking in philosophic substance. Others missed the famous names that seemed to be replaced by obscure ones.

Schlesinger issued an able defense of the series at a session of the American Historical Association. He pointed out the multiplication of original sources for social history—diaries, personal correspondence, newspapers, travel accounts, advertisements, artifacts, museum relics, etiquette books, cookbooks, popular songbooks, as well as scientific publications. As for the presence of more obscure figures and the alleged tendency to omit unusual facts, he stated that social history emphasized "the uncommon importance of common folk and common things." Furthermore, he added, "Social history does not ignore the exceptional but focuses on processes rather than problems." [12] This emphasis on "social processes" reflected the early influence of Darwinism and its use by Ogburn and other sociologists. Younger historians were to try to advance social history toward greater philosophic and "interdisciplinary" integration. However, they did not usually go as far as American historians of the European scene did (like Hayes, for example), in integrating political history closely with social and intellectual history. However, they gave increased attention to the common bond of social experience between the United States and Europe.

Schlesinger's own volume in the series, *The Rise of the City,* also reflected a developing category of social history, urbanization, in which McMaster had also been interested. There are various explanations for the vogue of urban historians (and urban sociologists and political scientists): the spectacular increase of population and the rise of large cities by the turn of the century; maladjustments, "the shame of the cities," and the festering slums publicized by the muckrakers Lincoln Steffens and Jacob Riis; the antimonopoly movement, which found outlet in the municipal reform and municipal ownership movements; the rapid country-to-city migration; the influence of the automobile upon the metropolitan community; and various related factors. If most Americans now lived in cities, as the census of 1920 indicated, then the quality of American life was indeed changing in conformance with urban patterns.

Frederick J. Turner once wrote Schlesinger that there would soon be an urban interpretation of history, just as there had been a frontier synthesis.[18] Sociologists were showing the way. At the University of Chicago, Robert E. Park and Ernest W. Burgess opened up a promising area of "ecological research" during the 1920s and 1930s. It resulted in a very revealing, though primarily descriptive, series of books on Chicago's distinctive areas—the Gold Coast and the Slum, Hobohemia (the Madison Street section), and other neighborhoods. The Lynds of Columbia published a major urban classic, a case study of a medium-sized city, *Middletown* (1925), which used the techniques of cultural anthropology to discover the unifying factors in the culture of Muncie, Indiana. Through their questionnaires, interviews, observations, and other methods the Lynds pictured the pressures for small-town conformity and intolerance that were described also in the novels of Sinclair Lewis and the essays of H. L. Mencken.

To a large extent, the historians of the city followed the narrowly descriptive tradition of McMaster and tended for many years to ignore the dynamic techniques of the University of Chicago sociologists of the "ecological school," the political scientists who studied urban behavior, and the imaginative Lynds. Journalists seemed particularly successful in depicting the political pressures and personalities of the large cities. But by the 'thirties, the influence of the social scientists upon urban historians affected many academicians. Among the best of the urban histories were those dealing with Rochester, New York, Chicago, Milwaukee, Holyoke, Norfolk, and Memphis. Carl Bridenbaugh showed the importance of cities for colonial civilization in three fascinating volumes depicting Boston, Newport, New York, Philadelphia, and Charleston; the first volume was *Cities in the Wilderness* 1938). But of all branches of social history, the problem of integrating the numerous facets of urban institutions and city life seemed to be the most difficult. It was too easy to be loosely topical and encyclopedic.

During the Great Depression, when environmental interpretations of history proliferated, there were social historians who showed dissatisfaction with the seemingly impossible demands of the New History. They felt it expected historians to master too many social sciences in addition to the traditional auxiliary subjects; besides it added a flood of subject matter without offering a basis for selection and organization. At a meeting of the American Historical Association in December 1939, a group of historians and other social scientists called for a "cultural approach to history." They were enamored of the unity and symmetry of cultural anthropology and social psychology, which provided a relatively integrated view of patterns of social behavior. They hoped that historians could utilize these methods of culture study to understand the basic assumptions of individuals and their frame of reference for living.

Caroline Ware, whose book *Greenwich Village* (1935) sought to exemplify these ideals, edited the papers and essays of the group in *The Cultural Approach to History* (1940). She stressed the value of local history as the life history of a community and called attention to such integrated regional studies as Walter Prescott Webb's *The Great Plains* and Rupert B. Vance's ecological interpretation of the South. Other contributors, some of them students of Schlesinger, stressed the need for the study of folklore, folk music, population movements, and other strands of social behavior. Within the next decades, the new vogue for American studies in university programs encouraged many interdisciplinary experiments. One such ambitious project was that of Merle Curti and others in *The Making of an American Community: A Case Study of Democracy in a Frontier County* (1959). This demonstrated the applicability of Turner's leading frontier theses to a Wisconsin county during 1840-80. By that time Curti could cite his indebtedness to various interdisciplinary conferences, the Center for Advanced Study in the Behavioral Sciences at Stanford, and his experience in the developing field of American civilization at the University of Wisconsin and elsewhere.

6

McMaster had opened the door wide to the study of immigration history, and within a brief compass had used immigration statistics and immigrant letters, as well as occasional European newspapers. Usually he emphasized native reactions to the foreigner rather than any internal view of immigrant life and institutions. Like so many of the Old Americans, he doubted the assimilability of the Irish and other groups, for he belonged to the New England Brahmins who felt threatened by the influx of Catholics and Jews into Boston. Descendants of the Puritans like Henry Cabot Lodge, also a historian who had been trained under Henry Adams himself, united to secure federal laws restricting immigration, particularly from southern and eastern Europe. Among historians of the period from 1880 to 1924 (the date of the major immigration restriction act), the myth prevailed that Anglo-American institutions grew out of Teutonic institutions and that "Nordic" peoples were superior to other races. Henry Adams, who preferred to stress Norman rather than Teutonic origins, nevertheless outdid the others in virulent anti-Semitism, for he identified the evils of finance capitalism with international Jewish machinations. Woodrow Wilson showed his ethnocentrism in an early edition of his general history by prejudiced comments on the Italians and other southern Europeans; this embarrassed him during the election of 1912 when the Republicans used this material against him.[14]

Journalists, lawyers, and businessmen among the Italians, Greeks, Slavs, and eastern Jews took up the defense of their people. The stakes were high, since the outcome of the great debate would influence the long-pending legislation restricting southern European immigrants. Most of these books were either filio-pietistic or obviously designed to combat the prejudices of the Nordic propagandists. The results too often were merely a list or a general discussion of immigrants who had made good in some outstanding way. Enlightened social-service leaders like Edith Abbott of the University of Chicago wrote favorable books on the immigrant and published documentary collections on immigration that had historical merit as well as practical policy implications. Professor Mary R. Coolidge, a sociologist, disposed of many West Coast myths regarding Chinese traits in a most searching and sympathetic study, *Chinese Immigration* (1909); and University of Chicago sociologists, following the reformist tradition of Albion Small, published studies that opposed the older ethnocentrism. Louis Wirth, for example, a German-Jewish sociologist, published a noteworthy dissertation, *The Ghetto* (1928). He pictured the West Side Chicago Jewish community with its amazing medley of eastern European traits, the peddlers ("the lapel-pullers") of Maxwell Street, and the surviving orthodox customs; he showed the interaction of the new Jewish immigrant from Poland and Russia with the older Occidentalized German Jew.

American historians were largely of northern and western European descent and often mastered the language of these immigrants. Scandinavians and Germans in particular produced many scholars capable of using the tools of social research. The Swedes and Norwegians, for example, were among the first to secure the benefits of a well-equipped band of historians to tell the story of their impact upon American society. At the University of Minnesota, George Stephenson wrote articles and published letters and records dealing with the Swedish-American colonies, made a special study of *The Religious Aspects of Swedish Immigration* (1932), and even attempted in 1926, with only limited success, a general history of American immigration. His colleague, Theodore Blegen, explored numerous facets of Norwegian-American life: Norwegian emigrant songs and ballads, the early Norwegian press, and other pioneer studies that were finally incorporated in a definitive work, *The Norwegian Migration to America, 1825-1860* (1931). Augustana College, too, had its able historians of Scandinavian America. These men used numerous immigrant letters, the Scandinavian newspapers, the formal records, and artifacts. Historians were at a disadvantage in competing with the sensitive pen of the immigrant novelist, Ole Rolvaag, who wrote *Giants in the Earth* and other revealing novels about the titanic struggle of the Norwegian pioneers of South Dakota during the 1870s. The Norwegian emigrant also had a noted literary interpreter at home in Johan Bojer, author of *The Emigrants* (1925).

German-American historians had been active since the mid-nineteenth century, but the most ambitious and comprehensive work came in 1909 from a Germanic scholar at Cornell, Professor Albert B. Faust. His two-volume study, *The German Element in the United States*, which received several literary prizes, added a great deal to the picture of German-American civilization, though its emphasis tended to be filio-pietistic.

Several decades later, a more scientific historian, Carl F. Wittke of Oberlin and Western Reserve University, did much to stimulate the entire field of immigration history, as well as to tell much more accurately and fully the story of the German-American. In his study *German-Americans and the World War* (1936), he dealt with the mob spirit that had led to the indictment of an entire people, stamped out the long-established teaching of German in many schools, and intimidated thousands with false blanket accusations of disloyalty. He contrasted the historical record of general wartime loyalty of the so-called "hyphenate" (German-American) with the charges made against them. In later books he traced the influence of German socialism upon the American labor movement, notably in two well-written biographies of two stormy "Forty-eighters," Karl Heinzen and Wilhelm Weitling. In the 'fifties, he drew together many little-known facets of German-American liberalism in *Refugees of Revolution,* wrote a pioneer history of the German-American press, and issued a rounded history of the entire Irish-American immigration.

In 1939, Carl Wittke published *We Who Built America,* which was later voted by scholars in a survey printed in the *Mississippi Valley Historical Review* as an outstanding work. It went far beyond George Stephenson's *History of American Immigration* in its broad treatment of social and cultural history, its depth, and its extensive sources, which drew heavily on the contemporary press. It began with the immigrant traffic of colonial times, stressed the reasons for emigration, gave particular attention to the Irish, the Germans, the Scandinavians, and the eastern Europeans, and discussed the "closing of the gates" through native pressures and discriminatory legislation. Among the varied facets covered were the immigrant press, distinctive cultural contributions, political behavior, the distribution of the immgrant groups, education, recreation, the churches, and the interaction of immigrant and native. The tone was sympathetic though objective. For the author, the son of a German immigrant of 1889, the story was partly one of self-identification with the entire stream of immigration regardless of origin. Speaking of his father, he said, "Unpretentiously, simply, and harmoniously, his life blended into the American stream, and became a humble but honorable fragment of forgotten thousands who have helped to build this nation." This was his central theme.

The south Italian had his most interpretive and objective scholar in Phyllis H. Williams, who possessed a background in social work. Her fascinating narrative, *South Italian Folkways in Europe and America* (1938), showed specifically the interaction of cultures between the homeland and the new country—an adjustment process that sociologists referred to as *acculturation,* as distinct from mere assimilation, in which one group adopts the culture of the other.

Among the younger social historians, Oscar Handlin of Harvard, himself of Jewish immigrant extraction, wrote an analytical history of the Boston Irish before the Civil War, and raised fresh questions regarding ethnic groups in several books and in *Commentary* magazine dealing with the Jews and other groups. He won a Pulitzer prize for *The Uprooted* (1951), which pictured the emigrant's painful break with his age-old native community and culture and his persistent sense of alienation in an individualist world of "separated men." The newcomer was adrift in a fluid society in which roots were difficult to grow; but the perceptive discovered that here men could enjoy the exhilarating experience of utilizing one's dormant capacities. Research on the Jewish immigrant was prolific and some of it had been sponsored since 1892 by the Jewish Historical Society. The most ambitious co-operative project of all came in the 1950s when Jewish community agencies aided interested historians to write individual histories of Jewish communities in the larger cities, a work that was co-ordinated under the direction of Allan Nevins of Columbia. The early volumes revealed a painstaking use of numerous local records, family letters, Jewish newspapers, and other fresh sources.

The Slavs and other eastern European groups also had their trained historians, such as Professor Joseph S. Roucek of the University of Bridgeport, who came of Czech origin; but this group had fewer historians than the older immigrant groups, for the general scholars were discouraged by the linguistic difficulties. Talented journalists like Louis Adamic of Yugoslavia and the contributors to his popular series on immigration covered most major nationalities, and made up in enthusiasm what they lacked in original source materials and scholarly method. Adamic's very human autobiography, *A Native's Return*, which depicted unforgettably the Slovene native and his naïve notion of America, was a best-seller; his phrase, "a nation of nations" expressed the idea of a federated culture. Native Americans of older ancestral groups took up the cause of the newcomer against the prejudiced native. Many scholarly histories were written on such related topics as nativism, "the Protestant Crusade," and the social and intellectual forces behind restrictionism. Merle Curti encouraged scholars to approach the subject from the immigrant's view, notably in studies of "the image of America" held by various European nationalities.

Before mid-century, the uncritical concept of Americanization and assimilation—which did not always indicate exactly what native standards were being held up for imitation—had been severely challenged. Native impatience with the slow process required for the immigrant to lose his cultural identity had been reflected in the popular phrase, "the melting pot." "Cultural blend" was increasingly preferred to the melting pot label as less destructive of worthwhile ethnic contributions. A sensitive representative of the Jewish immigrant intellectual, Horace Kallen, professor of philosophy of the New School for Social Research, who had been born in Silesia, pleaded for the concept of "cultural pluralism." He suggested the human need for a rich diversity in machine-age America and for a federative rather than a tightly amalgamated culture. In the New Deal years, this tendency toward cultural pluralism was reinforced by the growing strength of all ethnic minorities, including the Negro and the American Indian. Cultural anthropologists, led by Franz Boas of Columbia and his prolific disciples, gave scholarly prestige to the ideal of cultural diversity working in democratic unity, and they successfully combatted the forces of racialism. Even the forgotten American Indian became the recipient of "A New Deal for the Indian," as Commissioner John Collier's program for the Indian was called. Respect for tribal culture was advanced through laws protecting Indian communal lands and a type of Indian education that recognized the creative values in traditional Indian life. All this had its equivalent in new histories of the Indian, which reflected a changed point of view.

The vast literature of American Protestantism was similarly enriched. William Warren Sweet of the University of Chicago focused upon the frontier as a force in church history, and his students published studies of the camp meeting and other institutions. Mormons competed with non-Mormons to write a history of that denomination. Alice Felt Tyler's *Freedom's Ferment* (1944) related the sectarian history of the ante-bellum years to Utopia-building. Very influential from the standpoint of methodology was *The Social Sources of Denominationalism* (1929) by H. Richard Niebuhr, which showed the evolution of sectarianism from an early stage of social protest to a more conservative position in keeping with the advancing prosperity made possible by the very tenets of hard work and thrift preached by the early leaders.

Especially important in the literature of the social gospel, which Ernst Troetsch had examined sociologically in 1912 in Germany, was C. H. Hopkins's *The Rise of the Social Gospel in American Protestantism, 1865-1915* (1940), which was actually a contribution to intellectual history, particularly in its explanation of the "doctrine of immanence." God's presence in secular society broke down the distinction between the secular and the spiritual and suggested a large role for the church in welfare, labor, and reform. Most enlightening in showing the historical origins of the principle of the separation of church and state was the monumental work of A. P. Stokes, *Church and State in the United States* (1950).

Catholic history advanced beyond the limited ecclesiastical studies to reflect the impact of the social studies. It was not uncommon for a Catholic professor like Aaron Abell, who dealt with the church and the labor movement, to write on a Protestant theme: *The Urban Impact on American Protestantism* (1943); nor wholly unusual for a Protestant historian like Robert D. Cross to write an excellent sympathetic volume on *The Emergence of Liberal Catholicism in America* (1958). Catholic historians developed a vigorous press, as well as a center for historical studies at the Catholic University of America, and various Catholic historical societies and national journals. Ecclesiastical historians were enriched by the expanding resources of the Baltimore Cathedral Archives and the University of Notre Dame Archives. Catholic leadership in America proved so popular a theme that biography became a dominant trend by mid-century. Especially well received was the outstanding two-volume life of James Cardinal Gibbons by John Tracy Ellis. Father Charles H. Metzger encouraged the organization of the extensive John Carroll papers and wrote on such themes as the Quebec Act and the Franco-American Alliance of 1778, both concerned with the role of Catholic influences in American history.[15]

Thus, the writing of American history took on larger dimensions due to the social historians. Each ethnic group helped to make America, as Carl Wittke had emphasized. Pennsylvania Germans, for example, as an entire historical literature demonstrated, had a decisive effect on colonial culture through their farming techniques, their music and art, their religious idealism, and their customs. Nineteenth-century Germans of the educated classes promoted progressive education, symphonic music, the adoption of calisthenics in the YMCA and the public schools, the antislavery crusade, reformist labor doctrines, Utopian colonies, and a high level of journalism.

Irishmen took the pick and shovel jobs in such numbers that native workers rose rapidly to take higher positions, while the new abundance of Irish domestic workers raised the social status of New England families. The Irish captured Tammany Hall and influenced the politics of the Empire State through New York City, especially in close national elections involving controversial British issues. They were foremost in shaping the organization and the parochial schools of American Catholicism. Two World Wars raised the "hyphenate issue" in varying degrees and tested the loyalty of ethnic groups affiliated with Germany and her allies.

Scandinavians played a significant role in the pioneer civilization of the Upper Mississipi Valley, as well as in twentieth-century social and political life. First-generation Italians brought their gift of song as well as their commercial skills. Eastern European Jews made the important garment industry influential in the history of welfare unionism, shaped the motion-picture industry for mass entertainment, introduced new techniques in vast department stores, while many of their children achieved eminence in the law, academic life, commerce, and medicine.[16]

Thus, the long and important story of America's diversity unfolded from thousands of books, monographs, theses, and articles. While much of the writing, as the younger historians complained, was largely descriptive rather than analytical, the quality steadily advanced, and the ethnocentric bias declined. The new generation of professional social historians were better equipped than McMaster, Eggleston, and even James Harvey Robinson in the interdisciplinary fields and methods, and improved results naturally followed.

Henry Adams and the Dream of a Science of History

1

Few historians of the nineteenth century seemed as determined as Henry Adams to share the prestige of the natural scientists by borrowing their methods. He was a friend of Sir Charles Lyell, the geologist, who had demonstrated the antiquity of the earth far beyond the brief span suggested by certain theologists. For years Adams lived in the London of Darwin, Spencer, and Huxley and was tempted, like other students of the social studies, to transform evolution into a precise historical process of stages and social adaptation, moving in some teleological way. Above all, he was aware of the revolutionary physicists, Thomson, Helmholtz, and Josiah Gibbs who were uncovering startling implications for the concepts of thermodynamics.

In his later years Adams took the idea of the dynamo from thermodynamics and applied it as a symbol of force to the field of historical development. "To historians," he thought, "the single interest is the law of reaction between force and force—between mind and nature—the law of progress." He found the social doctrines of Auguste Comte, "father of sociology," grist for his philosophy of history. Comte's positivism offered a theory of social reform that seemed scientific. It was based on the idea that society had evolved from its two earliest stages of theology and metaphysics into a scientific or "positive" stage. Adams spoke of "phases" instead of stages and was anxious to assign mathematical values to them. Like so many other social scientists, he admired the positivists because they seemed to be working toward a science of society based on irrefutable laws.

For a time he felt that the theories of Karl Marx and the socialists might actually have found the large measure of predictability in history which they claimed. "By rights," he wrote of himself in his autobiography, *The Education of Henry Adams*, "he should have been also a Marxist, but some narrow trait of the New England nature seemed to blight socialism, and he tried in vain to make himself a convert." During the long years after he had written his monumental *History*, his philosophy of history gradually moved toward scientific pessimism and determinism. He saw society as moving through calculated phases which would inevitably lead to collectivism and technological efficiency. He called publicly for a "law of phase" for history which would be the equivalent of Gibbs's celebrated law of phase in physics. But by that time he had ceased to write history.

This dream of transferring scientific certainty to history and the other social studies had influenced Richard Hildreth, whose *History of the United States* wavered between Jeremy Bentham's counsels to achieve mechanical objectivity and his own emotional bias. Long before Adams died in 1918, his original contemporary, Frederick Jackson Turner, had transmuted social Darwinism into a formula whereby western history was seen through the evolution of the frontier. Turner avoided outright prediction, but his idea of ever-evolving frontier stages left their clear implications of inevitable development. By 1890 the social sciences tended to emphasize the inevitable evolution of social institutions (property, law, the family, religion, capitalism, etc.) from a simple stage to a complex one. Social scientists were usually optimists, believers in progress, quite unlike Adams, who thought that social and racial energy would inevitably be dissipated.

There was another concept of scientific history which was more congenial to the optimistic free-will atmosphere of western Europe and America. This was the idea of historical objectivity belonging to the critical tradition of Thucydides. Henry Adams himself had been an American pioneer in harnessing critical principles to history-writing through the new seminar methods. Instead of borrowing generalized principles from physics or biology, the seminar historian invoked the searching questions of the courtroom to establish evidence, demonstrated a large measure of personal detachment, and handled the sources critically, particularly in the matter of meaning, authenticity, and dependability. He followed the highly fruitful example of the German philologists.

Natural history, like physics and biology, also left its imprint upon "scientific" historians through the monograph. Early in the nineteenth century German and French botanists, zoologists, and mineralogists had popularized the "monographie" or monograph which was a treatise on a single species, genus, or larger group of plants, animals, or minerals. It was an attempt to turn away from the general treatise in the interests of specialization and the division of labor. So it was with historians. Increasingly they rebelled against the broad encompassing histories of Bancroft, McMaster, and others and singled out a single institution or event for isolated study. Often the results were profitable and enriched historical knowledge and understanding. But very often the monograph afforded an easy escape from philosophic integration.

Adams was totally innocent of that type of "scientific" monograph which consisted solely of unrelieved factualism. He never tolerated the kind of unimaginative writing that was devoid of hypotheses and conclusions. While he was indeed a Comtian positivist in search of the laws of society, he did not believe that his fellow-historians should become mere fact-collectors as Comte expected. To those willing to become hewers of wood and drawers of water for the sociologists, there was the temptation to present discrete facts heavily bolstered by footnotes, to put together a narrative indifferent to literary charm, and to deny responsibility for integration on a high level. For such allegedly scientific historians, who might invoke the current relativistic anthropology in their defense, value judgments were obsolete.

In so far as the factual monographists had any philosophy of history, it was the easy notion that every historical event was unique and that the very idea of a philosophy of history was an anachronism. Even before the twentieth century began, these historians not only rebelled against the tight syntheses borrowed directly from physics and biology, such as those of Adams and Turner (later), but dismissed the search for "laws" and even the concept of historical causation as futile. The factualists had little use for the comparative method so fruitful in sociology, anthropology, and biblical criticism. History was too little an art to be a branch of literature and lacked most of the qualifications for a social science. Literally taken, the idea that history consisted of wholly unique facts made even history itself impossible, for at the core of historiography was the idea of change and development—a process assuming some continuity, direction, and meaning. Aristotle had long ago exposed the fallacy of uniqueness by demanding a context of classification to make each fact meaningful. Uniqueness was a half-truth useful for the unimaginative.

The academic historians of Henry Adams's generation tended to hail Leopold von Ranke (1795-1886) as the great master and pioneer of scientific history in the sense of objective, critical narrative. Born in Saxony, Ranke studied theology and classical philology at Leipzig. He became interested in Roman history, in which Niebuhr had introduced new concepts of research; then he made German history his specialty during a long lifetime. In 1833 he introduced the noted seminar method at the University of Berlin and attracted brilliant students, who later became leading historians in various countries. His seminar methodology stressed legal rules of evidence, the rejection of mere hearsay, and a reliance on the witness closest to the event. Under his inspiration archival studies became a major discipline.

Ranke and his circle represent a turning point in historiography. Not only did they make scientific methods the cornerstone of a new professionalization of history, but they broke the iron grip of the philosophers on their discipline. To them such philosophers of history as Hegel and others who superimposed formulas like progress on the actual events of the past had to be replaced by craftsmen of empirical research. This war against pseudo-history led Ranke to overstate his case to such an extent as to give the impression that he was childishly naïve in his epistemology; critics charged that he believed that the past could be completely recaptured by the scientific historian. He had written in his early years too emphatically:

> History has had assigned to it the task of judging the past, of instructing the present for the benefit of the ages to come. To such lofty functions this work does not aspire. Its aim is merely to show what actually occurred.

Furthermore, he continued to say even in his old age that he had tried "to avoid all invention and imagination in my works and to stick to the facts." Admirers pointed out that Ranke's famous *History of the Popes* must have been uncommonly objective because the work pleased both Protestants and Catholics.

Ranke's objectivity has been misunderstood because of his insistance that the historian must not intrude his judgments upon the narrative. He was after all a devout man who believed in eternal moral standards and in the idea that God acted through history. It was very important to the development of historiography that Ranke stood successfully against the use of the new natural sciences as a tool of deterministic historical interpretations and against the ideas of extreme philosophic necessity or inevitability. As a moral man, he believed in the existence of free will. Each epoch was to him "immediate to God" and hence contained essential qualities of individuality and uniqueness as be-fitted God's will. This emphasis on the uniqueness of facts and the idea of "irreducible individuals" was taken by many disciples here and abroad to sanction the total elimination of philosophy as an ally of history. Such superficial practitioners reduced history to a surface narrative, to the dry monographs and pedantic footnotes associated with the "scientific school," and lent color to the charge of Beard, Robinson, and the "relativists" that Rankean objective history was history without an object.

The same insistence upon suspending moral judgments as irrele-vant encouraged the rise of an amoral *historicism*. This made history the measure of all values and disregarded outside ethical judgments imposed upon the flow of recorded events. "Scientific" disciples among the Prussian school chose the road of *Realpolitik*, which permitted the end to justify the means by ignoring ethical value judgments. These historicists often saw the lives of great men as expressions of mere impersonal social forces. Ranke's emphasis on the primacy of foreign policy and the state, which he thought of as a search for a peaceful equilibrium between the great powers, became transformed by certain disciples into a nationalist, imperialist, and militarist formula. Few historians have seen the tragic influence of Ranke as well as the Dutch scholar, Pieter Geyl, who rejects historicism but recognizes that Ranke was no historicist.

Henry Adams owed much to Ranke. As already noted, he was a pioneer in teaching the meticulous critical methods of the German and introduced the scientific seminar and the archival diligence so popular in the German universities. However, he devoted years to diplomatic history not because of Ranke but because he became in-terested in the subject when his father was American minister to Eng-land. Taking Rankeism at face value, he took issue with the statement that history could show what actually occurred. Being too closely wedded to the natural science ideal, he disagreed with Ranke's in-junctions against historical predictability and imaginative generaliza-tions. But Adams's actual histories were well within Ranke's canons of scientific history; and his own formulas derived from natural science produced no history whatever.

Rationalism was a major ingredient in the new scientific history, despite Ranke's mysticism, and Henry Adams shared fully in this trend. Even in later years, when he wrote so appreciatively of the age of faith and the cult of the Virgin in *Mont-Saint-Michel and Chartres,* he regretted that he could not find salvation in the certainties of the church. The "higher criticism" movement of the nineteenth century had gone far to shake the historicity of the Bible even before Darwin went to work. Comparative religion as a discipline shook the inspired uniqueness of the Bible by showing parallel accounts of the Creation, the flood, and rituals in various religions. Early anthropologists, some of them products of Ranke's seminar, depended wholly on rational explanations of social institutions. Among the laity, there were many thousands of admiring listeners for the lectures on agnosticism of Robert Ingersoll, disciple of Thomas Paine.

The well educated had at least a bowing acquaintance with the books of the dogmatic Irish rationalist, William E. H. Lecky (1838-1903), author of *History of the Rise and Influence of Rationalism in Europe* (1865) and the even better-known *History of European Morals from Augustus to Charlemagne* (1869). Suggestive of Adams's plan for his *History* was Lecky's most-praised work, the eight-volume *History of England in the Eighteenth Century* (1878-90), which the American greatly admired. Adams, too, was then working on a political history which contained significant chapters on social and cultural developments.

Lecky liked to depict the decay of theology, the triumph of rationalism, and the warfare between reason and theology. Within the same tradition was the English-born American scientist and historian, John William Draper (1811-82), a New York University research chemist in radiant energy, and the author of rationalist works on topics similar to those dealt with in Lecky's books. His *History of the Intellectual Development of Europe* (1863) used an evolutionary approach (then novel in history), and the popular and rationalistic *History of the Conflict Between Religion and Science* (1874) inspired numerous debates in the lyceums of that era.[1] To him the Catholic Church was the chief foe of science throughout history. Andrew D. White, another early disciple of Darwin and Spencer, was trained in history under German and French scholars, gave research courses in scientific history at the University of Michigan, and became one of the first presidents of Cornell University. He served as a minister to Germany and Russia and became in 1884 the first president of the new American Historical Association. He called for a philosophic approach that would *not* be "value-free." Like Draper, he depicted the clergy as allies of obscurantism, but included both Protestant and Catholic churches in his indictment.

This rationalist milieu stimulated Adams's interest in science. It also strengthened his desire to use deterministic interpretations of history and left him nothing but contempt for the great man theories of history. He wrote emphatically in 1882 to William James, "With hero-worship like Carlyle's I have little patience. In history heroes have neutralized each other, and the result is no more than would have been reached without them." One can therefore understand his enthusiasm for the English physical environmentalist, Henry Thomas Buckle, who set aside any biographic approach to history for an inductive study of large masses of men which afforded—so Buckle thought—the possibility of discovering physical, moral, and intellectual laws of universal validity. This was good doctrine to Adams. He lamented the failure of historians to embrace natural science, except for such rare geniuses as Buckle. In his *Education* Adams wrote with his usual exaggerated pessimism:

> Since Gibbon, the spectacle was almost a scandal. History had lost the sense of shame. It was a hundred years behind the experimental sciences. For all serious purposes, it was less instructive than Walter Scott and Alexandre Dumas.

2

Henry Adams shamelessly misled his own readers in his classic autobiography, *The Education of Henry Adams*, by picturing himself as a failure in life who had learned little of value in school and college to equip him for the new age of science. His younger brother Brooks was amused (if he was amused at anything) by this pose and explained after Henry's death, "He was not a failure, for he succeeded, and succeeded brilliantly, in whatever he undertook, where success was possible." Although Henry loved to affect pessimism in his writings and he sustained a great shock in the suicide of his wife, his many years were spent among unusually devoted and talented friends in Cambridge and Paris. Unlike his kinfolk, he had not the slightest desire for public office, not even the presidency of the American Historical Association that was thrust upon him. His wealth, inherited largely from his Brooks grandfather, made it easy for him to travel and study abroad and to carry on his vast and expensive archival researches comfortably and to follow his inclinations generally.

His *Education* dwelt on the abiding influence of noted ancestors upon his life. Born in Boston in 1838, he knew his grandfather, John Quincy Adams, during impressionable early years; and the tradition of John Adams, who died finally in 1826, and of Abigail was still fresh. His father, Charles Francis Adams, was also a major statesman who ran in 1848 as the vice-presidential nominee of the Free Soilers and won a seat in Congress as a Republican in 1859. When Lincoln appointed him minister to Great Britain, he took Henry with him as his private secretary. Minister Adams proved so effective as a diplomat that he helped to win support for the Union at a time when Anglo-American relations determined in part the fate of the United States.

Brooks Adams offers a clue to the pessimistic interpretation held by his brother (and to some extent himself also) regarding the downward trend or "degradation" of the democratic dogma. In the "heritage of Henry Adams"—to use Brooks's chapter title—was revealed John Quincy Adams's lasting shock at his defeat in 1828 by Jackson and the unlettered hosts of Democracy. The defeated president, who believed that his program alone advanced the welfare of the people, even confessed privately that the defeat shook his faith in God—an inconceivable thing for a family so steeped in religious tradition. Brooks and Henry, who subscribed to the idea of the steady deterioration of "social energy," following an analogy from the second law of thermodynamics, saw in all this the decay of democracy. The high level of public morality and intellectuality in Washington's day had deteriorated under the spoils system of Jackson and reached the bottom under Grant. In fact, Henry even used the theme of decline in his popular novel *Democracy*, which portrayed the cynicism of corrupt men in the nation's capital.

Harvard of course was the only college for an Adams, and it left a decisive intellectual influence on him, despite all of Henry's flat denials in *The Education*. Among his teachers were James Russell Lowell, Louis Agassiz, and Professor Francis Bowen, who also speculated upon the possibility of a science of history. Nor did Harvard show the bad judgment that Adams attributed to the president when the latter invited him to teach medieval history (to which was added American) in 1870. When he introduced the seminar in history at Harvard, he had as an assistant, Henry Cabot Lodge, and his students' papers were published as *Essays in Anglo-Saxon Law* (1876). It is apparent from these essays (he wrote the introduction) that Adams, like other prominent historians of his day, taught the "germ theory," with its emphasis on how democratic institutions evolved from the Anglo-Saxon peoples. He advised Lodge, "Learn to appreciate and to use the German historical method, and your style can be elaborated at leisure." Here was the Ranke tradition. From medieval history, Adams turned to lectures and seminars in American colonial and early national history. He even assured friends that history as a profession paid well in money and prestige, as witness the examples of the New Englanders Prescott, Motley, Parkman, and Bancroft. But he failed to make the money they did.

Like other distinguished New England historians, he edited the *North American Review* and contributed articles and book reviews. In a lengthy paper on Captain John Smith he raised a controversy by questioning the story that Pocahontas had interceded dramatically to save him from imminent death. He thought it suspicious that Smith had omitted this tale in his earliest narrative, one written soon after the event, and published it first in a much later history. When he reviewed George Bancroft's *History,* he criticized its chauvinistic tone and its naïve support of man's inherent democratic faith and its belief in human perfectibility. One of his early books, *Documents Relating to New England Federalism* (1877), included the first publication of a polemic of John Quincy Adams, who had courageously voted for Jefferson's Embargo (which hurt New England commerce) and attacked the Essex Junto of his section and party for their plot to secede from the United States.[2]

Looking about for a large historical era to make his own after the fashion of the great New England historians, he chose the fourteen years following the time that John Adams left office in 1801. After a dozen years of research both here and in several European countries, he published nine volumes during 1889-91 as *The History of the United States of America During the Administrations of Thomas Jefferson and James Madison.* He had served a special apprenticeship for this work by writing detailed biographies of Albert Gallatin, Jefferson's secretary of the treasury, and John Randolph, erratic gadfly of the Virginian Republicans. Gallatin appeared as a man of high integrity, a gifted economist, and an energetic organizer and leader (like J. Q. Adams) in internal improvements. Adams believed that the basic practical questions of history were usually economic. Privately, he asserted that Gallatin "was the most fully and perfectly equipped statesman we can show." But Gallatin's later biographer, Raymond Walters, Jr., feels that Adams neglected the private life of the statesman and permitted the book to follow the documents so mechanically as to forsake the critical duties of the historian. The Randolph biography was much less successful because of the eccentric personality involved and Adams's desire to show the inconsistencies of the men who had replaced Washington and John Adams. By the time that Adams had been fairly launched into his researches for the Jefferson and Madison administrations, his prejudices became cumulative. He wrote to Samuel J. Tilden: [3]

> To do justice to Gallatin was a labor of love. . . . I cannot say as much for his friends Jefferson, Madison, and Monroe, about whom I have been for years hard at work. In regard to them I am incessantly forced to devise excuses and apologies or to admit that no excuse will avail. I am at times almost sorry that I ever undertook to write their history, for they appear like mere grasshoppers kicking and gesticulating on the middle of the Mississippi River. There is no possibility of reconciling their theories with their acts, or their extraordinary foreign policy with dignity.

Meanwhile he searched arduously for material in the archives of England, France, and Spain, aided by generous government policy. In the United States, he enjoyed unrestricted access to diplomatic papers. The British government, remembering his father, even changed official rules to allow Adams to examine the most confidential files. While recent critics have sometimes held that Adams left the bulk of the then available sources untouched, it is difficult to imagine how one would go about exhausting the enormous sources of such a vast period.

3

The nine volumes of the *History* focused on a central diplomatic and military theme—the coming of the War of 1812 and the actual conflict itself. For the sake of public curiosity, as he privately admitted, he gave the Burr Conspiracy disproportionate space. And only a New Englander could feel justified in devoting so large a part of the Jeffersonian section of the work to the Embargo.

Yet historians single out the all-too-brief 155 pages of introductory social and cultural history in volume one as most revelatory of the genius of this work. These early chapters actually portray the relative backwardness of the nation in 1800, not too far removed in some respects from the technology of Saxon times, especially in rural communities. Even in intellectual New England, where the schools were comparatively excellent, the educational system was antiquated in many ways, he thought. Harvard "resembled a priesthood which had lost the secret of its mysteries, and patiently stood holding the flickering torch before cold altars, until God should vouchsafe a new dispensation." A narrow alliance of clergy and magistracy then dominated New England, even though orthodoxy had been reduced to a shell. New York, Virginia, and South Carolina were ruled by family oligarchies. Newspapers flourished, but their quality was depressing. With his caustic humor, he observed: "The student of history might search forever these storehouses of political calumny for facts meant to instruct the public in any useful object." He felt no need to mince words over the prevailing intellectual poverty; for even Philadelphia, the literary as well as political capital of the United States, lacked an intellectual society. His conclusion was not unexpected: "The labor of the hand had precedence over that of the mind throughout the United States."

On the other hand, he defended the average American of 1800 from the charges of crude materialism and greed leveled by English poets and travelers. He was struck by the American faith in the future, a highly imaginative belief for which no underlying substance seemed to exist. He said that "the average American" was more intelligent than the average European of that day and that his gift for invention was converting the democratic instinct into practical shape. Beneath the forces of natural selection America was evolving into an advanced technical society. But there was still "a disproportion between the physical obstacles and the natural means for overcoming them." Conservatism struggled with the force of the innovating spirit:

> The task of overcoming popular inertia in a democratic society was new and seemed to offer peculiar difficulties. Without a scientific class to lead the way, and without a wealthy class to provide the means of experiment, the people of the United States were still required by the nature of their problems, to become a speculating and scientific nation.

Adams enriched his picture of 1800 with significant questions that he knew so well to ask, with the hypotheses that underlay his philosophy of history, and with his intensive reading and thinking about the Jeffersonian epoch. He showed unusual subtlety in the evaluation of psychological factors and tried to probe the inmost motives of Jefferson the man at the time of his central decisions. Unfortunately, he regarded Jefferson as a failure and manipulated the facts in order to prove that the Virginian contradicted almost all his principles in practice and that those principles he did retain were so contrary to the facts of political life that they cost the nation dearly. Adams conceded that the Sage of Monticello had integrity and faith in democracy and that he furthered the cause of science. In fact, he stated flatly, "According to the admitted standards of greatness, Jefferson was a great man." But there Adams left the reader waiting vainly for adequate examples of this statement.

The historian felt—and modern historians would disagree—that Jefferson's reforms while governor had "crippled and impoverished the gentry, but did little for the people, and for the slaves nothing." In a letter to George Bancroft, who was reading the Adams manuscript evidently from a good Democratic point of view, Adams gave his frank appraisal of Jefferson: "My own opinion is that J. *was* a coward, as he proved by resigning his governorship of Virginia in the face of a British invasion." This judgment was strongly implied in the volume itself when Adams dealt with Jefferson's Embargo as an unmanly evasion of the duty to fight when the national honor was at stake. Even Richard Hildreth could not surpass Adams in such derogations of Jefferson.

Adams considered Jefferson to be narrowly Virginian in his prejudices against centralized government. Such ideas of limited government were imposed on the nation in "as real a revolution in the principles of our government as that of 1776 was in its form." Thus spoke the grandson of John Quincy Adams, the champion of internal improvements for the nation and strong congressional action against slavery. The historian made it obvious that he had little sympathy for the agrarian philosophy of Jefferson. The idea that the farmers were a chosen people "clashed with his intellectual instincts of liberality and innovation." Yet this Moses, as Adams described him, leading the forces of democracy, showed no aptitude whatever for mixing with the multitude.

In his catalogue of inconsistencies, Adams liked to point out that this man whose inaugural address called for "Absolute acquiescence in the decisions of the majority" was none other than the recent co-author of the Kentucky and Virginia Resolutions—which Adams took to be an extreme statement of the states' rights philosophy. Jefferson the strict constructionist later found constitutional authority for the purchase of Louisiana and other measures requiring a liberal interpretation.

Like his distinguished grandfather, Adams looked upon the New England way of life as the best, derogated the South, and neglected the West. "During the administrations of Jefferson and Madison, the national government was in the main controlled by ideas and interests peculiar to the region south of the Potomac and only to be understood from a Southern standpoint." Again, like his grandfather, he sympathized with an enlightened Indian policy even if this meant praise for Jefferson. Adams made it clear that he saw no real solution possible for the Indian question and disposed of it by invoking the law of nature and the "survival of the fittest."

But unlike John Quincy Adams, who supported the Embargo, Henry Adams flatly denounced it as Jefferson's mistaken policy of "peaceable coercion," involving withdrawal without dignity and imposed upon a people without any explanation as to the motives of the government. Measured by Jefferson's states' rights theory, it was not even constitutional. Henry saw these events through the spectacles of his own diplomatic years in England during the Civil War, when Lincoln and Charles Francis Adams displayed Yankee firmness toward British provocations. Thus the Jefferson-Madison policy of Embargo and commercial boycott seemed not only ineffectual, but most likely to precipitate war. "Jefferson and his government had shown over and over again that no provocation would make them fight; and from that moment that this attitude was understood, America became fair prey." Such a policy, he thought, was even more destructive than war. Echoing the Spencerian idea of struggle, Adams asserted vigorously his admiration for the martial spirit:

> If war made men brutal, at least it made them strong; it called out the qualities best fitted to survive in the struggle for existence. To risk life for one's country was no mean act even when done for selfish motives; and to die that others might more happily live was the highest act of self-sacrifice to be reached by man. War, with all its horrors, could purify as well as debase; it dealt with high motives and vast interests; taught courage, discipline and a stern sense of duty. Jefferson must have asked himself in vain what lessons of heroism or duty were taught by his system of peaceable coercion. . . . Jefferson lost his vast popularity. America learned that she must fight with the weapons of other races. . . . She could not much longer delude herself with hopes of evading laws of nature and instincts of life.

The Embargo seemed of such overwhelming importance to Adams that he devoted 322 pages out of 474 in volume four. Madison, the ostensible subject of the second four volumes, is almost buried as a colorless man, "among the weakest of Executives," an irritating man who had a "feminine faculty of pressing a sensitive point." This unworthy successor of Jefferson tried to turn the clock back by vetoing internal improvements and by surrendering national powers. Usually Madison confined himself timidly to the policies laid down by Jefferson and to the wishes of Congress. All this differs markedly from the much more convincing picture of Madison presented recently by a careful biographer, Irving Brant. By this time, as Adams admitted privately, he was rapidly losing interest in his *History*.

Finally, when Adams reached his denouement, the military story of the War of 1812 (which he obviously enjoyed), he devoted over a hundred pages of volume six and practically all of volumes seven and eight to it. His military and naval history was of high professional quality, judging from the praises of military historians. In 1944, the *Infantry Journal* assembled this material on the War of 1812 and made a book of it.

Especially significant, in view of his dream of achieving a science of history, is the final concluding chapter on social and cultural history at the end of this period. He felt that the story of Jefferson and Madison was interesting to Americans as types of character rather than as sources of power. Once more, he was back to the Greek scientific search for permanence behind change, an anti-historical outlook. If consistently carried out—and it was not—this meant that Adams looked upon the record of the past as mere raw data for the really important task of discovering social laws. This was worthy of Comte and the positivists who had done so much to teach this ideal.

In this chapter Adams wrote that America was a vast stage, a laboratory in which one could study undisturbed the social evolution of democracy. Europe's fierce struggles and class conflicts confused the picture and made it impossible to use its experience as material for a science. It gave prominence to the hero, the dramatic individual, and scarcely featured society as an organism. If history were to become a true science, it must seek its laws not in the complicated story of rival European nationalities, but from the economic evolution of a great democracy. He lamented the lack of a scientific history along the lines of natural science:

No historian cared to hasten the coming of an epoch when man should study his own history in the same spirit and by the same methods with which he studied the formation of a crystal. Here were the best opportunities to be scientific and study the evolution of a *race*, not merely an individual. . . . In a democratic ocean science could see something ultimate. Man could go no further. The atom might move, but the general equilibrium could not change.

He thought that Americans were especially worth study "if they were to represent the greatest democratic evolution the world could know."

It was understandable that Adams paused to criticize another keen historian and observer of American ideas and institutions, Alexis de

Tocqueville, who studied history by methods not at all analogous to those used in studying the formation of a crystal. His *Democracy in America*, which appeared in English translations in 1835 and 1862, offered a scientific comparative method devoid of the determinism of natural science. De Tocqueville could have been speaking of Henry Adams when he took issue with the historical determinists:

> If this doctrine of necessity, which is so attractive to those who write history in democratic ages, passes from authors to their readers till it infects the whole mass of the community and gets possession of the public mind, it will soon paralyze the activity of modern society and reduce Christians to the level of Turks.

Adams's *History* largely escaped the determinism expressed in the final chapter. Jefferson and Madison are not merely "types" but human beings, and the choices of that time were very real choices, not mere reflections of some collective necessity. Good and evil were standard ideas in every Adams household.

While the *History*'s art has a timeless quality and has been appreciated not only by historians but by other discerning readers, it failed to reach the mass audience of Bancroft, Parkman, and McMaster. Only three-thousand sets were sold during the entire first decade of publication. The work was on too high a level of analysis to interest readers content with a simple dramatic narrative.

The *History* has continued to be praised by important critics. Carl Becker has written, "A history which for clarity, tight construction, and sheer intelligence applied to the exposition of a great theme, had not then, and has not since been equalled by any American historian." Henry Steele Commager, who edited one version of the *History*, commented, "With the exception of Francis Parkman's *France and England in North America*, it is the only major work yet produced by an American historian of which it can be justly said that age cannot wither it nor custom stale its infinite variety." [4] Its aspiration toward a scientific philosophy of history attuned to the analogies from Darwin, Spencer, Thomson, and Gibbs has interested professional critics and biographers, but usually passes over the head of the average reader. Adams wrote in a succinct, concise prose, in the intellectual tradition of the Puritan "plaine stile," which was enlivened by his own intimate identification with the men and problems of their day. His understanding of personality has even been compared with that of his gifted friend, the novelist, Henry James.

Adams's success in depicting social history is so great, despite his untenable preconceptions, that one regrets that his magnum opus devotes so little space to it. He chose the familiar path of politics, diplomacy, and military affairs so well trodden by the Adams family. Within this sphere, he showed such prodigious industry and such keen understanding that a generation went by before revisionists had made serious inroads on his work. While the books of Adams's illustrious New England contemporaries are now obviously dated, the *History* can still be, and is, assigned by professors to students mature enough to read it.

The reputations of Jefferson and Madison have now been refurbished through many histories and biographies. Julius Pratt in his *Expansionists of 1812* (1925) converted most historians to the thesis that the War Hawks had much more to do with the coming of the war than commercial causes. The Burr Conspiracy is now interpreted according to far more complex motives and facts than the *History* suggests. Adams had described Burr only in terms a Hamiltonian might have used. Despite these and even more serious revisions, much remains that is usable—the War of 1812 in its various phases at home and on the battlefield, the chapters on social and cultural history, and the intricacies of diplomacy during the Jefferson and Madison administrations.

4

One of Adams's appreciative critics, Max I. Baym, has seen reflected in him the whole romantic tradition in Europe through his pose of aesthetic pessimism, particularly his idea of heroic failure. Adams's preoccupation with science in the *History, Education,* and essays is set against the French-inspired sentimentalism and subjective romanticism which appears notably in *Mont-Saint-Michel and Chartres.*[5]

In 1904 he published privately this book-length essay on the medieval world of the great cathedrals of France. It is easy to agree that this was his greatest literary achievement, although it was not history in its usual developmental form. It is indeed a *tour de force* in aesthetics, combining the historian's insight into the medieval spirit with Adams's own lifelong search for certainty. Ralph Adams Cram, the noted American architect of the Gothic revival movement, wrote an enthusiastic introduction to the edition of 1913 sponsored by the American Institute of Architects. His praise was unqualified: "*Mont-Saint-Michel and Chartres* is one of the most distinguished contributions to literature and one of the most valuable adjuncts to the study of medievalism America has thus far produced." Though it was cast in the misleadingly simple form of a travel guide, its intellectual and aesthetic depth became clear almost at the outset. Cram believed that Adams had captured the spirit of the age by projecting himself into its thought, emotions, and art-expression.

Even in a study of American history-writing, one cannot neglect this outstanding work. Before writing this book, save for his early teaching of medieval history at Harvard and his long residence in Europe, Adams had been largely concerned with the American scene. The era of cathedral building and famous shrines afforded him an opportunity to probe men's motives as he had in the *History*. He continued to ask questions about the influence of energy and force in history. He also probed the role that women had played as a unique force for civilization, and contrasted the power of the Virgin for the age of faith with that of the dynamo for the era of the Chicago World's Fair of 1893:

> The twelfth and thirteenth centuries, studied in the pure light of political economy, are insane. The scientific mind is atrophied, and suffers under inherited cerebral weakness, when it comes in contact with the eternal woman—Astarte, Isis, Demeter, Aphrodite, and the last and greatest deity of all, the Virgin. Very rarely one lingers, with a mild sympathy, such as suits the patient student of human error, willing to be interested in what he cannot understand.

He saw in the seeming structural instability of the Gothic cathedral, especially its delicate equilibrium tending to endanger the line of safety, a symbol of "the uncertainty of logic, the inequalities of the syllogism" that were propped up by faith and human aspirations. He found a basic parallel between theology and science. The law of energy tended toward an ultimate unity, just as religion sought it in the nature of God.

5

The classic autobiography, *The Education of Henry Adams,* privately printed in 1906, was intended as a kind of sequel to *Mont-Saint-Michel,* with, as he explained, "the three last chapters of the *Education* being Q.E.D. of the three last chapters of *Chartres.*" Biographers tended to discount Adams's confession of failure, his constant self-deprecation, and even his scientific pessimism. Written when Adams was committed to a mechanistic philosophy of history, the autobiography depicts the tragedy and failure of an eighteenth-century man in an iconoclastic nineteenth-century world. Educated to believe in progress and human perfectibility, he was upset by Grant's inefficient and corrupt administration and by the policy of drift.

Much of the volume throws fresh light on significant historical incidents and trends. There is much on our diplomatic relations with England during the Civil War, when he wrote articles for the press while acting as Minister Adams's private secretary. His picture of the Grant era and of Congress represented much research as well as good reporting. Above all, his survey of changing intellectual fashions—allowing for his increasing bent toward mechanical scientism at the time—has challenged the interest of readers ever since. His final chapters presented a plan for a science of history which would make old-fashioned descriptive and literary history obsolete: "A Dynamic Theory of History" and "A Law of Acceleration." He thought that he had found an excellent illustration of the historical dissipation of energy in the dissolution of the Roman empire, and he leaned upon analogies taken from Newton's principles of gravitation:

A dynamic theory, assigning attractive force to opposing bodies in proportion to the law of mass, takes for granted that the forces of nature capture men. . . . The result might have been stated in a mathematical formula as early as the time of Archimedes, six hundred years before Rome fell. The economic needs of a violently centralizing society forced the empire to enlarge its slave system until the slave-system consumed itself and the empire too, leaving society no resource but further enlargement of its religious system in order to compensate for the losses and horrors of the failure. For a vicious circle, its mathematical completeness approached perfection.

But when Adams tried to convert professional historians to the cult of scientism, they balked, even though they were quite willing to make him president of the American Historical Association—a position that he accepted without appearing personally to deliver the annual address. Not even the adverse criticism of physicists, who indicated that Adams had misapplied his analogies from science, could deter the "physicist-historian"—to use his own phrase. While social Darwinism was distorting the aim and methodology of sociology, ethnology, law, and other social studies for an entire generation, Adams tried to wed historians to dubious analogies from the second law of thermodynamics. Fortunately, the very complexity of physics to the lay mind undoubtedly deterred any of his admirers from becoming pioneer devotees of scientism, despite the fact that most historians of the time, of whatever philosophical persuasion, thought of themselves as scientific historians.

In 1910 Adams must have mystified many historians—at least those who had not taken his Newtonian vocabulary too seriously—by a little volume entitled *A Letter to American Teachers of History*. This appealed to them to throw off their "inertia" and to consider the inevitable future relationship between history and physics. He surveyed the history of recent contributions to physics since the formulation of the law of conservation of energy. This had held that the quantity of matter in the universe remained invariable, the sum of movement remained constant, and that energy was indestructible. But since the 1850s a new school of physicists had announced a second law of thermodynamics. This did not deny that the universe was a closed box from which energy could not escape, but added that "the higher powers of energy tended to fall lower, and that this process had no known limit." In other words, there was a constant dissipation of energy to do useful mechanical work in closed systems. This was the law of "entropy." In biological evolution, he believed, the ascent of man occurred at the expense of energy. Thus, he denied the optimistic implications of Darwinian evolution. Similar conclusions regarding man, he said, were being reached in the various social studies. What would be the future of history in a world that was running down and had been running down for some time? Certainly the doctrines of upward progress and human perfectibility made no sense.

He went on to speculate upon a new chronology with "changes of phase" such as a "Mechanical Phase of 1600-1900" fixed by a certain mathematical value expressed in numbers. One could measure the time phase when society moved from one form of thought to another. This type of speculation, with many of the same illustrations and arguments, had appeared a year before in his essay, "The Rule of Phase Applied to History." He ended on an obscure note, which indicated how little progress he had made in creating a history shaped in the image of the second law of thermodynamics:

Always and everywhere the mind creates its own universe, and pursues its own phantoms; but the force behind the image is always a reality,—the attractions of occult power. If values can be given to these attractions, a physical theory of history is a mere matter of physical formula, no more complicated than the formulas of Willard Gibbs or Clerk Maxwell; but the task of framing the formula and assigning the values belongs to the physicist, not to the historian.

The erratic assumptions beneath Adams's scientism have been thoroughly explored by Professor William Jordy. Adams's results could scarcely have been better, even if he had been more expertly equipped in physics than was the case. He failed to recognize the inferential nature of historical facts as compared to the immediate data, subject to check, that scientific facts involve. Considering the highly subjective quality of historical facts—and not the least those culled by Adams himself—the dream of a science of history in the image of mathematical physics seemed doomed from the beginning.[6]

Adams's determinism seems to have colored, even if it did not originate from, the surprising anti-Semitic doctrines that Adams expressed most emphatically in his correspondence during the Bryan free silver campaign (which he supported financially) and the depression of the 'nineties. This was an era when he was warned by his family that his large inherited wealth was in jeopardy. His reaction was to condemn the capitalism of England and France as Jewish-dominated. To the Jewish financiers, he attributed an all-pervasive force. His flare for comprehensive formulas of a mechanistic nature led him to accept the current cosmology of the anti-Semites, who made the Jewish financier a focal source of energy in the deterioration of the world of the small entrepreneur. Therefore, Henry Adams actually thought of *three* primary sources of pervasive historical energy—the Virgin for the religious impulse, the Dynamo for the spirit of technology, and the International Jew for modern finance capitalism.

By the 'nineties, hundreds of Boston Brahmins had yielded to anti-Semitism, tormented by the spectacle of the new immigration with its Jewish and Italian elements. Thus they organized the first effective immigration restriction league since the days of Chinese exclusion. The Populists, too, in many cases, associated their hatred of the hard-money creditor class with the machinations of the Bank of England and the scheming of the Rothschilds. It is therefore not surprising that Adams showed no sympathy for Captain Alfred Dreyfus when his trial for treason took on the form of an anti-Semitic plot.[7]

Brooks Adams shared with his brother Henry not only prejudices against Wall Street and Jewish capital (though both expressed these largely in private letters) but also a determination to create a science of history based—at least in part—on the principle of the dissipation of energy. In 1896, he published an analytical historical work, *The Law of Civilization and Decay*, which began with the downfall of Rome—a tragedy that he ascribed to capitalistic usury; the book went on to trace the conflict of debtors and creditors up to modern times.

Henry contributed many suggestions and did some actual editing, but he disagreed on many basic points of interpretations. The Bryan free-silverites hailed the book as a scientific exposition of their cause.

Brooks explained his underlying science of history in a preface:

> The evidence, however, seems to point to the conclusion that, when a highly centralized society disintegrates, under the pressure of economic competition, it is because the energy of the race has been exhausted. Consequently the survivors of such a community lack the power necessary for renewed concentration and must probably remain inert until supplied with fresh energetic material by the infusion of barbarian blood.

In 1943, Charles Beard wrote an appreciative introduction to a new Knopf edition of *The Law of Civilization and Decay*. He did not dismiss the hope that history might some day become a science, but he rejected Brooks Adams's cyclic theory of history, just as Beard had previously quarreled with Oswald Spengler's idea that history moved in endless cycles. He could not agree with Brooks that society moved from barbarism to civilization and then back again—from "a condition of physical dispersion to one of concentration and then disintegration." Brooks had suggested that cosmic energy inspired this social treadmill in which fear, greed, and the domination of priests and soldiers were the main factors. His somber view of the Middle Ages contrasted decidedly with the exhilarating aesthetic one that Henry Adams offered in *Mont-Saint-Michel*. Brooks Adams confessed to his brother that his own books were neither history nor literature but brochures intended to throw light on specific current crises such as the free-silver fight.

In the end Henry Adams drew back in fear from the radicals and the portent of socialism dominating the next generation. Besides, he disliked the prospect of southern and western farmers allied with city laborers trying to run modern society. "Much as I loathe the regime of Manchester and Lombard Street in the nineteenth century," he wrote privately, "I am glad to think that I shall be dead before I am ruled by the Trades Unions of the Twentieth. Luckily society will go to pieces then." In another letter, he identified the Jew with capitalism. "It is the socialist—not the capitalist—who is going to swallow us next, and of the two, I prefer the Jew."

Henry Adams's distrust of corporations and speculation—Lombard Street—went back a full generation. In 1870, while denouncing the crimes of Jay Gould and James Fisk, he had declared ominously in an article for the *Westminster Review* on "The New York Gold Conspiracy": [8]

The belief is common in America that the day is at hand when corporations far greater than the Erie—swaying power such as has never in the world's history been trusted in the hands of mere private citizens, controlled by single men like Vanderbilt, or by combinations of men like Fisk, Gould, and Land, after having created a system of quiet but irresistible corruption—will ultimately succeed in directing government itself. . . . The corporation is in its nature a threat against the whole world.

His eldest brother, Charles Francis Adams, a prolific part-time historian with Comtian beliefs in a scientific history, a man who had fought at Antietam and Gettysburg and had become an economist and business administrator hostile to railroad buccaneering, had much the same to say. Writing in 1869 for the *North American Review*, he freely predicted the dire consequences of Gouldism:

As the Erie Ring represents the combination of the corporation and the hired proletariat of a great city; as Vanderbilt embodies the autocratic power of Caesarism introduced into corporate life, and as neither alone can obtain complete control of the government of the State, it, perhaps, only remains for the coming man to carry the combination of elements one step in advance, and put Caesarism at once in control of the corporation and of the proletariat, to bring our vaunted institutions within the rule of all historic precedent.

The remedy, he thought, lay in "a renovated public opinion," but he saw no hope of this. Later he urged partial public ownership of the railroads as the only effective alternative to corporate abuses, but he did not favor government regulation. Unlike his more sedentary brothers, he entered the speculative world of Jay Gould and even became president of the Union Pacific during 1884-90—until Gould forced him out—and head of the Kansas City stockyards. But after retirement, he devoted himself to history and educational reform. With Brooks and Henry, he shared a common interest in the history of Massachusetts and in the role of the Adams family; especially original was his two-volume work, *Three Episodes of Massachusetts History* (1892), which examined the Puritan theocracy with a critical eye.[9]

The three remarkable brothers also shared to a considerable extent similar social ideas and philosophies of history, especially the belief that history should record a past usable for future reformers. Brooks and Henry Adams were almost monists in their belief that natural science would reveal the underlying principle of history. Yet when it came to their social principles their faith in mechanistic laws was overruled by an even stronger faith in men. They had much of Ancestor John Adams's suspicion of the rising world of speculative finance heralded by Alexander Hamilton. As it was, their reformist sympathies led them to the Mugwumps. Their father, Charles Francis Adams, had been a rallying symbol for the Mugwumps, those Republican independents who rejected the unbearable Grantist corruption and hoped that a civil service controlled by an enlightened public opinion would promote justice. Possibly, Henry Adams had lost some of this original fervor with the years, but the Bryan campaign of 1896 succeeded for a brief time in reviving these dormant sympathies.

No formula can easily dispose of the versatile and often inspired Henry Adams (and of Brooks Adams). Even historians who brush away his untenable historical analogies from physics are often awed by his strange gifts of prophecy. Although the predictions regarding the future course of world affairs are often quite wide of the mark, many of his impressions have turned out correctly and show a rare perceptive quality. Otherwise, what else can one say of a man who forecast a coming conflict with an expanding Germany, her alliance with Russia, an "Atlantic System" consisting of the United States, England, and France aimed at central and eastern Europe, the rapid growth of revolutionary socialism, and even the bifurcation of the world between the United States and Russia? Historians, for all their justified impatience with prophecy, especially when it is based on dubious premises, nevertheless turn prophet when they construct their image of the past. The nature of written history derives form not only from past and present considerations but often from its presumed meaning in the present light of an anticipated future. Henry Adams contemplated power politics without mysticism but with flashes of historical insight into the future—as our generation is now aware.

Turner and the Moving Frontier

1

Frederick Jackson Turner of the University of Wisconsin and Harvard believed with Henry Adams that it was possible to make history a science with methods similar to those of the natural sciences. He would make Darwinian evolutionism rather than the second law of thermodynamics the mainspring of his system. Both men also sought analogies in geology. On at least two occasions, Turner quoted Adams approvingly for the observation that history should aspire to the kind of precision that marked the study of the formation of a crystal. Darwinian assumptions in biology underlay his famous concepts of frontier and section. Fortunately for history, both fell far short of converting their discipline into a non-humanistic science. Both men became president of the American Historical Association and won an enviable professional reputation. Each in his important writing revealed that he viewed history not as a rudimentary type of biology, geology, or physics, but as a wholly different kind of discipline concerned with men who frequently upset admirable "laws" and predictions by simply choosing to act in unforeseeable ways. The two historians believed that by studying masses of men (rather than ruling elites) in the unspoiled New World environment they could discover certainties akin to those of the scientists.

Turner far exceeded Adams in influence. In fact no man shaped twentieth-century histories of the United States as much as Turner did. His reputation grew even after social evolution, upon which he depended so much, lost its respectability among social scientists. Yet his output was rather modest by academic promotional standards, and his writings were burdened with needless repetition and seemed quite vulnerable to criticism. His brief seminal paper of 1893, "The Significance of the Frontier in American History," delivered before the American Historical Association at Chicago's famed Columbian Exposition, contained most of what he had to say during his entire career. His later writings were mere commentary upon the theme that America was overwhelmingly the product of frontier social forces. But even critics felt that somehow Turner's greatness transcended their bill of particulars.

The facts of his early life go far to explain his frontier interests. He was born in 1861 in a Portage, Wisconsin, frontier community between the historic Fox and Wisconsin rivers, where the old fur-trading routes were common knowledge and a youth might even meet an occasional Indian. He loved outdoor sports, fishing especially, learned something of journalism from his father, a newspaperman and Republican politician, and even gathered a year's experience as a Madison reporter. He took his first two degrees at the frontier-minded University of Wisconsin and in later years lectured on the theme that the state university was the best hope for replacing the vanishing frontier influence.

His master's thesis, not surprisingly, was on "The Influence of the Fur Trade in the Development of Wisconsin." His learning had not been parochial because among other things he had been closely associated with Professor William F. Allen, a specialist in Roman history and a man of broad interests who had studied with Heeren of Gottingen—Bancroft's teacher—and now taught the critical methods of the new German historiography. Allen had also introduced Turner to intensive readings in western history.

In 1888, Turner temporarily left his alma mater to work toward a doctoral degree at the pioneer graduate institution, the Johns Hopkins University, where Herbert Baxter Adams, his future thesis sponsor, had successfully introduced the Ranke-type historical seminar. Adams had studied with the foremost historians of Heidelberg and Berlin and, following the trend in Germany and in England, became concerned with the evolution of social, economic, and above all, political institutions. Thus, his doctoral dissertation dealt with the European as well as colonial origins of the New England town meeting.[1]

Like so many of the budding American historians who took their Ph.D.s in Germany, H. B. Adams found a starting point in the flattering account given by Tacitus of the primitive German tribes within the Roman empire. He sought to discover the origins of western democratic institutions in certain alleged equalitarian practices of the ancient Germans. Tacitus had marveled at the strength and bravery of these tribesmen; he had been impressed by the majority rule of the Germans, who brandished spears to indicate assent or openly murmured their dissent. German nationalists like the historian "Vater" Jahn encouraged the social-athletic *Turnverein* to help remold the modern German into the heroic form of the tough tribesmen. Scholars both here and abroad looked to the Teutonic forest for the origins of parliamentary institutions, trial by jury, and other democratic practices. To Tacitus, as to Turner, it was significant that the great open spaces of the forest frontier lands had produced this independent, democratic folk.[2]

Schoolboys, familiar in those days with Caesar and the Commentaries, knew something of those German frontier tribes, which had destroyed five consular armies and three of Caesar's legions in a protracted but hopeless struggle for independence that lasted 210 years before mighty Rome won. Turner was already bent upon the idealization of the American frontier and forest, but it would be a grave mistake to assume that he rejected the forest myth of Tacitus and H. B. Adams. He rebelled in 1893 merely at the current *exclusive* emphasis on Teutonic origins, although he did not quarrel with the chauvinistic Anglo-Saxon overemphasis in history and international affairs. This is quite clear from his famous essay of 1893: [3]

> In the settlement of America we have to observe how European life entered the continent, and how America modified and developed that life and reacted on Europe. Our early history is the study of European germs developing in an American environment. Too exclusive attention has been paid by institutional students to the Germanic origins, too little to the American factors. The frontier is the line of most rapid and effective Americanization. The wilderness masters the colonist. . . . Little by little he transforms the wilderness, but the outcome is not the old Europe, not simply the development of Germanic germs, any more than the first phenomenon was a case of reversion to the Germanic mark. The fact is that here is a new product that is American.

So while Adams taught or wrote about the Germanic origins of New England towns or on Saxon tithingmen in America, Turner gave only formal lip service to the idea that early American institutions required a basic Germanic origin. He made some concession to the Adams "germ theory" school while writing his dissertation on the Wisconsin fur trade, subtitled "A Study of the Trading Post as an Institution," by tracing it back, even to Phoenician days! The thesis also showed its debt to almost all the books of Francis Parkman on the West. Except for the first few pages on transatlantic origins of the trading post, the book is wholly within an American context with little reference to other factors.

Turner entered Johns Hopkins at a time when history was becoming a professional study, not a mere adjunct to literature. The American Historical Association was formed in 1884, local historical societies multiplied, archival collections in Washington and the states were amassed and classified, and Congress showed greater solicitude over the record of the past. In fact the AHA in its second annual meeting of 1885 formally called for more research aids for students of the West: "Resolved, That it is especially important that the beginnings of history in our newer Territories and provinces should be fully and carefully recorded." They specified the need for more local historical societies, the preservation of local newspapers and documents, and the encouragement of town activities to preserve records and maps. Ten years later at another AHA session, Turner scoffed at this step as hopelessly inadequate, as "mere antiquarianism." What was needed, said the student of H. B. Adams, was more training in institutional and social investigation.

Some of the new enthusiasm for history both here and abroad sprang from nationalist sources. Turner witnessed the rise of such patriotic societies as the Sons of the American Revolution, the Daughters of the American Revolution, the Colonial Dames of America, and the United Daughters of the Confederacy. The East had led the procession of states eager to record their past, beginning with the Massachusetts Historical Society founded in 1791. Most of them stressed the antiquarian and genealogical approach that Turner abhorred. They were usually privately supported, unlike the societies of the Mississippi Valley, which flourished generally on state grants.

Turner and his friend Reuben G. Thwaites, another frontier historian, helped to found the new State Historical Society of Wisconsin in 1887 as a sponsor of far more humanistic researches than those usually associated with genealogy and antiquarianism. Thwaites, for example, translated or edited such vast collections as the *Jesuit Relations and Allied Documents* (1896-1901). He also edited the eight-volume *Original Journals of the Lewis and Clark Expedition* (1904-05), and put all students of the West in his lasting debt by the monumental thirty-two-volume series of *Early Western Travels* (1904-05). Other states in the Mississippi Valley followed this dynamic leadership. The culmination to this activity came in 1907, when secretaries of the historical societies of the Mississippi Valley states met in Lincoln, Nebraska, to organize the Mississippi Valley Historical Association. By 1914, it was to have its own journal, and its original regional emphasis (which began with the expectation of affiliation with the AHA) gave way to a comprehensive national program.[4]

Literary history did not yield without a struggle to the German-inspired scientific historians. It was difficult for Turner and his school to compete in fine writing with Prescott, Motley, Bancroft, Irving, Parkman, and others of that generation. New editions of these masters were usually available and popular. The writing of western history, the public had been led to expect, must be dramatic and exciting. "Much has been written from the point of view of border warfare and the chase," complained the man from Wisconsin in 1893, "but as a field for the serious study of the economist and the historian it has been neglected." Largely to the category of literary historian—so Turner thought of him—belonged the versatile Theodore Roosevelt.

One of Turner's close associates at Johns Hopkins was another future president, Woodrow Wilson. He had given up in disgust an uninspiring and profitless Atlanta law practice to pursue a history doctorate. Wilson's own historical talents were none too much for the critical role that awaited him, but he was acute enough to be among the first to recognize the importance of Turner's theory of the moving frontier. This appreciation of the West enriched Wilson's histories, such as the five-volume *A History of the American People,* which was also inspired by Green's social-political history of the English people, and *Division and Reunion* (1918). However, even the generous application of the Turner thesis did not save Wilson's historical writings from mediocrity. Wilson, together with such Southern liberals as John Spencer Bassett, William P. Trent, and Walter Hines Page, represented a University that was then staffing most of the Southern colleges. After Adams left, Southern scholars deserted Johns Hopkins for the conservative Dunning seminar at Columbia.

Turner returned to Wisconsin from Johns Hopkins with his new doctorate and remained there until 1910, when he went to Harvard. At Harvard he brought large numbers of graduate students to the study of history. In the classroom his warm personality and freedom from dogmatism charmed students. Besides, he had something definite to offer in the way of method as well as factual instruction. He made fruitful and imaginative use of maps and statistical charts to show significant relationships between frontier sections and national legislation or the significance of population trends. His seminars stressed the critical Ranke test for the trustworthiness of witnesses. He called attention to transferable methods from geography, economics, politics, religion, psychology, and other disciplines. His students found his approach unique for breadth and inspiration.

2

In the education of Turner, as in that of Henry Adams, the natural sciences were basic. The prestige of Darwinism during the 1880s and afterwards led many social scientists to borrow the ideas of primordial germs, evolutionary stages, recurrent social processes, natural selection, environmental adaptation, and the survival of the fittest. Condorcet and other social evolutionists had depicted long before Darwin the advance of cultural history as a series of progressive stages; Montesquieu saw national traits as a product of the physical environment, climate particularly; Auguste Comte's positivism had its law of the three (cultural) stages; and Buckle, among many others, had tried to make a science of geographic determinism.

Turner was particularly impressed by the researches of Professor Friedrich Ratzel (1844-1904), evolutionary zoologist and geographer of the universities of Munich and Leipzig, who had won wide acceptance for his "anthropogeography" or "human geography." But he did not feel that geography alone modified society, for he stressed cultural "diffusion" concepts which explained how social growth occurred through rivers, trade routes, and population movements. He not only spoke of evolutionary social processes but originated the "culture area" concept, which is somewhat similar to Turner's "section," with its relative internal homogeneity of culture. Even more specifically, Ratzel had written on the influence of the West on the American character and institutions.[5]

In his paper of 1896 read before the American Historical Association, "The West as a Field for Historical Study," Turner praised the new (1893) edition of Ratzel's geography of the United States, particularly his significant chapter on "Space as a Factor in the United States." In examining the influence of the sense of space, Ratzel said of the West, "The breadth of land has furnished the American spirit something of its own largeness." He went on to stress, as Turner was to do, the problems of western settlement, land cultivation, the utilization of resources, and the political importance of these processes.[6] At that 1896 session, the commentator on Turner's paper was Professor Andrew C. McLaughlin, substituting for Theodore Roosevelt, who failed to come. McLaughlin fully shared Turner's enthusiasm for Ratzel and called attention to the influence of the West in fostering a sense of destiny among Americans, and in affecting politics, home life, and national development.

Ratzel's chief disciple in America, Ellen C. Semple, was a stimulating contemporary who knew Turner's work as well as the German's, even if she stressed diffusion far more than social evolution. In her influential book, *American History and Its Geographic Conditions* (1903), she acknowledged part of Turner's thesis: "The acquisition of the new West prolonged greatly the most distinctive feature of American anthropo-geographic conditions—the abundance of free land." Her own emphasis on diffusionism led her to accept only so much of Turner: "American soil and the barrier of the Atlantic had modified European institutions and character in the hands and persons of the colonists somewhat; but their gaze was seaward towards the English palace and council hall where their destiny was decided." But she, like Turner, emphasized the influence of western waterways and the Appalachian barrier upon colonial history; to them the sense of American nationality grew out of frontier isolationism.

Turner's specific frontier stages, ranging from the nomadic to the settled community, were not unlike those of the famous German economist, Karl Bucher, who recognized three universal stages of economic development: the hunting stage, the pastoral stage, and the agricultural stage. Even Turner's "section" develops like the noted recapitulation idea of the evolutionists—widely quoted in support of Darwinism—which said that ontogeny (the life history of an individual organism) recapitulates phylogeny (the history of the race). Culturally applied, this would mean that each frontier section would repeat the social processes from primitivism to a sedentary society.

Many of Turner's key generalizations were founded on the results of graphs and map studies which showed the lines of the advancing frontier, the sectional influence on politics, population movements, and other major problems. He owed a good deal to the techniques and findings of Francis A. Walker, a federal statistician, an economist, and a former Commissioner of Indian Affairs, who published census studies while superintendent of the ninth and tenth censuses (1870, 1880), taught at Yale, and then in 1881 became president of the Massachusetts Institute of Technology. No less important to Turner were the geographic charts of Henry Gannett, the chief geographer of the

United States Geological Survey after 1882 who won acclaim as "the
father of American map making." One of Turner's outstanding seminar students, O. G. Libby, used the political map-making technique
most effectively in his oft-quoted study of the geographical distribution of the state votes on the proposed federal constitution. Charles
Beard was to base much of his argument in *An Economic Interpretation of the Constitution* upon Libby's evidence.

Perhaps the most fundamental fact in Turner's background was his
obvious acquaintance with much of the literature and with the central
ideas that made up the image of the West since colonial times. While
he was too sophisticated to accept the Noble Savage idea that the
French *philosophes* talked about or the Puritan notion of "choice seed"
planted in the wilderness, he accepted the popular belief that the
frontier had a beneficent transforming influence upon eastern migrants.
The Turnerian theory that cheap lands meant an outlet and "safety-
valve" for urban labor surpluses can be traced back as far as Benjamin
Franklin. George Fitzhugh, proslavery propagandist, wrote in *Canni-
bals All!* (1857) that class war was checked in America by the fact
that "in forty-eight hours, laborers may escape to the West and become proprietors." Jefferson, friend of the West and sponsor of the
Lewis and Clark explorations, often speculated on the significance of
the frontier and cheap land for a democratic self-reliant nation of
small farmers; and he had commented on the various stages of the
frontier advance westward.

Professor Henry Nash Smith has portrayed the history of the symbols and myths of the American West in *Virgin Land* (1950), reflecting so many of the underlying themes in Turner's writings: The western hero, the West as the Garden of the World, the Utopia of yeoman
farmers, primitivism, and some of their variations. When Turner delivered his paper of 1893, Americans had already reached the stage of
nostalgia for a vanished frontier, and its myths were treasured as a
national heritage. Dime novels and western theme melodrama had
created an exciting stereotype of the West. It would be most surprising, indeed, if quite a few of Turner's auditors at Chicago's World's
Fair did not walk over to the stellar attraction of Buffalo Bill and the
Wild West show.

3

Turner stated part of the frontier thesis in his doctoral dissertation
on the Wisconsin fur trade. There is, for example, the social evolutionary notion of recurrent social processes: "The occupation of the

backlands of the South affords a prototype of the process by which the plains of the far West were settled, and also furnishes an exemplification of all the stages of economic development existing contemporaneously."

Surprisingly, when Turner published a paper in 1891 on "The Significance of History" in the *Wisconsin Journal of Education,* he not only had little to say about the frontier influence, but he seemed to be stressing the germ theory and diffusionist viewpoint of the eastern scholars like his sponsor, Herbert B. Adams. He praised the English economist, Thorold Rogers, author of *The Economic Interpretation of History,* for opening up the possibility of rewriting history from an economic point of view. Only in this way could historians write of the masses and of the rise and fall of nations. They must drop their concern with "the brilliant annals of the few," the court intrigues, and palace life. As for the historians' ideals of history, whether they were moralistic, philosophic, religious, or political, these depended on the particular age. Schelling had emphasized the philosophic idea of "a moral order of the universe ruled by cosmic forces from above." Herder taught the doctrine of growth and the historical development of cultural germs. Niebuhr had helped to found the modern historical school by reconstructing Roman history from institutions of known reality "as the botanist may infer bud from flower." Today, an era of technology fostered "an age of socialistic inquiry," an inquiry into the economic basis of society. "Each age writes the history of the past anew with reference to the conditions uppermost in its own time." Herder was right that society grows, and Comte was right that society was an organism. This meant that history was a comprehensive "biography of society in all its departments."

He did not believe that the "real event of our age" changed, but that our conceptions of them did. From his strong organic viewpoint, he held that history was ever "becoming" but never completed, and that the aim of history was to know what came into the present from the past. This idea was restated in his theory of two histories: The "objective" side were the events themselves; the "subjective" was our conception of them. His idea, sometimes called "presentism," was neatly put: "For the present is simply the developing past, the past the undeveloped present. . . . The goal of the antiquarian is the dead past; the goal of the historian is the living present."

Despite this emphasis on the present as the principle of selection, Turner was too rarely explicit as to where he stood on current issues, and then he did not always appear consistent. Yet he held (as so many

Greek and Roman historians had said) that history afforded a training ground for statesmanship, which would in turn lead to the amelioration of society. Later he was to indorse generally the western demands for democratic reform—but with exceptions.

Theoretically, Turner seemed committed at every essential point to what James Harvey Robinson later called the New History: the expansion of historical subject matter to include practically every phase of social development, the use of techniques drawn from all the relevant social studies, and the belief that this kind of history would improve the social order. Turner concluded, "Historical study has for its end to let the community see itself in the light of the past, to give it new thoughts and feelings, new aspirations and energies. Thoughts and feelings flow into deeds."

There is only the briefest reference to the protest movements of his day in the seminal essay of 1893, "The Significance of the Frontier in American History." He was concerned with the theme of the closed frontier. His starting point was the fact stated by the census superintendent of 1890 that the decennial frontier line had become so broken by isolated bodies of settlement by 1880 that it could no longer have any place in census reports. He went on to show how pivotal the frontier had been hitherto in shaping the nation. He declared his independence of eastern historians who had overstressed the germ theory of American institutions or had been preoccupied with slavery or some other special theme:

> Up to our own day American history has been in a large degree the history of the colonization of the Great West. The existence of an area of free land, its continuous recession, and the advance of American settlement westward, explain American development.

Our history had an evolutionary basis, first in institutions along a limited area such as the Atlantic Coast, and, secondly, in the recurrence of the processes "in each western area reached in the process of expansion"—a reference to the frontier "section" which he developed in later years:

> This perennial rebirth, this fluidity of American life, this expansion westward with its new opportunities, its continuous touch with the simplicity of primitive society, furnish the forces dominating American character.

This frontier, which must now be studied scientifically, was no mere fortified boundary line running through a dense population, as in Europe, but moved always "at the hither edge of free land."

He quickly traced the successive frontiers, beginning with the tide-water region, then the piedmont beyond the "fall line," and thence to the trans-Allegheny settlements. Like Ratzel, he held that regional isolation increased the peculiarly American traits. Each frontier met its problems by an experience in part gained from previous frontiers, thus fostering continuity and development, as in the case of the mining experience of Wisconsin, Illinois, and Iowa, which was applied to the mining laws of the Sierras.

Ever attentive to the geologists, Turner compared the method of analyzing the successive frontiers to the technique of geology in comparing older and newer rock formations. He saw "much truth" in the observations of the economic determinist, Achille Loria, who believed that the study of colonial life would clarify European development, presumably by revealing various recurrent historical processes that moved in inevitable stages. This currently popular aspect of "inevitability" was of course part and parcel of the social evolutionary errors of that day. Thus, in speaking of the various frontier stages, Turner could say that "the evolution of each into a higher stage has worked political transformations." Perhaps the most quoted sentences of this essay hinge on the social evolutionary idea:

> Stand at Cumberland Gap and watch the procession of civilization, marching single file—the buffalo following the trail to the salt springs, the Indian, the fur trader and hunter, the cattle-raiser, the pioneer farmer—and the frontier has passed by. Stand at South Pass in the Rockies a century later and see the same procession with wider intervals between. The unequal rate of advance compels us to distinguish the frontier into the trader's frontier, the rancher's frontier, or the miner's frontier, and the farmer's frontier.

This was no less than a mechanical process—so a reader would infer. "Thus," he observed, "civilization in America has followed the arteries made by geology, pouring an ever richer tide through them, until at last, the slender paths of aboriginal intercourse have been broadened and interwoven into the complex mazes of modern commercial lines."

Following the suggestions of certain geographers (e.g. Ratzel), he argued that the Indian frontier was a consolidating agent in our history, because the colonial need to meet such dangers overcame particularism and hence fostered nationalism. Besides, he thought, the increasing distance of the moving frontier from England encouraged self-reliance and independence. He stressed the East-West transfer of culture, together with the frontier influence on these customs and institutions: "The experience of the Carolina Cowpens guided the ranchers of Texas." Here he ignored the overwhelming Spanish-American influences of the Southwest: the *vaquero* (cowboy), the *rancho*, the *lariat*, the *chaparejos* ("chaps"), the *rodeo*, and even the *juzgado* ("hoosegow"). Again, following the inspiration of contemporary geographers, he pointed out such neglected social factors in history as the role of the salt springs in Kentucky settlement-founding and the influence of favorably situated soils and the mines.

He offered this major proposition: "The legislation which most developed the powers of the national government, and played the largest part in its activity, was conditioned on the frontier. Writers have discussed the subjects of tariff, land, and internal improvements, as subsidiary to the slavery question." But he weakened this highly plausible remark in the extravagance of the next sentence: "But when American history comes to be rightly viewed it will be seen that the slavery question is an incident." His favorite whipping boy in this regard was Professor Hermann von Holst of the University of Chicago, the popular author of the recently published seven-volume *Constitutional and Political History of the United States* (1876-92). This man, who fled the hated czarist autocracy to which he was born a subject, had so intense a hatred of slavery that Turner (and others) felt he had converted six of his volumes on constitutional history from 1828-61 to a mere history of slavery. Von Holst's dubious theory that the war was a slaveowner's conspiracy had a moralistic basis that Turner's scientism avoided, despite his insistence that history should serve social amelioration.

American nationalism was fostered by the frontier, urged Turner, not only by its pressures for national legislation in regard to land, tariffs, and internal improvements, but also by the frontier assimilation of nationalities derived from the East and Europe. On the other hand, New England was sectional because it represented an intensive English quality in Puritanism; tidewater English planters also retained their regional quality through their English heritage. By moving westward, these qualities declined, although Turner thought that the "greater New England" influence all the way to the Great Lakes, as in the Western Reserve, was a transplantation of the Puritan conscience. Otherwise he held to this argument for nationalism: "Mobility of population is death to localism." Even the fierce struggle of the sections over slavery did not diminish—except by way of exception— the fact of nationalism.

Like many others before him, Turner believed that the frontier's most important effect was in promoting democracy and individualism both here and abroad. Frontier individualism, often anarchic and rebellious, produced manhood suffrage and equalitarianism through new state constitutions and assured the triumph of Jackson and William Henry Harrison. Free land gave strength to individualism because "economic power secures political power." On the unfavorable side was the fact that the frontier was intolerant of administrative experience and education and hence gave rise to the spoils system, "lax business honor, inflated paper currency and wild-cat banking." In recent times, Populist agitation had revived these traits, which Turner looked upon as survivals of an earlier barbaric state. "A primitive society," he said, "can hardly be expected to show the intelligent appreciation of the complexity of business interests in a developed society." Bryan and Altgeld were not for Turner.

Yet Turner seemed sympathetic to the frontier debtor classes in their recurrent struggles against the eastern creditors—a struggle that was not altogether unlike the Populist and Bryan battles. In fact he made the East-West struggles of each frontier a frequent theme of his writings. Even frontier primitivism, aside from lawlessness, is described most sympathetically:

That coarseness and strength combined with acuteness and inquisitiveness; that practical, inventive turn of mind, quick to find expedients; that masterful grasp of material things, lacking in the artistic but powerful to effect great ends; that restless nervous energy; that dominant individualism, working for good and for evil, and withal that buoyancy and exuberance which comes with freedom—these are traits of the frontier, or traits called out elsewhere because of the existence of the frontier.

But he concluded his address for the Columbian Exposition quite soberly by reminding his auditors that after four centuries from the discovery of America, the frontier was gone. He expected that the intensive frontier experience of America would leave lasting results, even though "never again would such gifts of free land offer themselves." The frontier would no longer be "a gate of escape from the bondage of the past." Therefore, the first period of American history had closed. He let others speculate in after years as to the implications of his "closed space" theory. He had no suggestion as yet to offer regarding social planning, despite the unmatched opportunity for him to demonstrate his theory that history had its uses as a tool of social action.

The thirty-two-year-old historian had laid out the fruitful hypotheses which were sufficient to occupy the research years of many disciples. Obviously he had not reached these conclusions independently, for his empirical research had been small and fragmentary before 1893—merely a few articles in fact. He was heavily indebted, as already noted, to Ratzel and other geographers, geologists, sociologists, philosophers, and, of course, historians. All were saturated with social evolutionism. In the next few decades, even after Darwinism was driven back to the confines of biology, Turner retained the basic theses of 1893 with surprisingly few modifications. One can only infer that many of these hypotheses were for him acts of faith whose truth must be assumed.

Turner's evolutionism, at the turn of the century, was based on the analogy between cultural growth or social inheritance and plant inheritance. He supplemented the non-Darwinian "germ" theory of the German idealistic philosophers and their American disciple, George Bancroft, who clung to the mystical notion that Teutonic institutions "unfolded" into modern Anglo-Saxon institutions of parliaments, juries, and equal suffrage systems. Turner's moving frontier quite eradicated the faintest traces of the ancient Teutonic forest by creating anew the *genus Americanus*. He wrote as if these newly born frontier traits would be transmitted like the evolving species of the French zoologist, Lamarck. These organisms evolved in response to the stimulus of the environment, and the changes were carried on through the inheritance of acquired characteristics. Darwin built upon this idea but emphasized the selective agency of the environment in creating new species. Frontier traits would evolve in the Lamarckian way in response to environmental stimulus, but surviving remnants would remain even after the frontier was gone. This Lamarckian viewpoint is evident in Turner's essay of 1896 for the *Atlantic Monthly*, "The Problem of the West":

> The history of our political institutions, our democracy, is not a history of imitation, of simple borrowing; it is a history of the evolution and adaptation of organs in response to a changed environment, a history of new political species. In this sense, therefore, the West has been a constructive force of the highest significance in our life.

Again, evolutionary thought is at the core of his theory of the "section" as expressed in an essay-lecture of 1904, "Problems in American History":

> The American physical map may be regarded as a map of potential nations and empires each to be conquered and colonized, each to rise through stages of development, each to achieve a certain social and industrial unity,

each to possess certain fundamental assumptions, certain psychological traits, and each to interact with the others, and in combination to form that United States, the explanation of the development of which is the task of the historian.

However, he made a major exception to the rule of independent (American) social evolution in the case of New England where he relied upon the diffusionist idea that cultural institutions and attitudes were borrowed from abroad. Thus in "Dominant Forces in Western Life," he traced Populist traits back to New England's Shays's Rebellion and even to Old England's Cromwellian revolution. But he stopped short of Herbert B. Adams's Teutonic Forest.

In an essay of 1895, "Western State-Making in the Revolutionary Era," published in the *American Historical Review,* he tried to make clear that each frontier section did not evolve independently of others. "The frontier did not proceed on the principle of *tabula rasa;* it modified older forms, and infused into them the spirit of democracy." He tried to forestall the criticism (which came anyway from Benjamin Wright, Jr., in later years) that the frontier did *not* actually foster new political institutions, for he was quite aware that western states usually accepted the laws and constitutions of the older states. He recognized the existence of sharp class antagonisms in frontier sections between debtors and creditors, small farmers, and planters, even if he preferred to emphasize geographic lines.

In "Problems in American History," Turner called for an evolutionary historical science based on a comparative study of social changes. Hence he urged the fullest co-operation of all social scientists, emulating the example of the men in physics, chemistry, and mathematics. Henry Adams, too, had forecast a future science of history, and both men urged a developmental study of masses of people in the New World. Thus the laws and tendencies of history could be derived if historians ceased to bury themselves in "the complicated story of rival European nationalities." [7]

When Turner was elected president of the American Historical Association in 1910, he elaborated further upon his theories of history in "Social Forces in American History." [8] This contained much familiar material expressed in his 1891 essay on "The Significance of History," but it went on to show the elements of subjectivism in history. Each age served itself by writing its own history, and he hoped that "history may hold the lamp for conservative reform." He asked for more scientific hypotheses based on fruitful analogies between his-

tory and geology and dwelt upon the "multiple hypotheses" of the
geologist, Thomas C. Chamberlin, and others: "He (the geologist)
creates a whole family of possible explanations of a given problem, and
thus avoids the warping influence of partiality for a simple theory."
This approach made Ranke's idea of sticking to the facts and seeing
the past "as it actually was" misleadingly simple. Turner argued for a
much larger relativist element in historical interpretation:

> Those who insist that history is simply the effort to tell the thing as it was,
> to state the facts, are confronted with the difficulty that the fact which they
> represent is not planted on the solid ground of fixed conditions; it is in the
> midst and is itself a part of the changing currents, the complex and interact-
> ing influences of the time, deriving its significance as a fact from its rela-
> tions to the deeper-seated movements of the age, movements so gradual
> that often only the passing years can reveal the truth about the fact and its
> right to a place on the historian's page.

To him the facts could be understood, then, only in a clear-cut frame
of reference.

4

In 1902, Turner looked ahead beyond the passing frontier to speculate upon the new economic stages of capitalism, economic co-operation, and monopoly in his Phi Beta Kappa address at Northwestern,
"Contributions of the West to American Democracy." [9] He said that
the frontier was not only individualistic but also fostered co-operation
and helpful governmental intervention, such as aid to the states for
education by gifts from the public domain and federal aid to the western railroads. The arid Far West required large-scale irrigation and
hence stimulated both private and governmental co-operation. "In a
word, the physiographic province itself decreed that the destiny of
the frontier should be social rather than individual."

With the passing of the frontier came the need for social control.
Class cleavages appeared "accentuated by distinctions of nationality"
—a reference to the New Immigration. Socialism, Populism, and Bryan
democracy had disturbed politics and a new global phase of American
history had begun with the Spanish-American War. But instead of
urging progressive panaceas, he clung to the frontier emphasis upon
the ideal of individualism. He argued that the new captains of industry, the Rockefellers, the Carnegies, the Marshall Fields, the Mark
Hannas, were the successors of the frontier heroes, George Rogers
Clark, Andrew Jackson, and William Henry Harrison:

Long after the frontier period of a particular region of the United States has passed away, the conception of society, the ideals and aspirations which it produced, persist in the minds of the people. . . . Even those masters of industry and capital who have risen to power by the conquest of Western resources came from the midst of this society and still profess its principles.

So, to answer his own question, he was apparently not worried whether democracy could survive under such enlightened industrialists and merchants. It *could*.

This line of reasoning led him to make a cheerful forecast of the coming victory of Bigness, in which industrial geniuses, as the pathfinders of democracy, would achieve the kind of consolidations best adapted to democratic social control:

Socialistic writers have long been fond of pointing out also that these various concentrations pave the way for and make possible social control. From this point of view it is possible that the masters of industry may prove not so much an incipient aristocracy as the pathfinders for democracy in reducing the industrial world to systematic consolidation suited to democratic control. The great geniuses that have built up the modern industrial concentration were trained in the midst of democratic society. They were the product of these democratic conditions. Freedom to rise was the very condition of their existence.

He even quoted the conservative authority of President Charles Eliot of Harvard, who said that the corporation was a strong supporter of democratic institutions. (Did he know that Eliot had denounced unions as hostile to liberty?)

Elsewhere, however, he expressed a fear that millionaires might dominate the private college, and he urged support of the state university as a democratic antidote. To him the state university offered a check against uniformity of thought, because it represented all classes. Had Turner been consistent and used his previous argument that Rockefeller, Hanna, and other latter-day "pathfinders of democracy" systematized monopoly and thus assured democratic control, he would have said that, since these wealthy men came out of an erstwhile frontier community, they could not possibly change the democratic quality of the private college. But he did not trust this line of reasoning, for he and such socially minded colleagues of the University of Wisconsin as Professor Richard T. Ely were concerned about the fate of Rockefeller's University of Chicago, where President Harper had ejected a critic of the great utilities by the name of Professor E. W. Bemis. While Rockefeller's biographer, Allan Nevins, denies that the oil magnate meddled with the institutions that he endowed—and this seems borne out by the minutes of the University—contemporaries like Ely believed that the Bemis case proved that the private university was dominated by the captain of industry.

5

In 1906, after publishing so many stimulating essays and addresses, Turner issued his first book, *The Rise of the New West, 1819-1829,* which appeared in Albert Bushnell Hart's comprehensive *American Nation* series of twenty-eight volumes (1903-18)—few of them in the same creative class as Turner's. (In the 1950s this series was replaced by Harper & Brothers with books that were much more analytical, readable, richer in sources, and rounded in subject matter—in the New History tradition—than the books they supplanted.) The period of 1819 to 1829 signified to him the American victory of economic and political independence, marked by westward expansion along the Gulf of Mexico, the rapid extension of the plantation system, the unilateral statement of the Monroe Doctrine, and the revolution in transportation and industry. The seemingly contradictory chapter title of "Nationalism and Sectionalism" reflected his idea that the United States "was more like an empire than a nation." He elaborated upon his famous idea of "sections"—that these regional units, not the states, were the basic federal components of the country. Each had its interests, demands, and leaders and often combined with other sections in a struggle for power. Changing political doctrines, as in the case of Calhoun and Webster, merely reflected changing sectional interests. By 1829, Calhoun led sectionalism upon the offensive against nationalism through his nullifying philosophy in the South Carolina Exposition. Most of the book was a period survey according to sections, though he admitted that the growth of American democracy, strongest in the West and the Middle region, cut across all sections and divided the people "on the lines of social classes." But his brief class analyses were usually buried in his quasi-geographic determinism.

As in his previous essays, he depicted New England as unique because of its non-frontier origins across the sea, particularly the social inheritance of Puritanism. He described the shift of the industrial center of gravity from the harbors to the waterfalls, from commerce and navigation to manufactures. Agriculture was in decline, and old settlers were deserting their worn-out lands that could not compete with the lands of the newer West. In church polity, the newer rural communities of Baptists and Methodists were assailing the conservative rule of the Congregationalists and Unitarianism, and liberalizing social reforms were gaining.

The Middle region was "a zone of transition" between East and West, North and South, involving a cultural mediation or interaction between sharply distinct areas. He mentioned the large non-English groups but made no attempt to explain their cultural influence, and he attributed the democratic reforms such as the public schools, modern prisons, and civic gains to western influences. As usual, Turner ignored parallel developments in England and elsewhere in western Europe, leaving the impression of frontier uniqueness.

In dealing with the South, Turner consulted his colleague and disciple, Ulrich B. Phillips, for his intimate knowledge of that area, and applied a strict sectional concept. This meant a changing, evolving series of "Souths." He showed how the former diversity of the South in population and economy gave way to assimilative influences and the extension of the cotton plantation to the Southwest. Politics reflected this transformation: Charleston, the center of the old plantation area and now in competition with the Southwest, led the revolt.

The chapters on western colonization, trade, and politics were more factual than was Turner's habit, but he repeated his characteristic generalizations. "The wilderness ever opened a gate of escape to the poor, the discontented, and the oppressed." The forest myth was given an uncompromising nationalistic form: "Western democracy was no theorist's dream. It came, stark and strong and full of life, from the American forest." He also described the colonization routes, the mode of travel, and the invasion of southerners into the Old Northwest.

Turner's scientism did not exclude personality altogether, even if free will and choice seem lost at times beneath deterministic environmental factors. He tried to understand the outlook and whims of John Quincy Adams and accepted the old Puritan's derogatory self-estimate, "I am a man of reserved, cold, austere, and forbidding manners." He preferred the more "engaging personalities" of Clay and Jackson, spokesmen for the West. Adams did not quite conform to the correct sectional pattern of New England, because he was an enthusiastic supporter of centralizing policies. Furthermore, Turner could not rob Adams of the honor of issuing the Monroe Doctrine, even though this policy seemed to belong to the western tradition of "pushing back Europe" from American borders. He offset this by dwelling on the role of Henry Clay of Kentucky, the real leader of our hemispheric policy through his Pan-Americanism.

The Rise of the New West was extravagantly praised by *The Independent* of June 28, 1906: "No more profound study of any period of American history has been written." This high judgment was shared by innumerable historians decades after the book appeared. Roosevelt and Wilson, Rhodes and McLaughlin were among the early enthusiasts, although they noted stylistic shortcomings.

During the 'twenties Turner lectured and wrote articles on the frontier section and other related concepts and added important modifications of his theories. These were collected in a posthumous volume in 1932 under the title, *The Significance of Sections in American History*, and awarded a Pulitzer Prize. The essays discussed the experience of sectional conflict and compromise, suggesting that postwar Europe had a model for federation in the history of the frontier sections. In "Sections and Nations," originally published in 1922, he insisted that he was not an extreme environmentalist but allowed for the diversity of human motives: [10]

No single factor is determinative. Men are not absolutely dictated to by climate, geography, soils, or economic interests. The influence of the stock from which they sprang, the inherited ideals, the spiritual factors, often triumph over the material interests. There is also the influence of personality. Men do follow leaders, and sometimes into paths inconsistent with the section's material interests. But in the long run the statesman must speak the language of his people on fundamentals, both of interests and ideals. Not seldom the ideals grow out of the interests.

This fresh emphasis upon free-will factors in history was indeed needed to offset the overwhelming impression of scientific determinism gained by readers from his previous writings. He was now concerned with the need for cultural diversity for a federated Europe, and for social experimentation. Thus, he interpreted the frontier-bred sections as possessing traits that acted as "restraints upon a deadly conformity." Yet a reader of his earlier writings might be led to expect that the recurrent revolutionary process and a frontier indifference to the fine arts could only lead to a growing sameness of culture. He had usually ignored the rich cultural borrowings from Europe and even now took a condescending attitude toward effete Europe, chided her addiction to force, and offered to teach her the democratic lessons to be learned from the frontier.

For fifteen years before his death in 1932, Turner gathered notes on a major work, *The United States, 1830-1850*, but he died before he finished his final chapters or revised his earlier material. Fortunately, his devoted student, Avery O. Craven, edited and brought out the volume in 1935, permitting no important changes from the original. Its 591 pages were almost double the size of *The Rise of the New West*. It gave much more descriptive factual detail than he usually offered alongside of imaginative generalizations. The Darwinian emphasis on "successive stages" was far less pronounced than before. Apparently thinking of his critics who were suspicious of his heavily patterned history, he said disarmingly, "Not all regions of property and prosperity voted Whig and not all the poor regions of rough country were predominantly Democratic. There were exceptions that prevent the historian from formulating a law of political distribution on physical or economic grounds." At this stage of his intellectual development, he could probably have added "or any other law."

Consistently, however, as in his first book, he used a regional and sectional approach. His sections of 1830-50 were now New England, the Middle Atlantic states, the South Atlantic states, the South Central states, the North Central states, and Texas and the Far West. As ever, he was alert to show relationships between physical environment and social institutions: "For example, the Disciples of Christ were proportionately strongest in the areas of rough country settled by the Southern-upland pioneers, and especially in the driftless area of southern Ohio and Indiana." Once more he used the theme of a Puritan New England conscience transmitted westward to greater New England; this time he showed the influence of the receding frontier on the older section:

Beyond any other New Englander, Emerson caught the spirit of the New West, America's youthful buoyancy, faith, and exaggeration, the belief in the perfectibility of the common man, the connection of wagon and star, the appeal to the imagination made by vast spaces, affording opportunity for a newer and finer society.

In dealing with the South Atlantic states, he rejected the notion of the "solid South," but he apparently agreed with U. B. Phillips in making the presence of the Negro the most important and determining social factor. He saw the South Central states mediating between a rising plantation society and a declining frontier, as the eastern planters brought their slaves into that area. For the North Central states, he called attention to the recurrent frontier types of the cowboy, lumberman, and the lawless character of the Far West.

He gave much more attention than before to European influences. When he discussed the coming of the Germans, he dipped into original German accounts concerning the reasons and background of emigration. The Irish, too, received more space. In dealing with Horace Mann's educational reforms, he devoted two sentences to the borrowings from Prussia (omitting Switzerland, France, and England), but minimized this by saying that the original autocratic assumptions were set aside by "distinctive marks of American democratic and individualistic ideals." Later, he retreated from the constant reiteration of indigenous frontier democracy: "But, far too frequently, the new Western commonwealths paid only lip tribute to the relations between liberty, democracy, and the public schools." Possibly he was thinking of the Hoosier schoolmaster and the hickory stick.

His final political chapters continued the usual frontier section theme connecting regional issues with national politics and legislation. Jackson, of course, was his hero, and his triumph was a pivotal fact for social democracy:

> The instincts of the American people in supporting him conformed to the general drift of the tendencies of this New World democracy—a democracy which preferred persons to property, an active share by the people to the greater system and efficiency of a scientific administration by experts or by an established elite who dealt with the people from above.

The last reference was probably to John Quincy Adams's ideal of scientific administration by the government of public lands and transportation.

6

The year of Turner's death, 1932, witnessed a most impressive adoption of the theory of the closed frontier by the Democratic presidential candidate, Franklin D. Roosevelt, whose Commonwealth Club address, delivered in San Francisco, was said to be the product of the social planner, Adolf A. Berle. The author had obviously read Turner's essay of 1893, and probably his plea for social planning as well. Here the ideas appeared unmistakably in their pessimistic form: [11]

> Our last frontier has long since been reached, and there is practically no more free land. More than half of our people do not live on the farms or on lands and cannot derive a living by cultivating their own property. There is no safety valve in the form of a Western prairie to which those thrown out of work by the Eastern economic machines can go for a new start.

This argument afforded a theoretical introduction to the NIRA based on the pessimistic assumptions of a relatively declining population, a finished industrial plant, and inevitable monopoly.

Meanwhile, social evolutionism had relaxed its iron grip over the social studies and angry critics felt encouraged to attack the master's theories. Besides, the depression years offered an intellectual climate favorable to class conflict theories, rather than geographic determinism. Louis Hacker of Columbia charged that Turner neglected the growth of monopolistic capitalism and imperialism, and that he disregarded the basic class antagonisms in American history and the European equivalents to American experience. Hacker considered the concept of the section as misleading. "Turner and his followers," he wrote in *Sections or Classes?*, "were the fabricators of a tradition which is not only fictitious but also to a very large extent positively harmful." Turner, as has been noted, did use the idea of class conflict as an integral part of his sectional analysis, and did discuss the rise of big business but the regional emphasis tended to blur the class factor.

Professor Fred Shannon, another friend of social planning, marshaled census data in approved Turnerian fashion to undermine the safety-valve theory of surplus labor. He cited the facts that American economic crises and strikes had not been averted by cheap or free lands, not even by the Homestead Act. He saw in the census figures proof that few industrial laborers became homesteaders. Migrants to the farms usually lacked capital and became tenant farmers or farm wage laborers. Cities were much better safety outlets for depressed farmers, judging by the heavy migration to the cities in the decades before 1890.

Benjamin F. Wright, Jr., a Harvard political scientist, made few concessions to Turner's idea that the frontier was an innovating political force—a position that Turner had actually qualified a good deal. It was obvious that western constitutions imitated eastern models, adhering to the single executive, bicameral legislature, the system of checks and balances, the court hierarchy armed with the power of judicial review, and the standard bill of rights, Wright took specific exception to the statement that the West was the leader in manhood suffrage. However, he conceded that the West accelerated the growth of the democratic movement while not changing its direction. He held that frontiersmen were among the underprivileged of the older states and hence chose to imitate those constitutional devices most calculated to increase their share of political power. Besides, the frontiersmen were so far from a radical outlook that they did not tinker with contractual rights, property safeguards, slavery, or the status of

women. But actually, there were many exceptions to Wright's assertions.

From Yale, George Wilson Pierson attacked both the contradictions
and lacunae in Turner's theses. How could the frontier be simultaneously a sectionalizing and a nationalizing force, he asked. Was it not
crude geographic determinism to make inert minerals transform an
entire society into new forms of economy? Was it not a gross materialist tendency to omit or minimize the force of tradition or habit?
Yet Pierson admitted that he would not discard Turner's entire thesis
nor overlook his insights. Too much remained that was quite reasonable and corresponding to fact.[12]

7

Turner's idea (borrowed from Loria) that the frontier had creative
innovative force was given fresh application by a "disciple," Walter
Prescott Webb of the University of Texas, who scarcely knew Turner
but shared in the mainstream of frontier thought. His book, *The Great
Plains* (1931), was the product of a man reared in that section and
convinced of its uniqueness. He professed to tell "what happened in
American civilization when in its westward progress it emerged from
the woods and essayed life on the Plains," and concentrated on this
flat, treeless, and semi-arid expanse of cattle frontier, mining frontier,
and homesteaders' lands stretching from the 98-degree meridian on
the East to the Rockies. Instead of using the Turnerian idea of repetitive sectional processes, he dwelt upon another—and primarily Lorian
—suggestion: the idea that each physical environment draws forth
unique cultural results:

> The frontier experiences on the Great Plains were not, moreover, a repeti-
> tion of frontier experiences in the region from which the settlers came. A
> frontiersman from the woodland region found on the Great Plains many
> novelties, many new experiences. Woodcraft was there displaced by plains-
> craft.

Thus, he showed how the Great Plains, which had baffled the
colonizing efforts of the Spanish, had been conquered by Americans
by such inventions as the six-shooter, which enabled the armed horse-
man to overcome the Indian mounted on a swift steed. Webb recognized the many contributions of the Spanish to the cattle industry,
but he stressed the newer range techniques of the Americans. The
homesteader used newly invented barbed wire to keep cattle away

from his crops and thus was able to dispense with the prohibitively expensive wood fences. He mastered the semi-arid soil through irrigation devices such as windmills and by dry-farming techniques. Webb pictured briefly and simply the cultural aspects of the story of the Great Plains—for instance, cowboy ballads and novels of adventure.

Among Turner's disciples was Avery O. Craven of the University of Chicago. He developed the suggestions of Turner and the geographers regarding the significance of soil exhaustion as a factor in historical change. First, he published a monograph on the influence of soil exhaustion in Virginia upon the life of that state and then wrote a biography of the Virginian, Edmund Ruffin, a distinguished agricultural reformer, as well as the fire-eating politician who claimed the honor of firing the first cannon at Fort Sumter. Ulrich B. Phillips of the University of Michigan, as noted elsewhere, also applied the Turner theories to the South by treating that region as an evolving frontier and plantation section.

In the Far West, Herbert E. Bolton of Stanford trained western historians to transcend the Anglo-American synthesis of Turner with an Anglo-French or an Anglo-Spanish viewpoint based on archives in Paris, Madrid, and Mexico City, as well as collections within the United States. The interaction of the Americas as a unit absorbed his attention and became the core of his most popular academic lectures. In this spirit he wrote several volumes on the significance of the Spanish borderlands in the light of frontier conditions, the colonization of North America, and the advance of Spanish conquistadors like Coronado or missionaries like Father Kino, ever stressing the role of geography, topography, and anthropology.

In 1911, Professor Bolton left Stanford for the University of California where he was not only a history professor but also the curator of the special Bancroft Library, which claimed over a million volumes by the 1940s. This involved a huge collection of Far Western and Latin American (particularly Mexican) materials in history and anthropology acquired from the successful California bookseller, publisher, and historian, Hubert H. Bancroft (1832-1918), who had spent much of a lifetime collecting manuscripts, rare books, maps, newspapers, scrapbooks, pamphlets, and numerous reminiscences of old settlers that had been dictated to him or his assistants. Bancroft boasted of the authorship of at least sixty volumes of histories and pamphlets dealing with California, other parts of the Far West, and Latin America. He made no secret of his "factory" of history-writing. Scores of untrained assistants prepared a master index of the collections or took notes copiously, while others wrote up assigned topics. The results were turned over to Bancroft, who could then take up the task of composition—or could turn it over to his staff. Other historians had used assistants, but none in quite this manner. Yet the Pacific Coast branch of the American Historical Association avowed in 1918, the year Bancroft died, that "he created the conditions which made possible the first scientific treatment of the history of one-half of our continent." And his sympathetic biographer, John Caughey, a specialist in California and western history, notes that many of the Bancroft volumes remain the best reference books in certain areas.[13]

Turner's ideas inspired men of stature to embark on investigations of new frontier questions: the influence of the frontier on diplomacy, land speculation, railroad colonization of public lands, conservation, agrarian discontent, the "sod-house frontier," fur trade problems, Indian influences, transportation studies, and the impact of sectionalism. At Harvard, Turner's former assistant, Frederick Merk, produced many frontier scholars as well as certain writings in this tradition.

One of Turner's contemporaries, Clarence W. Alvord (1868-1928) of the University of Illinois (and Minnesota) joined the master (and many others) in demonstrating the influence of the West upon British imperial diplomacy. He was born in Massachusetts of old stock and had studied in Berlin as well as with the rising history department of the University of Chicago. His chief work was *The Mississippi Valley in British Politics: A Study of Trade, Land Speculation, and Experiments in Imperialism Culminating in the American Revolution* (1917). He stressed the Imperial Perspective which looked to decisions made in London regarding the fate of the transmontane West acquired from France in 1763. Most important were his arduous efforts to discover and publish innumerable documents, such as the *Kaskaskia Records* (1909) for the old French settlements in Illinois, and the fourteen volumes of the Illinois Historical Society *Collections*. He was not only editor of the excellent *Centennial History of Illinois* but wrote the first volume in that series. Finally, he was one of the chief founders of the (originally) regional journal, *The Mississippi Valley Historical Review*. However, another disciple of Turner, James Alton James, took issue with Alvord's imperial perspective when the latter maintained that it was Lord Shelbourne's good intentions rather than George Rogers Clark's conquest which gave the United States the Old Northwest at the peace table in 1783. James's own biography of Clark minimized the transatlantic factor.[14]

At the University of Wisconsin the Turner tradition continued to dominate graduate studies under Frederic L. Paxson, author of *The Last Frontier* (1910),[15] John D. Hicks, and Merle Curti. Hicks took up the theme of the passing frontier in *The Populist Revolt* (1931), an interpretation of rural revolt behind the Farmers' Alliance and the People's party. He declared that "it was only as the West wore out and cheap lands were no longer abundant that well-developed agrarian movements began to appear." The first chapter, "The Frontier Background," concluded that the building of the transcontinental railroad was the beginning of the end of frontier conditions. He dwelt upon the rural parts of the Central states, where farmers struggled with failing crops, low prices, debts, and taxes. Populism left a heritage of democratic electoral devices, currency reform, rural credit, and the national control of business. *The Populist Revolt* won scholarly acclaim, but its sales were modest (like most history books of the time). It was readable, comprehensive, and based on large amounts of letters, government materials, representative newspapers, pamphlets, and special studies.

Merle Curti tested parts of the Turner thesis successfully in *The Making of an American Community: A Case Study of Democracy in a Frontier County* (1959). Aided by a very competent staff and vast amounts of local records, diaries, newspapers, correspondence, and interviews, he constructed the most analytical study of a county ever done by a historian. Trempealeau County in southwest Wisconsin illustrated Turner's frontier stages of early development, showed that frontier individualism existed side by side with social planning, and pictured the social mobility of the New Immigration as well as the Old. Here New England institutions such as the township were carried over and permitted democracy to flourish vigorously at the grass roots.

Turner's disciples often spoke of striking analogies to the frontier process discernible in the forests and plains of other countries but failed to convince the generality of historians. Russian Siberia of the nineteenth century, with its cheap lands, primitive settlements, and great resources, displayed some democratic traits among the peasantry that marked them off from their fellows in other parts of the Czarist domain; but their cultural inheritance, tight government controls, and special environmental factors overcame the latent democratic qualities. New France of colonial times also showed wilderness independence for a time before it yielded to the conservative and centralizing qualities of church and state. Australia, too, seemed to resemble superficially a frontier environment, but its vast arid section and national policies favored monopolistic ranch owners and irrigation companies rather than the small farmer pictured by Turner.[16] Besides, the younger historians were much more suspicious of analogies based upon geographic determinism than their elders had been. Too few were willing to accept Walter Webb's imaginative theory of a world-encircling frontier developing since 1500 and conditioning the rest of the globe in the style suggested by Turner. The cultural approach to history, with its idea of the diffusion or borrowing of culture, seemed more convincing.

8

By the mid-twentieth century, courses in western history were not as popular as during the 1930s, but they continued to reflect the influence of Turner. His scientism, particularly his social evolutionism, aroused critics, but none could deny the amazing amount of ideas that were still usable. It was no longer necessary for anyone to point out the importance of the West as a key to American development. If anything, the danger remained that teachers of American history would ignore European influences and seek historical explanations solely in indigenous frontier developments. Few textbooks troubled to point out that European equivalents existed for the allegedly unique democratic movements stemming from western experience. The advance of intellectual history, it is true, inevitably suggested some affinities with the European mind.

Turner had stimulated economic and technological studies of America. Hundreds of theses and general books had traced the influence of land policy, transportation, and the economic bases of sectional pressures on state and local politics. The story of the struggle of creditor and debtor classes, going far beyond Bryan to colonial times, was now easily recognizable for the various "sections" of America. His ideal of the New History had been reinforced by James Harvey Robinson and his followers, and his focus on the present as the point of departure for historians had become a commonplace, despite protests that violence was being done to the integrity of the past. Map and graph studies had become so prolific that few thought of them as particularly Turnerian. With the passing of the Great Depression and the New Deal, fears receded that the Closed Frontier had ended American dynamic growth. Like Turner in his later years a new generation believed in the need for social planning to meet urban conditions.

☆ 11 ☆

Von Holst to Dunning:
Abolitionists and Revisionists
(1880-1910)

1

Historians of the 'eighties and 'nineties discovered their epic in the
Civil War. The war-guilt controversy North and South gathered fuel
from the publication of numerous relevant autobiographies, reminiscences, biographies, private letters, and official collections. GAR committees and patriotic societies, as vigilant sentinels of the Union cause,
perused history textbooks, while Southern historical societies spurred
on teachers and research men to examine the Lost Cause. Although
Congressmen had kept historians on short rations since those distant
years when they aided Jared Sparks in publishing revolutionary records, they were now eager to respond generously to the insistent demands for the publication of Civil War records.

Therefore, Congress voted ample funds to publish and distribute
widely entire sets of the 128 volumes of the *Official Records of the
Union and Confederate Armies* (1880-1901). Nor did the Congressmen
neglect the Navy, for they financed the publication and free distribution of a parallel naval series of thirty volumes which appeared during
the years 1894-1922. Southerners preferred the term "War Between
the States" as more in keeping with the rightness of the state sovereignty position than the derogatory label of "War of the Rebellion"

attached to the official volumes, but they were content with the huge quantity and objective presentation of the Confederate documents.

Hermann Eduard von Holst (1841-1904), one of the most vehement abolitionist historians of this era, reflected the European tendency to see the sectional struggle almost entirely in moral terms centering upon the evil of slavery. He was born into the decayed German gentry of the Baltic provinces of Russia, one of ten children in a Lutheran minister's household. Financial difficulties did not prevent him from supporting himself through *gymnasium* and the University of Heidelberg. He was trained by the Prussian school of historians, among them Treitschke, which meant he received a large dose of German unification and of the virtues of Prussian centralization as against states' rights. In his *History* he was to cite approvingly a comment of Bismarck made in 1872 that the lesson of the American Civil War was unification: "Sovereignty can only be a unit and it must remain a unit." He transferred to America the lesson that Germany was best served by unification and escape from petty state sovereignties.

Von Holst could not remain in Russia. His hatred of Czarist autocracy grew following the attempt on the life of Alexander II in 1866, when the police arrested numerous suspects. In Leipzig he published an attack on the regime which promptly led to an order for his arrest, but von Holst chose to go to America rather than Siberia. In New York City he encountered great difficulties in finding suitable work. He turned to manual labor, lived in a cold room with other laborers, and finally took up tutoring. Fortunately he secured a historical research commission from Bremen merchants, and well-wishers aided him to obtain a teaching post at the University of Strasbourg, which was reorganized as a German institution following the Franco-Prussian War. There he began his ambitious multi-volume work, *The Constitutional and Political History of the United States*. The first volume was such a success that he gained a professorship at the University of Freiburg. This position enabled him to continue his research in London and in the United States.

President William R. Harper of the University of Chicago sent him a generous offer in 1892 to come as chairman of the history department in the newly established institution. His vigorous lecturing style and emphatic opinions won him student enthusiasm, but his sweeping generalizations and references to American naïveté and superficiality annoyed others. Ill-health led to his early retirement.[1]

The first volume in the German edition of von Holst's *History* circulated in 1874, and the American translation came two years later;

thereafter, the German and American editions of the other six volumes appeared about the same time until the last was printed in 1892. During the 'eighties he also published biographies of John C. Calhoun and John Brown. Primarily concerned with political and constitutional history, he depended upon such political sources as the *Congressional Globe;* his use of newspapers, though not too extensive by present-day standards, was novel enough to inspire Rhodes.

The *History* reflected von Holst's dogmatic nature, his use of absolute moral judgments, and his tendency to praise or arraign key historical figures. The collective "slavocracy," however, was the chief villain of his piece. His analytical approach, largely topical, often resulted in profitable insights, but it sacrificed the art of narrative. More of a political scientist at heart than a historian, he neglected historical development for constitutional philosophy.

In the first volume, *State Sovereignty and Slavery,* he stressed the binding nature of sovereignty and argued that the Union was actually older than the states. In fact he condemned practically all particularist tendencies in American constitutional history, seeing in them factors causing the Civil War. To him the Constitution was filled with dangerous ambiguities; yet, Americans tended to think of that document as the divine product of the unique wisdom of the founding fathers rather than of economic and political necessities. This reference to divine inspiration, he said in a caustic aside, "is one of the standing formulas in which the self-complacency and pride of a people who esteem themselves special objects of the care of the Ruler of the Universe, find expression." His own belief was clear enough: "The historical fact is that the Constitution had been extorted from the grinding necessity of a reluctant people." The political thinking of Americans seemed to him more superficial and immature than that of Englishmen or Germans, though superior on concrete questions. Furthermore, in the United States the masses were moved by vague maxims of inconsistent idealism, while their leaders worshiped the masses. The poison of state sovereignty and localism led political parties and leaders to represent localities rather than the nation and to act as "the mere mouthpieces of their immediate constituents." Calhoun and his disciples did not invent nullification and secession, for these grew out of the life and circumstances of the people and the ambiguities of the Constitution. There was at least a residuum of truth in many of his critical comments about the course of American development.

The second volume, *Jackson's Administration—Annexation of Texas,* showed how a sinister manipulative slavocracy absorbed Texas, provoked the war with Mexico, and tried to spread slavery westward. Presidents Polk, Pierce, and Buchanan were mere "doughfaces" serving every bidding of the slavocracy. Of Polk's war declaration he wrote, "The very school boys laughed at the fable of the 'urgent necessity' of defending Texas." The next volume, *The Annexation of Texas—Compromise of 1850*, pictured slavery as a parasite which devitalized the South: "She [the South] saw the North, like the giant in the fable, filled with fresh strength at every contact with the earth, while her own flesh shrivelled on her bones and her sinews relaxed."

The preface to his fourth volume, *Compromise of 1850—Kansas-Nebraska Bill*, stated confidently that "other investigators will have to reckon with my labors" and launched on the theme of the irrepressible nature of the conflict between slavery and freedom. However, as he was too much the moralist to deny personal guilt and responsibility in history, he did not stress the inevitable. The Kansas-Nebraska Act came as a climax in a highly moral drama, and its chief proponent, Stephen A. Douglas, was pictured as a liar, an irresponsible manipulator, and a cheap politician. Von Holst believed that Douglas was motivated by a desire to defeat Pierce; he hoped to win southern support for the presidency by repealing the Missouri Compromise.

The final volume concluded with von Holst's central theme of "the dark powers which unbound the furies of civil war." These were the doctrine of non-coercion (of a state by the federal government), the slavocratic interpretation of state sovereignty, and slavery. Much as he admired Lincoln as a democrat and opponent of slavery, he felt that the President tended to follow the same non-coercion theory that had paralyzed Buchanan into dangerous inactivity. However, Lincoln had been able to act because the Southern Confederacy provoked actual war. He looked sympathetically upon John Brown's attack on Harpers Ferry as an act that awakened the conscience of a nation. Brown was no lunatic but, as his behavior under interminable questioning revealed, a man of great dignity and calm bravery, quite conscious that his enterprise was doomed from the beginning.

Von Holst's brilliance did not win him a large or lasting following, for his weaknesses were too great. However stimulating his insights and syntheses and meticulous the accuracy of his facts, he lacked attractive literary qualities and he held *ex parte* theses that became quickly outdated early in the twentieth century. He gave only the most cursory attention to the economic and social forces beneath constitutional developments and produced oversimplified explanations of great historical movements. But unlike the next generation of "scientific historians"—at least a large branch of them—he had no fear of expressing a definite philosophic position or of reaching conclusions.[2]

2

Much more urbane in temperament, but no less sincere in his anti-slavery sentiments, was James Schouler (1839-1920), a New Englander educated at Harvard. The son of a Scottish immigrant who edited a Whig newspaper and of a mother belonging to an old New England family, he had studied law, volunteered in the Civil War, and enjoyed a lucrative law practice until progressive deafness led him to make a career of writing legal treatises and histories. He commenced research in the 1870s on what became a seven-volume *History of the United States of America under the Constitution*, but the publishers were wary and the first volume did not appear until 1880; four more were issued by 1891, a sixth in 1899, and a seventh, after an even longer wait, in 1913. Meanwhile, in 1891, Herbert Baxter Adams of Johns Hopkins invited him to give a course of lectures in American history, and he remained there until 1908.

Like von Holst, he chose to write on the era between the formation of the government and the Civil War; later he advanced into the Reconstruction period. The "venerable" Bancroft's ten volumes, which Schouler admired, began with colonial foundations but never went beyond the writing of the Constitution. McMaster's eight volumes from the Revolution to the Civil War began to appear in 1883 and were completed in 1913. More important was the inspiration of Richard Hildreth's *History of the United States*, covering the colonial and early national period to 1821. Schouler's preface of 1880 rated Hildreth above the others:

We can find but one work, that of Mr. Hildreth, which shows the diligent research of a scholar among the accumulated records of 1783-1821, a work of whose high merits as to the three final volumes I may be permitted to speak after a minute comparison of almost every page with authentic materials elsewhere gathered.

But he quickly added that he differed from Hildreth in many particulars and estimates; and he had consulted many new collections dealing with key figures.

Schouler anticipated Ulrich B. Phillips's thesis regarding the racial factor in Southern history. He said that slavery "came to exist purely as a race institution; as the subjection, not of debtors or vanquished enemies, but of an alien, uncouth-looking people, whom the Caucasian could hardly regard without mirth and contempt, even when moved to compassion for their wrongs." He did not necessarily share this opinion and added his observation, "Americans boasted their descent from Indian chiefs, but none took pride in an Ethiopian pedigree." Like von Holst he frequently made moralistic judgments. He liked to contrast the freedom-loving, progressive Northern states with the medieval, reactionary South.

Like von Holst and Hildreth, he felt that economic pressures were the chief forces behind the Constitution. But he would not accept the extreme centralizing philosophy of the German or the ideas expressed by Hamilton in calling for more power at the Capitol. While he conceded the ability of the secretary of the treasury, he criticized his distrust of the people, his conceit, and personal weaknesses. "Hamilton frankly avowed his conviction that mankind were vicious, except a few choice spirits, and should be ruled upon that theory," he wrote, adding that Hamilton showed "eccentricity of thought, that confident reliance upon his unaided judgment, and that equally confident way of impressing his convictions upon others as truth eternal, which aided so greatly to benumb his capacity for successful leadership in a republic like ours." Yet Schouler spoke of Hamilton's "truly noble disposition," while he was criticizing his neglect of the nation's welfare:

To Hamilton belongs the lasting honor of founding the national credit of this new Union at the outset upon the firm rock of punctilious good faith. But State credit was not placed by his endeavors on an equally sound basis, his controlling purpose being to make the influence of the thirteen commonwealths wholly and forever subsidiary and dependent upon the nation.

Just as Schouler was ready to disparage Hamilton's extreme centralization, he had only praise for Jefferson's policies, denying that the states' rights sentiments of the Kentucky and Virginia Resolutions resembled the nullificationism of Calhoun. When he wrote volume two dealing with the Jefferson-Madison administrations, he took notice of the recent *History* of Henry Adams, whose anti-Jefferson comments annoyed him:

An extensive and valuable work, which shows much scholarly research, and brings to view many important facts from foreign archives hitherto inaccessible; but which appears to be written, one must regret to add, in quite a disparaging strain.

When Henry Adams read this, he chose to distort this comment grossly in his own inimitable way:

Happening to take up a volume of a certain Mr. Schouler's history, I was struck the other day by finding a prefatory remark in which Mr. Schouler said that he had stolen out of my books all that seemed to him worth taking, and that anyway, my history was not good for much, because of its depreciatory spirit.

Totally unlike Adams's judgment of Jefferson is Schouler's admiring observation. "A parting radiance, indeed, lingers about this second administration of Jefferson, to be remembered like that of the last sunset before a storm at sea; it was a miniature golden age of American history."

His fears of Hamiltonian institutions did not prevent his criticizing Jackson's methods of waging war on the second United States Bank, for he considered that institution far less severe in its regulatory policies than similar central banks abroad; despite certain abuses, it had rendered very useful services to the financial structure of the country. Jackson's naïve policy of fostering the state banks merely created a composite monster:

We have found no fault with Jackson's policy of suppressing the Bank by vetoing its recharter, but with his meddlesome transfer of the deposits, and most of all because he battered away at this old temple of the faith without the least conception of what new one should be erected in its stead.

By the time Schouler reached his final volume in 1913, which covered the years 1865-77, he had to compete with James Ford Rhodes's extensive history, which began with the Compromise of 1850 and also halted—temporarily, as it turned out—with 1877. Schouler was generous in his evaluation:

I have relied greatly upon the judicious and accurate recital of Mr. Rhodes, with whose general views I find myself in harmony. But I have studies and recollections of my own to present for those eight important years.

Later, in the same volume, he added:

James Ford Rhodes, who has composed the standard narrative covering this Reconstruction period, is justly considered a fair-minded and painstaking historian, accurate and resourceful in his general work. But I think his chapters which relate to the years 1865-1869 are quite unjust to [Andrew] Johnson.

This disagreement about President Johnson grew out of Schouler's use of new correspondence and a logical reassessment of the evidence

cited by Rhodes and by William Dunning, who had discovered that
Johnson's first congressional message had been written by George
Bancroft. Schouler revised downward the older friendly treatment of
the Radical Republicans. He rejected Rhodes's emphasis on Johnson's
crude frontier antecedents and character and said that the same could
be said of Lincoln. In defending the moderate Lincoln-Johnson Reconstruction policy, he attacked Thaddeus Stevens as "coarse and
abusive" and minimized Charles Sumner's sympathy for the Negro.

Schouler's animated style was most effective amid these numerous
controversial issues, but he lost many readers by his incredibly ill-
advised chapter organization. While he improved upon von Holst by
inserting at least a chapter on social history in each volume and satisfied any reader's desire for political detail, he chose to arrange each
chapter according to congressional sessions and presidential administrations, thus imposing a most unconvincing political synthesis within
brief two-year periods. Fortunately, Schouler wrote too well to lose
himself in the bare annalistic organization characteristic of the medieval chronicles, but his organizing principle was not too far from it.
He did not apologize for his overemphasis on politics: "History, in
short, is the record of consecutive events—of consecutive public
events."

The narrative suffered at times from eccentric language and flagrant
anti-Irish prejudices. When he dealt with the anti-Catholic riots of
1834, he was much more incensed by the riots promoted by the Irish
themselves. "Here in the earliest riots, Irish Democrats, an unwashed
crowd, were the aggressors." Speaking of their anti-abolitionist and
election riots, he observed tartly, "Unlettered and boozy foreigners,
the scum of European society, made a large fraction in the commo-
tions we have mentioned."

In this volume, as in later professional papers, he stated his belief
that the historian must make evaluations according to his own per-
ceptions and judgments. "It is not in nature to be impartial as between right and wrong, honorable and dishonorable public conduct."
The historian, he made clear, must commit himself throughout but
must also seek to discover the atmosphere of the time and its standards. No neutrality was possible. His aim, he said, was to furnish "in
the true sense a history of the people of the United States, their virtues, their errors, and their wonderful development."

Like McMaster, he held no brief for radical panaceas but glorified
the "common people" and extolled the gains of Progress. "Progress is
the law of our being." He did not deny the role of the great hero of

the age in creating achievement, but he attributed a far more basic influence to the common man in making these gains possible. It was not the individual mind that swayed American politics but the "majority or average mind." The leader who unites the highest expression of thought and action, he said, rarely appears in modern days.

In various addresses and essays assembled later in *Historical Briefs* (1896), Schouler offered interesting insights into history. In 1889 he told his colleagues of the American Historical Association that he disagreed with the positivists who believed in the possibility of forecasting history. He believed that the complex interaction of persons and things which affected thought and feeling made historical forecasts forever uncertain. "Let us reject, therefore," he said, "the idea of an *a priori* history and whatever conception conjures up a human mind planning history in advance and then executing it. . . . There is no rigid scientific development to the human race." But the complex times did call for more specialization in the study of history. "In the present age one must be ignorant of much if he would be proficient in something." [3]

Schouler shook the confidence of critics by using an unusually large amount of secondary writings as well as a preponderance of formal political sources. Professor Lewis E. Ellis, who has made a careful analysis of Schouler's sources, shows that in the volume dealing with the years 1865-77 Rhodes is cited 235 times, while the second most-quoted source, Gideon Welles's *Diary*, is cited 53 times; and too much reliance was placed upon biographical sources. In the volume covering the Constitutional era 1783-1801, the *United States Statutes at Large*, a rather formal political source, is cited 123 times, with Hamilton's *Works* in second place with 53 citations and the *Federalist Papers* at the very bottom with one. [4] Schouler would not have been perturbed by these facts, for he had always paid homage to the primacy of politics and the great usefulness of secondary sources:

Original records and information are preferable to all others; but secondary sources of knowledge I have largely accepted as a labor-saving means, where I could bring my own accumulated knowledge and habits of verification to bear upon them so as to judge fairly of their comparative worth.

His writings, indeed, show eagerness to discover and use manuscript collections and other new sources unknown or ignored by other historians and biographers. But his methods did not permit him to make the novel revisions of historical evaluations and facts that his abler contemporary Rhodes did. Still, he could construct a fresh vivid pic-

ture of men and events by carefully reconsidering familiar facts and
judgments; but this virtue was not "research."

3

Far more skillful and successful as a narrative historian was the
retired Cleveland coal and iron executive who was Schouler's favorite
—James Ford Rhodes (1848-1927). His family came from New England, and he was born in Cleveland, where Puritan ideas and institutions continued to exist. His father, Daniel P. Rhodes, was a native
of Sudbury, Vermont, and a lifelong friend of his neighbor and cousin,
Stephen A. Douglas, whom young Rhodes knew as a frequent visitor.
Like Douglas, the elder Rhodes was a staunch Democrat—a "copper-
head" his son called him—who soon became a wealthy real-estate man
and a pioneer in the Ohio coal and iron ore industry. Eventually,
James trained himself to enter the business with a brother and a distinguished brother-in-law, Marcus Alonso Hanna, who had married
his sister. Altogether the prosperous Rhodes family belonged to the
scintillating and conservative Cleveland elite, which included John
Hay, the novelist and future secretary of state, and John D. Rockefeller, who organized the Standard Oil Company in 1870, both of
whom the future historian admired.

Rhodes did not go to Harvard but enrolled in various collegiate
courses as a special student (he ignored the standard classics and
mathematics requirements for the degree) at New York University and
the University of Chicago. He attended history lectures at the Sor-
bonne, studied metallurgy in Berlin, and observed various iron and
steel works in Europe. He read widely, and thought of a career in
journalism. Although he preferred concrete narrative to abstract or
philosophic books, he claimed to have discovered inspiration in
Draper's *Intellectual Development of Europe* and Thomas Buckle's
analytical *History of Civilization*.

"One evening in 1877, while reading Hildreth's *History of the United
States*," he afterwards recalled, "I laid down my book and said to
myself why I should not write a history of the United States." Then
he embarked on a plan of note-taking and study and planned retirement. By the age of 37 he had earned sufficient wealth to support
himself in the expensive career of historian, and was still young
enough to begin a new vocation. Soon he moved to Boston, city of
eminent historians and outstanding historical collections at Harvard

and the Athenaeum, where he could also meet the Brahmins whom he admired. He could afford to hire assistants to copy documents both here and abroad, and he even found time to serve on Rockefeller's General Education Board. Among his stimulating dinner guests were Theodore Roosevelt and Charles Francis Adams, Jr.[5]

Beginning in 1887 he devoted his entire time to the first two volumes of his *History of the United States from the Compromise of 1850 to the Final Restoration of Home Rule at the South in 1877.* By 1906, when all seven volumes had appeared, he decided to go ahead with the next period from Hayes to McKinley, and finally, in 1922, he brought forth volume nine, which ended the story with the Roosevelt administration. Reviewers lavished generous praise on the first seven volumes, but were less enthusiastic about the histories since 1877, despite the obvious advantage Rhodes had in a personal knowledge of so many of the chief participants. Like Schouler, he concentrated on political history, except for a single chapter devoted to social history in each volume. He wrote clearly and vigorously in a plain style that his Puritan ancestors would have approved of, although his rationalist outlook, apparently affected by his father, Buckle, and Lecky, suggested the late nineteenth and early twentieth centuries.

He began his first volume with a long background survey, drawing much of his material from Bancroft and to a lesser extent from Hildreth as well. In fact, Bancroft's name appears at least twenty-four times in the footnotes of the first forty pages. When Rhodes came to slavery, which he treated as a central theme in the antislavery spirit of von Holst and Schouler, he made his abolitionism unmistakable:

In spite of misrepresentation, obloquy, and derision, the abolitionists continued to apply moral ideas and Christian principles to the institution of slavery. The teachings of Christ and the Apostles actuated this crusade, and its latent power was great.

He stressed the influence of William Lloyd Garrison. "It was due to Garrison and his associates that slavery became a topic of discussion at every northern fireside." His picture of slavery was the standard abolitionist one: Planters lived in fear of insurrections, practiced slave-breeding, used cruel overseers, broke up slave families by sale, and earned great profits. Cotton fostered slavery and slavery was the cause of the Civil War. *Uncle Tom's Cabin* he praised as substantially true. "The South could not in 1861 justify her right to revolution, for there was no oppression, no invalidation of rights. She could not, however, proclaim to the world what was true, that she went to war to extend slavery." The only unusual note for an abolitionist was Rhodes's occasional reference to the racial inferiority of the Negro.

Scores of pages were devoted to the controversial Kansas-Nebraska Act and to the base motives of Stephen A. Douglas. To the surprise of anyone who expected that the link between the Rhodes family and Douglas would be reflected in a favorable interpretation of that statesman, James Rhodes indicted the "Little Giant" in no uncertain terms. He quoted approvingly from a letter of 1854 written by John Van Buren, "Could anything but a desire to buy the South at the presidential shambles dictate such an outrage?" The Clevelander could see no other motive because the Democrats needed no fresh issue, preferring to let things drift along, and Douglas was therefore not helping his party. All that the Democrats needed to succeed in 1856 were such mild programs as tariff reduction, economy, and "a just foreign policy." Douglas wished to dominate his party nationally, just as Clay had done among the Whigs. As an abolitionist, Rhodes had no use for Douglas's popular sovereignty doctrine, which meant to him that a few thousand uneducated territorial pioneers could compel Congress to abdicate its right to decide a question that demanded the most sagacious national statesmanship.

It is possible, as some have suggested, that Rhodes was now prejudiced against Douglas by the fact that the historian was personally a losing party in a lawsuit brought by Douglas's heirs. But actually, Rhodes had long broken with his father's political beliefs and had come to share the dominant views of von Holst and Schouler regarding the guilt of Douglas. Later historians, beginning with Professor Frank H. Hodder of Kansas, produced evidence to show that Douglas may have been influenced to repeal the Missouri Compromise of 1820 as embodied in the Kansas Bill by his need for Southern votes to open the territory for a transcontinental railway. Besides, it is clear that the current sectional quarrel over the enforcement of the Fugitive Slave Act was making the Compromise of 1850 partly inoperative and reawakening a new slavery crisis even before the passage of the Kansas-Nebraska Act. Therefore, Douglas is not usually given the full onus of responsibility for precipitating the crisis that led directly to the Civil War. Others have pointed out how little in fact Douglas actually profited from the Deep South in the struggle for the presidential nomination of his party in 1860 or in winning the election. In 1934, a journalist, George Fort Milton, revised the von Holst-Schouler-Rhodes assessment of Douglas and the causes of the Civil War in *The Eve of Conflict: Stephen A. Douglas and the Needless War*, which showed the senator as a great compromiser and pragmatic statesman who sought to avert conflict between the extremists. As a result of this revisionist trend, the Rhodes-Schouler view had few academic supporters by mid-century.

Rhodes had little but praise for the new Republican party and John Brown. "Never in our history," he wrote of the Republican Convention of 1856, "and probably never in the history of the world, had a more pure, more disinterested, and more intelligent body of men banded together for a noble political object than those who now enrolled themselves under the Republican banner." They were an elite of clergymen, college professors, writers, scientists, and school teachers. Like von Holst and Schouler, he denied that John Brown was insane, even if he did not comprehend government by discussion, and that his martyrdom strengthened the public opinion behind Lincoln's war on slavery.

Rhodes minimized economic factors, despite his industrial and technological background and the fact that he was the author of a short treatise on Cleveland's coal and iron industry which glorified the industrialists. One exception, however, was the tariff, which he discussed in order to argue for the abstract advantages of free trade, although he had called for protection for the iron and steel industry in 1883. He surprised those who expected a former industrialist to espouse a high protective tariff, although Andrew Carnegie was also coming around to free trade in his *Autobiography*. Instead, Rhodes tried to show that economic paternalism invited inefficiency; he attributed the sensational progress of industry to a competitive situation in which the brilliance of the engineer and the manager's ability and patience promoted economies, efficiencies, and new inventions. He deplored the "ignorance" of the businessman on the tariff issue. In a later volume he extolled the technological contributions of John D. Rockefeller and of other entrepreneurs whom he knew well. Otherwise, Rhodes was an economic conservative who opposed inflationism, blamed labor troubles on agitators and foreigners, and assumed that it was the essential duty of the enlightened businessman to provide national leadership. He confused his economics at times with ethnic prejudices and a class bias:

If it be true that, with this growth of enormous fortunes, poverty has become more abject, this tendency had begun before the war, and has been the result rather of the constantly deteriorating character of the European immigration than of industrial changes on our own soil.

Generally, Rhodes clung to the story of political machinations and maneuver that he understood so well. He gave many pages to the controversial Crittenden Compromise, which offered Lincoln a deal by which the slavery crisis and perhaps the impending war itself could be averted in return for a guarantee to the South that slavery would be forever safe below a line of 36 degrees 30 minutes all the way to the Pacific.

Southerners were usually pleased at his conciliatory references to their people, a fresh note among historians since 1861. Jefferson Davis was sympathetically pictured on the eve of war as a man distraught by the crisis and by insomnia, and as praying for peace. It was also pleasant for ex-Confederates to read that secession was a popular movement, not a conspiracy. Neither side, he said, avowed its true aim: "The North went into battle with the preservation of the Union blazoned on its banner, the South with resistance to subjugation."

Rhodes's account of the Civil War is a major part of the *History*, for it occupied most of volumes three to five. He benefited greatly, as Schouler had done, from the newly published official records of the Union and Confederate armies. Later, in 1913, he prepared a book of Civil War lectures, and four years later wrote an entirely new history of the war, in which he ignored most of the criticism of his earlier presentation. When he dealt with life behind the lines, he went hastily over social developments and concentrated at length on domestic and foreign politics. Much as he admired Lincoln, he did not feel that his restraints upon civil liberty were justified; in fact, the President accustomed Congress and the people to arbitrary power, which was "relished by each party or faction if exercised to further its particular ends." He likened the North to a dictatorship and the South to a vast socialist state—both evil.

Rhodes left his most lasting influence on historiography by his circumstantial account, based on fresh sources, of the errors of Radical Reconstruction. In 1902, John W. Burgess in his *Reconstruction and the Constitution* had already started reassessment of the Radicals and their motives. Rhodes's racism, like that of Burgess, put an extremely low estimate on Negro potentialities and hence expressed itself in a willingness to take the Southern side in the controversy over the freedmen. Rhodes relied on the current racial errors of the anthropologist, Daniel G. Brinton, for the "fact" that the Negroes suffered arrested mental development after the age of thirteen or fourteen. "Three and a half million persons of one of the most inferior races of mankind had through the agency of their superiors been transformed from slavery to freedom," said Rhodes. He argued that the North acted without knowing anything about the Negro uprisings—the Black Terror—that Southerners feared, but his honesty led him to report that the large-scale Louisiana race riot grew out of direct white attacks rather than Negro provocations.

Although the Negro historian, Dr. W. E. B. Du Bois, was to use many of Rhodes's facts regarding Carpetbag legislatures to reach quite different conclusions, the Clevelander had little to say about the solid welfare achievements of the Negro legislators and their white allies, for he preferred to dwell on their corruption.[6] Radical Republican leaders like Thaddeus Stevens appeared only as bitter and vindictive. Andrew Johnson appeared as crude, semi-literate, and so incompetent that he played right into the hands of the extremists. His great error lay in failing to persuade the South to ratify the Fourteenth Amendment, thereby inviting the Radicals to do their worst. As for the Reconstruction Acts of March 1867, Rhodes could not find enough words of excoriation: "No law so unjust in its policy, so direful in its results had passed the American Congress since the Kansas-Nebraska Act of 1854." This meant "negro rule forced on the South at the point of the bayonet," while Negro suffrage "consolidated nearly all decent white men into the Democratic or conservative party." Rhodes did favor the Lincoln-Johnson idea of granting limited Negro suffrage based on educational qualifications, but his facts raised doubts whether this objective would be fully acceptable to the South. He praised the Southern people for their integrity and courage under the Carpetbag yoke.

According to his detailed analysis of the disputed election of 1877, the Electoral Commission had acted in a partisan manner, but Hayes was legally entitled to the presidency, while Tilden had the moral title. He was disappointed in the latter: "Tilden did not rise to the emergency. In quiet times he would have made a good President but he was entirely lacking in both the physical and moral courage needed in a leader during the turbulent times which succeeded Election." But the country would have preferred him to Hayes.

With the appearance of his volumes dealing with the Hayes-McKinley years and with the Roosevelt era, Rhodes thought of himself as a historian of contemporary times after the model of Thucydides and Herodotus. He showed himself the conservative businessman in discussing the railroad strikes of 1877, the Haymarket Riot, the Pullman Strike, and the inflationist movements. His heroes were Grover Cleveland and his fellow-Ohio conservatives McKinley, Mark Hanna, and John D. Rockefeller. He refused to probe the labor conditions behind the Haymarket Riot, but stated without evidence—since it does not exist—that the actual anarchist bomb-thrower was known, because he had been arrested and released for lack of evidence. He thought it significant that six of the eight who stood trial for the bombing were Germans, and so, he said, was the original bomb-thrower.

Again, he took the conservative side in defending Cleveland for selling government bonds disadvantageously (from the national viewpoint) to Morgan to maintain gold payments, admired his sound money policies, and supported his dispatch of federal troops to Chicago during the Pullman Strike. Reminiscences and full-length portraits characterized these final volumes. He could draw a fresh portrait of brother-in-law Mark Hanna, and he praised him as a foe of the Cleveland urban political machine, an active friend of the labor unions, a civil service reformer, and a public-spirited kingmaker. But he severely criticized President McKinley (as the Spanish ambassador had done) for his ineptness in yielding to the jingoes and in provoking "the unnecessary war." Here was a combination of the economic conservatism and anti-imperialism taught at the time by William Graham Sumner, the sociologist. Rhodes's anti-imperialism, it will be recalled, was previously expressed in his condemnation of the annexing of Texas and the war on Mexico.

He had only praise for Rockefeller and condemnation for the anti-Standard Oil muckrakers like Henry D. Lloyd and Ida Tarbell. "The management of the Standard," he said, "was one of efficiency in every direction. . . . For efficient cooperation the United States never saw the equal of the Standard." Toward the end, his use of original sources declined markedly, and when he came to Roosevelt he supplemented his memory by recent biographies.

While Rhodes was as subjective in approach as von Holst or Schouler, he went beyond them in the detective work of historical research. This is clear from his solutions of problems that he published in *Historical Essays* (1909). Present-day readers still find it fascinating to follow his convincing logic in the paper, "Who Burned Columbia?" Here he took up the puzzle as to whether General Sherman or the Confederate General Wade Hampton burned this capital of South Carolina. Rhodes demolished both theories and then demonstrated that the fire was due to marauding Confederate soldiers aided by convicts and escaped Union prisoners, all of whom helped to sack the city.

In 1899, when Rhodes was elected president of the American Historical Association, he discussed some of his historical theories and paid his respects to the progress of scientific methods in teaching and research, singling out the influence of Darwin. Yet Rhodes, unlike his contemporaries Frederick Jackson Turner and John Fiske, made only the most cursory use of social evolution. Nevertheless, he held forth: [7]

Evolution, heredity, environment, have become household words, and their application to history has influenced every one who has had to trace the development of a people, the growth of an institution, or the establishment of a cause. Other scientific theories and methods have affected physical science as patently, but none has entered so vitally into the study of man.

This promising line of speculation only led him to raise another question, "But do we write better history than was written before the year 1859, which we may call the line of demarcation between the old and the new?" To him the classical historians Herodotus and Thucydides were among the best, and one reason for their superiority was the fact that what they wrote was practically contemporary history. "It is easier to describe the life you know than one you must imagine, which is what you must do if you aim to relate events which took place before your own and your father's time." This argument of course was intended to raise his own stock academically and to meet the criticisms of those who doubted that contemporary history was really history at all. The man who knew so many of the chief characters in American history since the time of Stephen A. Douglas was indeed a part of all that he had transcribed, just as Thucydides had been. The Greek historians whom he regarded as the greatest of all time had long ago refuted the hasty dictum that history within the memory of men living cannot be truthfully and fairly written.

Rhodes shared with McMaster the honor of being a pioneer in the regular use of newspaper sources for history, although he gave most credit to von Holst. He explained how the paucity of political materials had led him to turn to newspapers for source information:

Boy though I was during the decade of 1850 to 1860, I had a vivid remembrance of the part that the newspaper played in politics, and the thought came to me that the best way to arrive at the spirit of the times was to steep my mind in journalistic material.

The ephemeral nature of the newspaper did not deter him: "Take the newspaper for what it is, a hasty gatherer of facts, a hurried commentator on the same, and it may well constitute a part of historical evidence." Besides, newspapers made history, as is evident in the case of the Spanish-American war in this country and in the Crimean war for England. Like McMaster, he believed that all studies of public opinion, especially during political campaigns, were best studied through the newspaper. He felt no superior reverence for moldy, often anonymous letters, which required the most meticulous handling by experts. "Some men have lied as freely in private letters as in public speeches," he observed. Newspapers could and should be checked for the same basic purposes as other documents. "The duty of the historian," he said, "is, not to decide if the newspapers are as good as they ought to be, but to measure their influence on the present, and to recognize their importance as an ample and contemporary record of the past." Yet Rhodes, unlike McMaster, missed the best potentialities of the newspaper—its great value in social history. In fact, the Clevelander once described social history cruelly as "the routine of work and the round of pleasures of the majority—those blank pages of history which, if written over, could indeed be tiresome." Yet he made exceptions in his actual *History* for random pages on manners and morals, schools and churches, sports, and everyday life. But Mc-Master, too, for all his emphasis on social facts, did all too little in making them an integral part of the entire American scene.

4

John William Burgess (1844-1931) of Columbia, once the protégé of George Bancroft, was no ardent abolitionist like von Holst, Schouler, or Rhodes, but he had always been an antislavery man and to a large extent he shared their research interests in the same historical periods. The son of a Tennessee slaveholder, but reared in the strong Unionist tradition of Henry Clay and the Whig party, he disliked slavery and secession, fought as a Union volunteer, and now wrote disparagingly of slaveholders as a class. Like Schouler and Rhodes he contributed heavily to the new "revisionist" and racist interpretation of Reconstruction, which assumed that the biracial legislatures failed because Negroes were inherently inferior and incapable of understanding their true interests.

From his education at Amherst, Burgess had acquired an Hegelian philosophy of history which was to permeate his writings. This was reinforced with an admixture of Prussian centralization theory and scientific historical method from Göttingen, Leipzig, and Berlin, where he studied during the 1870s. Thus, he retained Hegel's idea of history as an idealistic unfolding of God's mind at a time when American historians (and Europeans, too) were showing increased suspicion or distaste for philosophic speculation in historical narratives. Nevertheless, he was devoted to genuine empirical research and the Rankean scientific method which stressed objectivity, the critical handling of documents for authenticity, and a careful evaluation of testimony as to reliability. He went beyond the average "scientific" historian, who was content with "facts" and looked askance at unimaginative syntheses, for he used a large interpretive canvas in the philosophic tradition.[8]

After teaching political science at Amherst from 1873 to 1876, he went on to a distinguished career at Columbia, where he organized graduate work in history and political science and was soon appointed dean of the faculty of political science. His influential disciples included William A. Dunning and Ulrich B. Phillips. Burgess and Dunning both published treatises that were important in American political theory.

Burgess's first history book, *The Middle Period, 1817-1858* (1898), contained no footnotes or bibliography, except for a short list of recommended books, which included Rhodes, von Holst, Schouler, and Hildreth. His facts and interpretations showed such little novelty that it seemed certain that he relied heavily on secondary sources. However, Burgess insisted that he had sedulously avoided all the histories written after 1865 and "all rehashes of them of later date." Proudly he declared, "In fact I have made it an invariable rule to use no secondary material; that is, no material in which original matter is mingled with somebody's interpretation of its meaning."

He liked to employ the Hegelian dialectic in history with its pendulum movement: "But in all the convulsions of political history, described as advance and reaction, the scientific student of history is able to discover that the zigzags of progress are ever bearing in the general direction which the combined impulses toward nationalism and humanism compel." He might have shown empirically, had he attempted a brief investigation, that European and American reform movements were closely related, but he was content to infer these facts from Hegelian principles:

While no actual connection can be established between the Revolution of 1830 in Europe and the Rise of Abolition in the United States, yet they belong to the same period of time, and harmonize in principle. The impulses which move the human race, or those parts of the human race which stand upon the same plane of civilization, are not broken by mountain heights or broad seas. Their manifestations appear spontaneously and coetaneously in widely separated places.

To him as to Hegel the history of civilization was an evolution toward individual liberty, equality, and fraternity. According to his version of Hegel's dialectic movement as applied to America, the period of 1800-30 had been one of selfishly conceived tariffs and of race domination, while the next thirty years were a swing toward world intercourse and human rights. Actually his own facts did not wholly support this formula.

Again like Hegel and Bancroft he relied upon a supernaturally inspired morality and presented history as "the reconciliation of men to the plans of Providence for their perfection." His preface made this very clear indeed:

Any interpretation of this period of American history which does not demonstrate to the South its error will be worthless, simply because it will not be true. In a word, the conviction of the South of its error in secession and rebellion is absolutely indispensable to the establishment of national cordiality.

There was no effort to qualify his judgment that "the Northern view is, in the main, the correct view." While he condemned slavery as an evil, he pointed out only environmental reasons for its existence, rather than any personal guilt. The climate, soil, and swampland diseases were the chief culprits. Georgia's founders, he said, had outlawed slavery, but geographic and economic factors had reinstated it. He could speak of slavery's champion, Calhoun, as "grave, pure, and patriotic," ranking him with the greatest Americans of his day and regarded slavery as ethically wrong but a necessity in the early development of the South after which it became increasingly an anachronism.

Curiously, like the proslavery philosophers, he attacked the intellectual basis of the antislavery movement, namely the natural rights philosophy, which produced the Declaration of Independence, "a humanitarian outburst," as he called it. He threw his heaviest shafts at abolitionism, "the literal interpretation of the Declaration of Independence," the Radicals' disregard of consequences. Abolitionists like John Brown ignored the constitutional pathways for progress, increased the tensions between the sections, and worsened the condition of the slaves. Individual freedom, he believed, could only be reached in gradual evolutionary fashion as part of a larger social development from barbarism to civilization.

Since he was primarily concerned with constitutional and political history, he dwelt at length on the nature of states' rights and its evolution under changing conditions. "Personally, I never had regarded the Union under the Constitution of 1787 as a confederation of sovereign states," he wrote in his *Reminiscences*. Even in boyhood he had learned the lesson from his Henry Clay Whig father and grandfather that the Union was "a nation holding exclusive sovereignty and exercising government through two sets of organs, each having its own constitutional sphere of action and limitation." This theme of nationalism versus particularism runs through the volume beginning with the first chapter, "The Nationalization of the Republican Party" and is stressed in another chapter, "The Beginnings of the Particularistic Reaction," dealing with the influence of slavery upon national policies.

The sequel to this crowded volume of politics and constitutional struggles which ended in 1858 was a two-volume work published in 1901 as *The Civil War and the Constitution, 1859-1865*. This stressed military history, except for the long, early section on the secession crisis and several brief chapters on domestic and international questions. An unusual chapter about antislavery sentiment in the South pictured a class war between townsfolk and planters, but on the social rather than the economic plane. He thought that the Southerners were moved by a general fear of slave insurrections and that the planters played upon this fear, for which there was some substance, in promoting the movement for secession. No evidence for this interpretation of the planter was given.

The third work in this series, *Reconstruction and the Constitution* (1905), had far more influence than the others, for it converted many to the revisionism which severely condemned the Radical Republican view of Reconstruction on racist grounds. Burgess may have written this about the same time that Rhodes was preparing his own revisionist views on Reconstruction. Burgess's fundamental racism, for all his antislavery sentiments, was basic. Like so many of his fellow-Hegelians who espoused the germ theory of cultural evolution, he believed in the superiority, uniqueness, and high civilizing mission of the Anglo-Saxon or Teutonic peoples. Imperialism was part of this pattern. The revisionists felt Reconstruction had failed because it had endangered white civilization.

His facts regarding Reconstruction greatly resembled those of Schouler and Rhodes, and his primary emphasis on constitutional questions was not enriched by any examination of economic determinants. In his preface he reminded his readers that he had previously insisted that the South must admit that secession was an error; now he called for a similar acknowledgment from the North regarding Reconstruction. The product of this error was the solid South. At this point he made clear his imperialistic and racist assumptions:

And now that the United States has embarked on imperial enterprises under the direction of the Republican Party, the great Northern party, the North is learning every day by valuable experiences that there are vast differences in political capacity between the races, and that it is the white man's mission, his duty and his right, to hold the reins of political power in his hands for the civilization of the world and the welfare of mankind.

He tried to be objective on many individual facts and judgments, but his over-all bias remained apparent. Sometimes his inconsistency was certain to confuse readers. In the beginning of his volume President Johnson was a man "of considerable intellectual power and of great will power," but within a few chapters he deteriorated into a low-born, low-bred, violent, obstinate, coarse, and vindictive man. Unlike later revisionists, Burgess defended the passage of the Civil Rights Bill, which Johnson vetoed, on the ground that it simply provided for equality before the law and granted no social equality or political privileges. Johnson blundered in opposing the bill, because he thereby encouraged Southerners to continue their discriminations against freedmen and provoked the Republicans to take extreme measures.

He agreed with Johnson and the South in opposing the way in which Congress tried to force the Fourteenth Amendment upon the former Confederacy. "The Southern statesmen knew that Congress had no power under the Constitution to require of new States obedience to anything as a condition of their admission to the Union but the Constitution as it was at the moment of their admission." As for the biracial Carpetbag legislatures, Burgess like Rhodes was denunciatory, calling attention to the plunder of state treasuries, the increase of taxes, the corrupt sale of franchises, and the celebration of "high carnival everywhere."

Not all scholars were pleased by *Reconstruction and the Constitution.* One eminent Southern historian handled it quite roughly in the *American Historical Review,* characterizing the book as a futile exercise in unrealistic political theory. Dogmatic assertions buried the actual Reconstruction narrative, and a colorless style made it worse.

While the reviewer found a few interpretations worthy of commendation, he challenged specific facts and inconsistencies in a most caustic way.[9]

5

Burgess had his most influential follower in William A. Dunning (1857-1922), whose interests and professional career paralleled that of his master in both history and political theory. The son of a cultured small town manufacturer in New York state, he came to Columbia, where he took up Burgess's favorite topic—the constitutional aspects of the Civil War and Reconstruction—and picked up some of his mentor's race interpretations. Like Burgess, too, he studied abroad at the University of Berlin and other places, where the Prussian enthusiasm for political centralization was in the ascendant, and he became a political theorist of note. However, he not only dropped the Bancroft-Burgess use of Hegelian historical theory but sought that particular variety of "scientific history" which eliminated as far as possible moral judgments. The positivists of Comte's day had hoped that the fact-collectors and the synthesizers would somehow come together to write a scientific history or a science of society, but the reaction against controlling philosophic formulas encouraged the historian to stop with mere fact-collecting. Dunning was too thoroughly trained in philosophy to operate without a conscious hypothesis, but he differed from Burgess in refusing to make the theoretical element too manifest at the expense of the historical narrative. Still, the careful reader could discover wherein lay his moral judgments, even without the aid of the Burgess-type asides and prefaces. He earned a surprising reputation for objectivity. James W. Garner, who was one of the ablest of his productive seminar students and the author of an outstanding monograph study of Reconstruction in Mississippi, paid this tribute:

By his detached objective treatment he succeeded in removing the many prejudices which hitherto had prevented an accurate analysis of the reconstruction period, and by his influence on other scholars he cleared the way for a thoroughgoing reinterpretation.

The fact that Dunning was not as dogmatic or aloof as Burgess undoubtedly enhanced this impression of detachment.

Dunning modified the Reconstruction story of Schouler, Rhodes, and Burgess but did not reverse it. In fact, he gave the highest praise to them in 1907: "The appearance of Dr. James Ford Rhodes's last two volumes, covering the years 1866-1877, in time to be used in the final revision of my manuscript, is a mercy the greatness of which cannot in a preface be adequately expressed." As far as social ideas were concerned, he had imbibed the Rhodes-Burgess view of racial determinism, as had his influential seminar student, Ulrich B. Phillips. In 1897, almost at the same time that Burgess published *The Middle Period*, Dunning republished a revealing article "The Undoing of Reconstruction" in *Essays on the Civil War and Reconstruction*. He attributed these ideas to Jefferson, Clay, and Lincoln:

> This was that the ultimate root of the trouble in the South had been, not the institution of slavery, but the coexistence in one society of two races so distinct in characteristics as to render coalescence impossible; that slavery had been a *modus vivendi* through which social life was possible; and that, after its disappearance, its place must be taken by some set of conditions which, if more humane and beneficent in accidents, must in essence express the same fact of racial inequality. The progress in the acceptance of this idea in the North has measured the progress in the South of the undoing of reconstruction. In view of the questions which have been raised by our lately established relations with other races, it seems most improbable that the historian will soon, if ever, have to record a reversal of the conditions which this process has established.

The rest of the volume was far less revealing of social ideas than this suggests; it mainly consisted of technical formulations of constitutional problems. He traced the way in which the Civil War, by destroying the right of secession, thereby destroyed the doctrine of state sovereignty. One of his few value-laden phrases refers to the "reckless enfranchisement of the freedmen and their enthronement in power." As he put it, "To stand the social pyramid on its apex was not the surest way to restore the shattered equilibrium of the South."

He showed surprising concessions to the Carpetbag regime, in his second book, *Reconstruction Political and Economic, 1865-1877* (1907), far more than either Rhodes or Burgess had been willing to make. With the aid of seminar-inspired monographs by Garner and Walter Fleming, he pointed out that there was quite another side to the extravagance of the Carpetbag legislators: Their deficits were partly due to highly useful but expensive projects, such as public schools and welfare institutions. To the whites, the significant fact was that the Negroes benefited most, since the ante-bellum planter had ignored such welfare needs for the Negro; hence the whites were angered. Besides, he observed, the heavy financial burden imposed by the Carpetbag legislatures could be partly attributed to their use of state credit in undertaking the costly but useful task of rebuilding the railroads.

Furthermore, Dunning even had an explanation for Carpetbag corruption—although he did not change his mind that Negro incapacity and ignorance was at the bottom of the failure of Reconstruction. "The form and manner of this corruption, which has given so unsavory a connotation to the name 'reconstruction' were no different from those which have appeared in many another time and place in democratic government." He cited the notorious Tweed Ring as an example of large-scale contemporary graft in the North. Quite acutely, he made this basic observation, "The really novel and peculiar element in maladministration in the South was the social and race issue which underlay it and which came to the surface at once when any attempt at reform was instituted." Since the Northern white carpetbaggers were enabled by Washington to make more concessions to Negro power than loyal white Southerners (the so-called scalawags) could, the latter lost out in the competition and eventually joined the conservatives.

All this, however, was within a racist framework of his own. Dunning was clear enough on this point. "The negro had no pride of race and no aspirations or ideals save to be like the whites," he said. For this "reason" the Negro wished the privileges of social equality, demanded mixed schools, and equal entree into hotels and theaters. Little wonder that Dunning attracted so many students with strong opinions on race.

His judgment on the Radicals did not differ greatly from the unfavorable views of other revisionists. There was little of scientific objectivity in this emotional attack on Charles Sumner, who had been warmly praised by Emerson and others:

However remote his doctrines from any relation to the realities of human affairs, he preached them without intermission and forced his colleagues by mere iteration to give them a place in law. He would shed tears at the bare thought of refusing to freedmen rights of which they had no comprehension, but would filibuster to the end of the session to prevent the restoration to the Southern whites of rights which were essential to their whole conception of life. He was the perfect type of that narrow fanaticism which erudition and egotism combine to produce and to which political crises alone give the opportunity for actual achievement.

On certain other controversial judgments, too, he did not differ greatly from Rhodes or Burgess. For example, he could not see that the so-called Black Codes passed by the unreconstructed Southern legislatures should have angered the North, for they seemed quite unlike slavery or peonage.

Thus, the second decade of the twentieth century opened with the revisionists well entrenched. Rhodes, Schouler, Burgess, and Dunning agreed that slavery was a sin but that racism was not. They gave academic respectability to the racism of the unreconstructed Southerner at a time when Negro disenfranchisement, lynchings, and racial discriminations were in full flower. Thomas Dixon's racist book, *The Clansman* (1905), became the enormously popular movie, *Birth of a Nation* (1915), depicting Southern Reconstruction as a movement led by Negro barbarism. In 1915 a second Klan was organized, and ten years later, its four millions were intimidating Negroes, Catholics, Jews, foreigners, and radicals and it was even becoming a major issue in party politics. The revisionists, often in the name of scientific historiography, colored the school textbooks as well as the newer biographies and histories of the Reconstruction era. Among the best-sellers was the revisionist book, *The Tragic Era* of Claude Bowers, and there were a host of friendly Andrew Johnson biographies.

By mid-century, historians apparently favored an economic interpretation of the undoing of Reconstruction, judging from the favorable reviews of C. Vann Woodward's *Reunion and Reaction: The Compromise of 1877 and the End of Reconstruction* (1951). While Paul Buck's *The Road to Reunion* (1937), a Pulitzer Prize winner, had stressed the social and cultural contacts between the sections after Reconstruction, Woodward dwelt upon the economic formula suggested by the New South of Henry Grady, editor of the Atlanta *Constitution*, who had pleaded with Northern merchants to cooperate with the South and to leave the race question to Southerners. Woodward thought that the old ante-bellum alliance of Northern and Southern Whigs was in effect revived on the plane of self-interest. Thus the Radicals were willing to abandon the Negro and to restore the conservative "Redeemers" in return for Southern votes not only to elect Hayes over Tilden but to secure congressional votes to sponsor transcontinental railroads, internal improvements, and other economic enterprises.

But there were scholars left with the impression that the non-economic explanation for the union of the Blue and the Gray might still have validity. The frustrating Reconstruction struggle had already blunted the Radical will to resist a Southern solution to the race question. The racial cracks in the righteous armor of the North, especially in the Old Northwest, were revealed by the strong resistance to the passage of the Fourteenth Amendment and by the hostility to Negro migrants from the South (or anywhere else). Much of the fervor of the ante-bellum crusade had spent itself, and erstwhile antislavery men even of such high character as Rhodes, Schouler, Burgess, and Dunning seemed convinced on racial grounds that Radical Reconstruction was a grave error.

☆ 12 ☆

Ulrich B. Phillips and the Image of the Old South

1

Southerners had long been unhappy over the Yankees' monopoly of American history-writing. School-textbook writers like Professor George F. Holmes of the University of Virginia began shortly after the Civil War to present the Confederate case against the angry New Englanders who pictured a slaveholder's conspiracy or a traitorous rebellion. The former vice-president of the Confederacy, Alexander H. Stephens, hurried to show that the South had fought for the "Grecian type of civilization against the Asiatic" in his two volumes of *The Constitutional View of the Late War Between the States* (1868-70). Belatedly, the harassed ex-president himself, Jefferson Davis, was at work on his own version, *The Rise and Fall of the Confederate Government* (1881). Mark Twain, who had informally and promptly severed his service with Confederate troops during the war, visited the South again and reported in *Life on the Mississippi*, "Mention of the war will wake up a dull company and set their tongues going when nearly any other topic will fail. In the South the war is what A.D. is elsewhere; they date from it."

Nostalgic Confederates quickly collected funds to start the filio-pietistic Southern Historical Society of New Orleans in 1869; a more critical later generation in 1896 set up the Southern History Association, which encouraged research and college teaching about the Old

South. Many bright Southern scholars clustered around Columbia University to study American history under William A. Dunning, who was not only stimulating but quite sympathetic to the Southern point of view.

The road to reunion between North and South, as already noted, consisted of economic bedrock as well as a growing racism in the North and the return of fraternal sentiment. Southern Bourbons—the planters and rising industrialists—were firmly in the saddle during the years between Reconstruction and the coming of the Dixie demagogues such as Ben Tillman of South Carolina. They had resumed the ante-bellum Whig alliance in Congress of merchants and planters. Their New South brought the cotton mills to the cotton fields, erected large factories making the popular "bright tobacco" cigarettes, attracted Northern capital for industry, and secured a plain understanding in the North that the race question was to be handled exclusively by Southerners. This Bourbonism, in the name of Retrenchment, Reconciliation, and Reform, partly undid the social gains of Reconstruction by strict economies at the expense of schools and welfare institutions for Negroes and the poorer whites. One of its persuasive spokesmen, Henry Grady, editor of the Atlanta *Constitution,* offered Northern audiences of merchants the benefits of sectional co-operation and offended few by asserting, "The South has nothing for which to apologize." But he argued that just as Americans had refused to quarrel over the status of the Chinese, so they must not dispute the treatment of the Negro accorded by the Southern white. The old Radicals were tired and failed to shake the new spirit of conciliation, while the Supreme Court decided that the Fourteenth Amendment did not offer social equality. The disfranchisement of the Negro proceeded apace (save where the Bourbons could count on his vote). Northern publishers gratified innumerable Northern readers by sponsoring the Southern sentimental "local color school," which pictured the Negro, when he was introduced at all, as a simple, kindly Uncle Remus. Ulrich Phillips, despite his intense awareness of race conflict, liked to think of the Negro in the sentimental terms of his fellow-Georgian, Joel Chandler Harris, assistant to Henry Grady.

The young Southern liberals who grew up after the Civil War might dislike industrial monopoly, protective tariffs, illiteracy, and backward social conditions, but they had little to say against the racial practices of the South—except for the unhappy expatriate George Washington Cable of New Orleans who protested against the convict lease system which bore heavily on the Negro, the economic discrimination, and the tendency to treat the Negro as a perpetual alien. Woodrow Wilson, a lifelong Jeffersonian, though sympathetic to many Bourbon ideas, shared the common hatred of Radical Reconstruction, but he could say, "I rejoice in the failure of the Confederacy. . . . We cannot conceal from ourselves the fact that slavery was enervating our Southern society and exhausting to Southern energies." He, too, showed a relative blind spot to Negro issues, both as a historian and as a statesman. Josephus Daniels, later Wilson's liberal Secretary of the Navy (and Franklin D. Roosevelt's ambassador to Mexico), was a North Carolina editor who attacked James B. Duke's monopolies, but he campaigned also to oust an outspoken history professor at Trinity College, John Spencer Bassett, who had blamed the South for its own backwardness and said that Booker T. Washington was the greatest man, next to Lee, who had been born in the South for the past century. Little wonder that Bassett left for Smith College in 1906. Another liberal critic of the South, Dean William P. Trent of the University of the South, was ostracized for his frank but carefully considered criticism of Southern reactionary ideals, and he, too, found it politic to leave—in this case for Columbia. Replacing the Bourbons came the demagogues who treated the Negroes as tools of the upper classes, disfranchised most of them, and permitted mobs to lynch or intimidate the freedmen.

The vogue for Southern history written by Southerners coincided with a racialism that was not confined to the South, but on a lesser scale common in the North and in Europe. Scholars, as already noted, had made the idea of Anglo-Saxon superiority part of their controlling assumptions. They shared to a surprising extent the enthusiasm for Spencerian ideas of the survival of the fittest, colonialism, immigration restriction of the lesser breeds without the law, and the Kipling refrain of the white man's burden. In those areas of the South where the plantation system had concentrated the Negro population, racialism was buttressed by the insecurity felt by white minorities. But by 1900 Southern historians could point out that even the chief Northern writers like Rhodes, Dunning, and Burgess were hostile to Radical Reconstruction. Reputations of such abolitionist heroes as Charles Sumner suffered during these years (Emerson had once said of him, "I never knew so white a soul.").

While it did not become fashionable to praise slavery and secession outright, a sense of nostalgia for the Lost Cause grew. Even more than before, the plantation South aroused romantic emotions, for this image contrasted pleasantly with the prosaic realities of industrialism. As far back as the 1830s, novel-readers had been given an attractive introduction to a semi-idealized plantation society by John P. Kennedy in *Swallow Barn,* and William A. Caruthers in *The Cavaliers of Virginia.* George Fitzhugh, proslavery extremist, had drawn a popular antithesis between the planter as an aristocratic descendant of the cavalier and the Puritan Northerner as the mean offspring of Saxon serfs. Post-bellum Southern romantics like Thomas Nelson Page of Virginia sounded the fresh nostalgic note that the glory was departed.

The patriarchal plantation image was given wide currency by Philip A. Bruce of Virginia (1856-1933), who wrote a large shelf of books about Virginia's institutional, social, and economic history during the seventeenth century. His father was the wealthiest tobacco planter in the state, and one of his uncles was James A. Seddon, Secretary of War under the Confederacy. As a planter's son he went to a traditional "old field" school, graduated from the conservative University of Virginia, and took a law degree at Harvard. He studied the county and parish records, the British State Papers dealing with the colonies, and the Peter Force Historical Tracts. He shared Phillips's enthusiasm for the planter class and their civilization; for he believed that the plantation, like Turner's frontier, bred self-reliance, independence, and hospitality. Bruce concluded that seventeenth-century Virginia, at a time when slaves were relatively few, was "a duplication of the English rural communities of that day" and that the Virginia gentry descended from the English squire ruling class. With the coming of slavery on a large scale, the small aristocratic class rose greatly over the non-slaveholding whites. Furthermore, he held that the gentry filled every public office of influence—a judgment which contemporary historians tended to accept. Phillips, too, believed that while most Southerners were small farmers—referring of course to the nineteenth century—political power inhered largely to the planters.

In 1910, Bruce was challenged by Professor Thomas Wertenbaker of the University of Virginia, who was later to become president of the American Historical Association. Wertenbaker's *Patrician and Plebeian in Virginia* and later books on similar topics drew proof from the land records that fully 90 per cent of the Virginians were simply hardworking small farmers. They had enough political strength, he argued, to act as a democratic check on aristocracy through their control of the lower houses of the colony and to halt the encroachments of the Stuart monarchs as well. However, this effort to posit a basic yeoman democratic force in the South, even if the discussion was limited to the seventeenth century, met considerable criticism. Louis B. Wright's

The First Gentlemen of Virginia (1940) showed both evidence and sound logic for the contention that small as the elite was—perhaps a hundred wealthy planter families—they clearly held dominance and cultivated the aristocratic tradition.

By 1890 Northern and Southern historians usually agreed that Radical Reconstruction had been a failure and that it had not squared with racial realities. Bruce went even further; he wrote in 1889 that the freedman showed little desire to work hard and his children even less so; so serious was the mortality rate among Negroes that the near-extinction of the race could be envisaged. Politicians of the Progressive movement, whether following the banner of Bryan, La Follette, Theodore Roosevelt, or Woodrow Wilson, reflected this atmosphere by their silence on the desperate status of the Negro in the South. This controversy had been settled once and for all, they thought, in 1877, the year of Ulrich B. Phillips's birth, by the great sectional compromises.

2

U. B. Phillips was born in the small community of La Grange, Georgia, where he had ample opportunity to work under the sun in the cotton fields, to watch the excitement of the camp meeting, to meet numerous ex-slaves as well as whites, and to acquire the traditions of the Deep South. In later years, he pointed out the effect of his early experiences upon his historical outlook:

A sympathetic understanding of plantation conditions was my inevitable heritage from my family and from neighbors, white and black, in the town of La Grange and Troup County, Georgia, where I was born and grew up. A deepening appreciation of the historical significance of the plantation and of the preceding frontier regime I owe to Dr. Frederick J. Turner of the University of Wisconsin, whose constant disciple I have been since 1898.

At the University of Georgia, he learned a good deal about the ante-bellum history of his state and the institutionalist approach and wrote his M.A. thesis on Georgia politics. His thesis sponsor was Dr. J. H. T. McPherson, who had taken his doctor's degree at the Johns Hopkins University where the institutionalists were dominant and had written on Liberia as the focus of Negro colonization movements. Most opportunely, Phillips attended the University of Chicago summer school where he studied with a visiting professor, Frederick J. Turner, who gave a seminar on American colonial institutions and offered lectures on the West. Out of Turner's lectures on sectionalism, particularly his observations on the effect of Nullification on Georgia politics, came Phillips's idea for his doctoral thesis published in 1902 as *Georgia and State Rights*. The study was completed under William A. Dunning at Columbia. It represented intensive research in numerous private letters, various local collections in Georgia libraries, and the collections of the Library of Congress.

At Columbia in 1902, while he was publishing his dissertation, one of his mentors, John W. Burgess, issued his revisionist *Reconstruction and the Constitution*. From the books and lectures of Burgess, Phillips carried away ideas that reappear in his own works as central assumptions: Slavery was an evil but grew inevitably as a product of climate and geography. Southerners had an exaggerated fear of slave insurrections, for slaves were usually contented. The real *bête noire* was abolitionism, which produced race tensions and drove Southerners to secession and war. Above all, the races differed in capacity, and, as Burgess put it, "it is the white man's mission, his duty, and his right, to hold the reigns of political power in his own hands for the civilization of the world and the welfare of mankind."

But the Hegelianism of Burgess had less influence on Ulrich Phillips than did the "scientific history" and cult of objectivity claimed by William A. Dunning, the young man's dissertation sponsor. The Dunning school, despite certain racist assumptions, offered a good deal of historical craftsmanship, for many a monograph of merit began in the noted seminars of this Columbia professor. The young students explored new state, county, and town records and forgotten local newspapers, as well as national sources. But even these illuminating sources could not overcome the preconceived racist assumptions of Walter Fleming, J. D. Hamilton, and other Dunning students. Some of the details of the story of Reconstruction that these seminars unfolded—large aspects in fact—did not agree with the Rhodes-Schouler-Burgess-Dunning accounts, but the total and unfavorable synthesis remained. Dunning (like Schouler) even anticipated Phillips's main idea that race was the central fact in Southern life and that slavery was primarily an institution of racial accommodation.

However, Phillips's graduate instruction was not limited to Burgess and Dunning; he also attended the lectures of other seminal teachers, notably those in European history under James Harvey Robinson, then the enthusiastic apostle of the New History, which expanded the subject matter of history to something as broad as the sociologist's idea of "culture." Phillips did give some attention to social history in later years, but he preferred Turner's emphasis on economic, geographic, and political factors.

Between 1902 and 1908, Phillips taught history at the University of Wisconsin, where he was associated with Turner and apparently derived his central concepts of plantation and frontier from the older man. At the same time Turner acknowledged his own debt to Phillips for the application of the frontier idea to the South and particularly for the role of the Negro as a modifying factor. Phillips continued his steady researches and publications on the South while he taught for two years at Tulane University (1908-11) and at the University of Michigan (1911-29), where he found a number of gifted graduate students. He then went to Yale where he stayed until his death in 1934.[1]

One brief but revealing experience in his life took place during World War I when he was Educational Director of the YMCA at Camp Gordon, Georgia, and later a captain of military intelligence. He was then writing his magnum opus, *American Negro Slavery* (1918). Apparently looking about him at Camp Gordon, he wrote in his preface regarding the psychology and behavior of the Negro troops, using language that reflected his kindly, paternalistic, and stereotyped picture of Negroes: "The negroes themselves show the same personal attachments to white men, as well as the same sturdy lightheartedness and the same love of laughter and rhythm, which distinguished their forebears." He compared the Negro non-commissioned officer with the ante-bellum plantation foreman and the white officer with the planter noted for tact and firmness. Freedom had made little change. The Negroes, as in the days of the Gold Coast slave traders, loved colors and finery, were obedient and humorous. Phillips thought that the West African climate prohibited mental effort of a severe or sustained character, "and the negroes have submitted to that prohibition as to many others, through countless generations, with excellent grace." He knew little about the contemporary Negro movements for racial equality nor about the reform programs of Negro organizations.

Phillips won his greatest praise from historians for his industrious use of newly discovered plantation records. He concentrated upon the plantation, although many others had dealt with it less analytically. Both the Southern frontier and the plantation were to him evolutionary forms in the Turner sense. But he did not go as far as Turner in creating historical theories, for he stressed the historian's task of acting as custodian of concrete facts. His racialist concepts were far milder than those of so many of the social scientists and politicians of his day and did not intrude directly upon his description of the plantation, but they did present controlling assumptions.

The books that Phillips wrote reveal that he was indebted more than he cared to admit to the classical trilogy on the Old South written during the 'fifties by Frederick Law Olmsted and compressed in two volumes as *The Cotton Kingdom* (1861). Although Phillips criticized this Northern observer as prejudiced against the South, he frequently drew upon the facts of Olmsted and used them to strengthen certain of its main theses, such as the inefficiency of slavery. Olmsted also had anticipated the central theory of Phillips that slavery did not pay but survived as a mode of race policing. The famous special correspondent for the New York *Daily Times*, later also noted as "the father of American landscape architecture," had spent fourteen months in the South and declared that not only was slavery inefficient, but that many Southerners he had met would have liked to see emancipation but dreaded the prospect of racial conflict thereafter.

Phillips and Olmsted differed in at least one basic way: Olmsted believed that if the planters could be convinced that slavery did not pay, they would take steps to end it. But Phillips, for all his emphasis on economic forces, believed that in the final analysis, it was not only the dollars and cents of slavery that mattered to the average Southerner but also the fact that the institution preserved the security of the tenuous biracial system. Both men blamed abolitionism for arousing sectional tensions, although Olmsted was an active Free-Soiler who worked privately with the New England Emigrant Society to create a free state in west Texas on the Kansas model. Both agreed that slaves were better off in bondage than in their original African home. But Olmsted vigorously disagreed with those (like Phillips) who attributed slavery to the necessities of climate; and he denied that the plantation was a kindly patriarchal institution—as Phillips maintained later. Despite these differences, the two men did a great deal to create the modern image of the Old South.[2]

3

Phillips's first book, *Georgia and State Rights*, traced the recalcitrant attitude of that state toward federal power since statehood. He held that Georgians acted as a united group, whether in ratifying the Constitution, condemning the iniquitous sale of the Yazoo lands, or in demanding the lands of the Creeks and the Cherokees. In Turner style, he drew his theme from a frontier determinant, Georgia's two frontiers. These acted as separate centers of emigration, one to the South in the direction of Savannah along the seaboard and the other at the edge of the Virginia and North Carolina settlements which overflowed into middle Georgia. Throughout his book, he related the political factions to the pressures of frontier and settled areas of Georgia. Again, as befitted a Turner disciple, he made frequent use of county charts and maps to illustrate the sectional and economic basis of party conflicts. With the skill of a craftsman, he showed the changing sectional bases of planter-small farmer rivalry throughout the state's history. Eventually the planter-aristocrat won dominance by infiltrating the frontier, west and southwest.

While Phillips was mildly critical of the Georgia frontiersmen who disregarded Indian rights, he had little love for the red men. The Cherokee, he thought, while not savage, were "heavy and stupid," except for the more intelligent half-breeds. He believed it rather peculiar for the federal government to treat Indian tribes as sovereign.

Secession and war, he made abundantly clear, grew out of the race question. He recorded the sustained conciliatory efforts of Georgia's planter-leaders, Alexander Stephens, Robert Toombs, and Howell Cobb to avert a break, but admitted that the South had not been consistent or thorough in its original desire to get rid of slavery. He defended the resentment against incendiary abolitionism: "There was a perpetual fear of slave insurrections," he asserted, but added that slavery was a mild patriarchal institution of generous masters whose kindness was reinforced by self-interest. Colonization of the Negroes in West Africa and the West Indies had grown out of fears of the Negro, and John Brown's attack on Harpers Ferry converted Georgia's non-slaveholders to secession. When the state debated secession in 1861, the difference between slaveholders and non-slaveholders was not pro and con but revolved around the question of immediate versus delayed withdrawal. He did not think that insurrections were common, but that Southerners held an exaggerated idea of them. "A slave insurrection was the one thing most dreaded by the Southern people. The improbability of its occurrence did not lessen its theoretical horrors."

In 1909, Phillips published two volumes of documents, *Plantation and Frontier*, to initiate a ten-volume series edited by his Wisconsin colleague, Professor Richard T. Ely, entitled *The Documentary History of American Industrial Society*. Here were little-known records of the large plantations, many from ante-bellum planter's manuscripts dealing with management, routine, staples, supplies, "vicissitudes," overseers, slave labor, fugitives, slave conspiracies and crimes, Negro qualities, free Negroes, poor whites, immigrants, migration, frontier society, manufacturing, and, very briefly, artisans and town labor. Many of the sources were drawn from newspapers—advertisements, editorials, news items, and letters to the editor.

The preface introduces his theory that the plantation was a unit developing inevitably under economic pressure and then, as the frontier disappeared, remolded the entire South into its cultural image as far as attitudes, customs, and beliefs were concerned. The plantation was not merely another institution dwarfed by the far more extensive nonslaveholding, small farm economy but the dominant institution of the South. "The plantation system was evolved," he said, "to answer the specific need of meeting the world's demand for certain staple crops in the absence of free labor." In doing so, it trained "a savage race" to fit to some extent within an Anglo-Saxon community and shaped the industrial, commercial, and social system as well as political policy of a vast section. While small farms existed in great numbers, the general order of life was determined by either the plantation system or the frontier. "Hence the antebellum South is peculiarly the region of plantation and frontier and a study of those systems may largely coincide with a study of Southern industrial organization and society."

In Turner style, he traced the historical stages of the plantation system in the West Indies and upon the mainland. When the stage of maximum productivity and prosperity was reached, there was a declining fertility of the soil and an increasing pressure of costs. Comparing the frontier and the plantation, he found that while the former had a lasting influence in giving a stamp of self-reliance and aggressiveness to men's character, the plantation had a more lasting influence locally and in giving a tone of authority and paternalism to the master class and one of obedience to the servants. After the close of the seventeenth century, the plantation problem was mainly the Negro problem and therefore of concern to both races. While the frontier and the Indian were transient factors, the staples and the Negro were permanent and had an intensified influence on Southern philosophy as the years passed. "It eventually overshadowed the whole South and forced the great mass of the people to subordinate all other considerations to policies in this one relation." So it would appear that Turner's frontier was far less important than Phillips's plantation in explaining the South.[3]

Phillips emphasized the planter's pivotal role in the South when he wrote a dedication in his next volume, *A History of Transportation in the Eastern Cotton Belt to 1860*, published by the Columbia University Press in 1908. Here was a lyric endorsement of ante-bellum Bourbonism:

> To the Dominant Class of the South who in the Piping ante-bellum time schooled multitudes white and black to the acceptance of higher standards who in the wartime proved staunch and who in the troublous upheaval and readjustment which followed wrought more sanely and more wisely than the world yet knows.

The "higher standards" could not refer to formal education, since the planter's record on public schools was less than mediocre. His reference to Reconstruction suggests that he had an enthusiastic regard for the anti-Radical Dunning school.

The eastern cotton belt was mainly in South Carolina and Georgia, and it extended from the southern edge of Virginia to central Alabama; it was the most active part of the ante-bellum South in transportation development and united a piedmont region of many hills and rapid streams. Phillips was interested primarily in the social consequences of transportation. He showed that the railroad actually intensified the one-crop system by enlarging the cotton-growing area. It helped some cities and towns to become "trade catchers" rather than "trade makers." An interior city like Atlanta gained at the expense of the older local seaports. In addition, the coming of the railroad demoralized the Negroes and influenced many of them to start roving.

Also very important as an obstacle to diversification was the planter's utter dependence on Negro labor and the slavery system. Since the plantation used "unfree, unwilling, stupid, and half-barbarous laborers, a premium was of necessity put upon routine." Besides, such a regime was safer in view of possible slave disturbances. In addition, slave labor was not only inefficient, but it "locked up" vast amounts of capital in labor that could have been better utilized under a diversified crop system worked by free labor. But slave prices, reflecting market and speculative factors, rose much faster than cotton prices. Phillips, however, implied that the passing of slavery aided the South economically and that slavery's justification depended on the policing argument.

In 1911, he edited for the American Historical Association many hitherto unpublished letters of Robert Toombs, Alexander Stephens, and Howell Cobb, Georgia's leading ante-bellum statesmen. These letters together with an intensive use of the *Congressional Globe* helped him to write a fairly interesting political history of one of the largest slaveholders, the federal senator, Robert Toombs. Phillips showed sympathy for the Georgia State Rights faction of James Jackson, Crawford, and Troup and their successors, which eventually included Toombs. They were staunch supporters of Indian eviction, a low tariff, government economy, and finally secession. Toombs had attended the University of Georgia when it was the planter's favorite school, before going to Union College, New York, and then he studied law at the University of Virginia. The author used much of the material and conclusions from his first book, *Georgia and State Rights*, but the planter's point of view seemed even more intrusive. He saw Toombs as a conscientious moderate who tried for years to avert war through Whig compromises, despite the risks that his delaying tactics meant for the South. Only on the eve of war did Toombs as a Democrat join Jefferson Davis "to strike for Southern independence." Phillips usually justified Toombs's decisions, even to the extent of supporting the extremists. He thought that Toombs was too cautious in 1851 and that he was inclined to minimize the danger that the North would interfere with slavery. He revealed his own position in these words:

If the great sectional conflict was indeed irrepressible (and no man could then nor can any man now nor hereafter be sure that it was by human means avoidable) wisdom required that the South should hasten the issue. The policy of Rhett, Yancey and Quitman was quite possibly the wisest for the South to adopt. Stephens said in after years that he would have advocated extreme measures of resistance in 1851 except that he did not believe the people could be made unanimous in its support nor that their leaders were sufficiently statesmanlike. Toombs was doubtless influenced by the same thoughts.

Phillips portrayed Toombs at the opening of 1861 as keenly aware that war would jeopardize everything and confident that Southern war preparations against the federal forts would intimidate the North and avert civil war. He hoped and expected that all the Southern states, including the border states, would secede and thus leave the Union with a *fait accompli* that would make coercion ridiculous. When his calculations failed, he held out to the end against the decision to fire upon Fort Sumter, an act which he said would amount to murder and suicide.

Once more Phillips won the praise of reviewers, above all the kind words of his master, Frederick J. Turner. His book's moderate pro-Southern view was no longer a novelty to Northern historians; indeed,

in temperate tones Phillips seemed to be reprimanding the extremists
on both sides. Some critics regretted that the biography submerged
so much of Robert Toombs's colorful personality beneath a flood of
political detail.

In 1918 Phillips wrote his most comprehensive book, *American
Negro Slavery*. By this time, his command of new original sources
such as letters, private records, and journals guaranteed a fresh treatment. He began with the background of the West African slave trade
and went on to deal with colonial slavery, the impact of the cotton
revival on slavery extension, the domestic slave trade, the plantation
system in all its aspects, the business side of slavery, the town slaves,
the free Negro, and slave crimes. While the Negro appeared occasionally as an insurrectionist as well as a docile plantation worker, the
sources did not permit Phillips to gain much insight into the aspirations of the Negro (assuming that the author was genuinely interested). The chapter on the Westward Movement in the South after
the American Revolution utilized the Turnerian idea of the evolving
section, beginning in this case with the eastern cotton belt.

One of Phillips's major contentions was that the plantation offered
the best school yet invented for the mass training of "that sort of inert
and backward people which the bulk of the American negroes represented." But he admitted that the pupils seldom graduated. He
thought that the Africans kidnaped as slaves were possibly better off
than those who remained in the jungle—which he assumed had been
their common home. Nor did he miss the opportunity to point out
that it was the New Englander who imported the slaves in the first
place and inflicted cruel punishments on them. Phillips even went so
far as to adopt the proslavery writer's argument that Jefferson's Declaration of Independence and the natural rights philosophy were
merely "the more glittering doctrines current in the philosophy of
the time." He seemed relieved to observe of the post-revolutionary
era: "On the whole the glamor of revolutionary doctrines was passing,
and self-interest was regaining its wonted supremacy." Along these
lines, he quoted favorably Thomas R. Dew's comment that slavery
was more or less essential for the advancement of civilization where
population was scant and currency little used.

Elsewhere he repeated his earlier arguments that slavery was more
costly than free labor; that it involved overcapitalization for the sake
of controlling labor; and that the planter was caught in a treadmill
where he was compelled to buy land and slaves to grow cotton with
which to buy slaves to grow more cotton. Rising slave prices did not

enrich planters unless they sold slaves speculatively. Besides, slavery handicapped the productivity of the whites who had to undertake supervisory tasks. Altogether, slavery prevented the growth of the real wealth of the South; population remained sparse, land values low, money scarce, and natural resources largely neglected. Only the control over the Negroes was assured through slavery. Otherwise the peculiar institution had as many drawbacks as attractions.

While he gave much more attention to slave insurrections than most historians did in his day, he minimized their importance, except to admit that they were sufficiently serious "to maintain a fairly constant undertone of uneasiness." Furthermore, he said, "their result was to restrain the progress of liberalism derived from economic causes." A generation later, historians of both races—and both sections —were to discover the existence of far more slave insurrections and plots than Phillips noted.

When he came to sum up American Negro slavery, he betrayed the emotionalism of one who was committed to a painfully defensive position:

There were injustice, oppression, brutality, and heartburning in the regime,—but where in the struggling world are these absent? There was also gentleness, kind-hearted friendship and mutual loyalty to a degree hard for him to believe who regards the system with a theorist's eye and a partisan squint.

Therefore he concluded that "it is impossible to agree that its basis and its operation were wholly evil, the law and the prophets to the contrary notwithstanding."

Except for the offended Negro scholars like Dr. Carter G. Woodson and contributors to his *Journal of Negro History,* the journals were usually very favorable. There seemed little question as to the author's contribution to the economics of Southern ante-bellum agriculture, his main emphasis. A competent specialist in the *American Historical Review* found it comprehensive, objective, and convincing; he was also impressed by the thesis of the contented slave. "The evidence of the confidence of the slaves in the integrity of the ruling race comes up as a fact too constantly to be ignored," he wrote.

In 1930, Phillips published his most attractive and illuminating book, *Life and Labor in the Old South,* which bore considerable resemblance to *American Negro Slavery.* He had pursued his researches in numerous Southern libraries, as well as in the Library of Congress. By this time the Southern literary renaissance of the 1920s had taken place, and Southern novelists, poets, playwrights, and essayists had made a sympathetic rediscovery of the Negro as art material. The Negroes, too, had had their literary expression in the Harlem renaissance, although this expressed a rather pessimistic note of racial frustration, marked by the occasional "back to Africa" theme that Marcus Garvey, the Jamaican race leader, had sounded. Phillips expressed his own sympathetic appreciation of these developments, though in language that suggested a link with the outmoded local color school of Uncle Remus's day. He regretted that he was "content to delve rather than soar":

> When I read of Howard Odum's Black Ulysses, of Du Bose Heyward's Porgy, of Stephen Benét's plantation mammy and her mistress, esteem for their creations is mingled with chagrin that my fancy is restricted by records. The characters portrayed by these writers are as true as the men and women who figure in my pages.

Actually, Odum, Du Bose Heyward, and Benét were closer to the actual Negro than Phillips, although in those days the treatment of the Negro, even by the best-intentioned, did not go much beyond the lyric phase.

Phillips's first chapter, "The Land of Dixie," begins with a summary of his entire interpretation of the ante-bellum South compressed within a single paragraph and introduced by his idea of climatic influence:

> Let us begin by discussing the weather, for that has been the chief agency in making the South distinctive. It fostered the cultivation of the staple crops, which promoted the plantation system, which brought the importation of negroes, which not only gave rise to chattel slavery but created a lasting race problem. These led to controversy and regional rivalry for power, which produced apprehensive reactions and culminated in a stroke for independence. Thus we have the house that Jack built, otherwise known as the Confederate States of America.

He pointed out the various climatic belts of the South and used these to explain the various regions which were controlled by growing seasons of varying length and different crops. But he went far beyond this reasonable position for the role of climate, and attributed to heat an entire array of Southern habits and problems: languid appetites, indolence, slow, slurred speech, soft manners, easy-going ways, and hookworm infestation. However, he was not much behind his noted but extreme Yale colleague in geography, Ellsworth Huntington, who found climate an all-powerful determinant on culture.

Life and Labor in the Old South was written in an engaging literary style, used a great deal of interesting narrative material, and offered more social history than Phillips had previously used. It began with the settling of the Old Dominion, went on to picture frontier expansion, then the coming of the cotton belt, and finally gave a detailed discussion of everyday plantation life. Unlike the previous works of Phillips, there was no explicit racialist statement. He approached closer to that aspect of scientific objectivity which avoids self-identification with the issues under discussion. His new urbanity even found expression in a favorable comment on George Washington Cable, the ex-Confederate writer who had forsaken Louisiana for Massachusetts, presumably because the South would no longer tolerate his criticisms of racial injustices.

In a chapter on "The Peculiar Institution," Phillips went much further than before in showing the drawbacks of slavery. He did not stack the cards so obviously in favor of the planter class. Actually, he had not changed his mind on the fundamentals of ante-bellum society, though he may have reflected the influence of teaching Northern students and of his association with Yankees. The chief theses of *American Negro Slavery* were all there: the unprofitableness of slavery, the plantation as a civilizing agency, and the cultural and economic unity of the patriarchal plantation. He gave the usual brief treatment, though with fresh illustrations, of "the plain people."

Specialists as well as general readers applauded the work. The eminent William K. Boyd of North Carolina, a student of Dunning, wrote in the *American Historical Review*, "Realism rather than romanticism, actuality instead of tradition, is the dominating motive throughout." To Boyd the book was "a delightful reconstruction of the antebellum plantation regime." [4] Charles W. Ramsdell, another Southerner who had studied with Dunning and became a president of the Southern Historical Association, liked the Phillips book, even though it lacked his favorite thesis that the South had been a colonial province of the North; he wished that Phillips had examined such questions as the increasing influence of Eastern financial power over southern agriculture before 1860. He also missed any adequate treatment of certain important industries and complained that only fifteen pages were devoted to the six-million non-slaveholders. But all this was offset in his mind by the immense solidity of the book, its objectivity mixed with sympathy, its easy style, unfailing humor, and apt quotations. [5]

That Phillips never changed his mind regarding the racial factor in Southern history became doubly apparent in 1939, five years after his death, when the American Historical Association published his series of public lectures delivered at Northwestern University, *The Course of the South to Secession.* The editor was his disciple, Professor Merton Coulter of the University of Georgia, whose own works reflected Phillips's defensive viewpoint. These lectures elaborated upon the same social interpretation that Phillips had written a generation before in his doctoral dissertation under Dunning on *Georgia and State Rights* and in his biography of Robert Toombs.

He looked upon the American Revolution as an act of secession, for the Enlightenment ideas of "the extreme left" behind the Declaration of Independence had nothing to do with the causes of the conflict, but were "philosophical gloss." Yet Phillips depended on an ideological interpretation that ran counter to this minimization of the weight of ideas in history. He deplored the evil consequences of eighteenth-century liberal "agitation" and, above all, of abolitionism in stirring up the sections against each other. John Taylor's abstractions, particularly his philosophical objections to the centralizing tendencies of Hamilton and the Federalists, were sympathetically reviewed alongside of the states' rights ideas of the later realistic Jefferson.

One of the longer lectures, "An Answer to Race," showed the planter's reaction to the race wars of San Domingo and to the Southern slave revolts and plots. Phillips tried to impress his audience with the needs of a white civilization and security in a heavily Negro area. Apparently he had changed his mind on one important fact, for he intimated that the Southerner's fear of race war was justified by actual outbreaks. He blamed the antislavery societies for creating an explosive situation. On the other hand, he was sardonic in speaking of the "socialistic acrobatics" of the extreme proslavery propagandists, George Fitzhugh of Virginia and Henry Hughes of Mississippi. The wisest ideological course for the South, he thought, was to take up the line developed by Edward A. Pollard, namely that the retention of slavery was "the crux of Southern purpose in the maintenance of white supremacy as a safeguard of civilization and orderly government." Slavery was primarily insurance against race conflict.

Phillips left his listeners without any doubt that he identified himself with the Southern Rights program and its obvious contemporary implications:

The doctrine of Southern rights was in essence that the community must possess, and be assured of possessing control of its own domestic regime, that the South must be and remain a white man's country not menaced with the turmoil sure to come from an incautious, extraneous elevation of the millions of Negroes out of their necessary subordination.

To him the Southern demand for congressional sanction of slavery was a "questionable dogma" intended merely to test Northern purpose.

This "white man's country" view of the road to secession had already been presented by Phillips in 1928 for general discussion before the American Historical Association as "The Central Theme of Southern History." He contended that the South had never had a "focus" in any geographic sense and that "Southernism" did not arise from any selectiveness of migration, or of a distinct religion or language, or a one-crop tillage, or the agricultural way of life. Beyond these factors, the Southerners were "a people with a common resolve indomitably maintained—that it [their section] shall be and remain a white man's country." As the Negroes became numerous enough to be a race problem, they were policed "in the interest of orderly government and the maintenance of Caucasian civilization." Only by such an explanation, he felt, could one account for the fervid secessionism and war sacrifices of the non-slaveholders.

He concluded that the Southern belief that the Negroes in the mass were incompetent for any good political purpose had led to disfranchisement of the blacks; furthermore, he implied that the sentiments and symbols of the Tillmans, the Vardamans, and the Watsons were "not wholly divorced from reason." His opposition to any program of racial civil rights may be inferred from his reference to the similarities of the Japanese and Negro questions. California with a small Japanese population had secured federal support for its discriminatory legislation, but the South, he complained, with 10,000,000 Negroes in their midst, could not expect more at best from the federal government than "a tacit acquiescence in what their state governments may do." Thus, the Solid South had emerged, "Political solidarity at the price of provincial status is maintained to keep assurance doubly, trebly sure that the South shall remain 'a white man's country.'" He made it clear, as he had in earlier writings, that the Road to Reunion was based on the acquiescence of the federal government to Henry Grady's formula of a New South co-operating with the North economically if the race question was left to Southern whites. During Phillips's lifetime, the Northern historian's readiness to be "objective" was not wholly a reflection of the age of science or of Ranke's injunctions. He, too, was slow in accepting the full implications of race equality as he observed the huge influx of Southern Negroes, the Chicago Race Riot of 1919, and the tendency to use informal means of segregation in housing and schools. But the search for democratic alternatives to domination and force was making progress when Phillips died in 1934.

4

The influence of Ulrich B. Phillips on Southern historiography, despite the challenge of recent critics, has been profound. With all his limitations, he raised the level of history-writing about the South and stimulated Southerners to write about their section. The movement led to the founding (at the time of his death) of the Southern Historical Association, and the appearance in 1935 of the first issue of the *Journal of Southern History*, which maintained high standards of research. Many a Northern scholar, too, had become an enthusiast of Southern history. Secondly, he probably interpreted the Southern white's mind more accurately than some of his successors; his Georgia environment helped him to see that the "white man's country" concept had far more influence on the ante-bellum Southerner than sectional economic rivalries alone. But, like the Southerner of 1861, he could not visualize the possibility that the race question could be handled in any other way than by force. Thus, by 1934 he had not budged from the traditional position that had kept the Negro waiting several centuries for complete naturalization as an American citizen. As we have seen, he shared the dominant racist views of his time, particularly those held by a number of eminent historians and other social scientists North and South.

Among his shortcomings was that he ordered his evidence in such a way as to justify slavery; the initial sin of the slave trade had been committed by others. He did not trouble to reconcile his argument that slavery was a civilizing institution with his factual finding that Southern states forbade the teaching of reading and writing to the slave—obviously for security purposes. Instead, he would contrast the alleged jungle origins of the Negro (slave ship records indicate that he came from the diversified West Coast, not from the primitive interior of central Africa) with the mild advances made by his sedentary descendant of 1861. The fact that Phillips could enumerate many brutalities in the slave system from sound historical sources did not prevent his drawing a predetermined conclusion that nothing must be done to disturb slavery as long as the race problem existed. The case of Ulrich B. Phillips illustrates how the subjective values of a historian may neutralize the most meticulous empirical research. To buttress his case, he had to fall back upon the dubious intellectual weapons of the notorious proslavery propagandists.

While most historians agree that Phillips oversimplified the "South" to mean little more than a plantation process of development succeeding an earlier Turnerian frontier process, he had a sound nucleus of reality to offer. Obviously he went too far in neglecting the life and influence of at least five million Southern whites out of eight million in 1860 who belonged to the small farmer class, but there was much to be said for his contention that the Black Belt concentrations of Negroes, where whites were in the minority, did much to generate race fears and suspicions which infiltrated the non-slaveholding areas or those with relatively few slaves. (This assumption, for example, is similar to the actual conclusions of Professor V. O. Key, who has proved by statistical methods that the racial attitudes of the South today are most intense in the Deep South and then taper off in the more heavily white communities of the upper South.) Plantation South Carolina, Mississippi, Alabama, Louisiana, and Georgia therefore could be expected to provide the most militant leaders for secessionism and war. Phillips recognized a number of other causes for secession, but he regarded them as quite secondary.

Therefore, Phillips, with all his racist misconceptions, seemed closer to a convincing explanation of why Southerners took the road to war than did later historians who assumed that somehow rival industrial and agricultural societies must fight. He refused to take stock in the theories of an "irrepressible conflict"; certainly he was too good a Bourbon to be interested in the theories of Charles Beard, Louis Hacker, and others who held that Northern capitalists and rival planter-aristocrats stood in mortal combat. He could have accepted the theories of Professor James Randall, and George Fort Milton, that emotionalism and "a blundering generation" had precipitated the war —providing that they understood that the fundamental basis for sectional peace to a Southerner would have been the continued acceptance of the Grady formula for compromise. Thus, the upgrading of the reputation of Stephen A. Douglas (and later of Andrew Johnson) by the Randall-Milton revisionists of the 1930s could be fitted into the Phillips's thesis. To this Georgian, who held no brief for strict determinism, the Civil War was indeed a needless war, as the revisionists and admirers of Douglas contended.[6]

Phillips's tendency to put heavy blame on the abolitionists (and to a lesser extent upon the Southern fire-eaters) for awakening the Southern fear that Northern interference in the race question was imminent would have made him at least moderately receptive to those who later emphasized the psychological and ethical factors, though he paid little attention to Northern public opinion as a factor. The vogue for psychology developed somewhat after the turn of the century, by which time Phillips had made up his mind to a large extent on primary and secondary issues of the Civil War. Thus in the 1940s and 1950s, Avery Craven of the University of Chicago blamed the war partly on a dangerous psychological stalemate between two irreconcilable sections to whom *"slavery had come to symbolize values in each of their social-economic structures for which men fight and die but which they do not give up or compromise."* (Italics his.) Craven added in this book, *The Growth of Southern Nationalism* (1953), "These values had been emphasized and reinforced by two decades of emotional strife, name-calling, and self-justification. Right and wrong, justice and injustice were in conflict. The destiny of mankind was at stake." Craven, however, traced these emotions to concrete issues such as expansion, lands, and tariffs which had come to be misrepresented by emotional abstractions and principles that could not be yielded. Craven and other historians went beyond Phillips in analyzing the Northern will to resist—nationalism, growing economic and social interdependence, the development of a new financial-industrial capitalism, and the incompatibility of Christianity, democracy, and progress with slavery. But this mid-twentieth-century position would in all likelihood have been inadequate by the Phillips test of the primacy of the Southern desire for a "white man's country." Slavery to him, as we have seen, was almost a *sine qua non* for Negro domination, although he was also interested in getting the same result by the post-bellum road that the South finally took.

The image of the Old South of Ulrich Phillips was often but not always reinforced by his doctoral students. His emphasis on the incendiary influence of abolitionism in greatly arousing the fears of race war among Southern whites led his disciple, Gilbert H. Barnes, to investigate the impetus behind the abolitionist leaders. His *Antislavery Impulse, 1830-1844*, which disposed of the myth that Garrison was the fountainhead of abolitionist activities, demonstrated a link between the evangelical fervor of the camp meeting and the techniques of Theodore Weld's abolitionists. Through the popular textbooks the Phillips point of view reached many undergraduates.

By the time of Phillips's death in 1934, the abolitionist interpretation of the Civil War had few academic supporters and the Lost Cause enjoyed the keen sympathy of popular novelists and moviegoers. Liberals and Negro leaders had protested in 1915 the showing of *The Birth of a Nation,* which pictured the old Klan (newly resurrected that same year) as the shield of Southern womanhood. Thereafter Hollywood found that their audiences liked the sentimental view of the plantation aristocrat, the portrait of the contented slave, and the minstrel interpretation of the Negro. Even the depression did not change this stereotype.

However, there were eminent Southern historians who preferred Jefferson to Jefferson Davis, Lincoln to Lee. The kindly William E. Dodd, who received his Ph.D. at the University of Leipzig and had left the University of North Carolina to teach at the University of Chicago, produced many graduate students who published liberal interpretations of Southern history. Dodd's own writings were unfortunately too hastily written to rank high as empirical research, but they provided many keen insights into the ante-bellum society. While he stressed the role of the democratic frontier in Southern history, he shared Phillips's idea that the plantation dominated the South. But he looked on the planters as oligarchs analogous to certain Northern industrialists of his own day; they had shaped the aristocratic philosophy of the Cotton Kingdom and led the way to a war against the Northern and Western democratic forces under Lincoln. Like other Southern historians, he felt suspicious of Northern financial and industrial exploitation of the agricultural economy of the South.

Dodd was no political historian in the narrow sense, although he understood the workings of power coalitions, for he also dealt with many everyday facets of Southern life, developed the theme of a popular small farmer's struggle for democracy against the planter (as in *The Old South* and *Expansion and Conflict*), stressed economic determinants such as soil exhaustion, and wrote many biographies and essays on Southern leaders from a democratic point of view. On the activist Negro, however, he had little to say. In most respects his liberalism dwelt upon Jeffersonian agrarian values (like Parrington), low tariffs, the rights of small nations (like his friend Woodrow Wilson), and kindred viewpoints. In later years, as Franklin D. Roosevelt's ambassador to Hitler's Germany, he proved a vehement foe of racialism and spoke to German audiences of that "other Germany" of the democratic Carl Schurz.

At Vanderbilt University, Frank Owsley and certain of his colleagues challenged the idea of Phillips and Dodd that a planter aristocracy had driven small farmers and poor whites into poorer lands. They emphasized the independent and relatively prosperous small farmers ("the plain people"), the wide diffusion of land ownership among them, the opportunity to rise to planter status, and the lack of class friction between yeoman and planter. Their critics argued that the planter did monopolize the best soils, produced most of the money crops, and lived much more prosperously than did the yeoman, who tended to cultivate subsistence crops such as wheat and corn on a far larger scale than cotton.

In 1940, Clement Eaton of the University of Kentucky arrested considerable attention for his anti-Confederate interpretations in *Freedom of Thought in the Old South,* which showed how the dominant pro-slavery forces erected an intellectual blockade against the inroads of the new liberal ideas. Free speech, popular education, and science suffered, while white illiteracy, shouting preachers, and duelists flourished. His excellent volume, *A History of the Old South* (1949), synthesized the newer researches and rejected U. B. Phillips's emphasis on climate, geography, and the struggle for "the white man's country" as the prime cause of the plantation system and the Civil War. However, like other historians, he appreciated many of Phillips's contributions to the economic history of the South.

Louisiana State University and its active press, although a beneficiary of Huey Long's largess to education, showed nevertheless the same objectivity as the Northern university presses and became a leading sponsor of Southern historical studies. One of its able historians, the indefatigable Wendell H. Stephenson, edited the noteworthy *Southern Biography Series* during the 1940s. He also became one of the chief editors of the scholarly series, *A History of the South,* issued mostly during the late 'forties and 'fifties and devoted to social, economic, and cultural as well as political history. At the same high level, Louisiana State University published for many years *The Journal of Southern History,* which at once took a leading place among regional journals of national interest. Scarcely of less importance for Southern studies and with no less devotion to the newer liberal spirit in the South was the University of North Carolina and its outstanding university press. Here Howard Odum, the sociologist, influenced historians as well as sociologists in regional studies; in fact, he and his colleagues sponsored so many "ecological" studies as to rank the University of North Carolina second in this field only to the leader, the University of Chicago. While scholarly liberalism in the South still tended to be economic and pro-New Deal rather than representing any frontal attack on segregation (as was generally true of Northern scholars as well), the naïveté of U. B. Phillips's racism retreated from the great centers of learning.

Even Phillips's unfailing urbanity toward individuals of both races did not charm the newly trained professional Negro historians like the rebels Dr. William E. B. Du Bois of Atlanta, Dr. Carter G. Woodson of Washington, Dr. Charles Wesley of Howard University, and many other able and outspoken young academicians of that race. They looked upon history as an instrument of racial salvation as well as a source of pride in race achievements. Therefore, they condemned Phillips's racialism, his stereotype of the happy-go-lucky Negro, and his assumption that Negroes had few cultural contributions to make in either the New World or in Africa. Unlike Burgess, Dunning, and Rhodes, they felt a keen sympathy for the Reconstruction experiment in political and social equality.

The brilliant and belligerent radical, Dr. Du Bois, came of mixed Negro and French ancestry and was reared in Great Barrington, Massachusetts, a small community with few Negroes. After he went South to study at a Negro college in a white community, Fisk University in Nashville, he rebelled against the ritual of Jim Crow. Finally, he discovered a haven at Harvard and earned all three degrees there, with his doctoral dissertation—which remained his best original work thereafter—on *The Suppression of the African Slave Trade from Africa to the United States* (1895). Before taking his doctorate, he used a Slater Fund award to study at the University of Berlin, where he listened to the lectures of Weber, Schmoller, Treitschke, and other leaders in economic and political history. For thirteen years he taught at Atlanta University and quarreled with Booker T. Washington and the Tuskegee conservatives. *The Souls of Black Folk* (1903) set forth his uncompromising stand on racial equality and castigated Booker T. Washington's acceptance of segregation, emphasis on vocational education for Negroes, alliance with business, and willingness to forgo the strategy of agitation. His own solution was embodied in the new National Association for the Advancement of Colored People, which he helped to found, and its outspoken organ, *The Crisis*, which he edited. The NAACP labored through the courts to secure the Negro's fullest rights under the Constitution.

By 1927, Du Bois felt captivated by the Russian Revolution, visited that country when Russian-Americans financed his trip, and emerged a confirmed Marxist who placed the slavery struggle and the Negro's current problems in a world setting of class conflict. These ideas were embedded in his widely read *Black Reconstruction* (1935), which depended more on the researches of Rhodes and other antislavery writers than on original sources. He reversed the Dunning interpretation by praising the racial contributions of Stevens, Sumner, the Freedmen's Bureau, and the Radical program. Above all, he showed in detail the positive achievements of the Negro in the so-called Carpetbag legislatures. While some reviewers complained of distortions and bitterness, others were persuaded that he had opened the door to a valuable reassessment of Reconstruction.

Dr. Carter G. Woodson did not follow the radical panaceas of Du Bois, but he was no less firm in fighting for racial equality. He was born in 1875, the son of a Virginia freedman, and he worked as a coal miner in his youth, deriving his education by home study until the opportunity came to enter high school and the University of Chicago, where he earned the first two degrees. Like Du Bois he entered Harvard; he wrote his dissertation on *The Disruption of Virginia*—a fitting subject for a son of West Virginia. He gave up a deanship at Howard University to devote the rest of his life (except for teaching at a Washington high school) to the promotion of Negro history by amateurs as well as professionals. In 1915 he established the Association for the Study of Negro Life and History, which introduced Negro History Week, Negro history bulletins, and conferences dealing with the subject. Most important, he founded that same year *The Journal of Negro History,* with an editorial board of scholars and literary contributors drawn from both races. Woodson urged historians to search for the historical role that Negroes had played in freeing themselves and in shaping their own destiny. He helped to raise the status of Negro historical studies to a high professional level. Not least among his intensive activities was the sponsorship of a special outlet for books about the Negro, the Associated Publishers.

Dr. Woodson emphasized his dislike for Phillips's *American Negro Slavery* by reviewing it adversely not only for the *Mississippi Valley Historical Review* but also—this time in an unsigned review—for his own *Journal of Negro History.* While he conceded that the book was better than most histories of slavery (at least in extent of subject matter), he thought that it was primarily an economic treatise concerned only with the Negro as property and definitely biased. He commented upon Phillips's "inability to fathom the Negro mind" and his tendency to emphasize the kindly planter and the contented slave.[7] Woodson's friend and successor as editor of the *Journal,* William M. Brewer, in another review, had much the same complaints against *Life and Labor in the Old South.* He added with obvious bitterness that the slaves were lumped together as a group "which is still the policy of white Americans in thinking of Negroes and prescribing a place for them." While he thought that this book was better than *American Negro Slavery*, it neglected the poor whites and free Negroes and showed that "Phillips is a disciple of the color line and a staunch defender of the faith in the South." [8]

Among the young gifted Negro historians was the Fisk-Yale-Harvard educated Dr. Charles H. Wesley of Howard, later president of Central State College at Wilberforce, Ohio. Like many talented Negroes, such as those of the Harlem Renaissance of the 1920s, he joined Dr. Woodson in calling for greater attention to the role of Africa in history and a more intimate interpretation of the Negro's past. His *Collapse of the Confederacy* (1937), unlike so many histories by Negroes, did not focus upon slavery alone but dealt with the entire Southern society and argued that the Confederacy lost the war because of weakness in morale rather than a shortage of weapons and men.

Another Harvard-trained doctor of philosophy in history was John Hope Franklin, a thoughtful, soft-spoken scholar who reflected the temperateness of the younger generation without sacrificing the activist Negro. His book, *The Free Negro in North Carolina* (1943), grew out of his dissertation and won very favorable notice; and his *From Slavery to Freedom* (1947) easily became the best textbook in the field because of its balance, thoroughness, and accuracy. Like Wesley (and some Negro novelists as well), he turned to a general picture of Southern society in *The Militant South, 1800-1861* (1956), which traced the tradition of violence and the martial spirit in that section's emphasis on filibustering expeditions, secret militant societies such as the Knights of the Golden Circle, dueling, and race police. Dr. Franklin's appointment to the History chairmanship of Brooklyn College, a large and outstanding city college in New York City, was an event in the history of racial integration.

Negro historical studies attracted innumerable whites as well. At Emory University, in Phillips's own state, Bell Wiley published *Southern Negroes, 1861-65*, which depicted genuine Negroes in wartime singing songs of freedom and quite familiar with the issue of emancipation. The standard picture of the loyal slave hating the Yankee and defending his master was challenged by the facts of wartime slave insurrections and plots, fifth-column activities behind the lines, and other evidences of a repressed people. At the extreme left were Marxist writers like Dr. Herbert Aptheker, author of *American Slave Re-*

volts (1943), who not only demonstrated the frequency of slave revolts and sabotage but interpreted them as an expression of class war.
Aptheker and other Marxists published narratives of Negro abolitionists. The Marxist novelist, Howard Fast, in the best-selling story,
Freedom Road, offered a fictional (and grossly exaggerated) class
struggle interpretation of Reconstruction along the lines of Du Bois's
Black Reconstruction.

While Negro sociologists like Franklin Frazier and Charles Johnson
stimulated Negro historical studies, the proponents of race relations
studies secured the sponsorship of the Carnegie Corporation in 1937
for a "comprehensive study of the Negro in the United States, to be
undertaken in a wholly objective and dispassionate way as a social
phenomenon." They found an outstanding scholar, a social economist
acceptable to both races in Gunnar Myrdal of the University of Stock-
holm. The result was the monumental study, *The American Dilemma*
(1944), which showed with considerable detail drawn from history
as well as sociology the ambivalence of a society ideally dedicated to
the equalitarianism of the Declaration of Independence but committed
to practices quite at variance with equality. It ended optimistically
with the statement that "we have today in social science a greater
trust in the improvability of man and society than we have ever had
since the Enlightenment." The ensuing enthusiasm for race relations
studies and courses and the Supreme Court integration decisions of
1954 showed that a new phase of Negro history had begun.

The central importance of Africa in Negro studies, which had been
emphasized by the Harlem Renaissance and dramatized by Marcus
Garvey's Back to Africa movement of the 'twenties, had its leading
white scholarly exponent in Northwestern's noted anthropologist, Melville Herskovits. He emphasized the provenience of New World Negro
culture in West Africa, made pioneer studies of African "culture
areas," and published interpretive descriptions of Negro societies in
Haiti, Brazil, and the Caribbean. He was a disciple of Franz Boas
of Columbia, who had led the scholars to defeat the racists of the
'twenties by dispelling the confusion over the nature of race and culture. Herskovits's challenging book, *The Myth of the Negro Past*
(1941), took issue with the social scientists who had assumed that
the Negro came to the New World "culturally naked," and it showed
evidences for considerable cultural borrowing from Africa. Among his
students were many apprentice historians as well as anthropologists;
he made Northwestern a center for a noteworthy African program.

While a new image of the Negro and his African past began to replace the Phillips interpretation, younger scholars took issue with the entire plantation hypothesis as well. One of the most analytical refutations of essentials in the Georgian's position came from Professor Kenneth M. Stampp of the University of California, although this was not the primary purpose of his book, *The Peculiar Institution* (1956). Stampp denied that climate and soil inevitably created the plantation; besides, it was older than slavery and survived its prohibition. Reasons of profit, rather than deterministic factors, led the colonial South to prefer the plantation to the non-slaveholding farm.

Stampp utilized the recent findings on Negroes and African studies by the anthropologists to demonstrate how relatively advanced the original African cultures were. He dismissed the plantation myths of the Negroes' inherent inferiority and submissive temperament. Phillips had made the Negro at once submissive and prone on occasion to slave plots, insurrections, and crimes. Stampp disagreed with Phillips and with those historians who followed this view that slavery did not pay economically. There were ample details of profitable slaveholding supported by efficient workers who were spurred on to do extra work by incentives of extra pay and positions of prestige among fellow-slaves.

So far from the truth was the idea that slaves were fit only for crude farm labor that Southerners talked about the desirability of greatly increasing the use of slaves in new Southern factories. Stampp went beyond Phillips in portraying the mistreatment of slaves, for he did not find that self-interest and humanitarianism were quite the checks that the older historian had imagined. From this analysis it followed that slavery would not necessarily die a natural death soon, even if left alone. One might logically infer from Stampp's facts that nothing short of force could dislodge slavery. However, Stampp did not press this latter point and tended to use a multiple approach freely in another book on the causes of the war, *And the War Came* (1950). His chief argument in *The Peculiar Institution* rested on the assumption that Southerners had freely made their choice to set up the slave plantation despite other—less profitable—alternatives.

Another acute Northern-bred critic, Richard Hofstadter of Columbia, pointed out in an article, "U. B. Phillips and the Plantation Legend," what a serious error the Georgian had made in drawing the materials for his picture of the Old South from the records of the largest plantations—which Phillips had done partly for the reason that these papers were the best preserved. Phillips magnified this error by depending on the case method, thus assuming that he was dealing with typical plantations. By omitting the smaller units, he was actually using a sample of about 10 per cent of all the slaves and less than 1 per cent of all the slaveholders. "For the most part," said Hofstadter, "he was concentrating upon the upper crust of the upper crust." Yet the critic added a compliment, albeit a heavily qualified one, that "so thorough was his work that granted the same purpose, the same materials, and the same methods, his treatment of the Old South is unlikely to be altered in fundamental respects." Possibly this comment was intended as a tongue-in-cheek appraisal.[9]

No other area in American historiography reflects so baldly the influence of subjective influences on historians as in the case of the Old South, the Civil War, and Reconstruction. Even those who did not go as far as Phillips in marshaling the evidence to establish an *a priori* thesis could not wholly escape taking a stand either overt or implied on the corrosive race issue. More than in other fields, the writer tended to draw conclusions that did not actually emerge from the evidence presented. Human values of course are not an indigenous part of the historical narrative; they are put there by a moralist disguised as a historian, and the conclusions are partly shaped by this fact. The mid-twentieth-century historian of the South could only claim that his facts are more accurate than Phillips, that he recognized many facets that had been neglected, that he used far more sources than seemed to exist a generation ago, and that he felt under greater compulsion to be objective, recognizing more than ever the grave likelihood that he would not wholly succeed.

☆ 13 ☆

Charles A. Beard and the
Economic Interpretation of History

1

Economic history in the form of a chronological summary of facts was quite common in the nineteenth century, and indeed was attractively presented by McMaster and others, but, on the other hand, only an elitist few like Richard Hildreth and those within the socialist or Marxist ranks had attempted a genuine economic synthesis of society. The bright young men of 1900-1920 seeking economic determinants for history, like Charles Beard and others in the Columbia School of the New History, felt the pragmatic urge to make history serve society by curing its social ills. It was not enough to commemorate the past and to assume like Tacitus that the great models of antiquity would suffice to teach an inspiring lesson for statesmen and ordinary citizens. One must apply the current lessons of the Industrial Revolution, experimental science, finance capitalism, and materialist factors to history rather than depend upon the ineffectual idealistic conceptions held by the Bancroft school.

European economic historians, some of them Marxists, led the way toward an economic synthesis. Since the 1870s, Marxians had followed their master's injunction to cease dwelling on personalities and isolated events and to make "personifications of economic categories." Non-Marxians were unwilling to go so far, but they shared in the search for the evolution and meaning of economic institutions. In

New History [margin handwritten note]

Germany, Werner Sombart produced studies of capitalism which tried to explain the motivations and methods of the entrepreneur. Richard Ehrenberg analyzed the origins and development of the great entrepreneurial fortunes as reflected in the rise of the Fugger bankers. Such studies had their American counterpart in Gustavus Myers, *The History of the Great American Fortunes* (1907) and, much later, in Matthew Josephson's influential volume, *The Robber Barons* (1934). British economic historians like Toynbee (the elder), the Webbs, and Thorold Rogers won the plaudits of American scholars for their perceptive historical analyses of economic influences in industry and agriculture. Christian socialism especially inspired European (and American) scholars to pioneer in "social economics." The Social Gospel was in its heyday.

The vast protest literature of Populism and Progressivism is too well known to require summary. At the University of Wisconsin, these currents were evident in the labor histories of John R. Commons and the reformist books of Richard T. Ely, the economist. Frederick J. Turner, while critical of the paper-money panaceas of the Populists, turned to the virtues of government planning and focused attention on the economic as well as geographic determinants of the frontier. He and his students thought of American history as partly determined by the struggle of debtor farmers and creditor merchants. Another regionalist, Ulrich B. Phillips, resisted the reformers, but helped to make Southern history a product of primary economic as well as racial factors.

At Columbia University, many students learned to interpret history from an economic point of view in the classes of Edwin R. A. Seligman, the son of a well-to-do banker, but a reformer nonetheless. He had been lecturing since 1886 on financial and industrial history. In 1903 Seligman published a very popular little book, *The Economic Interpretation of History,* which explained the inadequacy of Hegel's idealistic theories and urged the need for systematic "laws of history" which recognized that economic conditions were the foundation of life. But he rejected "economic determinism" or any other kind of determinism as false and argued that it was wholly unnecessary to embrace the socialist program in order to profit from the economic interpretation. Charles Beard read this book and apparently agreed with its main tenets.

One of Turner's students, Algie M. Simons, became for some years an ardent socialist committed to an economic interpretation of history that was definitely Marxist. His *Social Forces in American History*

(1911) circulated for years as a pamphlet and used a vituperative Marxist jargon to describe class conflict in American history. He saw the Revolution as an economic struggle led by colonial merchants. When he came to the movement for the Constitution, he anticipated to a surprising degree Beard's thesis that four interest groups representing the industrial and mercantile creditors of the East imposed that document upon the farmer-labor debtors of the interior. (Hildreth, Libby, and J. Allen Smith also expressed similar economic interpretations.) "The wageworking, farming, and debtor class naturally had no desire for a strong central government," observed Simons. Like Beard after him, he argued that due to wholesale disfranchisement, the Constitution was ratified by a minority. Even his conclusion bore some resemblance to Beard's, although couched in offensive language:

> To sum up: the organic law of this nation was formulated in secret session by a body called into existence through a conspiratory trick and was forced upon a disfranchised people by means of a dishonest apportionment in order that the interests of a small body of wealthy rulers might be served. This should not blind us to the fact that this small ruling class really represented progress, that a unified government was essential to that industrial and social growth which has made this country possible.

Simons, like Beard in *The Rise of American Civilization,* looked upon the Civil War as a struggle between rival capitalisms, one industrial, the other agrarian. Both agreed upon the economic outcome:

> Out of the Civil War was born the elements of present society. It created the great capitalist and the great industrialist and the mechanical foundation upon which these rest. It placed these in control of the national government.

But, as a good Marxist, Simons went on to predict the ultimate seizure of political power by labor. Beard never subscribed to the Marxist dialectic of class struggle, though he stressed the role of interest groups in molding politics.[1] Neither Simons nor Beard knew how much businessmen hated abolitionists and worked for peaceful compromises to avert war.

Charles Beard became closely identified with a brilliant Columbia colleague, James Harvey Robinson, and with the New History, which became the creed of so many other distinguished men of that university. In fact, both men published a very popular two-volume textbook, *The Development of Modern Europe* (1907-08). They protested the overemphasis upon politics and wars and called for more attention to such fundamental economic matters as the Industrial Revolution, commerce and the colonies, the internal social reforms of the European states, and the general advance of science. Since Robinson did all too little research, the exemplification of this program could be claimed only by Beard.

In this text, both writers took up the pragmatic idea that history should justify itself by its usefulness for the present. They complained that text writers usually failed to connect the past with the present, sometimes with the excuse that we should avoid distortion or bias. Their own position was made crystal-clear:

> In preparing the volume in hand, the writers have consistently subordinated the past to the present. It has been their ever-conscious aim to enable the reader to catch up with his own times; to read intelligently the foreign news in the morning papers.
>
> There has been no distortion of the facts in order to bring them into relation to any particular conception of the present and its tendencies. Even if certain occurrences of merely temporary prominence have been omitted as irrelevant to the purpose of the work, this cannot mean any serious loss.

Here was the emphatic expression of what came to be called "presentism," which had certain relativist tendencies. They became more manifest in Beard's later years.

Robinson complained in *The New History* (1912) that historians seemed to justify facts for their own sake. Mere name-listing and an emphasis on extraordinary events destroyed perspective, even when the narrative was told interestingly. To him the true principle of selection was, "Is the fact or occurrence one which will aid the reader to grasp the meaning of any great period of human development or the true nature of any momentous institution?" But he rejected the idea that reliable "lessons" could be learned from past events. Such beliefs assumed that conditions remained sufficiently uniform to give precedents a perpetual value. Actually modern conditions changed so rapidly that it would be risky to apply past experience to solve current problems. Like Beard he castigated the oft-repeated claim as to "what history teaches."

Instead of seeking lessons from the past in this uncritical way, Robinson urged a pragmatic evolutionary approach to history that would enable people to understand themselves and the problems of mankind. One would use history just as one applied personal history. In both cases the present was not self-explanatory but required the aid of experience and memory. Thus a "Godlike knowledge of all history" afforded a corresponding insight into the best methods of

alleviating mankind's ills, but not because the past offered "lessons."
History would serve us because our present institutions and ideals had
an evolutionary continuity from the past. Without history we would
lose effective adjustment to our environment. Through this pragmatic
New History, especially through intellectual history, we would overcome anachronisms in our attitudes and understand how to dissolve
the bonds of prejudice.

Robinson also urged historians to ensure practical results by using
the discoveries of the anthropologists, economists, psychologists, and
sociologists. As in the case of Turner's similar ideas, this implied the
integration of cultural processes. Thus, he expanded the subject matter of history to benefit human society now and in the future. The
common man would occupy a large part of this story, and he, too,
would study history.[2]

As a partial relativist, Robinson attacked the alleged objectivity of
the Ranke school. Beard afterwards recalled his *bon mot* that "objective history is history without an object." To Robinson history was not
an accretion of fixed truths, but a changing organic thing in the Darwinian sense. It was bound to alter its ideals and aims with the general progress of society and the social sciences. Ranke had theoretically
at least subordinated the present to the past, for he held that every
epoch was "immediate to God" and hence important for its own sake.
Unlike Robinson, he called for the primacy of foreign policy in historical interests with a focus upon the state as the central fact of human
existence; yet, he taught the virtues of objective history which had
universal validity.

Mid-twentieth-century critics feared that Ranke's value-free objectivity had weakened the resistance of the German intellectual to the
immoralities of Hitlerism, but this was scarcely fair to a highly civilized man, nor a correct estimate of his influence. On the other hand,
not a few "presentists" felt so shocked by the Nazi horror that they
saw practically all of modern German history, from Luther to Hitler,
telescoped in a totalitarian pattern.

2

Charles Austin Beard was born in 1874 in Knightstown, Indiana, the
son of a successful town banker, newspaper publisher, and large-scale
farmer. His parents belonged to the conservative Whig-Republican
tradition, with its emphasis on property rights, but their son did not
quite receive the conservative Methodist education which they ex-

pected DePauw College would give him, for while there the young
Beard came under the unsettling influence of the faculty radical,
James Weaver, the Populist leader. Thereafter, the young man spent
four stimulating years in Europe, where he learned a good deal about
Bismarck's pioneer welfare laws, which were intended by its sponsor
to kill socialism with kindness. More important, in England he came
into intimate contact with the Christian socialists, the reformist Fabi-
ans, the semi-socialist British Labour party, and the Settlement movement inspired by Oxford. John Ruskin's books on social reform impressed him greatly. While actively engaging in reformist projects
such as workers' education, he took up studies at Oxford under disciples of Stubbs and wrote a thesis on the Justice of the Peace. However, Beard would not subscribe to Stubbs's notion of the Teutonic
origins of democracy.

In 1904, he took his doctor's degree at Columbia and studied with
John W. Burgess, but his independent mind made him reject the latter's emphasis on the state and his Hegelianism; instead he sought
economic explanations from such men as E. R. A. Seligman, and also
learned much from William Dunning and James Harvey Robinson.
Beard was a professor of politics from 1907 until 1917, when he resigned because of friction with the high-handed trustees and because
of the dismissal of some of his colleagues. The classroom lost a gifted
teacher, because his warm personality, stimulating questions, unorthodox yet well-balanced mind, and rich background left a lasting impression on his students.

Meanwhile Beard became actively engaged in public administration
work and in urban and state planning, particularly as a staff member
of the New York Bureau of Municipal Research and its Training
School for Public Service. He was an enthusiast for city planning during these pioneer years and even went to Tokyo as a consultant to
assist in the reorganization of that city's administration after an earthquake. Later he published an important book on this experience. As a
political scientist, he wrote books which stressed the dynamics rather
than the pure mechanics of governmental structure. This was reflected
in his widely used textbooks *American Government and Politics* (1910)
and *American City Government* (1912), among others. It was still not
uncommon for a versatile man to win distinction as a historian and a
political scientist simultaneously. After all, Beard's own Columbia
mentors, William Dunning and John W. Burgess, had done so.[3]

In 1912 Beard published *The Supreme Court and the Constitution*
and inadvertently delighted conservatives by proving that the Su-

preme Court under John Marshall had *not* usurped the right to declare national laws unconstitutional. On the contrary, as he demonstrated, this idea of judicial review had been affirmed by the authors of the *Federalist Papers*, accepted by the other founding fathers, and pressed by members of the pre-Marshall court, as well as by those who ruled on *Marbury vs. Madison*. Afterwards Beard recalled the tense atmosphere of Progressive controversy at that time. Ex-President Theodore Roosevelt in the name of the New Nationalism had attacked the court's right to declare laws unconstitutional and had proposed the recall of judicial decisions. The same political background also was widely associated with *An Economic Interpretation of the Constitution* (1913), which was quickly picked up by both Progressives and the Old Guard as grist for their propaganda mill. But Beard insisted, "I had in mind no thought of forwarding the interests of the Progressive Party or of its conservative critics and opponents." Yet, he issued a new edition of his book on the Supreme Court in 1938, and saw it offer ammunition to those opposed to Franklin Roosevelt's court reform proposals. Apparently, Beard was too good a Whig philosophically, too staunch a believer in the balance of social interests through a system of checks and balances, to aid even Progressive factions if they threatened it.

An Economic Interpretation of the Constitution, for all its indebtedness to previous writers, retained a fresh Whig synthesis of its own that was by implication friendly to the rights of property. Its air of detachment and ultra-scientific guise was presented in a style so flat that it fitted Jeremy Bentham's prescription for scientific history. The author made considerable use of the actual Treasury records in order to discover the individual security holdings of the members of the Convention. However, he made no pretense to exhaustive research, frankly pleading that this was a fragmentary study intended to suggest new lines of historical inquiry for others. Besides, he hoped to persuade scholars to drop narrowly political history in favor of "the real economic forces which condition great movements in politics."

To make clear where he stood, he began with an evaluation of the chief contemporary schools of historical interpretation. Obviously he was not with those who pursued Bancroft's mystic conception of the movement for the Constitution—"the movement of the divine power which gives unity to the universe and order and connection to events." Next, he disposed of the Teutonic hypothesis of Stubbs as productive of little besides narrow studies of local government. Finally, he showed little enthusiasm for the so-called objective or scientific writers who deliberately avoided hypotheses, dwelt upon neutral facts, and seemed absorbed in critical editions of documents. Apparently Beard did not even then consider himself a member of the objective school of historians in the current sense, for he used the term in a special way when he spoke of his own writings. Against the pretensions of these three schools, he set up the virtues of the various economic interpretations of history conceived in social controversies. Too few besides Turner and his disciples had done much with such a synthesis, and the majority seemed content to ignore it or to treat it with contempt. The "theory of economic determinism," he said, had not yet been tried out in American history.

Later he tried to explain away his unfortunate phrase "economic determinism" as too sweeping. What he had written, he said, was "an economic interpretation," not the *only* one, nor did he pretend that it was *the* history of the formation and adoption of the Constitution. In 1935, he was to say retrospectively and emphatically, "I have never been able to discover all-pervading determinism in history. In that field of study, I find, what Machiavelli found, *virtu, fortuna,* and *necessita,* although the boundaries between them cannot be sharply delimited." But one should always ask of those who urged abstractions like national power or states' rights, "What interests are behind them and to whose advantage will changes or the maintenance of old forms accrue?" One of his major contributions to historians and political scientists was the central importance of pressure groups.

Beard noted a tendency, developing since the Civil War, to forget the realistic economic interpretations of the Constitution that had been stressed in John Marshall's biography of Washington, in Hildreth's writings, and in other ante-bellum books. Instead, the academicians were absorbed in a superficial and abstract interpretation of states' rights and national sovereignty. They saw the Constitution as a popular product of all of the people after a sectional debate in which "straight-thinking national men" defeated "narrower and more local opponents." When he investigated the economic interests behind the convention members, he received, as he later recalled, "the shock of my life."

In this book, and many times afterwards, he attributed his economic philosophy in part at least to that eighteenth-century realist, James Madison, and his Tenth Number of the *Federalist Papers.* Beard usually chose to quote the economic emphasis of Madison, without noting other parts of that essay which contain non-economic implications:

The diversity in the faculty of men, from which the rights of property originate, is not less an insuperable obstacle to a uniformity of interests. The protection of these faculties is the first object of government. From the protection of different and unequal faculties of acquiring property, the possession of different degrees and kinds of property immediately results; and from the influence of these on the sentiments and views of the respective proprietors, ensues a division of the society into different interests and parties. . . . The most common and durable source of factions has been the various and unequal distribution of property. Those who hold and those who are without property have ever formed distinct interests in society. Those who are creditors, and those who are debtors, fall under a like discrimination. A landed interest, a manufacturing interest, a mercantile interest, a moneyed interest, with many lesser interests, grow up of necessity in civilized nations and divide them into different classes, actuated by different sentiments and views. The regulation of these various and interfering interests forms the principal task of modern legislation, and involves the spirit of party and faction in the necessary and ordinary operations of the government.

Beard said admiringly, "Here we have a masterly statement of the theory of economic determinism in politics." It was no European importation, and it came straight from a man who had played a large role in the Constitutional Convention. Pointing out that the Madisonians disregarded ultimate motives in order to concentrate upon economic advantages, Beard concluded, "The whole theory of the economic interpretation of history rests upon the concept that social progress in general is the result of contending interests in society—some favorable, others opposed to change."

Following the quantitative approach of Libby and Turner and the scientific methods of the positivists, he set about discovering the amount and geographical distribution of money and public securities held by the men who sat in the Constitutional Convention. Their securities, it seemed fair to conclude, would appreciate in value under a strong federal constitution which protected creditor interests. This did not mean that Beard had any desire to write a muckraking volume in the contemporary mode, for he mentioned the "names of hundreds of patriots who risked their money in original certificates or received certificates for services rendered." He was primarily interested in showing that the founding fathers were fully aware of economic realities. "Did they," he asked, "represent distinct groups whose economic interests they understood and felt in concrete, definite form through their own personal experience with identical property rights, or were they working merely under the guidance of abstract principles of political science?" Furthermore, he considered their handiwork a great success, not a sinister or undesirable document. "As a group of doctrinaires, like the Frankfort assembly of 1848, they would have failed miserably; but as practical men they were able to build the new government upon the only foundations which could be stable: fundamental economic interest." So spoke the disciple of James Madison.

At the conclusion of what he termed with some justice a "long and arid survey," he described the movement for the Constitution as a product of four interest groups: money, public securities, manufactures, trade, and shipping. It was made possible by excluding representatives of a large propertyless mass who were disfranchised. The convention members were with few exceptions "immediately, directly, and personally interested in, and derived economic advantages from, the establishment of the new system." Examining the various parts of the Constitution, he stated flatly, "The Constitution was essentially an economic document based upon the concept that the fundamental private rights of property are anterior to government and morally beyond the reach of popular majorities." Thus, he held in his neutral language that the chief architects were "a consolidated group whose interests knew no state boundaries and were truly national in their scope."

Beard's interpretation aroused much more attention than that of Simons or of J. Allen Smith, for he was already a widely known historian. Some academicians cut him altogether. Beard later recalled the tempest he had evoked:

> When my book appeared it was roundly condemned by conservative Republicans, including ex-President Taft [who attacked it as another muckraking book] and praised with about the same amount of discrimination, by Progressives and others on the left wing. Perhaps no other book on the Constitution has been more severely criticized, and so little read. Perhaps no other book on the subject has been used to justify opinions and projects so utterly beyond its necessary implications.

An aggrieved New York Bar Association even summoned him to appear before them, and, when Beard declined, they expressed deep resentment. The austere Albert Bushnell Hart of Harvard looked upon the book as something almost indecent, as did President Nicholas Murray Butler of Columbia, who had never enjoyed Beard's bold opinions. On the other hand, a rapidly increasing band of eminent historians like William Dunning praised it highly. Others who did were William E. Dodd, Edward Channing, Max Farrand, and the brilliant journalist, Walter Lippmann. Despite its radical flavor, the main ideas of the

Robert E. Brown

book gained general acceptance in college textbooks and even in high-school texts during the next two decades. For the progressive *New Republic* as well as for the younger scholars, it was a classic. Beard apparently did not change his mind on essentials, for in the 1935 edition he felt it necessary to make few changes.

A generation later, in 1956, Robert E. Brown of Michigan State University aroused angry critics by assailing the scholarship and balance of *An Economic Interpretation of the Constitution*. He complained of the heavy reliance on secondary and fragmentary sources for such crucial facts as those concerning the property interests of convention members, the exaggerated estimate of the proportion of disfranchised citizens, and the unproved assumption that farmers were a debtor class. There were few extremes of wealth and property in that day, and the class differences were not as sharp as Beard had suggested. Brown's book may well have inspired a fresh revision movement seeking a new balance between economic and non-economic factors.

3

Historians came to show special favor for Beard's next important work, *Economic Origins of Jeffersonian Democracy* (1915). His frontis-piece contained a significant quotation from Frederick J. Turner, "We may trace the contest between the capitalist and the democratic pioneer from the earliest colonial days." He also quoted a prediction by one of the most brilliant of the younger historians, Carl L. Becker, that "American history would shortly be rewritten along economic lines." To Hildreth was given credit for raising the question whether a majority in the ratifying conventions actually favored adoption and for pointing out the economic interests of the supporters of the Constitution. Now, in this new book, Beard argued that the capitalist-agrarian party divisions over ratification were the same as those which created Federalists and Republicans after 1789. He showed the continuity of party beliefs among the founding fathers before and after the Constitution and tried to establish the fact that Washington and his government were partisan. Thus he explained the struggle over Hamilton's program and the Jay Treaty, though he identified the contending Congressmen with the interests of their constituents rather than their own.

There is a striking section on John Taylor and the democratic politics of agrarianism, which is set against John Adams's theory of the ruling aristocracy of wealth. While Taylor called for a republic based on substantial equality as against Adams's theory of ineradicable inequality, he was himself a well-to-do planter and federal politician of Virginia. Taylor held the radical theory that the older aristocratic ruling classes originated by exploiting the masses and sustained their power by psychological devices such as loyalty to the throne and altar. Recently, he argued, a new capitalistic class came into existence out of Hamilton's system with its inflated public paper, bank stock, and a protective tariff; they relied on new psychological devices of "public faith, national integrity, and sacred credit." Their wealth grew at the expense of "productive labor," particularly labor on the land. Thus developed the capitalist-agrarian conflict which originated the party system.

To counter what he regarded as the parasitic activities of the stock-jobbers, Taylor recommended the drastic cure of outright confiscation without compensation. As it happened, even Jefferson's alliance of landholding and laboring classes did not, in Beard's analysis, mean any fundamental break with the Federalist philosophy. He tried to demonstrate that the Federalists had learned enough about Jefferson's intentions to feel that even with the Virginian there was no danger that the Hamilton economic system would be destroyed. Politically, Jefferson's idea of political democracy was far from radical. "The fact is that, notwithstanding his generous use of the phrase 'popular rule' Jefferson was as anxious as any Federalist to guard against 'the tyranny of majorities.'" He wished to see the election of a Virginia senate based on property and indirect election, though he was advanced enough to favor the ratification of the state constitutions by the people.

Beard said that Jefferson recognized that his party was based on agrarian interests, but he favored practical concessions to the opposition and distrusted "the mobs of the great cities." Neither Republicans nor Federalists were "enamored of an equalitarian political democracy" as far as suffrage was concerned. The final evaluation showed no warmth for the Jeffersonian position:

Jeffersonian Democracy simply meant the possession of the federal government by the agrarian masses led by an aristocracy of slave-owning planters, and the theoretical repudiation of the right to use the Government for the benefit of any capitalistic groups, fiscal, banking, or manufacturing.

This volume, like its predecessor, had the same quality of detachment and objectivity; the author avoided taking sides or expressing value judgments. Though Beard later earned a fine reputation as a stylist, he chose the arid form of one who was trying to make a scientific demonstration "upon a statistical basis," as he put it. Like so many rising social scientists, he had faith in the possibility of using measurable qualities in historical analysis. Gradually, he changed his mind in these matters until he was ready to make overt judgments. His efforts suggest those of one phase of Hildreth's development when the historian's ideal was a scientific objectivity presented in a flat expository style.

4

In 1927, Charles A. Beard and his wife Mary Ritter, a gifted De Pauw graduate he had married in 1900, collaborated in a fascinating two-volume work, *The Rise of American Civilization,* which fully exemplified the spirit of the New History. His introduction reflected the pragmatic spirit of Robinson, "The history of a civilization, if intelligently conceived, may be an instrument of civilization." Furthermore, "If the history of a people is a philosophy of the whole social organism in process of becoming, then it ought to furnish material with which discernment can be whetted." As an example of this social philosophy, he pointed out that modern business enterprise rested upon the whole heritage of western civilization—religious, legal, moral, crafts and skills, and the arts and sciences. Business enterprise would fail if left to cogs and robots. He cited Buckle for authority that material advances, such as the invention of gunpowder, changed the moral and intellectual order.

Although Beard acknowledged—but all too briefly—that there were non-economic determinants in the history of colonization—religion, love of adventure, curiosity, restlessness, domestic unrest, and personal ambition—his chief guideposts remained economic, with the rivalry of social classes playing a large part. He quoted approvingly Sombart's idea that history was a world struggle over feeding places on the earth and the distribution of the earth's resources.

When he came to the Revolution, "The Clash of Metropolis and Colony," he made it an organic part of rival imperialisms of that era:

> Out of the interests of English landlords and merchants, illuminated no doubt by high visions of empire not foreign to their advantage, flowed acts of Parliament controlling the economic undertakings of American colonists and measures of administration directed to the same end. These laws and decisions were not suddenly sprung upon the world at the accession of George III in 1760.

To him, as to Simons, Schlesinger, and others before and after him, the American merchants furnished the mainspring of resistance. Most colonists were voteless or apathetic. He pressed this point, just as he had pressed the role of disfranchisement in defeating the popular will over the Constitution: "As far as balloting was a measure of popular support, not more than one-third of the adult white males in America ever set the seal of their approval on the Revolution by voting for its committees and delegates." With Lecky he felt that the Revolution was a product of "an energetic minority who succeeded in committing an undecided and fluctuating majority to causes for which they had little love and leading them step by step to a position from which it was impossible to recede."

Such interpretations challenged the older view of George Bancroft, who simplified the effects of mercantilism to mean English exploitation of the colonists, which led the latter to make war (though Bancroft stressed the influence of ideas). Louis Hacker, whose book *The Triumph of American Capitalism* (1940) paralleled many of Beard's views of rival capitalisms at work in history, applied this idea to the pressures on colonial mercantile capitalism. Hacker insisted that the breakdown of the mercantile system reflected the inability of both English mercantile capitalism and colonial mercantile and planter capitalism to operate within a contracting sphere in which clashes of interest were becoming sharper. Other historians like Charles McLean Andrews and Lawrence Henry Gipson found much to say in defense of mercantilism and saw benefits as well as drawbacks in the system.

Beard was so interested in the historiography of the American Revolution that he paused to poke fun at the World War I propagandists who helped the alliance with England by suggesting that the Revolution "was more or less a moral and tactical error on the part of the Patriot Fathers." The real question regarding the motive of the historian should be, he said, "Is he preparing to unite the English-speaking peoples in the next war?" For himself, he avowed only the objective ideal of seeking the facts which conditioned the struggle between the men who governed England and those who ruled the colonies. In later years, he ceased to be certain that it was as simple as that. Finally, the Revolution appeared to him as a major social change from which many important social changes flowed—emancipation, penal reform, religious freedom, and the abolition of entails and primogeniture.

While Beard might dislike the Hegelian tendencies of Bancroft, in which motivating ideas often had a disembodied form, he did not deny the power of ideas and the diffusion of attitudes from abroad. In this respect, he limited his heavily economic interpretations. Thus in an excellent chapter in *The Rise of American Civilization,* "Democracy: Romantic and Realistic," he showed a full appreciation of the impact of European thought on America, the effect of romanticism, the new concept of progress, and evolution. His anti-monistic position was emphatically stated:

> Had there been no significant changes in the economic structure of the nation, had there been no novel social forces let loose in the national arena, had there been no additional impacts from Revolutionary Europe, the great concepts of human rights and human equality, professed if not always followed by the Fathers, would have altered the intellectual climate for philosophy, letters, and the arts.

But he added that there were technological and scientific changes which had their effects on the mind.

Just as Turner stressed sectionalism more than slavery as a major cause for the Civil War, so Beard (like Simons) turned to a class analysis—the irrepressible struggle between industrial-commercial interests and the planters. Abolitionist agitators alone could not bring about war, because propertied interests did not respond to mere appeals and the anachronistic planters were after all "fighting against the census returns." War was bound to come between these factions who sought a redistribution of power while echoing moral pronouncements. The Republican platform of 1856 avoided special favors to industry and attracted free farmers who opposed the plutocracy of the East and the planting aristocracy of the South. So far was the nation from any crusade for the antislavery cause that in 1856 they repudiated even the mildest antislavery program. Therefore, like the Revolution and the Constitution, the Civil War was promoted by minority interests. He did not ignore other factors: John Brown's raid aggravated "the jangling nerves of a people already excited by fears of a race war and continued disturbances over the seizure of slaves under the fugitive slave act."

More significant to him was the fact that in 1860 the planter's program stood diametrically opposed to the measures which business enterprise deemed essential to its progress—tariffs, ship subsidies, and a national banking and currency system. "Many an orator who might have forgiven the South for maintaining a servile labor system could not forgive it for its low tariff doctrines and its opposition to centralized finance." Thus he disposed of the popular Rhodes interpretation of the Civil War as the product of a moral struggle over slavery, since the slave system did not stand in isolation from other factors. Slavery was a labor system upon which rested the Southern aristocracy opposed to industrial capitalism. Self-interest, not abstractions, alone counted as a consistent factor.

Logically, therefore, the war appeared to him as "the second American Revolution," because "the capitalists, laborers, and farmers of the North and West drove from power in the national government the planting aristocracy of the South." In so doing they gained protective tariffs, the immigration of contract labor, and a northern transcontinental railroad route. Fond of economic interpretations based on the collusion of interest groups, Beard explained the Fourteenth Amendment as a conspiracy of Radicals and the new corporate interests. This meant that business was to be specially protected in the federal courts against state regulation.

He found the thesis of triumphant capitalism useful in explaining the Gilded Age as a cultural expression of an imitative American plutocracy. "Imperial America" had devised a system of acquisition and enjoyment by industrialists and well-to-do farmers encouraged by government favors. Americans raided foreign lands on predatory expeditions in the name of moral purposes. When he came to America's entrance into World War I, he leaned heavily on the conspiratorial thesis of Senator Robert La Follette, long before it was reinforced in 1934 by the Nye Munitions Investigation. Here was the sinister situation in 1917 as he saw it:

> At best, American investors who had staked money on the Anglo-French side, munition makers who had accepted the paper of London and Paris in return for supplies, merchants and manufacturers who had huge Entente credits on their books were placed in a serious dilemma; they were in danger of immense losses unless the United State government came to their rescue. No doubt the war dirge raised by these selfish factions was adequately financed, astutely managed, and effectively carried into strange out-of-the-way places as well as into the main highways.

As a good New History man, he brought his two volumes right up to the morning newspaper and offered a convincing synthesis of the Harding-Coolidge era of business leadership. Despite his criticisms of America's shortcomings, he was then as always optimistic about his country's future. His final chapter, "The Machine Age," offered encouragement and drew its inspiration from Thorstein Veblen's admiration for creative technicians as against the parasitic leisure class. The present current of mass opinion reassured him as to the future of America—the faith in democracy and in the ability of the undistinguished masses (not heroes or classes alone) to meet issues as they arose. Through "the invention of invention" would come an ever-wider distribution of the blessings of civilization. He was ever a believer in the possibilities of social planning and of materialist progress. "If so, it is the dawn, not the dusk, of the gods."

5

The Great Depression upset this relatively optimistic mood and led him to excoriate the illusions of the 1920s and the "rugged individualism" of Hoover. His new volume covering the 1930s, *America in Midpassage* (1939), suggested the skeptical view of his literary contemporary John Dos Passos, whose *USA* was a left-wing social history of a generation. Beard had always been a social planner opposed to the laissez-faire assumptions of Adam Smith. New Deal controls over production, he said, were not less consistent or unfamiliar than similar objectives of corporations in the past. It did not represent a class revolution, for conservatives, too, were driven by the cataclysmic events to support government enterprises. A new democratic social conscience was born. "In the realm of gentility a primary assumption had long prevailed to the effect that, in the main, idleness and poverty were due to defective minds or bodies, or to congenital improvidence."

More emphatically than ever, he proceeded to treat foreign affairs as organically linked with domestic policies. For a half-century before 1929, he pointed out, Americans had been told that prosperity depended on operations abroad rather than at home. Imperialism had been justified to dispose of agricultural and manufacturing surpluses. Beard as a social planner apparently did not believe that capitalism required the urgent disposal of "surplus value" abroad, as the Marxists insisted. When imperialism and "money-lending adventures" failed, liberal internationalists had urged that free trade could work a miracle for the economy. But these alternatives were no longer usable by the 1930s. Pressure groups were busily at work to advance steel and shipbuilding interests by combatting disarmament movements, such as in the Shearer lobby of 1929-30. They used ingenious propaganda methods in the newspapers, lecture halls, and organization presses. Other pressure groups—the sugar lobby, for instance—now sponsored Philippine independence.

The startling revelations of the Nye Committee of 1934 regarding the war pressures of the munitions industry had already absorbed Beard when he wrote on this theme for *The New Republic*, although his thinking—as already noted—had long flowed in this channel. Nye did not need to convince Beard that the pressures for America's entrance into World War I had originated in ties of patriotism, salesmanship, corruption, and international lobbying. The Senator had even reported sinister plans for a coming war. Said Beard: "For a nation that liked to think of itself as pacific, non-militaristic, and dedicated to liberty and democracy, the vision of the coming 'day' was informing, to some extent shocking, in any event educative." As for the League of Nations, the author blamed the "Collective Internationalists" under Wilson's leadership for using a war born of imperialist rivalries to impose an idealistic scheme of permanent peace, thus disregarding the actual imperialist settlement in Paris. The unrealistic Collective Internationalists drew their "world image" from the international free-trade system of Cobden and Bright. They disliked the current unilateral agreements and managed currencies. But the fact was that England and the United States were abandoning the free traders.

As an alternative to the imperialists and internationalists he saw the rise of a new critical school which sought vast welfare advances in the United States and a much more modest national defense "under prudent policies by small but appropriate military and naval establishments." Instead of urging the white man's burden type of imperialism, he was concerned with keeping out of war and avoiding foreign commitments, with substituting abundance for scarcity, and in establishing a sound and efficient domestic economy. This was obviously Beard's program; he denied that it was isolationist in the Lodge-Harding-Coolidge sense or chauvinistic. He preferred the term "Continental" or American civilization for this school. He believed in a plural universe free from evangelistic exhorters who would attempt to impose their ways on others, and he rejected wars for trade promotion, colonial expansion, or ideologies. His "continentalism" rested on the assumption that science and technology had broken Adam Smith's theory of regional specialization and regional monopoly. The machine and invention had greatly lessened the dependence of nations on imports of manufactures and raw materials. Furthermore, the Continentalists were not necessarily opposed to a league of nations—so long as it was "constituted for other purposes than the perpetuation of historic wrongs."

Actually, he greatly preferred the isolationism of Ambassador Joseph Kennedy to the interventionist foreign policy of Franklin D. Roosevelt, who disturbed him by moral diatribes against Germany, Italy, and Japan. Beard of course was no fascist, but he was ever suspicious of efforts to reawaken Wilson's missionary diplomacy. He suspected that the Administration was pursuing policies and making bellicose statements ardently desired by bureaucratic interests, rabid peace societies, and belligerent labor elements. These were strong enough to override middle-class liberals and Middle West agrarians. Labor was in danger of being destroyed by the peacetime mobilization act of 1938 and by the influence of the armament industry.

In an unusually large section devoted to social and cultural history, he applied vigorously the Veblenian analysis of the corruption of culture by finance capitalism. He made no effort to conceal exactly where he stood on these controversial questions. He showed how the entertainment world had succumbed to block booking, with its tendency toward commercial concentration; exhibitors were forced to take a complete set of motion pictures good or bad as a condition for getting any films. Movie themes reflected the morals of "pecuniary respectability," but this involved sex, fantasy, war propaganda, crime, wealth, and splendor. Movie competition and the Depression injured the legitimate theater. Despite the mediocrity of the Federal Theater, he showed a sympathetic attitude because it symbolized the obligation of the government toward the arts. The state of literature seemed much more wholesome than that of the radio and movies. In one section devoted to social-intellectual history, "Frames of Social Thought," Beard stressed the advent of collectivism over laissez-faire. He closed with a hope that "the humanistic wing of American democracy" would provide the economic and cultural foundations indispensable to a free society.

Beard combined his economic syntheses increasingly with studies in the history of ideas, a pioneer field in which he was a master. Unfortunately, his study of the "idea of civilization in the United States" in *The American Spirit* (1942), a sequel to his *Rise of American Civilization*, seemed to lack informing direction, though it contained many shrewd insights. In 1934, he had published a more successful book in the history of leading concepts, *The Idea of National Interest: An Analytical Study in American Foreign Policy*. The title was inspired by reading a volume of 1918, "What Is National Honor?" Beard took his cue from Secretary of State Hughes, who had frankly stated, "Foreign policies are not built upon abstractions. They are the result of

practical conceptions of national interest arising from some immediate exigency or standing out vividly in historical perspective." Beard
often said much the same thing.

Significantly, as a "realist," Beard also sought authority in the hard-
bitten propositions of Alfred Thayer Mahan, strategist of seapower:
"Self-interest is not only a legitimate but a fundamental cause for national policy, one which needs no cloak of hypocrisy." Beard's view
had much in common with Mahan, Washington's Farewell Address,
and the realistic axioms of the younger political scientists and theorists
such as George Kennan and Hans Morgenthau.

The task as he saw it was to explore the use of the formula of "national interest" by responsible statesmen and publicists, to discover the
patterns of conduct embraced by the formula, and to examine the
social and economic conditioning of this historical development. He
began with his favorites, the founding fathers, whose conception of
national interest appeared in the *Federalist Papers,* the Constitution,
and in Washington's Farewell Address. He showed how the whole
weight of government activities eventually came into play to protect
the material basis of national interest—concessions, privileges, investments, trade promotion, tariffs, armaments, merchant marine subsidies, and immigration restriction. Wilson had been the most active foe
of the idea of national interest, in so far as he made a conscious effort to limit it by invoking an abstract moral purpose, as in his famous
Mobile Speech and in the idea of "peace without victory." But his
moral individualism pushed the United States into war.

Taft, Coolidge, and Hoover induced American businessmen to believe that their interest depended upon the continuous expansion of
foreign trade, but they were refuted by the Depression, which demonstrated that expanding outlets for surpluses would not exist forever. At this time Beard believed that President Franklin D. Roosevelt
had forged a new conception of national interest. In it was the central idea that "by domestic planning and control the American economic machine may be kept running at a high tempo supplying the
intra-national market, without relying primarily upon foreign outlets
for 'surpluses' of good and capital." But Beard's suspicions of the New
Deal had already been aroused, for he noted that the Roosevelt Administration had made no corresponding adjustment of foreign policies; instead, it was spending more money for naval construction, which
implied the older policies of international relations. The author expanded this theme later in *America in Midpassage* in the semi-isolationist form of Continentalism.

Many readers enjoyed Beard's venture into political theory in 1943, *The Republic: Conversations on Fundamentals*. This revealed both his perennial faith in America's future and his undeviating confidence in the realistic wisdom of the founding fathers. Now he gave much more attention to the principle of checks and balances, which was after all a central theme of his friend James Madison. "I believe that our Republic, with authority and liberty constantly readjusted under constitutional principles, will long endure, forever, I hope." He saw the United States as unique, not a product of cyclic development, nor an imitation of Europe. To those who still thought of him as an economic determinist, he said:

> But according to my world-view, our universe is not all fate; we have some freedom in it. Besides fate or determinism there is *creative intelligence* in the world, and there is also *opportunity* to exercise our powers, intellectual and moral. America is well endowed with such powers.

Beard lost many of his admirers by opening a severe revisionist attack on the alleged role of Roosevelt, Stimson, and Hull in bringing this country into World War II. He was not alone (nor was he the first) in this movement, but his prestige gave his words wide notice. *President Roosevelt and the Coming of the War, 1941* (1948) was bolstered by the unusual quantity of revealing sources made available through the various official reports on Pearl Harbor, Secretary Stimson's diary, and other current records.

He called attention to the antiwar pledges of Roosevelt in the campaign of 1940, implying a deliberate violation of faith, but he did not mention that the President could scarcely guarantee against an actual attack by a foreign foe. Like other revisionists, he concentrated on the presidential provocations given the Axis nations and the Administration effort to maneuver the Japanese into firing the first shot—an idea that seemed to be implied in Secretary Stimson's diary. Did Roosevelt force the issue of war on the theory that the Axis must be defeated and that the end justifies the means? If so, all expectations of perpetual peace and security derived from this assumption had been disappointed. The argument that Hitler's victory would turn this country into an armed camp meant nothing, because these evils—including a large permanent conscript army, heavy outlays for arms, a huge national debt, and grinding taxes—came anyway. Beard's severe attack on Roosevelt as the arch-plotter of war almost repudiated the theme of his *New Republic* articles on "The Devil Theory of War," which blamed relatively impersonal social-economic forces rather than sinister politicians for provoking war.

His book lent prestige to those congressional and newspaper isolationists who opposed the supremacy of the Executive in foreign policy. He assailed the current practice of giving power to the President to effect commercial treaties and entangling international loans at will. "At this point," he charged, "the American Republic has arrived under the theory that the President of the United States possesses limitless authority publicly to misrepresent and secretly to control foreign policy, foreign affairs, and the war power."

Isolationist historians were encouraged by Beard's volume to expand his indictment of the Roosevelt regime before Pearl Harbor. Professor Charles C. Tansill, who had shown anti-Wilsonian interpretations in a previous book, *America Goes to War* (1938), a relatively plausible account of our neutrality policies of 1914-17, now dropped all restraints in his *Backdoor to War* (1952) in an effort to place the responsibility for a war policy on Roosevelt. Like Beard, he believed that the President took a major provocative step in his Quarantine Speech against Japan to cover up the shortcomings of the New Deal and to divert attention from his blunder in appointing a former Klansman, Hugo Black, to the Supreme Court. Even the disgraced Admiral Husband E. Kimmel and his counsel each published books for the defense, which charged that the attack on Pearl Harbor came because Roosevelt had "planned it that way." William Henry Chamberlin, once a decided "liberal" historian but now a conservative columnist for the *Wall Street Journal*, developed the Beard arguments in *America's Second Crusade* (1950). Critics frequently described Tansill's book, as well as those of other revisionists, as a mere diatribe against the Roosevelt Administration. Historical opinion clung to those labeled by Harry Elmer Barnes, a "revisionist" critical of the Allied point of view in two world wars, as "court historians." This referred particularly to the well-documented and circumstantial account of William L. Langer and S. E. Gleason, *The Challenge to Isolation, 1937-1940* (1952), and its sequel, *The Undeclared War, 1940-41* (1953). Langer and Gleason, together with other academic writers, demolished many of the sinister charges of the revisionists. Among other evidences, they cited the public opinion polls to show that Roosevelt did not move as fast toward interventionism as public opinion demanded. Coming not long before his death, Beard's intemperate volume cost him dearly in reputation.

6

Charles Beard undoubtedly stimulated the interest of some if not most of his fellow-professionals in the philosophy of history, for he loved to explore the unspoken assumptions that lay behind the façade of history-writing. During the 1930s, when seminars tended to pay homage to Leopold von Ranke's ideal of objectivity and the tradition of "scientific history," historians sometimes labeled Beard and Robinson historical relativists who denied the belief in historical certainty.

Historical relativism meant different things to various historians, for none denied that photographic truth regarding the past was impossible. Usually it offered the skeptical idea that a historian could not escape the vast array of conditioning forces that stood between him and total objectivity: his culture, class, "frame of reference" (the dominating and often uncritical assumption from which he operated), and his psychological make-up. Therefore, each generation had to write a new history, even without important new facts, and no one could say if it was a "true" history. The past was dead and one knew only the present; therefore, the historian engaged in the subjective pastime of reconstructing the past in his mind with blunted tools. The inherent skepticism of this position drove away most historians; and Beard, among other thoughtful historians, looked for self-critical procedures and verifiable methods to escape the relativist's dilemma. He would redefine "objectivity" to conform to man's potentialities.

Beard's views were elaborated in his presidential address, "Written History as an Act of Faith," delivered before the American Historical Association at its meeting in Urbana, Illinois, during late December 1933.[4] His argument was tightly knit. The raw materials of history, "history as actuality," consisted of everything done and thought in the past; it differed from "history as record" found in documents and archaeological remains. But the final inescapable definition of history was history as thought. "It is thought about past actuality, instructed and delimited by history as record and knowledge—record and knowledge authenticated by criticism and ordered with the help of the scientific method."

He went on to argue that his own idea of historical knowledge had been commonly held for a century or more by those who had stated that each historian was a product of his age, the spirit of the times, his nation, race, group, class, and section; therefore, the selection and arrangement of facts were determined by this. Obviously, selection as an act of thought was also an act of choice, conviction, and interpretation respecting values. But this supportable view had been over-thrown by Schoolmen, and particularly by Leopold von Ranke, who believed that it was possible to describe the past as it actually was. (Present-day students of Ranke deny that the German had so naïve a conception of historical knowledge.) Falling back upon a social interpretation of ideas, Beard accounted for this by arguing that Ranke was a member of the ruling classes who wanted to overthrow history as a vehicle of revolutionary propaganda and to transform it into a cold, factual value-free narrative.

Beard view of Ranke

The Rankeans later received reinforcement from the vogue of natural science which invaded history and which implied a neutral attitude. "Truths of nature, ran the theory, are to be discovered by maintaining the most severe objectivity; therefore the truth of history may be revealed by the same spirit and method." But later developments changed the attitude of historians, particularly when it became apparent that "one is more or less a guesser in this vale of tears." To escape this unpleasant truth, the "objective" historian turned to minute historical subjects, such as the price of cotton in Alabama between 1850 and 1860 or the length of wigs during the reign of Charles II. They held the pleasing but false assumption that this made possible history as it actually was, for by dealing with an isolated area they escaped all the ramifications of it.

Although he was aware that natural science no longer hypnotized historians as in the days of the younger Turner and of Henry Adams, Beard thought that a strong warning was justified now:

The supreme command is that he [the historian] must cast off his servitude to the assumptions of natural science and return to his own subject matter—to history as actuality. The hour for this final declaration of independence has arrived: the contingency is here and thought resolves it.

Applying a social interpretation of ideas, he said that natural science dominated Western thought only for a brief period and as an outgrowth of the conflict between theologians and scientists. Ten years later, in 1943, Beard took a much more benign attitude toward the tyranny of natural science over history, for he wrote a rather sympathetic introduction to a new edition of Brooks Adams's *The Law of Civilization and Decay*, which reflected the inspiration of the second law of thermodynamics. While he rejected Adams's cyclical theory of history, he seemed quite complaisant about the possibility that history might become a science. But now he denounced thinking by analogy as a form of primitive animism and singled out Oswald Spengler (whom he had recently criticized at length) as an example of a man who had abused biological analogies in creating an elaborate cyclic history. As for physics, he said that its data was not identical in nature with historical occurrences. Besides, the facts of history were beyond the reach of mathematics, which was powerless to assign meaningful values to "the imponderables, immeasurables, and contingencies of history as actuality."

He then turned to attack the new school of historical relativism:

[Historical relativism] was the formula that makes all written history merely relative to time and circumstance, a passing shadow, an illusion. Contemporary criticism shows that the apostle of relativity is destined to be destroyed by the child of his own brain. If all historical conceptions are merely relative to passing events, to transitory phases of ideas and interests, then the conception of relativity is itself relative. When absolutes in history are rejected, the absolutism of relativity is also rejected.

He predicted that the skepticism of relativity would also disappear like the earlier formulas. However, his own insistence that historical knowledge was heavily conditioned and hence relative to many environmental factors, made it difficult to be certain just where Beard parted company with the relativists.

Against relativism he projected an "absolute"—"the absolute totality of all historical occurrences, past, present, and becoming to the end of all things." Beard, like Carl Becker, had two main histories: history as actuality and history as thought. Presumably the historian should aspire to bring the two as close together as possible. Examining the various aspects of historical knowledge, he concluded that only a mixture of subjective and objective procedures was possible in the search for certainty:

The historian who writes history therefore, consciously or unconsciously performs an act of faith, as to order and movement; for certainty as to order and movement is denied to him by knowledge of the actuality with which he is concerned. . . . His faith is at bottom a conviction that something true can be known about the movement of history and his conviction is a subjective decision, not a purely objective discovery.

All this did not mean that the historian must abandon the scientific method. "The inquiring spirit of science, using the scientific method, is the chief safeguard against the tyranny of authority, bureaucracy, and brute power. It can reveal by investigation necessities and possibilities in any social scene and also offerings with respect to desirabilities to be achieved within the limits of the possible."

hist, as act of faith

Beard therefore still clung to the meliorist New History of his friend Robinson and the reformism of John Ruskin, William Morris, and his Oxford preceptors. While he had pointed out that even the scientific method possessed limitations for historians and that a science of history was an illusion, he urged all to continue their "tireless inquiry into objective realities, especially economic realities and relations." He recommended the concept of "frame of reference" for all historical knowledge, thereby suggesting how close he came to that historical relativism that he denied. Any selection or arrangement of historical facts, he declared, was "controlled invariably by the frame of reference in the mind of the selector and arranger." The address ended with his own "guess" that the world was moving toward a collectivist democracy rather than toward a dictatorship of the right or left.

These ideas of historical knowledge were further elaborated in an article, "That Noble Dream," which appeared in the *American Historical Review* in 1935. Once more he took up the cudgels stoutly against "so-called objective history" of the value-free variety and urged the New History (this would seem to be the inference) which threw light on "the quandaries of life" to facilitate adjustment to reform. Particularly, he took sharp issue with a critic, Theodore C. Smith, who had deplored the efforts of innovators—quasi-relativists presumably—to destroy "that noble dream" of objective history by using economic interpretations flowing from Marxist inspiration. Again, Beard raked Rankeism over the coals and called attention to the mistaken assumption of the objective historians that history existed as a discrete object outside the mind of the historian and could be reproduced objectively independent of the writer's conditioning influences. What were the consequences of this kind of history?

It condemns philosophy and throws it out of doors. As practiced, it ignores problems of mind with which philosophers and theologians have wrestled for centuries and have not yet settled it to everybody's satisfaction. As developed into historicism, it takes on all the implications of empiricism, positivism, and, if not materialism, at least that rationalism which limits history to its purely experiential aspects.

The American Historical Association, he held, was never committed to Ranke, for at its very inception in 1884, the president, Andrew D. White, declared that he wished no "neutral value-free history" but sought philosophic synthesis. Besides, Ranke was not objective but a Prussian reactionary who dwelt upon mystical concepts of God's dominating presence in history and neglected social and economic factors. Beard denied once more that his own economic interpretation was based on Marx but said he drew directly from James Madison and the founding fathers, among others. It was without the Marxian insistence upon an inevitable conflict of classes. No historian acquired "the colorless, neutral mind" merely by declaring his intention to do so. Like Mannheim, Beard went on to say, "Rather do we clarify the mind by admitting to cultural interests and patterns—interests and patterns that will control or intrude upon the selection and organization of historical materials." [5]

While historians generally remained suspicious of integrated philosophies of history and philosophical abstractions in general, many were quite enthusiastic about economic history and even economic interpretations of history during the Great Depression. The influence of Turner and Beard was manifest in the college classroom of those years; and there seemed little danger that any revival of natural science analogies would invade history-writing and teaching. By mid-century, it became clear that Beard had led many of the younger historians, particularly those in intellectual history, to re-examine the lessons and errors of their craft through the study of historiography, a subject which steadily increased in academic popularity and sophistication. [6]

[margin annotation: Influence of Beard]

7

Over the years, Charles A. Beard was not only creative, but unusually prolific and versatile. A careful survey of his writings by Howard Beale and his associates shows that in European history alone—not counting textbooks—he completed eight volumes totaling 3510 pages, while in American history he finished twenty-one volumes of 8443 pages—altogether nearly 12,000 pages. His fifteen textbooks aggregated nearly 8500 pages and brought the total of all his books to forty-nine volumes and over 21,000 pages. His writings had both high quality and tremendous popularity. In a day when able historians congratulated themselves if their trade sales exceeded 2000 copies and college texts reached a 50,000 sale mark, Beard's publishers (usually Macmillan) disposed of over 11,352,000 books, about half of them textbooks. At least three Book-of-the-Month Club adoptions, together with many foreign editions and a huge *Life* edition of over 4,000,000 copies of *The Republic*, swelled his sales.

His magnum opus, *An Economic Interpretation of the Constitution*, did not quite sell 8000 copies, though, while his books on American foreign policy alone sold almost 170,000. Aside from massive Book-of-the-Month Club adoptions, the regular edition of *The Rise of American Civilization* sold over 71,000 copies and the regular edition of *America in Midpassage* reached almost 34,000. Extraordinarily popular both here and abroad was a short one-volume history intended for the general reader and written with Mary Beard's collaboration, *A Basic History of the United States* (1944), which was eventually distributed to over 649,000 people. Japan and Germany led the procession of foreign readers. Some of the earlier judgments regarding pressure interests were tempered. Besides these and many other books, he edited influential volumes or symposia on American civilization and poured forth a steady stream of thoughtful articles in professional, popular, and social action journals. Little wonder that Beard's point of view penetrated so many books about the United States, especially during the critical years of the Great Depression when the economic viewpoint was uppermost.

8

Charles Austin Beard, whatever his shortcomings—and these were far from overwhelming—was indeed a giant in our midst. He practiced in the New History what his colleague James Harvey Robinson merely preached for the most part. His study of the origins of the Constitution was far more influential than other histories of his day in applying the concept of pressure or interest groups to a document that had seldom (outside of Hildreth, Allen, and certain socialists) been scrutinized in this way. He contributed, inadvertently perhaps, to the tradition of native radicalism by locating the idea of conflicting interest groups within an American (Madisonian) framework. Like Jane Addams, pioneer of the settlement house movement, he helped to carry the social idealism of the Oxford reformers to America. He made a new generation of American historians more aware of their philosophical assumptions and more understanding of scientific method, and he stimulated the study of historiography. His well-stocked mind, freed of teaching obligations, wandered in search of a synthesis amid the fields of political behavior, social forces, diplomatic history, political theory, and social and intellectual history. He did not confine his analysis to economic interpretation, although he usually stressed it, but he encouraged many to embark upon this fruitful path and to escape the aridity of formal narrative. Thus he helped to keep historians abreast of parallel advances in the other social studies and to increase the dimension of depth among his fellow craftsmen.

☆ 14 ☆

Parrington and the Rise
of Intellectual History

1

By the time World War II began, historians of the American past were no longer so suspicious of the academic standing of intellectual history, although many complained with some reason that it was ill-defined and amorphous. They were often quite willing to give enthusiastic praise to the intellectual historian, as well as to the historian of philosophy, literature, or art, but the bulk of monographs and graduate theses continued to fit within the well-worn grooves of political, constitutional, economic, and narrowly descriptive social history. The current attacks on democratic thought by communists, fascists, and Nazis galvanized social scientists, literary historians, and art historians to reformulate the meaning of freedom. As to the definition of intellectual history, apart from the older and similar disciplines, many historians tended to agree with Crane Brinton: "The intellectual historian is interested in ideas wherever he finds them, in wild ideas as well as in sensible ideas, in refined speculation and in common prejudices; but he is interested in these products of men's mental activity as they influence, and are influenced by, men's whole existence." Abstract ideas for their own sake, then, were not enough.

Cultural nationalism, developing during an age of rapid national maturity, stimulated hundreds of books and articles on American thought, attitudes, folklore, philosophy, and literature. Reputations like that of Henry James, who had once been classified with the genteel tradition, and evaluations of art movements like the Hudson River school, once treated as merely derivative, soared to a high plane. Sometimes the leaders in this movement for intellectual history were specialists in European currents of thought like Arthur O. Lovejoy and Crane Brinton, although teachers abroad were not too far ahead of their American confreres in dropping the traditional subject matter. In one area of intellectual history political theorists of course had long been concerned with the historical meaning of technical concepts like sovereignty and natural rights.

The movement for modern intellectual history was stimulated by Karl Lamprecht's *Kulturgeschichte,* which offered an evolutionary integration of social and intellectual history. In this country, Turner, Robinson, Beard, and the New History group sought a systematic integration, or at least co-operation between the disciplines, and sometimes invoked such magic terms as "cross-fertilization," a phrase that Beard himself decried as hopelessly infected with outmoded biological analogies. The new *Journal of the History of Ideas* (1939), edited by philosophers, welcomed qualified contributors from all the social studies. During the period from 1930 to 1935, the interdisciplinary approach was greatly aided when ten constituent national societies sponsored the ambitious *Encyclopaedia of the Social Sciences,* edited by Edwin R. A. Seligman and Alvin Johnson. For this, American and European experts in practically every social science were invited to use highly sophisticated methods of analysis and to emphasize intellectual trends. The whole project was integrated by long introductions, particularly in the first volume, and by frequent cross references, although no effort was apparently made to impose any particular theories upon the writers.

Philosophers and theologians had long been absorbed by the history and meaning of certain ideas, but intellectual historians invoked interdisciplinary methods in co-operation with literary historians. In the late 1940s they sponsored at least fourteen regional societies and published the official journal, *American Quarterly,* through a Committee on American Civilization at the University of Pennsylvania. Their articles frequently reflected the writer's efforts to draw together the techniques of several academic disciplines.

Intellectual history, as already shown, was not new. Historians of both Europe and America wrote significant books on the ideas of progress, Calvinism, capitalism, romanticism, and the guiding assumptions behind social and economic institutions. Charles Beard had pioneered in exploring the axioms and uncritical assumptions behind the serious ideas as well as the catch phrases in our history. The results were often devastating.

Finally, social historians of the New History school hastened the rise of intellectual history by including at least a survey of intellectual and aesthetic movements. Arthur M. Schlesinger, Sr., as we have seen, had been an editor and contributor of the *History of American Life* series (1928-43) which touched at least upon the chief intellectual trends and personalities. Such Schlesinger doctoral students as Merle Curti often chose to penetrate into the social analysis of ideas and attitudes. Increasingly, it became difficult for social historians of a perceptive type to deal with their specialty without a theoretical framework of leading ideas and scientific hypotheses, and a genuine awareness of the controlling assumptions behind their work. Like the relativists, they spoke of "a frame of reference" which gave specific meaning to ideas and attitudes by providing the social context.

2

Among the Americans who prepared the way for Vernon L. Parrington's type of intellectualized literary history was Professor Moses Coit Tyler (1835-1900), although the two men differed in many essentials. Tyler was born in Calvinist Connecticut, educated in the Detroit public schools, and studied theology at Yale and Andover. After graduation, he served as a Congregational minister at Oswego, New York, in 1859, but apparently found the orthodoxy too confining and left for an active career as a reform journalist in the fields of temperance, abolition, and women's rights, among others. Only in 1867 did he find a congenial career as a professor of rhetoric and English literature at the University of Michigan, where he proved himself an able teacher, and studied deeply in colonial history. He was influenced toward an environmental approach to history by reading Buckle intensively and appreciating the "civilization" point of view of man's past.

In 1881 Cornell invited him as professor of American history—one of the first in this country—and here he remained until his death. Using original sources and approaching his subjects in the current German critical fashion he wrote *A History of American Literature during the Colonial Time* (1878) and *The Literary History of the American Revolution* (1897). He also published critical biographies of George Berkeley, Timothy Dwight, and Joel Barlow and devoted some of his efforts to the founding of the American Historical Association. Tyler's chief biographer, Howard Mumford Jones, noted for books on the relationship of American literary history and ideas, praised him: "His power of portrait painting, sympathetic analysis, and clear synthesis of ungrateful material is immense." Tyler's attractive style as well as scholarly synthesis led to a vogue for his chief work as late as the mid-twentieth century.

He left an interdisciplinary method for intellectual historians, though he dealt with a sequence of writers in a political setting expressing ideas of "the spirit of the age," quite unlike the agrarian economic approach of Parrington. He was inspired by the keen French literary critic, Sainte-Beuve; some felt he had been influenced by Taine, but Professor Jones finds that Taine was too prone to oversimplification of literary history to have served as Tyler's model.[1]

By the time Tyler died at the end of the century, young Vernon L. Parrington (1871-1929) had already tested agrarian ideas and found to his liking the rebellious Populist spirit of his fellow-Kansans. He was born of Scotch and English ancestry in Aurora, Illinois, the son of a school principal who became a Union captain and a Kansas judge. He attended the Presbyterian-affiliated College of Emporia for several years and then finished at Harvard. He was later to discount his years at Harvard because of its alleged genteel tradition, and indeed his writings revealed that his experience in the Populist center of discontent had been far more influential.

Emporia recalled him to become an instructor of English and French during 1893-97; from there he went to the University of Oklahoma (1898-1908), until, as he put it, a "political cyclone" cost him his job. Thereafter he found a more fruitful and congenial atmosphere at the University of Washington, where he remained until his death. Students admired his original comments in literature, and his name became a proud tradition of the University, for he was also a poet and a writer of fine prose. His friend and colleague, J. Allen Smith, who had left his impress on Beard also, influenced his emphasis on economic determinants in literature. In fact, Parrington was to dedicate his magnum opus to this man, "Scholar, Teacher, Democrat, Gentleman."[2]

Parrington did not attract national attention until in 1927 when he won a Pulitzer Prize for the first two volumes of his *Main Currents in American Thought*. The third volume, tragically, was suddenly shortened by his death. Although he had finished only half of it, his publishers wisely decided to construct a book out of his early completed chapters and the illuminating notes and comments. By a striking coincidence, the first two volumes appeared simultaneously with the Beards' venture in *kulturgeschichte, The Rise of American Civilization,* which included several substantial chapters on American cultural history, also written from an economic point of view. Both shared the reformist temper of the Populist-Progressive era, even though it was now the age of Calvin Coolidge.

Those who looked for a history of American literature in the usual belletristic tradition were bound to be disappointed, but instead they learned a great deal about the social ideas of American literary men, politicians, journalists, and diverse writers of influence. The judgments were striking and original, but unfortunately quite vulnerable to the researchers of the next few decades; too often Parrington was cruel to constructive conservatives or overgenerous to agrarians. But even by the mid-century, after revisionists had taken a heavy toll of these interpretations, there remained a vast amount of trustworthy intellectual history.

Parrington made his position clear at the outset: "The point of view from which I have endeavored to evaluate the materials is liberal rather than conservative, Jeffersonian rather than Federalistic, and very likely in my search I have found what I went forth to find, as others have discovered what they are seeking." He acknowledged a special debt to the critical historians of the past twenty years, who had been so successful in studying the revolutionary and constitutional periods. Furthermore, he wished to offer "some account of the genesis and development in American letters of certain germinal ideas that have come to be reckoned traditionally American." This meant that he would "follow the broad path of our political, economic, and social development, rather than the narrower belletristic." He was concerned with the social forces that were "anterior" to literary schools and movements and were their source.

The first volume began with the rise of Puritan New England up to the triumph of Jeffersonianism and back-country agrarianism. The next volume stressed the creative influence in America of French romantic theories, the rise of capitalism, and the transition from an agricultural to an industrial order. The third and incomplete volume tried to show the "beginnings of dissatisfaction with the regnant middle class, and the several movements of criticism inspired by its reputed shortcomings."

The French romantic theory which he emphasized so much meant equalitarianism and the rejection of the Puritan conception of degraded human nature for the idea that it was potentially excellent and almost perfectible. It provided an intellectual justification for native agrarianism. Competing with it was realistic, materialistic English liberalism emanating from the commercial towns; this considered human nature as acquisitive and demanded that social and political philosophy conform with capitalism rather than the rights of man. Its principle of laissez-faire "reduced the citizen to the narrow dimensions of the economic man, concerned only with buying in the cheapest market and selling in the dearest." The kind of colonial liberalism that Parrington held dear was a strain that ran through Roger Williams, Benjamin Franklin, and Thomas Jefferson. Their opponents were John Cotton, Jonathan Edwards, and Alexander Hamilton. "The Carolinian Seeker [Williams] and the Jacobean theocrat, the colonial democrat and the colonial Calvinist, the Physiocratic republican and the capitalistic financier embody in concrete form the diverse tendencies of primitive America."

Quite proud of his realism, Parrington accused previous literary historians of leaning too heavily upon the genteel tradition to permit themselves "to enter into a world of masculine intellects and material struggles." By ignoring the polemics of colonial literature in favor of mediocre verse, they missed the creative thinkers of the time. He, too, began with Puritan New England, but he felt its first democratic influence was the freehold tenure system of landholding and believed that the mercantile spirit acted as a favorable creative factor. Puritanism itself was no friend of equalitarianism:

> It was rooted too deeply in the Old Testament for that, was too rigidly aristocratic. It saw too little good in human nature to trust the multitude of the unregenerate. . . . That the immigrant Puritans brought in their intellectual baggage the system of Calvin rather than of Luther must be reckoned a misfortune, out of which flowed many of the bickerings and much of the intolerance that left a stain on the pages of early New England history.

Luther was more mystical and more practical than Calvin partly because his inspiration came from the New Testament, which fostered tolerance of opinions among believers. Calvin was "ardently Hebraic exalting righteousness above love, seeking the law in the Old Testament and laying emphasis on an authoritarian system. The one was implicitly individualistic, the other hierarchical in creative influence."

This analysis scarcely rested on the bedrock of history and convincing theological philosophy. But Parrington was building on opinions of Luther and Calvin widely held in his day; unfortunately too much of his Puritan analysis depended on this dubious antithesis. He drew little distinction between the mild English seventeenth-century Calvinism and its harsher Genevan variety. Thus, his hero, Roger Williams, drew his libertarianism from Luther's idea of justification by faith with its favorable implications for political liberty. On the other hand, John Cotton and the Mathers belonged to Calvin's rigid system and to the foes of democratic liberalism. Calvin's reactionary theology represented "a composite of oriental despotism and sixteenth century monarchism, modified by the medieval conception of a city-state." It lingered on because it rigidly suppressed free inquiry.

When Parrington spoke of the principles of Separatism, he praised its ideal of Congregationalism allied with the separation of church and state; and he contrasted it with the Presbyterian synodical organization favorable to a theocracy. But for the Calvinistic Massachusetts Bay Colony he had a consistently unflattering characterization based largely on an anti-capitalist economic analysis. The Boston leaders were the product of a caste society laden with class prejudices: "They were potential capitalists, eager to accumulate ample landholdings, keen to drive a bargain, given to trade and with as sharp an eye to the main chance as any London merchant."

As for the origin of the theocratic principle itself, he charged that it grew out of the self-interest of the lay and clerical leaders who plotted in advance to endow their charter prerogatives with divine sanction. Even the famed town meeting—which was not contemplated under the charter—did not hamper the power of these magistrates, because the right of voting was limited to freemen subject to veto. Eventually, as Parrington interpreted it, the opportunistic leaders would transform their clerical provincial aristocracy into a secular power. He had little that was favorable to say about the cultural achievements of the theocratic oligarchy: "A world that accepted Michael Wigglesworth for its poet, and accounted Cotton Mather its most distinguished man of letters, had certainly backslidden in the ways of culture."

The tragedy of Puritanism was reflected in the "anachronism of Jonathan Edwards," a great but futile thinker who lived darkly in the bright eighteenth century of Benjamin Franklin: "Cut off from fruitful intercourse with other thinkers, drawn away from the stimulating field of philosophy into the arid realm of theology, it was his fate to devote his noble gifts to the thankless task of re-imprisoning the mind of New England within a system from which his nature and his powers summoned him to unshackle it." This gross underestimate of Edwards, which ignored his use of Enlightenment philosophies, was later revised by historians of philosophy and intellectual history. Edwards was a true Calvinist, but he did not depend upon the seventeenth century for intellectual sustenance. In contrast with this portrait, the author pictured the liberal Franklin enthusiastically, admiring his modesty, open-mindedness, charity, and devotion to the common welfare.

In depicting the American Revolution, he drew obviously upon the economic interpretations of Algie Simons and J. Allen Smith, although he insisted that the Revolution was basically a popular movement. Present-day historians tend to agree with this judgment: "The movement of resistance thus set on foot by the class conscious merchants eventually slipped from their control and passed into the hands of the Sons of Liberty, who drove faster and farther than conservative businessmen would willingly follow." Unlike later historians, however, he idolized Sam Adams as a "pure democrat" and a militant idealist who had long been unappreciated.

When he came to agrarianism and capitalism during 1783-87, he made considerable use of Beard's economic interpretation and his own favorite theme of French physiocratic influences upon the small freeholder's democracy. The economic basis of politics, he held, was not seriously questioned until French romanticism popularized the ideal of social equalitarianism. Neither England nor America, as their suffrage restrictions showed, challenged the fact of property rule. While the rising middle class established a new philosophy of capitalism evolving from Locke to Adam Smith, French intellectuals like Rousseau fostered "a passionate social idealism" based on a much higher opinion of human nature than competition revealed.

There is more resemblance to Beard in The Great Debate, dealing with the framing of the Constitution, for both men stressed and quoted at length from the economic philosophy of politics and history contained in James Madison's Tenth Number of *The Federalist Papers.* Not only did Parrington take seriously *An Economic Interpretation of the Constitution,* but he agreed with its sequel, *Economic Origins of Jeffersonian Democracy,* in which political parties are shown to have emerged in an economic setting from the debate over the Constitution. As a product of French and English liberalism and the democratizing influence of the frontier, Jefferson naturally fares much better than Hamilton, the architect of capitalism and industry, "but from whom our democratic liberalism has received nothing."

The second volume gives unusually generous and thoughtful attention to the ante-bellum South. Here again, as in the first volume, the high value of the individual characterizations is sometimes marred by sweeping syntheses which do not fit all the known facts. Jefferson's Virginia, its liberal leaders, and its agrarian philosophy attracted him —except for its older and fortunately passing Federalist elements:

> The history of the Old Dominion is an easy chapter in the textbook of economic determinism. . . . Established as a slave economy, it adopted an agrarian economy, espoused a republic, and accepted the doctrine of democratic equalitarianism. . . . During the noonday of its power its influence was always on the side of local democratic freedom and the common well-being. It opposed the encroachments of the centralizing state and the spirit of capitalistic exploitation.

All this was changed after 1830. "A new generation, trained in the school of Sir Walter Scott, fell to the pleasant task of portraying the familiar plantation life in glowing colors and investing it with romantic charm." This plantation tradition, he felt, grew out of the writings of the Virginia romantics. Parrington here exaggerated the weight of the alleged early democratic Virginian tradition and the supposed role of Sir Walter Scott in shaping the aristocratic ante-bellum South. He conceded that Virginia's generous outlook did not take root in the exploitative and imperialistic black belt. Apparently he admired the genius of Richmond's Edgar Allan Poe, even if he refused to consider him as a suitable subject for social-economic analysis. Poe was too puzzling for convenient social formulas. Maryland's Whiggish John Pendleton Kennedy also attracted him, despite his conservative economics and politics.

One striking philosophy that Parrington attributed to reactionary Southern leaders like Calhoun was the peculiar ideal of a Greek democracy. It held: "Democracy is possible only in a society that recognizes inequality as a law of nature, but in which the virtuous and capable enter into a voluntary co-partnership for the common good accepting wardship of the incompetent in the interests of society." Applying this to slavery Calhoun greatly injured agrarian democracy; and William Gilmore Simms of Charleston, for all his picaresque realism and talents, also fell under the sway of the same Charleston aristocracy that snubbed him. Parrington could have borrowed this notion of a Greek democracy for slaveholders from George Fitzhugh's *Sociology for the South*, published in 1854 as a justification for slavery.

Andrew Jackson naturally served him as a symbol of the authentic agrarian tradition of Jefferson and John Taylor, because his fight on the Bank and internal improvements nullified "the victories gained by the middle class during the boom period of nationalism." Increasingly, Parrington distrusted the methods of capitalistic finance. He saw redeeming features in the conservatism of James Fenimore Cooper: "An individualist of the old English breed, he could not be intimidated or coerced in the matter of his rights by any clamor, whether of newspapers or mobs." Cooper had a mediating mission: "He must discover some working agreement between the old America and the new, between the reputed excellencies of the traditional aristocratic order, and the reputed justice of the democratic ideal." Horace Greeley was forgiven his ties to Whiggery because he championed the great exploited classes of farmers and wage-earners against the middle class.

The third volume (again suggestive of Beard's analysis) tried to show the triumph of the coercive centralizing state controlled by the Jay Cookes and the Vanderbilts and the slow decay of romantic optimism and decentralization. At the same time, the author explained, the rise of mechanistic science and the emergence of a spirit of skepticism led to doubts regarding the ideal of democracy. History had again changed the definition: "Interpreted by the coonskin Jacksonians it meant political equalitarianism; by the slave economy it meant Greek democracy; by the industrial economy it meant the right of exploitation. It has changed service with each new master." He proposed to show the conquest of America by the middle class, its custodianship of democracy, and its philosophy. This overlordship was challenged by democratic agrarianism organized in third party movements; and a new proletarian philosophy came out of the ferment of the French Revolution. Finally, the agrarians were defeated by the victorious middle class.

The final volume of the trilogy included an addenda with many revealing and often pessimistic selections regarding the intellectual drift of the 1920s. None exceeds in bitterness the critique of our contemporary civilization, with Sinclair Lewis used as an exponent of the hollowness of our materialistic-urban-industrial-capitalist culture. In a sardonic essay, Parrington paid high tribute to this novelist's view of the tawdriness of our mass culture. Lewis had exemplified the thesis "that the *genus Americanus* is cousin-german to the scoffing Mr. Mencken's lately discovered *boobus Americanus*." Parrington was dismayed by the younger intellectuals, who thrived on the wartime discovery of the moron by the army intelligence tests, thus urging the futility of mass democracy and the need for a Nietzschean elite group of rulers. He hoped that this view of human nature would not turn out to be the last word in social philosophy for the next generation.

Boldly he essayed sweeping judgments upon recent figures. He looked upon Henry James, the idol of the next generation of critics, as rootless: "No other American has so hated and feared contamination from the vulgar. He was thus the last flower of the Genteel Tradition transplanted to an environment more congenial." Like Mencken, he admired the mediocre James Branch Cabell—"The Incomparable Mr. Cabell"—best known for his fanciful tales. He praised the basic economic interpretations of Charles Beard and of J. Allen Smith as the guide to Progressive doctrine, and thought that the muckrakers had proved that America was not the equalitarian democracy that it professed to be. From the beginning, he maintained, democracy and property had been at odds in a ceaseless conflict between man and the dollar. The recent critical studies of the Constitution revealed undemocratic premises in conflict with the idealism of the Declaration of Independence, and this was also reflected in the current drift toward plutocracy. But Parrington had no real solution for the nightmares that he had raised.

A product of the Progressive era, he shared to a large extent the indictment of the great American fortunes held by Gustavus Myers and the arraignment of business and politics offered by the muckraker. His strictures on capitalism were not, as is obvious, those of the socialists, but of an obsolete agrarianism. Greatly outweighing his faulty economics were his flashes of insight into American writers and political leaders. He was ever alert to the impact of European upon American culture, and he brought to light in all his volumes many a neglected poet, novelist, essayist, critic, and seminal thinker, whose contribution to belles-lettres was small but who offered great insights into the American mind. Like Taine, whose critical method influenced him, he constantly sought a large synthesis—sometimes, it is true, at the expense of sound history—and his emphasis was usually heavily weighted upon American political and social theory. Still, with all his shortcomings, he had much to say of worth even to a generation entering the second half of the twentieth century. Few could deny that he had stimulated immensely the search for the interdisciplinary aspects of American studies.

3

The immediate reception of Parrington's work was usually enthusiastic, and the award of a Pulitzer Prize to this comparatively unknown middle-aged writer surprised even his University of Washington administrative superiors—no admirers of his in any case. Henry Seidel Canby wrote in the *Saturday Review of Literature* that this was a work of the first importance, lucid, comprehensive, accurate, vivid, challenging, original, and sometimes brilliant. He believed that the patent Jeffersonian partisanship was actually a source of strength, not weakness, and he liked particularly the fresh appraisals of the less-noted writers. The least successful evaluations were the aesthetic ones.[3]

Kenneth Murdock, Harvard's specialist in Puritan literature, was greatly impressed by this use of literature as a source for historians and admired many of the biographical and critical sketches. To him, Parrington's application of new tests to familiar figures led to real revelations. On the other hand, he was not satisfied that Parrington had read enough of the original writings—he wanted *all* of the writings of a subject read—and he felt that too often the author had withheld evidence unfavorable to his judgments, as in the case of the Tory, Thomas Hutchinson.[4]

Professor T. V. Smith, philosopher at the University of Chicago, did not think that the author's bias would prevent this work from remaining the best history of American literature, one that would discourage the dry-as-dust emphasis in English in favor of a lively expression of human emotions, passions, and interests.[5] A lengthy but unsigned New York *Times* review gave unqualified praise to the author, even ranking the book above the Beards' current *The Rise of American Civilization.* The reviewer refused to concede that Parrington had ever permitted his sympathies to betray him into a flagrantly unjust judgment. "Biographically," he wrote, "it is unquestionably the best historical study that this country has yet produced."[6] Such high evaluations of Parrington certainly carried over through the Great Depression, when social and economic interpretations were uppermost even in belles-lettres and were encouraged by liberals, leftists, and doctrinaire radicals.

Marxist literary and historical critics were not altogether satisfied with Parrington's version of "economic determinism." The acute leftist critic, Granville Hicks, wrote an extensive critique for *Science and Society* in 1939 which criticized Parrington for failing to recognize the logical ultimate of his devastating social analysis—some form of socialism. Early in his career, the professor had revealed his attitude when he spoke of Harvard as "the apologist and advocate of capitalist exploitation." But his "economic determinism" was most contradictory, for, while his villains showed excesses of property consciousness, his heroes were usually idealistic, individualistic, or collectivistic, and cast in no consistent economic mold. Thus, Sam Adams was a man of reason, Jefferson a free soul, Freneau an idealist, and Joel Barlow a man with a sensitive social conscience. Parrington, said Hicks, "is forced to admit that Jefferson's plan for an agrarian democracy could not have been realized, and that Hamilton's labors for the establishment of capitalism were in effect progressive." This, it will be noted, was also the conclusion of later biographers of Hamilton.

Hicks (and others, too) considered Parrington in error for arbitrarily creating a dichotomy between English liberalism and French humanitarianism. Actually the terms were not mutually exclusive, and both expressed middle-class economic factors. The persistent dual classification of conservatives and liberals disregarded the biographic and historical facts. Hicks was perhaps the first critic to note that Parrington operated from a prejudice in favor of the alleged orderliness of the Enlightenment and showed a bias against the machine. This seemed to him to account for the savage onslaught upon the Gilded Age. Finally, he found many of the biographic analyses wrong.[7]

Lionel Trilling, a less doctrinaire critic of the mid-century, also took exception to Parrington's biographic judgments, particularly the flattering comparison of Cabell with Melville, the dismissal of Henry James as an escapist, and the refusal to deal with Edgar Allan Poe at length because he could not conveniently be fitted within the author's theory of American culture. Trilling's evaluations, often severe, reflected the reaction against Parrington after the Great Depression:

> Parrington was not a great mind; he was not a precise thinker, or, except when measured by the low eminences about him, an impressive one. Separate Parrington from his informing idea of the economic and social determination of thought and what is left is a simple intelligence, notable for its generosity and enthusiasm but certainly not for its accuracy or originality.

Yet, Trilling actually conceded quite a bit to the claim for Parrington's originality, for he stated flatly that the University of Washington professor "had an influence on our conception of American culture which is not equalled by any other writer of the last two decades." Furthermore, he added along this line, "whenever the liberal historian of America finds occasion to take account of the national literature, as nowadays he feels it proper to do, it is Parrington who is his standard and guide."[8]

Another latter-day critic who was apparently impressed by the studies of Hicks and Trilling was the historian, Richard Hofstadter. Then at City College of New York, he showed that Parrington had exaggerated the influence of French economic thought on the Jefferson tradition. Actually, Jefferson had "only toyed" with the physiocratic theories and had rejected the central idea of taxing agriculture primarily as inapplicable to American thought and conditions. While there still remained the central Jeffersonian and physiocratic idea of the primacy of agriculture, this notion was far older than the physiocrat philosophy. Hofstadter remarked on how impotent the economic thought of the Jeffersonians and Jacksonians had been to produce a design for American agrarianism: [9]

> At best their philosophy led to a negative conclusion: abandon the national banking system, reduce expenditures, cut taxation, divorce government from finance, democratize incorporation, keep hands off. Such devices might impede the advance of capitalism, but never prevent it.

Yet, neither Hofstadter nor any other responsible historical critic was prepared to remove Parrington's work from its pedestal as a great classic on American civilization. Even by mid-century, the scholarly process of riddling books that had once changed our minds had not quite disposed of *Main Currents in American Thought*.

4

At Harvard, particularly, where the Puritan tradition stood high and cultural nationalism there as elsewhere had replaced the skeptical Mencken spirit of the 1920s, revisionists displayed a keen appreciation for colonial New England that Parrington had lacked. In the researches of Kenneth Murdock, Perry Miller, Samuel Eliot Morison, and Ralph Barton Perry, the Massachusetts Bay Colony reappeared in an inspiring humanistic light, quite different from the portrait of gloomy misanthropes associated with the myth of American Puritanism. They discarded the grim caricature of Calvinist fanatics which Hawthorne had fastened upon his readers and in which H. L. Mencken had delighted.

The younger critics did not agree with Parrington or Max Weber, who would make Calvinism a force for exaggerated economic individualism or capitalism. Likewise they denied the historicity of the fanatical Puritan soured by a rigid theology lampooned in Oliver Wendell Holmes's "One Hoss Shay." Miller was impressed by the essential agreement between Puritans and Anglicans on basic dogmas and said that "about ninety per cent of the intellectual life, scientific knowledge, morality, manners and customs, notions and prejudices, was that of all Englishmen." Puritan preachers did differ from Anglican priests in their concern with more technical theological theories for the layman, their rejection of the hierarchy, and their belief that the Bible contained a complete constitution for church organization. Extreme Puritans like Cotton Mather thought of the Bible as a guide for the minutiae of daily life.

Perry Miller, who wrote a biography of Jonathan Edwards that showed him to be almost the antithesis of the same man discussed by Parrington, described the Puritans as humanists, heirs of the Renaissance as well as the Reformation. The Massachusetts Bay leaders, inspired by the philosophers of Cambridge University, thought of Christianity as a religion of cultivated reason rather than a sponsor of "enthusiasms." For them, therefore, a learned clergy was a necessity. They shared the Englishman's love of beauty; their "plaine stile" and meetinghouse had a beauty of their own. Above all, their asceticism was not wholly unique for their day and fell far short of the saintly hair shirt. Nor was the witchcraft craze and other intolerant practices limited to this people, as other historians showed.

Most impressive to Miller was the rich intellectual life of early New England, which Parrington had minimized. The heritage of Cambridge, from which so many Puritans came, was transmitted to Harvard, the Cambridge Press, the private libraries, and, even beyond this, to the efforts of the leaders to initiate tax-supported schools that would offer more than the mere ability to read and write. By the 1940s the revisionists had raised the reputation of the Puritans to new heights. Many of the Harvard group discounted the heavy social emphasis of Parrington's intellectual history and implied that ideas in themselves were far worthier of study than mere attitudes or beliefs confined in a rigidly deterministic framework. They did not neglect scientific interpretations, however, and were hardly less sparing of basic value judgments than Parrington had been, even if their style was more circumspect.

5

Out of the progressive Middle West of Beard, Turner, and Parrington came another rebel, Carl Lotus Becker. Born in 1873 in Blackhawk County, Iowa, he went on to academic training at the University of Wisconsin, where he acquired an admiration for Turner, studied history at Columbia, and taught in this field during 1902-16 at the University of Kansas. His really distinguished professorial career began in 1917 at Cornell University, where this serious and kindly man attracted large undergraduate classes in European history and turned out some of the best-known graduate scholars on the French Revolution. One of his most thoughtful books dealt with the Enlightenment, *The Heavenly City of the Eighteenth Century Philosophers* (1932). Like Charles Beard, with whom he was often compared, he enjoyed a reputation as a historian of European as well as American history, though his total output was slender indeed by comparison. Beard once considered Becker to be a pioneer exponent of the economic interpretation of history, but this judgment scarcely holds true of most of Becker's writings.

Of Beard's work, which he admired, Becker singled out *The American Leviathan* as one of the best, particularly for its realistic description of actual government. "The real Leviathan is not government, but society—this amazing and arresting and formidable phenomenon we call American civilization." As a relativist (at least he came close to it), he agreed with Beard that subjective elements made up a large part of historical theory. Beard had this in mind when he observed, "The theory that the Constitution is a written document is a legal fiction." It was always changing, for the judges constantly reinterpreted it.

There were important differences as well as similarities between the two: Beard stressed an economic interpretation of history, while Becker emphasized the role of ideals in most of the early chapters of *The United States: An Experiment in Democracy* (1920). Becker used Lecky's work a good deal, but he disagreed with the Irishman's notion of the Revolution as sordid and a "mere money dispute." Very different was his own statement: "American patriots came to think of themselves as hazarding their lives and their fortunes for the sake of a new social order, the ideal society founded upon the enduring principles of liberty, equality, and fraternity." The Revolution, then, was not a minority movement of interest groups but a contest for the rights of man. This idea was universalized in the Declaration of Independence, which appealed to the rights of all men. He idealized Washington as heroic, admirable, and broad in vision. However, Becker did recognize the colonial class divisions which gave the Revolution something of the character of civil war.

Becker's treatment of the Constitution, like Beard's, gave most attention to the checks and balance system as a key to liberty. "The whole history of the United States has been a process of trying to get more democracy," he wrote. Little, however, was said of the economic origins of parties, or the "moneyed class of Federalists," or of other factors stressed by Beard. His interpretation of the Civil War sounded as moralistic as that of Rhodes.

However, he leaned upon Frederick Jackson Turner and even insisted that "It is partly to the credit of the government that America is, as yet at least, a nation of small freehold landowners." His image of this country consisted of quiet towns, villages, and farming communities, where immigrants could be diverted from the crowded eastern cities. He quoted Turner approvingly in stating that westward expansion involves in every generation a return to simple and primitive conditions of life—"a perennial rebirth." Out of this process had come traits and ideals such as individual initiative, self-confidence, contact with hard realities, and mobility free from provincialism. In these latter chapters he reverted to economic analyses and accepted the pessimistic implications of the passing of the frontier, particularly the disappearance of the old equality of opportunity, the concentration of industrial power, the creation of a permanent class of wage-earners, and the rise of slums among exploited immigrants: "Political democracy we have; but the old economic democracy is rapidly becoming a thing of the past." The common faith in the eighteenth-century ideal of equality, he thought, reflected a cultural lag, because the solid base of our equality was not free government but a fortunate economic situation.

Surprisingly, in view of his earlier idealistic treatment, he ended up with an economic indictment that could have been written by Algie Simons or Beard:

In the economic sense, there is for the great mass of men and women neither liberty nor equality. Without a much greater degree of both than now exists, the personal and political liberties which have been so hardly won through a century of struggle lose half their importance, and democracy itself is scarcely more than a pious hope.

He feared that the concentration of economic power in the hands of a few would lead to their control of the state and to the subversion of democracy. But he saw hope in the growing power of the trade unions as a corrective to the power of capitalism. So his book on American democratic ideals ended well within the realm of the economic interpreters of history.

In 1910 Becker wrote an interesting essay, "Kansas," which tried to show that there was an intellectual "West" as well as a territorial "West." He spoke of Puritanism as a kind of frontier in the perennial rebirth of the intellectual frontier. Kansas and the Middle Border had inherited this return to the primitive in the evolution of the frontier. Yet, their strong individualism, which stressed achievement and rebelled against machines and "mortgage fiends," also contained large elements of conformity. Real toleration in fact seemed foreign to America.[10]

Becker's next book *The Eve of the Revolution* (1921), an outstanding contribution to the *Chronicles of America Series,* combined political and intellectual history. At the very outset, he suggested a rather subjective idea of history. It resembled the imaginative psychological techniques which Thucydides used to re-create a historical situation:

In this brief sketch I have chiefly endeavored to convey to the reader, not a record of what men did, but a sense of how they thought and felt about what they did. To give the quality and texture of the state of mind and feeling of an individual or class, to create for the reader the illusion (not delusion, O able Critic!) of the intellectual atmosphere of past times, I have as a matter of course introduced many quotations; but I have also ventured to resort frequently to the literary device (this, I know, gives the whole thing away) of telling the story by means of a rather free paraphrase of what some imagined spectator or participant might have thought or said about the matter in hand.

The result was not at all fictional, nor an abuse of quotations, but a sound, objective, and fascinating narrative of the coming of the Revolution. His explanations do not seem economic or materialistic—though he apparently believed that these qualities underlay intellectual realities—but rested upon the power of motivating ideas. He described both personality and environment, but he seemed most interested in the power of the mind in directing history. This is exemplified in his comment on the Declaration of Independence:

It is to these principles—for a generation almost obscured, it must be confessed, by the Shining Sword and the Almighty Dollar, by the lengthening shadow of Imperialism and the soporific haze of Historic Rights and the Survival of the Fittest—it is to these principles, these "glittering generalities," that the minds of men are turning again in this day of desolation as a refuge from the cult of efficiency and from faith in that which is just by the judgment of experience.

This idea was the central theme of his next and most famous book in the American field, *The Declaration of Independence: A Study in the History of Political Ideas* (1922). In this long essay, he analyzed the structure, drafting, and philosophy of the Declaration. He recognized that it was not intended as an objective historical statement of the causes of the Revolution, but merely furnished a moral and legal justification for rebellion. Step by step, the colonists modified their theory to suit their needs.

Whenever men become sufficiently dissatisfied with the existing regime of positive law and custom, they will be found reaching out beyond it for the rational basis of what they conceive ought to be. This is what the Americans did in their controversy with Great Britain.

Becker, like his fellow-scholar of the New History school, James Harvey Robinson, author of *The Mind in the Making* (1921), then recently published, fully appreciated the tendency of men to rationalize, but he also respected the innate value of moral ideas.

Becker's fondness for Turner did not prevent him from dropping the frontier approach and making a thorough analysis of the impact of the French Enlightenment and of British and Continental ideas upon the Declaration. In comparing the underlying assumptions of the French and American Revolutionary philosophers, he pointed out that nineteenth-century democracy tended to be anti-revolutionary on the whole, even though the abolitionists appealed to a revolutionary higher law. Elsewhere, Becker used Turnerian ideas to show how the bountiful New World environment produced sturdy American roots for its democracy.

His philosophy of history is clearly given in a presidential address, "Every Man His Own Historian," before the American Historical Association of December 1931. It contained his subjective emphasis, his considerable relativism, and the New History idea that the present should be the central guide of the historian. "Let us admit that there are two histories," he said, "the actual series of events that once occurred; and the ideal series that we affirm and hold in memory." The first was absolute and unchanged, but the second was relative, "always changing in response to the increase or refinement of knowledge." Historians sought to make the two histories correspond as much as possible.

As for the present, it was gone before full awareness took place. One had only a "specious present" which actually telescoped successive events in a single instant; the first event is past before the last took place. Only rhetorically can we speak of the "present hour," for it is already in the past. "In this sense all *living* history," as Croce says, "is contemporaneous; insofar as we think of the past . . . it becomes an integral and living part of our present world of semblance." We seek the past so that what we are doing may be judged in the light of what we have done and what we hope to do. This is living history—the present memory of events that have occurred in the past, things said and done. From these assumptions he concluded with a quasi-relativist interpretation regarding historical knowledge: [11]

It must then be obvious that living history, the ideal series of events . . . since it is so intimately associated with what we are doing and with what we hope to do, can not be precisely the same for all at any given time or the same for one generation or for another. History in this sense cannot be reduced to a verifiable set of statistics or formulated in terms of universally valid mathematical formulas. It is rather an imaginative creation.

History, he believed, is the artificial extension of social memory springing from impulse to enlarge the range of immediate experience. It was a mistake to think of history in every age as valid if the facts related were true, or invalid solely because the facts were inaccurate or inadequate. The subjective factor was denied respectability. "To select and affirm even the simplest complex of facts is to give them a certain place in a certain pattern of ideas, and this alone is sufficient to give them a special meaning." Historical facts, he argued, were not material substances like bricks. Even more clearly, he went on to elaborate the subjective nature of history:

Since history is not part of the external material world, but an imaginative reconstruction of vanished events, its form and substance are inseparable: in the realm of literary discourse, substance, being an idea *is* form; and form, conveying the idea is substance. It is thus not the undiscriminated fact, but the perceiving mind of the historian that speaks.

Like Beard he protested against the tendency of "scientific historians" to be discouraged by the "debris of exploded philosophies" and to turn away from interpretation altogether in favor of a rigorous examination of facts on the assumption that the facts speak for themselves: "Thus the scientific historian deliberately renounced philosophy only to submit to it without being aware. His philosophy was just this, that by not taking thought, a cubit would be added to his stature." He must renounce omniscience. Each generation will see the past and the future in the light of its own restricted experience.

Again, like Beard, he stressed the fact that the historian could not escape his conditioning. From the philosopher Alfred North Whitehead he borrowed the felicitous term "a climate of opinion," the atmosphere in which we live and think. Man and his world were ever in the process of becoming. Even the most striking events, he thought, "must inevitably, for posterity, fade away into pale replicas of the original picture, for each succeeding generation losing, as they recede into a more distant past, some significance that once was noted in them, some quality of enchantment that once was theirs."

Historians were not only suspicious of philosophy, as Becker and Beard had charged; they were also unhappy over the relativist position. Charles H. McIlwain, the noted political theorist and historian, was not alone in objecting to the selection of facts in the light of the present rather than the past. He feared that it endangered objectivity and impartiality; besides, the past could and should be written in the light of the past—its values, proportions, and modes of thought. The present must not be read into the past.

Becker discounted the Marxian philosophy of history. He believed that an intelligent person might regard the Marxist approach as an illuminating interpretation of the past without subscribing to it as a law of history. Secondly, that even if one were convinced that Marxism was valid, he might still have excellent reasons for refusing to support the communist cause. As a liberal, he rejected the idea of an inevitable class conflict, though he believed that history did reflect the fact that each new ruling class represented the mode of property owning. He had no faith, he said, in force and repression as the primary means of achieving the good life: "I have no faith in the infallibility of any man, or of any group of men, or of the doctrines or dogmas of any man or group of men, except in so far as they can stand the test of free criticism and analysis." [12]

Altogether, Becker, Beard, Turner, and Parrington represented a pragmatic revolt in which history served the statesman and reformer of each era by an even more deliberate design than that envisaged by the classical historians. Where they dealt with ideas, concepts, and attitudes, they made intellectual history serve the goal of social action. Like many other progressives, they found a subjective emphasis the best key to a changing world, but they did not permit their limited relativism or scholarly skepticism to undermine a serviceable idea of historical truth or knowledge. In the era of Stalin and Hitler, men like Carl Becker strengthened the ideological props of democracy.

6

Within the same pragmatic and reformist revolt, but perhaps more influential in encouraging historians to offer new courses in social-intellectual history, was Merle Eugene Curti, another Mid-Westerner.

He was born in Papillion, Nebraska, and attended the Omaha high schools; thereafter he was an eager student at Harvard, learning much about the New History from Morison, Turner, and Schlesinger, and dedicating his best-known book, *The Growth of American Thought* (1943), to Turner. His doctoral thesis, published as *The American Peace Crusade*, examined the ideas, personalities, organization, and history of the peace movement. For his comprehensive book, *The Growth of American Thought*, he was awarded a Pulitzer Prize and, most fittingly, the Frederick Jackson Turner professorship at the University of Wisconsin.

Students of method in the social analysis of ideas profited much from his earlier book, *The Social Ideas of American Educators* (1935), written while he was a professor at Smith College. Like Parrington, he tried to examine the social beliefs that underlay the technical work of influential men. He considered the extent of social and economic conditioning that affected the leading American educators—time, place, class, currents of ideas, social and economic tendencies, and temperament. In addition, like Beard, Becker, and others he gave close attention to the impact of European ideas upon America.

Curti used the relativist emphasis of the other progressives: "Much of the confusion and inconsistency in the social thinking of educators has been due to the fact that they have been for the most part unaware of their own frame of reference." By making these ideas and half-hidden assumptions clear he hoped to help those trying to bring equalitarian measures to education. Apparently his yardstick in this field was John Dewey, philosopher of instrumentalism, although he did not fail to survey the criticisms of Dewey. He liked this quotation: "Democracy has to be born anew every generation and education is the midwife."

Dewey's faith in intelligence and the school as a guide to a democratic order was reflected in a critical attitude toward economic competition, although he definitely rejected class war. He wished the school to cease overemphasizing the mere symbols of knowledge, to make first-hand contact with experience, and to encourage the child to make a critical adjustment to social life. Thus, the school would become an agency to break down class barriers and distinctions. All this was very far indeed from the colonial conception of schools as means of preserving orthodoxy in religion, trade, and social life. To a large extent, the nineteenth century had not changed this goal.

Some of Curti's most original analyses dealt with conservative educators. He was very critical of America's leading Hegelian, William T.

Harris, the United States Commissioner of Education who cast himself as the chief interpreter of German philosophical thought in America. To Curti, Harris's Hegelianism helped to standardize the American school system within a conservative ivory tower: "It rationalized the victory of nationalism, imperialism, and industrial capitalism by insisting that true individualism could be realized only by subordinating the individual to existing institutions." Likewise suspect were the theories of the dominant psychologist of Columbia, Edward Lee Thorndike, who implied that heredity is more important than environment and taught a restricted idea of "transfer of training" which encouraged a more utilitarian emphasis in the schools.

Curti's *The Growth of American Thought* (1943) is too comprehensive for summary here, but it was immediately recognized as a pioneer effort to integrate American social and intellectual history in a single volume, stressing the viewpoint of liberal democracy. Drawing upon an unusual variety of sources, the author went beyond Parrington and others in seeking ideas and popular attitudes in records of cultural agencies, folklore, theological treatises, essays of all types, novels, poems, newspapers, and, not least, in dime novels. Curti described his book as a social history of American thought, perhaps a socio-economic history of American thought. He believed that intellectual history should deal not only with the great thoughts of Americans but with their informal notions, dominant beliefs, values, and even casual attitudes. These were usually related to their institutional framework and the interaction of European and American influences.

The young intellectual historians, he pointed out, had quite a different task from the traditional philosophers. The former dealt to a large extent with the "exterior" of ideas in their social setting, while the latter were concerned with the intrinsic validity of the "interior" of ideas. Curti did not renounce either purpose for himself but admitted that the limited nature of the book did not furnish an opportunity for an exhaustive analysis of the "interiors" of the ideas and systems of thought discussed. Others like John Bury wrote profitably upon the interior of a single idea, Progress, and Curti hoped for similar studies of liberty, security, militarism, collectivism, and loyalty. By the 1950s he and his associates were absorbed in a social analysis of the history of philanthropy.

7

Ralph Henry Gabriel of Yale, an older contemporary of Curti's, enriched intellectual history by somewhat different methods. He had dropped his early vocation for the ministry, first in order to study geology, then to become a historian. In 1940, he published *The Course of American Democratic Thought*, in which he traced the vicissitudes of certain social ideals in our history since the mid-nineteenth century. A second edition, more optimistic than the first, which had appeared during the fall of France, was issued in 1956. He chose these three historical tenets of American democracy for scrutiny:

Americans by 1815 had formulated three major beliefs, each a complex of ideas. The first tenet assumed the dignity of human personality and asserted the conviction that that dignity could be realized only when the individual was free to express himself and to participate in decisions of vital import to him. The second tenet assumed that principles of universal validity underlie the common life of men in society, the application of which to affairs makes possible the realization of freedom and dignity. The third tenet asserted that the nation created in 1776 exists as a corporate entity not only to further the peace and security of its citizens but to aid—at home and, by example, abroad—the cause of freedom and humane living. . . . Their history after 1815 provides the theme of this book.

His religious background explains in part at least his attack on ethical relativism—the idea that truth varied from individual to individual (or group) and had no objective standard. This did not mean that he rejected altogether the epistemological relativism of the mid-nineteenth-century intellectual historians. As a student of William Graham Sumner, he early recognized that historians were conditioned by their culture: "Ideas arise out of social situations and persist because they have utility," he wrote. He was particularly concerned with the idea of a fundamental moral law which had dominated the nineteenth century, had been secularized during the scientific era, and then had declined under the ethical relativism of Sumner. Herman Melville was rejected by his own century because he denied its belief in the free individual and the moral law and insisted that evil was permanent. But the twentieth century understood him and bought his books. Gabriel thought it noteworthy that, while Europeans turned to doctrines of class struggle, Americans were attracted by a religion of humanity and a new rationalism based on the fundamental moral law.

In his criticism of scientific relativism, Gabriel examined the skeptical assumptions of legal realists from Oliver Wendell Holmes, Jr., to Thurman Arnold and Jerome Frank. The author had no sympathy for political realists like his colleague Nicholas Spykman, who found the ultimate reality in the power struggle. Total war, said the latter, was the result of a long historical process. This cumulative power struggle tended to wipe out the historic distinction between peace and war, because it went on without pause.

Gabriel saw victory in the struggle against ethical relativism. Intellectuals who had yielded to the relativism of William Graham Sumner were aroused by the war and realized that they lacked a sound democratic faith from which to denounce Hitlerism and Stalinism, Gabriel declared. Fortunately, gains had been made in securing the rights of minority peoples, despite the evolution of McCarthyism. Legal realists who had once portrayed the goal of law as the mere arbitrary will of judges now conceded that the goal was justice. Power politics was now being put in a context of moral law, and more reliance was being put on ideals rather than empiricism.

The Course of American Democratic Thought interpreted intellectual history largely as an expression of the urban elite. Hence, it omitted rural reactionary movements such as the Klan, the Fundamentalist crusade, the persecution of minorities, and various facets of King Mob. Within its designated limits, however, the book presented certain historical ideals effectively and in an attractive literary form.

8

By mid-century, the literature of American intellectual history had reached great volume and high quality. The influence of Darwin on social ideas was expertly described in Richard Hofstadter's *Social Darwinism in American Thought, 1860-1915* (1944). Hofstadter began with the reception of evolution in America, its enthusiastic champions John Fiske and Asa Gray of Harvard, the scientific contributions of O. C. Marsh to Darwin's proofs, the influence of Spencer's ideas of the survival of the fittest, and the use of Social Darwinism by reformers and conservatives.

Historians trained in science issued analytical narratives of the New Geology, the New Physics, and the New Biology. Broadly trained social scientists published outstanding biographies of William James, Thorstein Veblen, Henry George, and Edward Bellamy. Historiography took on richer dimensions as historians and graduate students sought to understand the social ideas and assumptions as well as the craftsmanship of American historians.

Parrington still had enthusiastic and discriminating disciples by mid-century. Henry S. Commager of Columbia wrote this high praise in *The American Mind* (1950): "My deepest intellectual debt is to Vernon Louis Parrington whose great study of American thought has long been an inspiration and whose disciple I gladly acknowledge myself." Commager looked upon him as a historian who struggled to rescue liberalism from the dead hand of the neo-Manchesterians and espoused a native radicalism—"a tough-minded radicalism on which protestants and rebels could confidently draw." Far from regarding Parrington's agrarianism as anachronistic, Commager asserted that the ideals of Jefferson and Emerson were more relevant to the problems of the twentieth century than anything that we could import.

The American Mind, purporting to be "An Interpretation of American Thought and Character since the 1880s," continued the liberal interpretation of Parrington without the exaggerated agrarianism; besides, it forsook emphasis upon individuals for the analysis of definite cultural movements. In his chapter on historians, Commager took issue with Beard's (and presumably Becker's) subjectivism and uncertainty, not because they were untrue basically but because they were harmfully exaggerated and unconstructive:

> The real objection to Beard's historism was not that it repudiated certainty but that it was sterile, and in a literal sense inconsequential. The doctrine of subjectivity and uncertainty like the doctrine of economic motivation was not a conclusion but a point of departure and everything depended on the route and the destination. That history was subjective and fragmentary and inconclusive—like almost everything in life—would be readily acknowledged, but if history was to be written at all it was necessary to go on from there.

Commager had already written an important original work in intellectual history in his biography *Theodore Parker* (1936), which pictured and interpreted the varied and influential career of the noted disciple of Emerson and Channing who tried to revitalize Unitarianism and to liberate it from its formalism. Parker, an eloquent and erudite lecturer and writer, fought against slavery, the exploitation of labor, unjust restrictions upon women, backward schools, and war. To him, as to many fellow-reformers, society rather than the individual created crime and poverty.

Inevitably, younger gifted scholars eclipsed Parrington's limited methods and rewrote political and economic, as well as cultural, history from the standpoint of ideas, attitudes, and class determinants. Arthur Schlesinger, Jr., of Harvard, son of the pioneer social historian, attracted attention as a youth with an excellent biography of the controversial author, Orestes A. Brownson. Later, in a vigorous and mature style, he analyzed the complex ideological skeins of Jacksonian democracy in *The Age of Jackson* (1947) and gave labor a major part in the creation of this new order. With an eye upon the revival of strong government under the New Deal, he criticized the surviving "Jeffersonian inhibitions" of weak government and pointed out the socially democratic heritage of Jacksonism which served the people by energetic measures against private monopoly. By the 1950s, logically enough, he turned to a multi-volumed history of the New Deal that probed into the intellectual assumptions as well as the deeds of the chief characters of the Age of Roosevelt. While his controversial reformist point of view, his syntheses, and his novel analogies aroused critics, few could dispute his brilliance.

The social study of ideas added a new dimension to diplomatic history, hitherto largely restricted to formal archival sources as in Ranke's day. Previously foreign affairs had been seen as the exclusive business of State Department officials, subject of course to Presidential intervention. There were those like the scholarly Samuel F. Bemis of Yale who elaborated most successfully upon the older archival tradition. But Charles A. Beard, ever given to a dynamic view of society, refused to confine his economic interpretation of history to domestic affairs, and studied interest groups as determinants of foreign policy. Among his lengthy ideological studies was *The Idea of National Interest* (1934); later he dwelt upon the "continentalist" or semi-isolationist theory which would preserve peace by minimizing internationalistic economic and political ties.

Beard decried Wilson's and Franklin D. Roosevelt's international idealism as unrealistic and provocative of war. A decade or two later, George Kennan, a onetime State Department expert and a diplomatic historian, offered many historical evidences of a moralistic idealism which ignored true national interests in dealing with Japan up to 1941 and with Russia since 1917. This antithesis between moralistic diplomacy and the necessities of power politics was elaborated so effectively by Hans Morgenthau of the University of Chicago Political Science staff that it awakened a national controversy over whether relativism was to run rampant in foreign affairs. Those historians who tested the charges of moralistic naïveté usually concluded that American diplomacy, including that of Wilson and Franklin D. Roosevelt, showed a realistic awareness of concepts like the balance of power and the national interest.

Hard-boiled diplomatic realism had its devotees among those who applied the seapower doctrines of Admiral Mahan or their equivalents in airpower as a basic determinant of diplomatic policy. A few historians of note even borrowed a controversial tool (somewhat tarnished by the Nazis) from geopolitics, which had won a separate maintenance suit against political geography, and studied the political community as a growing organism determined by pressures of population, living space considerations, and economic needs. Some, like Julius Pratt of the University of Buffalo, explained the coming of the Spanish-American War partly in terms of the impact of chauvinistic ideologies, as in *Expansionists of 1898* (1936); [18] and Albert K. Weinberg also made an ideological analysis of national expansionism in *Manifest Destiny* (1936).

Especially successful among those diplomatic historians who looked for social determinants was Thomas A. Bailey of Stanford, who supplemented archival resources by a variety of informal sources dealing with domestic pressures. Most expressive of his point of view was a general discussion in *The Man in the Street* (1948) which pointed out the damage done to consistency, wisdom, and security in foreign affairs by pressures from ethnic groups, domestic politics, chauvinism, isolationist prejudices, Manifest Destiny ideas, and newspaper and radio interests. Such warnings were at least partly heeded in the years ahead. By mid-century, the conduct of foreign affairs reflected this dynamic approach, in which ideological factors were recognized as of major importance. The State Department struggled to find the intellectual tools with which to combat the spread of subversive isms in the uncommitted parts of the world. The United States Information Agency and other official groups sponsored cultural programs in a cold war that could not be won with conventional weapons.

☆ 15 ☆

Allan Nevins and Recent Historiography

1

Few American historians of the mid-twentieth century represented so effectively and in such varied ways the chief trends of recent history-writing as Professor Allan Nevins of Columbia. His retirement in 1958 did not cut off a prolific and productive lifetime of creative writing in biography, business history, social and cultural history, and the background of the Civil War. Without sacrificing scholarly standards he made history an adventure for the many.

This hard-working son of an Illinois farmer was born in 1890 in Camp Point, Adams County, not far from the banks of the Mississippi and the state line of Missouri. As a boy he knew the tedium of farm work, the rounds of rural life, and the long hours of labor; and as a historian he continued to work endlessly, often without pausing for lunch. A Calvinist background and somewhat Victorian inclinations (or so he thought) shaped his outlook.[1] Fellow-historians marveled at his industry and some intimated without evidence that his nineteen volumes of history, eleven of biography, and scores of other voluminous writings on which he had collaborated must have been due to a corps of anonymous assistants and graduate students. Only Charles Beard, who had not been handicapped by numerous academic chores once he had left Columbia, was among the able few who could rival Nevins in the output of first-rate history.

Like other local sons of middle-class farmers, he had the opportunity
of attending the University of Illinois, where he earned two degrees by
1913, taught English there for a year, but did not go on to the Ph.D.
Thereafter, until 1927, he turned to newspaper work, became an editorial writer for the New York *Evening Post* and *The Nation,* a literary
editor for the New York *Sun,* and a member of the editorial staff of
the New York *World.* While living in New York City he managed to
write the first history of his alma mater, *Illinois* (1917), by examining
newspaper files, interviewing officials and alumni, reading state reports and student publications, and gathering other materials. His obvious devotion to the University did not prevent him from being objective, and he did not resort to anecdotes or trivia in tracing the
state university movement as against its sectarian rivals. He began
with the influence of the federal land grants, noted the unique services of Governor John Peter Altgeld in helping to transform the "cow
college" to major status, and ended with the emerging institutional
activities. Finally, Nevins saw in such progressive state schools the
means of disseminating practical idealism, for they worked as a leaven
upon the social mass. This early book was undistinguished in style,
but it set a high standard of informative analysis for future college
histories—a research area which Nevins always urged scholars to investigate.

Out of his extensive newspaper experience came one of the best
histories of journalism, *The New York Evening Post* (1922). It was
no mere technical summation or hasty portraits of editors but illuminated metropolitan journalism since 1800 and the influence of the
Post in national affairs. The William Cullen Bryant papers and other
family papers, as well as the New York press, enabled him to show
intimately the role of the *Post* in such crusades as the war against the
Tweed Ring and its part in party politics. Here again he added new
dimensions to the writing of a history of the press, for he dealt with
the *Post* as an organic thing, shaping as well as being shaped by the
metropolitan environment.

While still a newspaper man, he wrote a number of books in American history that continue to circulate actively in libraries and college
courses. In 1923, he published *American Social History Recorded by
British Travellers,* a most revealing book, and the next year appeared
a major work in the neglected field of state history—*The American
States During and After the Revolution 1775-1789.* He called attention
to the need for expanding the subject matter and method of the field:

In general, American historiography has treated each Colony separately till 1775, but with the year of independence has suddenly ceased to regard the thirteen commonwealths as separate entities, and followed only their collective fortunes. No real attempt has been made to synthesize State history for this period, or any other.

He showed that, while the states retained a colonial heritage of suffrage and religious restrictions, the new states also preserved much of seventeenth-century English democracy and experimented successfully in the forms and principles of government. Although Nevins did not carry out his plan to write a series of state histories, others (some of them his graduate students) published excellent books in this field.

For several years more he combined his editorial duties with history-writing and sporadic college teaching. Then in 1931, he became a professor of American History at Columbia University, remaining there except for distinguished visiting professorships both here and abroad and special war-time duties until his retirement. Despite his activities in directing graduate students, he found time to travel in search of source materials and to write books, which gained ever-increasing prestige. Steadily his style improved, especially by the 1930s, until the discriminating reviewers praised him for his ability to re-create historical situations vividly, yet without poetic license. Twice he won the Pulitzer Prize, in addition to academic prizes. Publishers sought him out to write readable textbooks or to edit entire series of biographies and histories.

Nevins was also among the early contributors in social history to the *History of American Life Series* with the issuance of *The Emergence of Modern America, 1865-1878* (1927). This period had been covered from the political and constitutional viewpoints by Rhodes, Dunning, and Burgess, but the versatile young author followed the series pattern of avoiding politics to the extent of omitting Charles Sumner and Thaddeus Stevens; and, like most of the other contributors, he tended to be descriptive or impressionistic rather than analytical. There was no doubt of his dislike of Radical Reconstruction and the use of Union bayonets in controlling the postwar South. The chapter headings are revealing: The Darkest Days in the South; The Industrial Boom in the North; Urban Living; The Taming of the West, etc.

He contrasted the boodling and financial recklessness of the era with the virility of other Americans, such as the hardy and picturesque cowboy, pointed out our growing intellectual maturity, and showed sympathy for the farmer's revolt against monopoly while deprecating his erratic reform ideas. Newspapers, railways, and public schools cemented the unity of post-bellum America, while the reconstructed South adjusted itself to "the healthful competitive forces, economic and social, of American life." A decade later Nevins seemed more disturbed over the chaos of competition and justified the necessity for economic consolidation, even semi-monopoly. His favorable view of business was already evident, for he held that the corrupt Fisks and Goulds were not typical of the American businessman. He preferred to think of Peter Cooper, the ironmaster and philanthropist, and of Abram Hewitt, steelmaker and reformer, as much more representative. Although he felt sympathetic towards labor and the unions, he was fascinated by the leadership of the new entrepreneurs. As yet, at this stage of his development, he seemed unable to make his social history absorbing, but his social outlook was already determined.

2

The art of biography fascinated Nevins throughout his life and led him to make his most noteworthy historical achievements. His ideal was not the notion of Carlyle or Emerson of history as a projection of the great man, though he left ample room for the role of personality. Biography was to him supplementary to history, and his desired objective was a life-and-times treatment which gave insights into complex movements. "It [biography] humanizes the past," he wrote in his *Gateway to History* (1938), "while at the same time it enriches the present by showing us life with a vividness and completeness that few men experience in life itself." In the 'twenties, the vogue for biography stemmed in part from the stimulating example of the Englishman, Lytton Strachey, who depicted eminent Victorians like Florence Nightingale and John Henry Newman with a realism in which sympathy and understanding were also present. Strachey was no "debunker" like the cynical New York businessman, William E. Woodward, who thought of George Washington as a cold-hearted land speculator and an inferior general.

Although Nevins believed that Strachey was an essayist rather than an historian, he shared his enthusiasm for honest biography, but his own portraits frequently revealed more moralistic judgments than psychological analysis. Some biographers of the 1920s like Dr. Katharine Anthony went so far as to interpret their subjects in semi-Freudian terms. Psychology was then the queen of the social sciences and reflected the introspective atmosphere and individualistic emphasis of the Lost Generation. Closer to Nevins in spirit was the former Progressive Senator from Indiana, Albert J. Beveridge, whose very sympathetic and successful *Life of John Marshall* (1916-19) reflected the business philosophy of the 'twenties; that generation admired the conservative outlook of Alexander Hamilton, the model for Secretary of the Treasury Andrew Mellon. This decade ended with the inauguration of the twenty-nine volume *Dictionary of American Biography* (1928-44). Written by over two thousand specialists, it was inspired by England's noted *Dictionary of National Biography*. In the second great wave of biographies during the prosperous 'forties and 'fifties, again an era of business leadership, Nevins found his milieu.

While still a newspaperman, Nevins tried to blend an interest in the romantic West with his interest in biography. He secured hitherto unused papers of John C. Frémont from his heirs and published in 1928 *Frémont, the West's Greatest Adventurer*. It delighted Willa Cather and other novelists of the frontier, and its tone was much livelier than conventional historical writing. Eleven years later (1939), "chastened in style and much enlarged in content," as the author wrote, he produced a much more critical book on the same man. He seemed fascinated by the dashing, scintillating personality of the versatile, adventurous Frémont. Yet, Nevins made no flattering claims for his hero, whom he spoke of as very rarely a Pathfinder and mostly a Pathmarker. Like certain previous writers, he concluded that it was fortunate that this man never became President, for he was too rash, tactless, and erratic in judgment. Frémont became a legend with a name that was to evoke "the fragrance of one of the truest love stories in American history." While an occasional specialist on the trans-Mississippi West like Professor Cardinal Goodwin complained that the book was too long and had little to say that was new, Carl Fish and other historians thought that it was an ideal biography.

In 1930, Nevins emerged from his studies in diplomatic history as well as biography to publish *Henry White: Thirty Years of Diplomacy*. This was the only authorized biography that Nevins ever wrote, but he denied that the family had influenced him and insisted that "the responsibility for every part of it rests exclusively with myself." The very wealthy White family turned over many new letters which made possible a somewhat different account of the diplomacy of Richard Olney and John Hay as well as White. While Henry White was no major figure, his biographer recognized this fact and did not go beyond praising his sterling character and diplomatic skill. One acute reviewer thought that the lavish use of personal correspondence did not make up for the failure to study the available archival sources, and, as a result, the diplomatic history lacked depth of penetration.

The author revealed unmistakable Anglophile tendencies, though his references in this and in other books to the creative Anglo-Saxon were cultural and not racial. "A life-long believer in a close friendship between Great Britain and America," he said, "he [White] lived to see the old hostility banished forever, and the two nations associates in war and partners in promoting disarmament and peace." White had served as an ambassador to Italy and to France; he headed the American delegation at the crucial Algeciras Conference, where he helpèd to prevent a conflict between Germany and France over Morocco. Like Nevins, he was an internationalist eager to see the United States enter the League. It was not easy for the biographer to be detached in dealing with a man who had died only recently; besides, Nevins almost never escaped the temptation to align himself with his subject in his various biographies, although his honesty led him to enumerate his heroes' drawbacks. Nevertheless, *Henry White* was a satisfactory performance. A very competent reviewer, Professor James A. Woodburn, considered this the most readable of volumes and concluded, "No student of the recent years, or of American diplomatic history, can afford to neglect this volume . . . the most important and valuable historical production of the year." [2]

3

The Great Depression did not greatly affect Nevins's pro-business outlook even when he took a sympathetic attitude toward the New Deal. His new heroes were the conservative Grover Cleveland, the reformist but wealthy ironmaker Abrám Hewitt, the traditionalist Hamilton Fish, and the super-entrepreneur John D. Rockefeller. Obviously he had no desire to satisfy the current demand for anti-business biographies. Gustavus Myers came back into notice in 1936 by arranging for a Modern Library edition of his *History of the Great American Fortunes*, which had been grist for the muckraking mill of a generation before. Myers had challenged the idea that "the great private fortunes were unquestionably the result of thrift and sagacious ability," but he regarded his own analysis as scientific, in contrast to the "sheer sensationalism" of muckraking. In 1907 reviewers had castigated his treatment of the Vanderbilts, the Jay Goulds, the Morgans, the Hills, and the Rockefellers as "Plutophobia." Now he had become a classic among liberals and leftists. Along similar lines, Matthew Josephson, a Columbia graduate, was popularizing a most derogatory term in *The Robber Barons* (1934) and *The Politicos* (1938). A vogue for economic history was then in full blossom, the disciples of Frederick J. Turner were directing attention in books and college courses upon economic aspects of western history, and Charles A. Beard's economic interpretation of history had become almost orthodox among the younger generation.

In 1932, Nevins chose to subtitle his *Grover Cleveland* "A Study in Courage" and thus subordinated somewhat the emphasis on the basic economic questions to the factor of Cleveland's strength of character, although the bulk of the narrative was devoted to the two presidential administrations. Aided by a vast unpublished correspondence, both personal and official, he was able to keep close to the private reactions of Cleveland, his alternations of exuberance and puritanical sternness, his simple and powerful emotions, his integrity, common sense, physical and mental strength, and cautious sagacity. He never surrendered "an iota of principle to expediency." But the biographer stated frankly that these qualities would not have been enough "but that the stars were with him." He was to express similar judgments on Rockefeller and Ford. Luck or chance and favorable environmental factors counted for a great deal in Nevins's interpretation of history, despite his concern for character and personality.

Cleveland's first term was successful because the "settled democracy" did not desire a new Jackson:

> Men expected Cleveland to display not an excursive boldness, but simply a greater honesty and earnestness than his predecessors, and he understood this perfectly. . . . Reconstruction was safely in the past, the agrarian problem, the labor problem, and the trust problem were only slowly coming to national attention, and belonged to the future.

While his first term, as Nevins saw it, stressed honesty and tariff reform, the second added to this "the principle of unyielding conservatism in all that affected finance and business." He observed acutely that to the support by reformers was joined the allegiance of "frightened Eastern capitalism," particularly bankers, utility magnates, large merchants, and railroad owners. Cleveland's low tariff ideas and internationalist leanings were very congenial to the author.

Nevins believed that Cleveland's anti-imperialistic philosophy, particularly as expressed in his rejection of the annexation of Hawaii, was much more important than his jingoistic language in the Venezuela boundary dispute with England. The latter message he attributed to the bad advice of Secretary of State Olney. Cleveland's firm anti-expansionism eventually led to better relations with Great Britain, a goal ardently desired by the writer, who liked to speak of "the great English-speaking nations" and the Anglo-Saxon heritage. The biographer also blamed Cleveland's friend, Olney, while he was attorney-general, for the misconception of the Pullman Strike that led the President to send federal troops to Chicago and to invoke the labor injunction. While Nevins sympathized with the progressive Governor John Peter Altgeld of Illinois, who protested Cleveland's military intervention, he argued that the governor should have moved faster in using the state militia. This statement overlooked the fact that Altgeld had consistently used militia that same year in the coal strikes whenever needed to preserve order, but never to break strikes; besides, the Chicago disorders began *after* and not before the arrival of Cleveland's troops. The author's admiration for the President did not prevent him from taking the labor side and from severely arraigning the labor policies of George M. Pullman and the organized railroad executives.

While other historians of the 'thirties sympathized with the Populistic demands for currency reform and inflation, Nevins preferred Cleveland's "sound money" gold theories and praised his courage in withstanding the storm of criticism that befell his hard-money policies. "He belonged to the Anglo-Saxon race which values character above everything else; and his career shows why that valuation is a just one." Thus, in the biographer's view, the President had saved the nation from abandoning the gold standard—"an abandonment that would have meant heavy loss and perhaps economic chaos." A few years later, undoubtedly, Nevins could have noted that the latter-day Bryanites among the New Dealers had embarked on similar inflationist currency experiments, which succeeded neither in raising prices nor in precipitating the economic chaos feared in 1896.

Arthur Cole and Elbert J. Benton, both eminent historians in this field, were impressed by the fairness, thoroughness, and brilliance of the Cleveland biography. "Mr. Nevins," said Cole, "has produced in every sense a stimulating volume such as might well have set the standard for the series of biographies which he edits and to which the work belongs." Benton as well as Cole liked Nevins's frankness in discussing the errors of his hero and added strong words of commendation,[3] "Probably no one will arise to deny that the author's objective has been brilliantly achieved." William Allen White of Emporia, writing in the *Saturday Review of Literature,* praised the book's scholarliness, honesty, charm, and intelligence.

In 1936, Nevins published *Hamilton Fish: The Inner History of the Grant Administration,* another life-and-times study based on a huge diary and many archival sources. While it exceeded 900 pages, it compressed the first sixty years of Fish's life in one hundred pages and the last twenty in thirty pages; the remainder dealt revealingly with the Grant administration. Although the author modestly stated that his book was intended for the general reader not the specialist and that he had left many problems for the monograph writers, the professional as well as general reviewers were usually enthusiastic.[4]

Grant's Secretary of State Hamilton Fish emerged from the book as a giant among cabinet pygmies. "Again and again he saved the government from misfortune, once or twice even from disaster." Yet Fish lacked quick perception, originality, or brilliance and was plainly a Whig-Republican conservative with a strong property consciousness. But he had clarity and soundness of judgment. He knew how to block the "sentimental imperialism" of Seward, Grant, and Sumner and the trend toward expansionism in Cuba, Santo Domingo, and Canada. "He helped to prevent a reckless realization of the doctrine of Manifest Destiny. The thoughtless masses were ripe for another movement of national expansion, or if not ready, could quickly have been made so." Fish's crowning achievement was of course in fostering good relations with Britain during the hot *Alabama* dispute and in bringing about a fair settlement.

4

With the lifting of the Great Depression and the coming of prosperity attendant and following World War II, the prestige of the businessman rose even higher than during the 1920s. Newspapers, magazines, and books told the prodigies of production wrought by the wartime industrialist that did so much to defeat the Nazis and fascists. The Robber Baron epithet did not fit those at the helm of General Motors, United States Steel, and the projects of Henry J. Kaiser. Nevins was now more in tune with his age when he set himself to the task of writing sympathetic biographies of Rockefeller and Ford.

The new vogue for business history was much more analytical than in the past without muckraking overtones. Businessmen and their public relations men were solicitous of academic as well as popular opinion. Business archives were organized under the direction of trained historians and opened to social science research. *Fortune* magazine and the President's Economic Advisors under the Maximum Employment Act issued many penetrating analyses of American business. These efforts were no longer solely the panegyrics that Bruce Barton had written of the businessmen during the 1920s. Objective studies of the entrepreneur and the philanthropist were fostered through generous scholarly grants at Harvard, Columbia, Wisconsin, Chicago, and elsewhere. The well-established *The Business History Review,* founded in 1927, issued many excellent articles on management and the entrepreneur, and *The Journal of Economic History,* begun in 1941, printed a number of evaluative articles on the social status of the top American business leaders. William Miller's study, "American Historians and the Business Elite," considered the careers of 190 corporation presidents at the opening of the century and questioned the Horatio Alger myth of easy social mobility among these men. Three-fourths came from old colonial families, not immigrants, four-fifths were sons of business and professional people; and a mere 2 per cent came out of the working class. Two-fifths had gone to college, and most of the rest to high school at least.[5] Even in the Horatio Alger stories, it will be noted, the hero usually rose out of a humble origin because of some wonderful stroke of luck, such as rescuing the daughter of a millionaire, rather than because of his ability and a favorable social environment.

But an increasing number of able historians, following the early European scholars like Richard Ehrenberg, student of the Fugger bankers, had lost interest in the Robber Baron approach and chose to concentrate on the history of managerial methods, technology, business and financial contributions, and the biographies of single banks, insurance companies, railroads, and industries. Nevins and Dr. Stanley Pargellis, a historian who headed Newberry Library in Chicago, urged businessmen to combat the anti-business prejudices of some historians by opening many more industrial and commercial archives. Not a few of the new business historians were associates, students, or friends of Nevins. Thus the Columbia professor revised the well-defined unfavorable image of the Standard Oil Company that came from Henry Demarest Lloyd's *Wealth Against Commonwealth* (1894), Ida Tarbell's *History of the Standard Oil Company* (1904), and John T. Flynn's *God's Gold,* the latter a more tolerant presentation which Nevins found partly salvageable. His associates, Ralph W. and Muriel E. Hidy, examined the technological history of this enterprise in *Pioneering in Big Business, 1882-1911: History of the Standard Oil Com-*

pany (1955). The Hidys were not directly concerned with moralistic, political, or social issues but focused on the technological and economic phases. In 1949, Ralph Hidy had made a close objective study of the complex international ties of finance in *The House of Baring in American Trade and Finance*. Business was now to be studied clinically under the microscope, not with the lenses of moral judgments alone.

In 1940 Nevins brought out both volumes of *John D. Rockefeller: The Heroic Age of American Enterprise*. He began by stating his intensive effort to be as objective as possible upon this controversial subject: "If the author brought any bias to his work, it was that of a convinced believer in a free competitive economy," he wrote, and added that the full account of Rockefeller's philanthropies was being told for the first time. Apparently the Rockefeller family felt no qualms about entrusting the family papers to this particular historian; critics and defenders of the oil tycoon were interviewed by the author; legislative reports, now duly tempered by personal and company correspondence, were not ignored. The facts were obviously meticulously examined, for Nevins took pride in correcting the presentations of previous writers, and the style remained absorbing throughout the entire long narrative.

Like John T. Flynn, he pointed out that Rockefeller's competitors were often worse in their business morals than Standard Oil; besides, this company had a remarkable story of solid pioneering contributions to industrial technology:

> It was to be vehemently denounced throughout most of the next generation and in part with good cause. But its success was not built upon dishonesty. The rebate contracts of 1877 were deplorable; the "massacre" of independent refineries had indefensible features. . . . The practices by which it earned merited castigation were fairly congenial to its contemporaries.

He thought that Standard Oil was entitled to recognition as "one of the most impressive industrial fabrics ever erected in any part of the globe" and that "impartial observers" had come to feel admiration for this creation. *The Age of Enterprise* (1942) by the business historians Thomas C. Cochran and William Miller accepted the Nevins-Flynn view that Rockefeller was not hated by his contemporaries primarily for his methods but because he was more adept than his rivals in using the means that lay close at hand.

Nevins was unstinted in his praise for Rockefeller's philanthropies and their administration. He did not agree with Flynn that Rockefeller was wholly naïve in his notion of stewardship for "God's Gold." "Rockefeller always dealt with his wealth in humility, not in arrogance. He never used it to minister to his vanity or power. Regarding it objectively, he never let personal prejudices or predilections impair the wisdom of its employment." Unlike Carnegie, Stanford, or Duke, he did not meddle with the men who directed these expenditures but kept his gifts on the very highest plane. Nevins of course knew that his own views were not held by contemporaries:

> The American people, as we have said, felt no great gratitude to Rockefeller for the distribution of a fortune which many regard as largely a historical accident. But reflecting citizens have properly felt a very warm gratitude to him and his son for the painstaking care, the wisdom, the unselfishness, and the fine public spirit with which the distribution has been made.

During his lifetime, Rockefeller gave to the public over $550 millions and left most of the remaining fortune to his son for the continuance of his philanthropies.

Whenever the evidence went against the Rockefellers, as in the case of the violent Ludlow, Colorado, strike, where their absenteeism encouraged gross abuses of labor by the manager, Nevins stated all of the relevant facts quite honestly, though he mitigated the charges by the most sympathetic treatment of the circumstances involved and went on to show that John D. Rockefeller, Jr., inaugurated reforms thereafter. The elder Rockefeller is usually treated much better than Standard Oil and praised as an organizing genius, keen mind, firm character, bold innovator, and "one of the most impressive figures of the century which his lifetime spanned."

Thirteen years after a very warm reception of this work, Nevins decided to revise it as *Study in Power: John D. Rockefeller, Industrialist and Philanthropist*. The second two-volume biography seemed to him practically a new book, because, while it preserved the main facts, it contained a great deal of hitherto unknown and highly illuminating material derived from recently discovered letters. This made possible a more intensive view of the organizing methods of the oil business and the personalities involved. Nevins was more convinced than ever that those who used the Robber Baron interpretation of 1865-1914 knew but one facet of the truth. "The constructive aspects of the transformation were in the long run more important than the destructive; the development of new wealth far outweighed the wastes of existing wealth."

One of Nevins's able Columbia colleagues in economic history, Louis Hacker, had collaborated with European historians to show that historians had erred in depicting the Industrial Revolution and early capitalism unfavorably, because they gave exclusive attention to the parliamentary investigations of the gross abuses of labor. Nevins agreed with this criticism:

Modern students of the Industrial Revolution in England have long ago agreed that early historians did it an injustice by writing their books out of the inquiries of the Parliamentary commissions which accumulated evidence of abuses as a foundation for reform legislation. That was part of the valid evidence but only part.

He could have added that the anti-business portraits of Gustavus Myers had depended upon legislative investigations. Yet, Nevins echoed a judgment on the wealth of these entrepreneurs that did not differ much from that of Myers:

In no true sense of the word did he [Rockefeller], Carnegie, and Henry Ford earn the huge accumulations which came to them. Only the special economic, legal, and fiscal situation of the United States 1865-1917 rendered it possible to make and keep so much money. Recognizing this fact, Rockefeller always regarded himself as a trustee rather than an owner.

Those who reviewed the Rockefeller biographies in either edition (although particularly the *Study in Power*) were frequently generous, if sometimes qualified, in their praise. Reginald C. McGrane, the economic historian of the University of Cincinnati, was impressed by Nevins's arduous research, the noteworthy revisions of so many phases of the Rockefeller story, and the absorbing style, but he felt that the author had contradicted himself to present the oil man favorably: "While Professor Nevins has not failed to criticize the Standard Oil and Rockefeller at times," he concluded, "he has written a very comforting history of the oil industry and of the rise of one gigantic corporation." [6] John D. Hicks shared much of this judgment. While he conceded that Nevins had made a most important contribution to American history, one of which the author might feel proud, there was obvious bias also: "The observer is apt to believe that if Rockefeller's critics have overplayed their hands, so also has his chief defender, Mr. Nevins." [7] Not all of the academicians were converts to Nevins's Rockefeller. [8]

No less ambitious in scope and sources than the Rockefeller biography was his two-volume work on Henry Ford, also cast in the life-and-times form, with considerable attention to the technology and entrepreneurial factors behind a leading industrial firm.[9] Ford's public relations men had not been idle in circulating the picture of an attractive industrial giant who might have become president, but in 1948 came a thoughtful but severe arraignment of the automobile magnate by Keith Sward, *The Legend of Henry Ford*. This showed a ruthless autocrat, sharp in his dealings with agencies and rivals, harsh in his labor relations, defiant of national authority in the guise of the National Labor Relations Board, and an irresponsible purveyor of anti-Semitism through his organ *The Dearborn Independent*. But Nevins did not wholly agree with Sward, of whose work he had this to say:

> The first attempted formal study, based on extensive research in printed sources and equipped with scholarly apparatus, of Henry Ford and the Ford Motor Company. While often perceptive, it suffers from bias, and from conclusions based on insufficient evidence. The heavily weighted pro-labor viewpoint of the author, a former CIO public relations counsel, governs the tone and character of the volume.

While Sward drew to a considerable extent from investigative materials aimed at Ford's abuses, Nevins went far beyond this to consult the vast Ford archives newly reorganized for the use of historians. One of Nevins's Columbia students who had been trained in his Oral History Research Office held a key position in the archives. As in previous books, Nevins began with an emphatic denial that this was in any sense an authorized work, but a product of a grant from the Ford Motor Company Fund to Columbia University in the interests of general business history and a project supervised by a special faculty committee. In fact, "the research has been done by University employees, working under ordinary academic conditions and with the usual academic salaries; all royalties on the volume are paid to the University." This statement also suggested the extent to which the author was accepting collaboration, though he insisted that he was responsible for the final product: "For all the faults and shortcomings of the history, the author alone is responsible." One of his chief collaborators in this and in previous works was the scholarly Frank E. Hill, whose name appears on a co-equal basis in volume two.

The book began with a vivid story of the pioneer development of transportation since the early stagecoach and came up to the rise of modern vehicles. Henry Ford's childhood in a rural setting was told in visual language:

The child Henry Ford toddled about on the Dearborn farm amid pleasant surroundings. The land, though a stiff clay and somewhat hard to work was fertile. Beyond the yard with its pump, beyond the evergreen shrubs and the orchard, well-cultivated fields were broken by patches of timber.

Nevins of New York City had not forgotten his rural past.

One of the chief episodes which pictured Ford in a most favorable light was the battle of his young struggling company against the arrogant patent claims of George Selden and the wealthy financiers and industrialists behind him: "Millions of dollars and the right to produce freely were at stake." Ford's victory in the courts not only opened his own path to great riches but freed automobile production for all, as against the payment of tribute in the form of large license fees to a monopolistic group: "To him it had been a fight for freedom in the deepest and most satisfying sense."

Up to 1914, Ford is an admirable man to his biographer, because he seemed to excel in all the traits that made American entrepreneurs examples for businessmen everywhere. There was well-directed hard work which led to the manufacturing and improvement of the early car models. He showed creative independence and initiative in designing, selling, and financing. His adaptation of the assembly line reflected an honest desire to enrich the masses by making cheap cars. Labor shared in the benefits that he dispensed. Especially praiseworthy to the author was the history of Ford's leadership in establishing the basic five-dollar day at a time when such a rate seemed fabulous. Sward had seen this as an effort to halt a costly turnover of labor in an industry marked by dreary repetitive manual operations; besides, it was expected to check radicalism and unionism and was minimized in actual operation. Nevins went into considerable detail to refute this view. The new wage scale was the capstone to "the most advanced labor policies yet known in large-scale American industry" at a time when Detroit was an open shop town. The Ford Company had long avoided the speed-up piece work system, led in the use of safety devices and regulations, checked the power of autocratic foreman and supervisors, paid efficiency bonuses, and instituted an eight-hour day. Even when his fellow-directors protested, Ford insisted on sharing profits with his men.

Nevins was much more impressed with Ford's "sociological" or welfare department than Sward, who regarded it as unjustified intrusion into the homes of employees. To the Columbia professor, this department deserved credit for its Americanization work, its vocational retraining of men, and the struggle against the slums. Furthermore, Henry Ford's philanthropies included work for the handicapped and even for large numbers of former convicts on parole. To Sward, these ex-convicts represented a group of necessity loyal to Ford himself and ready to do his bidding in fighting incipient unionism.

Ford's naïveté on matters outside of auto-making led him to trust his own intuitive judgments in areas quite foreign to him. He never outgrew the habit of making startling and irresponsible statements to the press, and he was eager to believe the emotional pacifists who urged upon him the Peace Ship venture to end the World War. He had been influenced by the peace movement and the peace sentiments of his beloved *McGuffey Readers*. Much more understandable were internationalist and pro-League sympathies which led him to support Woodrow Wilson and James Cox. While his growing popularity brought him a surprising number of supporters for the United States Senate and even for the White House, it seemed to Nevins that he was motivated by much more than a desire to sell more cars.

After 1916, Ford displayed autocratic tendencies toward his associates and his workers, and his increased reliance on intuition in social issues led him into strange bypaths. His worst and most injurious adventure was the manufacture of anti-Semitic charges and legends by staff members of his *Dearborn Independent*. They collected, elaborated upon, or invented a large stock of anti-Semitic canards, such as the alleged world conspiracy in the "Protocols of the Elders of Zion." Even when it was demonstrated that this conspiracy had been concocted by Czarist agents, the *Dearborn Independent* editors were not disturbed. Eventually, these Ford writers, who were not all enthusiastic about this assignment, overreached themselves by making conspiratorial charges against an able Jewish lawyer, Aaron Sapiro, who promptly began a heavy libel suit which attracted embarrassing national notoriety to Ford, who had been accustomed to newspaper praise in the past. Ford settled the case out of court at the first opportunity, especially when it became evident that his car sales might suffer. Although Nevins, with his customary urbanity, explained Ford's anti-Semitism as rural loutishness rather than bigotry, he did not minimize the facts themselves; in fact, he explored a variety of theories regarding the manufacturer's behavior. He showed that Ford was obviously lying when he pretended publicly that he had paid no attention to the activities of the *Dearborn Independent*. Furthermore, Nevins was quite aware that the injury inflicted on the Jews could not be ended by Ford's apology; these articles were widely read and translated by anti-Semites abroad. (Sward even linked this influence with the Nazis.) Ford's very prestige in rural America and abroad gave this hate literature validity and perpetuated its life.

Both Nevins and Sward were severely critical of Ford's use of the unsavory ex-prize fighter, Harry Bennett, as head of the Ford Service Department. Bennett's picked men intimidated alleged labor agitators and won a reputation as a local Gestapo. Nevins preferred to think of Ford's motives as merely naïve rather than sinister; his family was concerned about threats to their safety. Although the second volume did not go much beyond 1932, Nevins did stigmatize Ford's labor policies during the Depression as indefensible. Sward, who brought the story through the entire New Deal years, had much more to say about Ford brutality and defiance of the National Labor Relations Board during these years. Nevins and Hill made their second volume much more critical than the first: "Since 1919 he [Ford] had been one of the last great despots of the industrial world, his dictatorial sway backed by complete ownership and large financial reserves."

When the books appeared, the reviewers seemed more impressed than ever. Even Harold U. Faulkner, an economic historian of Smith College who had always been critical of industrial monopoly and big business, gave the biography unqualified praise. In his judgment the work superseded all others on the subject because of its comprehensive research, accuracy, tone, and style. "It is no glorification of Ford or big business," he believed.[10] A more detailed review in the *Mississippi Valley Historical Review* held a similarly high estimate. The reviewer was especially impressed by the fact that Nevins and his aides had to peruse archives containing over six million manuscripts and 100,000 photographs. But he thought that even more explicit value judgments could have been expressed by the biographer.[11]

5

Perhaps the best-written and most valuable historical work of Allan Nevins were the *Ordeal of the Union* (1947) and *The Emergence of Lincoln* (1950), each a substantial two-volume set. With all his facility in research, he was able to go over the much-worn period of 1847-61 and emerge with a fresh, lively narrative. Nevins's contributions did much to clarify the picture of ante-bellum America. He shared with Ulrich Phillips the belief that the race problem was the central one for a people irrevocably committed to "a white man's country"; both agreed that the abolitionists were incendiaries. But while Phillips justified the planter's point of view, Nevins did not, though he went along in pointing out that the North, with its exclusion of free Negroes, did nothing to alleviate the race issue and much to aggravate it. Neither of these historians was content with the view of James Ford Rhodes that the Civil War was a moralistic crusade over slavery.

These volumes were also unique in the way they exemplified Robinson's New History idea—in fact, much better than the older Columbia professor had done. The subject matter was as broad in social, cultural, intellectual, and political history as any devotee of this school could require. Nevins did not have the reformist emphasis that the older leaders of the New History had had, but he was not unconcerned with the present-day significance of historical situations. Besides, his use of cultural history had close relevance for the main theme and was an effort to acquire deeper understanding of the Civil War by synthesizing the various strands of historical development.

As in previous volumes, Nevins could refer quite honestly to his extensive labors in tracking down letters and other sources, this time through wide travels both North and South. Once more he invoked the goddess of objectivity as his ideal and stated frankly that this work would be primarily a narrative history. Only this, he thought, could "lay bare the inner meaning of the crisis," though room would be found for purely analytical and descriptive elements in the nation's civilization. He looked for a number of dominant themes or clues:

Most of the forces created by science, invention, and business technology thrust toward unification. This tendency had to contend against centrifugal impulses born of the wide spaces of the land, the varied national origins of the people, and the existence of two utterly different labor systems.

Sometimes the slavery theme seemed too narrow to contain the entire narrative structure, and the author was led to observe how the everyday life of the nation was not concerned with the political struggle over human bondage.

The first chapter began with a sensitive literary narrative that reflected the author's belief that historians must develop a feeling for the physical setting as part of the malleable whole. He was with Scott at Chapultepec:

On the high Mexican plateau the September nights are chill. The first gray glimmer of day was appearing outside Winfield Scott's headquarters on the craggy height of Tacubaya, less than a mile from Chapultepec on its sister hill, when the sentries' challenges rang out to halt a group ascending the slope.

Imaginative as this paragraph is, Nevins could actually document practically all of it. The sources exist. Irrefutable common sense fills in the gaps.

Nevins had far too much to cover of an area traversed by so many specialists for him to attempt an entirely new story. But there were few topics to which he did not add new facts and often interpretations. Besides, his selection of monographic theses were usually well blended into a total picture that was his own. He examined the growing factionalism within the Democratic party after the Wilmot Proviso proposal and concluded that the politicians of the Old Northwest had not conspired to induce David Wilmot to present an incendiary measure barring slavery from all lands acquired from Mexico as a result of the war. President Polk seemed wise to the author in following Calhoun and his Southern lieutenants in fixing the Oregon northern boundary at 49 degrees, instead of resorting to the dangerous slogan of "Fifty-four-Forty or Fight"; Polk had bravely disregarded the resentment of the Northwest. In fact Nevins regarded Polk as one of America's great presidents, and he had published a diary which put a favorable light upon the man. As an inveterate seeker for moderate solutions, he praised the architects and the ideas of the Compromise of 1850, particularly Clay and Webster. "No man loved the Union more strongly than Webster, and none had done more to instill in Americans a noble spirit of nationality."

Douglas, who has been praised by so many revisionist historians as no less important in achieving the Compromise than Clay and Webster, was not exonerated for his part in upsetting that settlement through the Kansas-Nebraska Act. However, Nevins constructed a single strand of complex motives, borrowed largely but far from exclusively from previous historians. As a businessman long interested in railroads, Douglas desired a northern transcontinental railroad from Chicago, his home; he may have believed that he could thus please the South and advance his presidential dream; he hoped to quash the slavery question in the territories by applying the squatter or popular-sovereignty idea to them; he had to appease the followers of Senator Atchison of Missouri; and he may have hoped to resolve the chaos in the Democratic party that had been induced through President Pierce's ineptitude.

Shrewdly and skillfully, Nevins reconstructed the elusive Atchison-Douglas maneuvers leading to the passage of the Kansas Act. He dismissed as a transparent rationalization the argument of Douglas that the principle of slavery restriction as expressed in the Missouri Compromise of 1820 had been dropped in the Compromise of 1850. Pierce, who had blocked Douglas's efforts to get a genuine test of popular sovereignty in Kansas, appears in a most unflattering light: "He was one of the quickest, most gracefully attractive, and withal weakest, of the men who have held his high office." For the imperialistic foreign policies of Pierce, such as the efforts to force Spain to sell us Cuba, he had only contempt: "Had our policy shown more honesty, more simple decency, it would have been both more reputable and more effective."

The author underlined the basic race factor as the prime cause of the sectional conflict, although he did not ignore other factors: "Everywhere, North and South, the free Negro offered a demonstration of the fact that the racial problem underlay the slavery problem, and that abrupt action in dealing with the 'peculiar institution' might well complicate the task of race-adjustment." Here again was the moderate speaking, the foe of violence; but he did not agree with Ulrich B. Phillips that slavery had much in its favor: "Slavery was the greatest misery, the greatest wrong, the greatest curse to white and black alike that America has ever known."

Like Frederick Law Olmsted, who visited the South during the 1850s (and quite unlike his friends Morison and Commager), he rejected the standard portrait of kindly planter paternalism:

> In reality, Southern kindliness was chiefly for Negroes in slavery and was that type of amiability always engendered in superior groups by an immutable caste system. It seldom extended to free Negroes, who were regarded with even greater hostility than in the North.

It was the caste system, then, which led planters to hate free Negroes. "If they grew numerous, educated, and economically secure, they would arouse the envious discontent of the slaves, become a rallying point against the existing order, and ultimately reduce slavery to atoms." The sectional quarrel between both sections over slavery and race adjustment was worsened by a schism in American culture:

> Differences of thought, taste, and ideals gravely accentuated the misunderstandings caused by the basic economic and social differences: the differences between a free labor system and a slave labor system, between a semi-industrialized economy of high productiveness and an agrarian economy of low productiveness.

The Emergence of Lincoln, two volumes which dealt with 1857-59 and 1859-61, continued the prologue to the Civil War. Nevins spoke

highly of his predecessors who had worked in the field—Rhodes, Mc-
Master, Schouler, and Edward Channing, "who brought a finished
scholarship to bear upon a succession of issues and aspects." But he
thought that historians put such an excessive emphasis on the politics
of this era that they regarded it too exclusively as one of turmoil.
"Yet in a broad view, the period stands conspicuous for a peaceful
growth and prosperity greater than any that Americans had previously
seen." California was now one of the wealthiest of states; Colorado had
become a rich mining frontier; scientific farming replaced subsistence
farming; and the East had become more intensely urbanized. "The
main impression given by American life in the fifties was of health,
strength, and constructive force."

Nevins hated war (though he supported the Roosevelt foreign policy
in World War II) and condemned the Civil War particularly, although
his precise reasons were not clear: "Secession had to be resisted; but
it would never have occurred had Americans realized what a great
war meant." Too many felt the lust for martial excitement, and some
from both sections later admitted that they would not have supported
a solution by war had they known of the horrors. Nevins had insisted
that the war was in part an utter failure of leadership to present the
facts of race adjustment in their true light. But he does not make clear
what the actual alternatives were for a confirmed Unionist or antislavery man in 1861. In fact he pointed out at length that the South
could not visualize race equality and that the North had no intention
of permitting large numbers of free Negroes to move there and to share
the benefits of integration. Not even compensated emancipation attracted more than scattered minorities. By 1859, as the author saw the
situation after John Brown's raid, there was little hope:

> The temper of both North and South had grown worse. At this eleventh
> hour, could the conservative forces of the nation be awakened? It did not
> seem likely. The country might yet regain the partial concord won in 1850
> —or it might slip swiftly toward disunion and war.

National leadership in the era between the two able presidents
Polk and Lincoln was at a low ebb. Pierce and Buchanan acted as if
they were paralyzed by the Kansas war and the presence of a mere
hundred slaves in a vast area. Nevins philosophized:

> Much that happens in human affairs is accidental. When a country is
> guided by true statesmen the role of accident is minimized; when it is not,
> unforeseen occurrences are numerous and dangerous.

That great accident was John Brown's raid on Harpers Ferry; it divided North and South more tragically than ever. The story of John Brown is told in detail, and Nevins indicated that this man was far more fanatic than saint, although not a madman in the usual sense. Brown was sane on all subjects but one—slavery and the possibility of ending it by a sudden stroke which would provoke slave uprisings. On this matter there was "a paranoiac flaw in John Brown's mind, the key to his type of reasoning insanity." So frightened was the entire South by John Brown that Democratic moderates like Douglas were destroyed politically. The aroused land of Dixie would only tolerate the presidential nomination of a man "whose friendliness to slavery was more fervent and unbending than Douglas's."

Nevins made his chief argument regarding the cause of the war clear through elaboration in each volume. Slavery and its complementary problem of race adjustment were the main causes of the war; had it stood alone, the slavery issue would have been resolved as an alternative to war:

Had it not been for the difference in race, the slavery issue would have presented no great difficulties. But as the racial gulf existed, the South inarticulately but clearly perceived that elimination of this issue would still leave it the terrible problem of the Negro.

Southern leaders refused "to nerve the people to pay the heavy price of race adjustment while the Southern rank and file would not pay the price of a rising social status for the Negro." But he confuses his reader at times by speaking of slavery as an "inevitable" or "irrepressible" cause of the war, particularly in *Ordeal of the Union.*

He rejected as almost wholly untenable the prevailing economic interpretations of the Civil War: "One fact needs emphatic statement: of all the monistic explanations for the drift to war, that posited upon supposed economic causes is the flimsiest." It was certainly not the tariff factor, because the South had secured most of its demands here, and its other economic grievances did not differ materially from those of the rural Northwest. He also saw nothing in the Republican platforms of 1856 and 1860 to incite the South to war. Undoubtedly the North felt that its political power was not commensurate with its social-economic strength, while the South feared that this power would be turned against slavery, thus endangering the white man's supremacy.

More than other historians of ante-bellum America, Nevins paid attention to the world setting of the slavery and the racial struggle, noting the abolition of serfdom or slavery in various parts of the world.

One great difference existed in the fact that the white South most feared racial amalgamation, while Latin America did not. Britain and France abolished slavery in their colonies, but only a very small fraction of the population consisted of a white elite, and presumably the social distance was so great that amalgamation was not feared.

Nevins felt that Lincoln understood the basic issues and correctly demanded that slavery be placed in a position where the public mind could rest assured of its ultimate extinction. Here were the questions:

> Was the Negro to be allowed, as a result of the shift of power signalized by Lincoln's election, to take the first step toward an ultimate position of general economic, political, and social equality with the white man? Or was he to be held immobile in a degraded, servile position, unchanging for the next hundred years as it had remained essentially unchanged for the hundred years past?

The Columbia professor was raising the ultimate questions which few had been quite ready to meet in 1861. There was little of the "revisionist" thinking which dwelt upon power factors, economic determinants, and psychological explanations.

Although rival economic and moral interpretations were still too strong to be swept away, even by Nevins's four massive volumes, the reviewers agreed in honoring their high literary and human interest qualities. John D. Hicks, reading *Ordeal of the Union*, was pleased to note that Nevins had not straddled the issue of the evil of slavery and had outdone himself by a very magnificent work.[12] Yale's distinguished intellectual historian, Ralph H. Gabriel, warmly endorsed these two volumes in detail, especially their richness of color and style.[13] Roy F. Nichols of the University of Pennsylvania, whose *Disruption of Democracy*, dealing with the 'fifties, had won a Pulitzer Prize, admired the books, though he deplored the tendency of Nevins to minimize the role of emotionalism as a cause of the war.[14] Two well-known Southern historians complained sharply of abolitionist bias and gross errors, but this reaction could have been foreseen.[15] Another severe critic, Avery Craven of the University of Chicago, a specialist in Southern history, who used a multiple approach to the causes of the Civil War, was unwilling to concede much more than literary and dramatic facility to the author. He regarded his interpretation as shallow and biased and, like Roy Nichols, preferred to stress the role of emotionalism:

> Moral issues, and issues having to do with the fundamental structure of society, had arisen and gotten into politics. Such issues do not lend them-

selves to toleration, rational discussion, and compromise. They crowded
reason aside and gave emotions full play.

To Craven, the conflict was much more "repressible" than it was to
Nevins, although the latter saw some possibilities for solution before
John Brown's raid.[16]

On the whole, the reviews were overwhelmingly favorable. The
writer himself was encouraged to plan an extension of the history to
1877, the end of Reconstruction, and thus to replace the numerous
volumes dealing with this entire period by James Ford Rhodes.

6

Those who thought of Allan Nevins as an industrious journalist (he
even spoke of himself in this modest way) gave him little credit for
abstract thinking or for any philosophy of history. They ignored the
logical construction of his historical thought and his thoughtful analysis of historical method and theory in *The Gateway to History* (1938).
In this book he gave considerable thought to the nature of history,
showed familiarity with European as well as American historiography,
and discussed many aspects of history as an art. His Columbia graduate course on American historians afforded him an outlet for his
studies in this field. *The Gateway to History* did not offer mere counsel
of perfection but stated ideas that were clearly practiced in his own
books.

Nevins's love of literary art and of imaginative, vivid language made
him enthusiastic about the great literary historians—Prescott, Bancroft,
Motley, Parkman, and Irving. Without compromise on quality, they
made books on history the fare of multitudes of intelligent readers.
Such work not only illuminated the past, but suffused a glow which
more than anything else—"more than the work of sociologists, economists, or political experts"—cast light on the immediate future. By the
1950s, as he noted, the writing of history and biography was very
frequently in the hands of men who had mastered the art of good
writing.

His admiration for the literary historians of the past did not imply
old-fogeyism, for he recognized the constant need for new historians
and perspectives to revise the viewpoints of an age that had gone:
"The lenses through which we look at the past must be refocused from
generation to generation." History-writing reflected the form and spirit

of its age and recorded the stages through which thought and feeling have passed.

On the question as to whether history is a science, Nevins offered a very qualified answer. He dismissed natural science analogies, although he liked to borrow Darwinian metaphors; but he believed that history was not inferior within its disciplined confines to the sciences as a critique of man. It was too "violently personal" to be a natural science although it was not behind biology, which also was incapable of discovering laws of "a purely timeless and mathematical character." Historians could discover certain uniform tendencies in human affairs:

The steady accumulation of data, together with an increasing ability to classify and analyze facts bearing upon individual psychology, communal psychology, economic changes, and the growth of institutions and mores, enables us to lay down more "laws" and to do so less tentatively.

But Nevins was too strongly a believer in the element of chance in history to leave much room for alleged laws of history. Events frequently presented themselves not as a logical chain "but a fortuitous string of occurrences, affected by chances of a thousand kinds."

His attitude toward the various types of history-writing was eclectic. He was ready to concede an element of truth in Carlyle's alleged emphasis on the role of the hero, but he thought that this individual became important largely as an expression of the *Zeitgeist*. He disliked relativism, but admitted, "Facts cannot be selected without some personal conviction as to what is truth, and cannot be arranged without the same conviction—and this conviction is a bias." Nevertheless, he stopped short of Beard's relativism, as revealed in "That Noble Dream." As he understood it, "The implication is that one set of assumptions would be chosen as sounder than another set, and an effort would be made to organize historical writing upon this set of preconceptions." This seemed to him no better than fascist pragmatism: "Those who have a higher ideal of truth will, while admitting that their effort to attain it is often doomed to failure, never give up the attempt."

Like most American (and even West European) historians, he felt suspicious of general philosophies of history such as that of Hegel, as distinct from specific interpretations of historical materials. "General philosophical concepts of history," he said, "will not bend to pragmatic tests." One such untenable concept was Oswald Spengler's idea of history moving in regular cycles of development. Nevins discussed at some length the various leading philosophies of history, but showed that he preferred the sophisticated common-sense view that it sufficed to have a generally reflective attitude toward history. Like Ranke, he did not reject the usefulness of philosophy, but opposed the tendency of so many formal philosophies of history to force the facts into a preconceived formula that was apt to run against the test of historical experience. He was quite willing to give careful thought to such reflective theses as Beard's synthesis of the Civil War as a sharp collision between a business civilization and an agrarian one (although Nevins never believed that this was a major "cause" for the war), because this theory could be tested.

He felt sympathetic to the broad social-science approach of the New History if this were not overdone. Any history that went too far in the direction of sociology fell into a limbo in which it lacked form and value. Sociology was certainly useful, but it offered no master key to history. There was danger that history turned over to sociologists would mean that it would be laid out in artificial and dogmatic patterns. Interpretation was essential, but so were facts, and the result of applying a pound of interpretation to an ounce of facts was disappointing. At the other extreme of narrowly descriptive social history, he deplored the lack of integration in McMaster, Oberholtzer, and certain of the authors in the *A History of American Life Series*. Finally, biography was a valuable supplementary element for history, with which it should be combined. It gave insights into complex movements: "It humanizes the past, while at the same time it enriches the present by showing us life with a vividness and completeness that few men experience in life itself." Thus spoke a highly successful biographer who took his own advice.

7

When Allan Nevins retired from Columbia University in 1958, he could look back upon a lifetime of achievement. He had opened many new facets of history—institutional research into the University of Illinois and the New York *Evening Post*, a venture into state history treated as a synthesis, and a decided revision of the Robber Baron portraits and business history through the greater use of personal and company correspondence, instead of reliance on exposé-type sources alone. Civil War revisionism had been enriched and given better balance through a fuller consideration of the race factor. It is surprising that in an age when the race adjustment factor in contemporary civilization had become so evident that there still remained so many "revisionists" who doubted that it could have been so important in the coming of the Civil War.

Nevins was a popularizer in the best sense of the word. He knew how to communicate a feeling for the past even to those whose interests lay far afield. His reviews and essays in *The American Heritage,* the New York *Times,* and the *Saturday Review of Literature* heightened the interest in American history for countless readers. Entire bookshelves of edited letters, usually made available for the first time, added freshness to the subject. He trained archivists through his Oral History project, which made tape recordings of important contemporaries permanently available and directed the theses of innumerable able graduate students. Faced by the rapid multiplication of historical sources, he called for more co-operative scholarship. His own life was one of such constant self-development, whether in literary style, historical method, or philosophical understanding, that his retirement year seemed to coincide with the apogee of his powers.

The success of Allan Nevins as a man who could make history live was cited in 1953 by a connoisseur of good writing, Professor Samuel E. Morison of Harvard, whose history department was studded with Pulitzer Prize winners. Morison had written histories of New England's life and culture, the biography of Columbus, and a monumental history of United States naval operations during World War II—all of them presented attractively as well as authoritatively. Like Nevins (and Theodore Roosevelt before him), he complained that history-writing in this country had descended to a mediocre level since the days of the craft-conscious William Bradford and Robert Beverley and the great literary historians of the nineteenth century. One side effect of German seminar training had been to produce dull monographs and uninspired scholars who toiled so that journalists, novelists, and freelance writers might spin. The public now preferred to learn their history through Margaret Mitchell and Kenneth Roberts:

> The few professional historians who have had a popular following or appeal during the last thirty years are either men like Allan Nevins who were trained in some juicier profession like journalism, or men and women like the Beards who had the sense to break loose young from academic trammels.

Although this was too harsh a judgment by 1953, considering the number of stylists among historians, there was substance in the charge. Morison called upon young historians to cultivate style and a disciplined imagination; to express themselves with clarity, vigor, and objectivity; to train themselves by such means as reading the ancient and English classics; and to enhance realism by making a direct contact with life through personal experience.[17]

8

The story of American history-writing may well conclude with the productive career of Allan Nevins. Although his students liked to speak of him admiringly as a maverick indifferent to the glories of the Ph.D. degree which he never attained and equally indifferent to the inner politics of the historical associations, he prepared a generation of Columbia scholars for professorial posts and he did become president of the American Historical Association in 1959. Preferring accurate narration to ambitious syntheses, he avoided the integrative approach of certain other noted Columbia historians—Beard, Osgood, Robinson, Burgess, Dunning, and Hacker. Like most historians of this era, he felt suspicious of abstract philosophies of history, of those who used "a pound of interpretation for an ounce of fact," or of those who emulated Spengler or Toynbee in a search for ultimates in historical meaning. He preferred to recapture the panorama of the past rather than to focus upon pressing social issues.

He and the average historian of the 1950s were no longer in search of scientific determinants in history. The Darwinian analogy in history (and in most of the social studies) had died within his lifetime, and the friends of Frederick Jackson Turner were trying to save the Master's teachings by stripping his theories of outworn evolutionary determinants. Beard's economic emphasis was under severe attack from younger historians, and even the Soviet Union's spectacular rise failed to make the Marxist economic synthesis palatable to the academician of the mid-century. Nevins's erstwhile colleague, Henry Commager, might speak of himself as a disciple of Parrington, but he carefully avoided the naïve Jeffersonian agrarianism as a *leitmotif*. Nevins and his generation gave much more attention to the role of accident and human personality as factors in a complex of multiple causation.

Attractive narrative drawn from rich sources and tempered by shrewd insights was the Nevins forte and the working ideal of many historians. He lamented the lack of stylists like Parkman or Bancroft, but it was indeed fortunate that their naïve ethnocentrism had greatly declined. Although Nevins showed sympathies for the role of the Anglo-Saxon, the day of the racist had gone. If Nevins was indeed the successor of James Ford Rhodes as the monumental historian of the Civil War, he and his fellow-historians were increasingly free of the anti-Negro or imperialist assumptions of Rhodes, Dunning, Burgess, and Phillips. While he might share the Phillips thesis that slavery and race adjustment were the main causes of the Civil War, he rejected the basic prejudices with which the Georgian had surrounded his total analysis. Thus, the historian had come abreast of the more enlightened concepts of race relations in the decade after Hitler.

Nevins could claim greater consistency of interpretation in his books on the entrepreneurs than those who swung to conservatism only in the Eisenhower years. He built on an optimistic faith in the continuing material and moral success of a civilization that was heavily indebted to the ingenuity of the businessman and technicians. But he laid no similar emphasis upon the constructive energies of organized labor, for he usually observed a passive though sympathetic role. In dealing with businessmen or politicians like Cleveland for that matter, he was concerned particularly with moral questions of character; Rockefeller and Ford (up to 1914) met his test, just as Cleveland did as a man of courage. By mid-century, few historians cared to defend the Robber Baron stereotype.

Although Nevins did his share of hasty writing (especially on diplomatic history) and was accused of a lack of penetration, his later works show a developing maturity that was far above the professional level. He did not scintillate like Henry Adams, but he also escaped the trail of erratic judgments that the brilliant New Englander left behind. His own personal values and beliefs are far less intrusive than those of most American historians since William Bradford's day. But they are present and direct his selection of materials. He is clearly on the side of late nineteenth-century liberalism—free enterprise (though unopposed to bigness), low tariffs, co-operative internationalism somewhat favorable to England, conservative credit policies, the ideal of objectivity, moderation, rational compromise, and the central role of integrity as a guide in politics and business.

Nevins has been as industrious as any famous historian in the utilization of monumental manuscript and archival sources, even introducing the "oral history" approach. While he has enjoyed the aid of competent assistants on a scale unavailable to most historians, none could minimize his amazing industry; those who sought him were apt to find him buried for many hours at a reader's desk in a library or an archives building. He cut long luncheon meetings short to hurry to do his research with the same personal application that he had made at his chores as a farm boy in Illinois.

But even as Nevins retired, there were young historians building upon the type of craftsmanship that he represented and going beyond him in the tools of analysis. Thus, it was clear that his skill as a biographer, which had lacked the psychological depth of a Lytton Strachey, would be supplemented by the new emphasis upon psychology and psychiatry—although the latter was not yet so clearly in evidence. The growing preoccupation with intellectual history meant added meaning by stressing the role of ideas in all aspects of history—an area that the narrative emphasis had neglected. Philosophers focused their attention on interpretations of history and helped historians to remove some of the naïve illusions of mechanical objectivity. Historiography demonstrated the wreckage of elaborate interpretations that told more about the historian than about the event. And such warnings could only spur on a more meticulous and critical search for a reasonable view of the past.

Bibliographic Notes

CHAPTER 1

BRADFORD, MATHER, AND THE PURITAN MISSION IN HISTORY

1. Samuel G. Drake (ed.), William Hubbard's *The History of the Indian Wars in New England* (Roxbury, Mass., 1865), *Introduction*, xxiv.
2. James W. Thompson, *A History of Historical Writing* (Macmillan, 1942), I, *passim;* Herbert J. Muller, *The Uses of the Past* (Oxford, 1952), 170-76.
3. Thomas G. Wright, *Literary Culture in Early New England, 1620-1730* (Yale, 1920), *passim.*
4. Arnold J. Toynbee (ed.), *Greek Historical Thought* (Mentor, 1952), *Introduction*, 53-9, 185-9.
5. Thompson, op. cit. I, 626.
6. "The Diary of Cotton Mather," Mass. Hist. Society *Collections,* 7th Series, VII, Part I (Boston, 1911), 548.
7. See S. E. Morison's *Introduction* to his modernized version *Of Plymouth Plantation, 1620-1647* (Knopf, 1952); E. F. Bradford, "Conscious Art in Bradford's History of Plymouth Plantation," *The New England Quarterly,* I (1928), 133-57. The Bradford text used here is the 1920 edition of William T. Davis.
8. See *Introduction* to Perry Miller and T. H. Johnson (eds.), *The Puritans* (American Book, 1938). Background material appears in Harvey Wish, *Society and Thought in Early America* (Longmans, Green, 1950), 24-33.
9. L. G. Tyler (ed.), *Narratives of Early Virginia, 1606-1625* (Scribner's, 1907), 326. Michael Kraus discusses many lesser-known colonial historians in *The Writing of American History* (Univ. of Oklahoma, 1953), 3-56.

CHAPTER 2

THE ENLIGHTENMENT: HUTCHINSON AND THE TORY EMPHASIS

1. Carl Becker, "Progress," *Encyclopaedia of the Social Sciences.*
2. In 1947 Dr. Louis Wright edited an attractive edition and wrote a useful introduction to Robert Beverley's *The History and Present State of Virginia* for the University of North Carolina Press.
3. R. C. Beatty, *William Byrd of Westover* (Houghton Mifflin, 1932).
4. Theodore Hornberger, "The Science of Thomas Prince," *The New England Quarterly*, 9 (March 1936), 26-42; Max Savelle, *Seeds of Liberty* (Knopf, 1948).
5. Taken from a microfilmed copy of Thomas Prince's *A Chronological History of New England* (in Western Reserve University Freiberger Library).
6. L. S. Mayo (ed.), *Hutchinson's The History of the Colony and Province of Massachusetts Bay* (Harvard, 1936), 3 vols.; James K. Hosmer, *The Life of Thomas Hutchinson* (Houghton Mifflin, 1896), 85.
7. "William Smith," *Dictionary of American Biography.*
8. "Cadwallader Colden," ibid.
9. Grace A. Cockroft, *The Public Life of George Chalmers* (Columbia U., 1939).

CHAPTER 3

JARED SPARKS AND THE DOMINANCE OF THE FEDERALIST-WHIG HISTORIANS

1. Orin G. Libby, "Ramsay as a Plagiarist," *Amer. Hist. Rev.*, 7 (1901), 697-703; S. G. Fisher, "The Legendary and Myth-Making Process of the American Revolution," Amer. *Philosophical Society Proceedings*, 51 (1912), 53-75; William Foran, "John Marshall as a Historian," *Amer. Hist. Rev.*, 43 (1937-38), 51-64; A. J. Beveridge, *John Marshall* (Houghton Mifflin, 1916-19), 4 vols., III, chap. 5.
2. W. A. Bryan, *George Washington in American Literature, 1775-1865* (Columbia U., 1952); Harold Kellock, *Parson Weems of the Cherry Tree* (Century, 1928).
3. H. B. Adams, *The Life and Writings of Jared Sparks* (Houghton Mifflin, 1893), 2 vols.
4. S. T. Williams, *Washington Irving* (Oxford, 1935), 2 vols. Probably the greatest George Washington biography came in Douglas S. Freeman's six volumes issued by Scribner's during 1948-54. Freeman's exhaustive researches and well-known dramatic presentation made Washington and his environment most convincing. The author dwelt upon the great crises in Washington's life in a more optimistic atmosphere than that of the tragic subjects in his definitive *R. E. Lee* (4 vols., Scribner's, 1934-35) and *Lee's Lieutenants* (3 vols., Scribner's, 1942-44). With Washington, said Freeman, "Disaster is never without hope."
5. Robert L. Brunhouse, "David Ramsay's Publication Problems, 1784-1808," *The Papers of the Bibliographical Society of America*, 39 (1945), 51-67.

6. Alice Brown, *Mercy Warren* (Scribner's, 1896); Maud M. Hutcheson, "Mercy Warren, 1728-1814," *William and Mary Quarterly,* 10 (1953), 378-402.
7. C. W. Cole, "Jeremy Belknap, Pioneer Nationalist," *The New England Quarterly,* 10 (1937), 743-51.
8. Harry R. Warfel, *Noah Webster, Schoolmaster to America* (Macmillan, 1936).
9. James K. Morse, *Jedidiah Morse, A Champion of New England Orthodoxy* (Columbia U., 1939).

CHAPTER 4

RICHARD HILDRETH, UTILITARIAN PHILOSOPHER

1. Martha M. Pingel, *An American Utilitarian: Richard Hildreth as a Philosopher* (Columbia U., 1948).
2. Donald E. Emerson, *Richard Hildreth* (Johns Hopkins, 1946).
3. Idem, "Hildreth, Draper, and Scientific History," in Eric F. Goldman (ed.), *Historiography and Urbanization* (Johns Hopkins, 1941); Alfred H. Kelly, "Richard Hildreth," in William T. Hutchinson (ed.), *The Marcus W. Jernegan Essays in American Historiography* (Univ. of Chicago, 1937).
4. See Arthur M. Schlesinger, Jr., "The Problem of Richard Hildreth," *The New England Quarterly* 13 (1940), 223-45.

CHAPTER 5

GEORGE BANCROFT AND GERMAN IDEALISM

1. "Romanticism," *Encyclopaedia of the Social Sciences.*
2. M. A. De Wolfe Howe, *The Life and Letters of George Bancroft* (Scribner's, 1908), 2 vols.
3. D. E. Lee and R. N. Beck have thoroughly explored the meanings of a confusing term in "The Meaning of Historicism," *Amer. Hist. Rev.,* 59 (1954), 568-77.
4. The best biography is Russel B. Nye's *George Bancroft, Brahmin Rebel* (Knopf, 1945).
5. Pieter Geyl has written a critical appraisal of Michelet in *Debates with Historians* (Meridian Books, 1958), 70-108.
6. This appears in George Bancroft's *Literary and Historical Miscellanies* (Harper, 1855), 408-35.
7. Among the more useful modern evaluations of Bancroft are N. H. Dawes and F. T. Nichols, "Revaluing George Bancroft," *The New England Quarterly,* 6 (1933), 278-93; Orie W. Long, "George Bancroft," *Literary Pioneers* (Harvard, 1935); Watt Stewart, "George Bancroft," in the *Jernegan Essays,* op. cit.
8. John W. Burgess, *Reminiscences of an American Scholar* (Columbia U., 1934).

CHAPTER 6

FRANCIS PARKMAN AND THE PAGEANT OF THE WILDERNESS

1. Most basic is Mason Wade's excellent edition of *The Journals of Francis Parkman* (Harper, 1947), 2 vols.; still useful is Charles H. Farnham, *A Life of Francis Parkman* (Little, Brown, 1900) and Wilbur L. Schramm's introductory essay to *Francis Parkman* (American Book, 1938).
2. Howard H. Peckham, *Pontiac and the Indian Uprising* (Princeton, 1947).
3. J. H. Kennedy expresses qualified praise for Parkman's treatment of the Jesuits in *Jesuit and Savage in New France* (Yale, 1950).
4. The most detailed of recent evaluations of Parkman's histories appear in O. A. Pease, *Parkman's History* (Yale, 1953); Joe P. Smith, "Francis Parkman," in the *Jernegan Essays,* op. cit.
5. Parkman in *The Nation,* December 23, 1869; Farnham, *Parkman,* 242-51, 268-9.
6. Theodore Roosevelt to Parkman, July 13, 1889, in Elting E. Morison (ed.), *The Letters of Theodore Roosevelt* I, 172-3.
7. *The Independent,* November 24, 1892.
8. Henry Adams to Parkman, December 21, 1884, in Harold D. Cater (ed.), *Henry Adams and His Friends* (Houghton Mifflin, 1947), 133-7.
9. George M. Wrong, *The Rise and Fall of New France* (Macmillan, 1928), I, 491.
10. A. L. Burt, *A Short History of Canada* (Univ. of Minn., 1942), 264.
11. Raymond C. Miller, "Theodore Roosevelt, Historian," in J. L. Cate and E. N. Anderson (eds.), *Medieval and Historiographical Essays in Honor of James W. Thompson* (Univ. of Chicago, 1938); H. J. Thornton, "Theodore Roosevelt," in *Jernegan Essays,* op. cit.

CHAPTER 7

FROM FISKE TO GIPSON

1. "John Gorham Palfrey," *Dictionary of American Biography.*
2. See the thorough study of Fiske in Patrick D. Hazard, "John Fiske as American Scholar," (doctoral dissertation, Western Reserve Univ., 1957).
3. James Schouler, "John Fiske," Massachusetts Hist. Soc. *Proceedings,* 2nd Ser., 15 (1901-2), 193-200.
4. George L. Beer, "John Fiske," *Critic* 39 (1901), 117-18.
5. J. B. Sanders, "John Fiske," *Jernegan Essays,* 144-70.
6. Dixon R. Fox, *Herbert Levi Osgood* (Columbia U., 1924).
7. Homer J. Coppock, "Herbert Levi Osgood," *Miss. Vall. Hist. Rev.,* 19 (1932-33), 394-403.
8. Grace A. Cockroft, "George Louis Beer," in Herman Ausubel et al. (eds.), *Some Modern Historians of Britain* (Dryden Press, 1951).
9. A. S. Eisenstadt, *Charles McLean Andrews* (Columbia U., 1956).

10. Lawrence H. Gipson, "Charles McLean Andrews and the Re-orientation of the Study of American Colonial History," *The Pennsylvania Magazine of History and Biography*, 59 (July 1935), 209-22.
11. S. E. Morison, "Edward Channing," Mass. Hist. Soc. *Proceedings*, 64 (1930-32), 250-84.
12. C. R. Fish, "Edward Channing," *Current History* 33 (1931), 862-7.
13. J. A. De Novo, "Edward Channing's 'Great Work' Twenty Years After," *Miss. Vall. Hist. Rev.*, 39 (1952-53), 257-74; Ralph R. Fahrney, "Edward Channing," *Jernegan Essays*.
14. Review in *Amer. Hist. Rev.*, 60 (1955), 614-15; also review by Stanley Pargellis, ibid. 60 (1955), 596-8.
15. L. B. Wright, *New Interpretations of American Colonial History* (Amer. Hist. Assoc., 1959).

CHAPTER 8

JOHN BACH MCMASTER AND THE RISE OF SOCIAL HISTORY

1. Lucy M. Salmon, *The Newspaper and the Historian* (Oxford, 1923).
2. Eric Goldman, *John Bach McMaster, American Historian* (Univ. of Penn., 1943).
3. J. B. McMaster, "The Social Functions of United States History," *The Fourth Yearbook of the National Herbert Society* (Chicago, 1898), 30.
4. See his lectures at Western Reserve University in 1903 along this line, "The Acquisition of Political, Social, and Industrial Rights of Man In America," (Cleveland, 1903); and his "Old Standards of Public Morals," *Ann. Rep. of the Amer. Hist. Assoc.* I (1905), 57-8; and his *With the Fathers* (Appleton, 1896).
5. William Hutchinson, "John Bach McMaster," *Jernegan Essays*, 122-43
6. R. F. Nichols, "Ellis P. Oberholtzer," *Dictionary of American History*
7. Review in the *Amer. Hist. Rev.*, 23 (1918), 676-8.
8. Edward Stanwood in ibid. 28 (1923), 337-9.
9. In ibid. 33 (1927), 162-4.
10. T. C. Smith in ibid. 37 (1932), 569-70.
11. In ibid. 44 (1939), 412-14. E. D. Ross in the *Miss. Vall. Hist. Rev.* 2 (1937), 341-50 and J. D. Hicks in the same journal, 24 (1937), 266-7 were no more enthusiastic than those in the *AHR*.
12. In William E. Lingelbach (ed.), *Approaches to American Social History* (Appleton-Century, 1937).
13. See William Diamond, "On the Dangers of an Urban Interpretation of History," in Eric Goldman (ed.), *Historiography and Urbanization* (Johns Hopkins, 1941).
14. E. N. Saveth, *American Historians and European Immigrants, 1875-1925* (Columbia U., 1948).
15. J. P. Cadden, *The Historiography of the American Catholic Church, 1785-1943* (Catholic U., 1944).
16. Summarized from H. Wish, *Society and Thought in Modern America* (Longmans, Green, 1952), chapters 10 and 11.

CHAPTER 9

HENRY ADAMS AND THE DREAM OF A SCIENCE OF HISTORY

1. For the historiographical background in Europe see G. P. Gooch, *History and Historians of the Nineteenth Century* (Longmans, Green, 1913), 87, 572-4; for a critical but well-balanced view of Ranke see Pieter Geyl, *Debates with Historians* (Meridian, 1958), chap. 1; much more favorable is Herbert Butterfield, *Man on His Past* (Cambridge U., 1955).
2. J. C. Levenson, *The Mind and Art of Henry Adams* (Houghton Mifflin, 1957); Elizabeth Stevenson, *Henry Adams* (Macmillan, 1955); Ernest Samuels, *The Young Henry Adams* (Harvard, 1948) and *Henry Adams, the Middle Years* (Harvard, 1958); and the excellent Introduction in Harold D. Cater, *Henry Adams and His Friends* (Houghton Mifflin, 1947).
3. Letter of Jan. 24, 1883, in Cater, op. cit. 125-6.
4. Henry S. Commager, "Henry Adams," *Jernegan Essays.*
5. Max I. Baym, *The French Education of Henry Adams* (Columbia U., 1951).
6. William Jordy, *Henry Adams, Scientific Historian* (Yale, 1952).
7. For numerous references to Adams and the Jews see the Index in Cater, op. cit. as well as other printed collections of Adams's letters.
8. For this and related essays see Charles F. Adams, Jr., and Henry Adams, *Chapters of Erie and Other Essays* (Holt, 1886).
9. Charles F. Adams, *An Autobiography* (Houghton Mifflin, 1916).

CHAPTER 10

TURNER AND THE MOVING FRONTIER

1. Fulmer Mood, "Turner's Formative Period," in E. Edwards (ed.), *The Early Writings of Frederick Jackson Turner* (Univ. of Wisconsin, 1938), 3-39; Carl Becker, "Frederick Jackson Turner," in Howard W. Odum (ed.), *American Masters of Social Science* (Holt, 1927), 273-318; and Ray A. Billington's informative historiographical survey in *The American Frontier* (Amer. Hist. Assoc., 1958); Wilbur R. Jacobs, "Frederick J. Turner—Master Teacher," *Pacific Historical Review,* 23 (1954), 49-58.
2. Cornelius Tacitus, "Germany and Its Tribes," in *Complete Works of Tacitus* (Random House, 1942), 709-32. See also James Malin, "The Turner-Mackinder Space Concept of History," *Essays in Historiography* (Lawrence, Kansas, 1946).
3. F. J. Turner, "Significance of the Frontier in American History," *The Frontier in American History* (Holt, 1921), 1-38.
4. J. L. Sellers, "Before We Were Members—The MVHA," *Miss. Vall. Hist. Rev.,* 40 (1953-54), 3-24.
5. Friedrich Ratzel, *The History of Mankind* (Macmillan, 1896), 3 vols. The first edition appeared during 1885-88.
6. In *Annual Report of the Amer. Hist. Assoc.,* 1896, I, 281-96.
7. F. J. Turner, "Problems in American History," *Aegis,* VII (1892), 72.

8. Reprinted in F. J. Turner, *The Frontier in American History*, 311-34.
9. Reprinted in ibid. 243.
10. F. J. Turner, *The Significance of Sections in American History*, 315-39. For an analysis of Turner's methods by one of his eminent students see Merle Curti, "The Section and the Frontier in American History," in Stuart Rice (ed.), *Methods in Social Science* (University of Chicago, 1931).
11. See Curtis Nettels, "Frederick Jackson Turner and the New Deal," *Wisconsin Magazine of History*, 17 (1934), 257-65.
12. The critical articles mentioned here are conveniently collected in G. R. Taylor (ed.), *The Turner Theses* (D. C. Heath, 1949).
13. John Caughey, *Hubert Howe Bancroft: Historian of the West* (Univ. of Calif., 1946); H. H. Bancroft, *Retrospection, Political and Personal* (New York, 1912).
14. Solon J. Buck, "Clarence W. Alvord, Historian," *Miss. Vall. Hist. Rev.*, 15 (1928-29), 309-20; Marion Dargan, Jr., "Clarence Walworth Alvord," *Jernegan Essays*, 323-38.
15. Earl Pomeroy, "Frederick L. Paxson and His Approach to History," *Miss. Vall. Hist. Rev.*, 39 (1952-53), 673-92.
16. For the application of the Turner ideas abroad see Ray Billington, *The American Frontier*, 22-9. An English historian, H. Hale Bellot, makes some cogent comments upon the recent historiography of the frontier in *American History and American Historians* (University of Oklahoma, 1952).

CHAPTER 11

ABOLITIONISTS AND REVISIONISTS: 1880-1910

1. E. F. Goldman, "Hermann E. von Holst," *Miss. Vall. Hist. Rev.*, 23 (1937), 515; C. R. Wilson, "Hermann Eduard von Holst," *Jernegan Essays*, 60-85; "Hermann E. von Holst," *Dictionary of American Biography.*
2. The best surveys of Civil War historiography appear in Thomas J. Pressly, *Americans Interpret Their Civil War* (Princeton, 1954) and Howard K. Beale, "What Historians Have Said about the Civil War," *Theory and Practice in Historical Study: A Report of the Committee on Historiography* (Social Science Research Council Bulletin 54, 1946); and Louis Ruchames, "Charles Sumner and American Historiography," *The Journal of Negro History*, 38 (1953), 139-60.
3. For a thoughtful evaluation of this and other presidential addresses of the American Historical Association up to 1945 see Hermann Ausubel, *Historians and Their Craft* (Columbia U., 1950).
4. Lewis E. Ellis, "James Schouler," *Jernegan Essays*, 84-101. Some of the best illustrations of the Reconstruction theories of the leading historians appear in Edwin C. Rozwenc (ed.), *Reconstruction in the South* (D. C. Heath, 1952).
5. The best biography of Rhodes is Robert Cruden, "James Ford Rhodes, Middle Class Historian," (doctoral dissertation, Western Reserve University, 1958); see also M. A. De Wolfe Howe, *James Ford Rhodes,*

American Historian (D. Appleton, 1929) and Raymond C. Miller, "James Ford Rhodes," *Jernegan Essays*, 171-90.

6. One critical reviewer, John R. Lynch, declared in *The Journal of Negro History* that ". . . so far as the Reconstruction period is concerned, it is not only inaccurate and unreliable but it is the most biased, partisan, and prejudiced historical work I have ever read." Ibid. II (1917), 345. There are some relevant comments on these race attitudes in John A. Garraty (ed.), *The Barber and the Historian; the Correspondence of George A. Myers and James Ford Rhodes, 1910-1923* (Ohio Historical Society, 1956).

7. In James F. Rhodes, *Historical Essays* (Macmillan, 1909), 2-14.

8. John W. Burgess, *Reminiscences of an American Scholar* (Columbia U., 1934); Bert James Loewenberg, "John William Burgess, the Scientific Method, and the Hegelian Philosophy of History," *Miss. Vall. Hist. Rev.*, 42 (1955-56), 490-509.

9. W. G. Brown in *Amer. Hist. Rev.*, 8 (1902-3), 150-52.

CHAPTER 12

Ulrich B. Phillips and the Image of the South

1. Wendell Holmes Stephenson, *The South Lives in History* (Louisiana State U., 1955), 58-94; Wood Gray, "Ulrich B. Phillips," *Jernegan Essays*, 354-73.

2. See Introduction by Harvey Wish (ed.), Frederick Law Olmsted, *The Slave States* (G. P. Putnam, 1959), 7-37.

3. See Avery O. Craven, "The 'Turner Theories' and the South," *Journal of Southern History*, 5 (1937), 291-314.

4. In *American Historical Review*, 35 (1929), 133-5.

5. In *Miss. Vall. Hist. Rev.*, 17 (1930-31), 160-3.

6. T. J. Pressly, *Americans Interpret Their Civil War*, op. cit.

7. Carter Woodson in *Miss. Vall. Hist. Rev.*, 5 (1918-19), 480-2 and in *The Jour. of Negro Hist.*, 4 (1914), 102-3.

8. In *Jour. of Negro Hist.*, 14 (1929), 534-6.

9. For recent historiography see Otis A. Singletary, *The South in American History* (American Hist. Assoc., 1957).

CHAPTER 13

Charles Austin Beard and the Economic Interpretation of History

1. William A. Glaser, "Algie Martin Simons and Marxism in America," *Miss. Vall. Hist. Rev.*, 41 (1954-55), 419-34.

2. Harry Elmer Barnes, "James Harvey Robinson," in Odum (ed.), *American Masters of Social Science*, op. cit. 321-408.

3. Howard K. Beale (ed.), *Charles A. Beard* (Univ. of Kentucky, 1954). A very valuable symposium.

4. In *Amer. Hist. Rev.*, 39 (1934), 219-29.

5. Very useful for the controversy over relativism, in addition to those sources mentioned, are Lloyd R. Sorenson, "Charles A. Beard and German Historiographical Thought," *Miss. Vall. Hist. Rev.*, 42 (1955-56), 274-87; Chester McA. Destler, "Some Observations on Contemporary Historical Theory," *Amer. Hist. Rev.*, 55 (1950), 503-29.
6. Somewhat in the Beard-Parrington-Curti tradition of studying social and economic ideas among representative Americans, Joseph G. Dorfman has made the most comprehensive survey of the economic ideas, attitudes, and beliefs of influential Americans since colonial beginnings. In so doing, he had added depth to American history. *The Economic Mind in American Civilization* (Viking, 1946-59), 5 vols.

CHAPTER 14

Parrington and the Rise of Intellectual History

1. Howard M. Jones, *The Life of Moses Coit Tyler* (Univ. of Michigan, 1933); John Higham, "The Rise of American Intellectual History," *Amer. Hist. Rev.*, 56 (1951), 453-71.
2. W. T. Utter, "Vernon Louis Parrington," *Jernegan Essays*, 399-408.
3. In *Saturday Review of Literature*, 3 (1926-27), 925-6.
4. In *Yale Review*, 17 (1927-28), 382-4.
5. In *International Journal of Ethics*, 38 (1927-28), 112-15.
6. New York *Times Book Review*, May 1, 1927, 32 (1927), 3.
7. Granville Hicks, "The Critical Principles of V. L. Parrington," *Science and Society*, 3 (1939), 443-60.
8. Lionel Trilling, "Reality in America," *The Stature of Theodore Dreiser*, (Indiana U., 1955), passim.
9. Richard Hofstadter, "Parrington and the Jeffersonian Tradition," *Jour. of the History of Ideas*, 2 (1941), 391-400; Oscar Cargill, who emphatically rejects Parrington's Jeffersonian agrarianism as oversimplified, proposes a new "Ideodynamics," a descriptive study of ideologies and of the forces which they exert, in *Intellectual America: Ideas on the March* (Macmillan, 1948), Introduction.
10. This and other significant essays appear in Carl Becker's *Everyman His Own Historian* (Crofts, 1935).
11. Ibid. 233-55.
12. Ibid. "The Marxian Philosophy of History."
13. Pratt's able colleagues at the University of Buffalo, Richard Heindel and Selig Adler also wrote from a cultural point of view.

CHAPTER 15

Allan Nevins and Recent Historiography

1. "Allan Nevins," in Stanley J. Kunitz (ed.), *Twentieth Century Authors* (H. W. Wilson, 1955); Robert J. Terry, "The Social and Intellectual Ideas of Allan Nevins" (master of arts dissertation at Western Reserve University, 1958).

2. In *Miss. Vall. Hist. Rev.*, 18 (1931-32), 108-11; see also Henry B. Learned's more qualified estimate in *Amer. Hist. Rev.*, 36 (1930-31), 843-4.

3. Elbert J. Benton in the *Miss. Vall. Hist. Rev.*, 19 (1932-33), 597-8; and Arthur C. Cole in the *Amer. Hist. Rev.*, 39 (1933-34), 351-3.

4. J. G. Randall praises Nevins's skill, readability, knowledge of the sources, and familiarity with the period in the *Amer. Hist. Rev.*, 42 (1936-37), 802-4.

5. *Jour. of Economic History*, 9 (1949), 184-208; see also critical view of Chester Destler, "Entrepreneurial Leadership among the Robber Barons," *Jour. of Economic Hist.*, 6 (1946), 28-49.

6. In *Miss. Vall. Hist. Rev.*, 28 (1941-42), 119-21.

7. In *Amer. Hist. Rev.*, 47 (1941-42), 163-5. Elmer Ellis thinks that the *Study in Power* excels the previous work on Rockefeller and "is certain to be a significant authority for many years." *Miss. Vall. Hist. Rev.*, 40 (1953-54), 751-2; Vincent P. Carosso praises its dispassionate quality among other virtues in *Amer. Hist. Rev.*, 59 (1953-54), 157-9.

8. Chester Destler upholds H. D. Lloyd's unfavorable picture of the Standard Oil Company against Nevins's favorable view in "Wealth Against Commonwealth 1894 and 1944," *Amer. Hist. Rev.*, 50 (1944), 49-72; and Thomas C. Cochran raises some fundamental questions concerning the "social desirability of monopoly through successful competition and the support of medical research and education from the tax levied on consumers by monopoly-supported prices." From "Inquiries into American Wealth," *The Virginia Quarterly Review*, 17 (1941), 310.

9. Two vols., (Scribner's, 1954, 1957).

10. In *Amer. Hist. Rev.*, 59 (1953-54), 956-7.

11. Reynold M. Wik in *Miss. Vall. Hist. Rev.*, 41 (1954-55).

12. J. D. Hicks on two vols. of *Ordeal of the Union* in *Amer. Hist. Rev.*, 53 (1947-48), 845-6.

13. In *Yale Review*, 37 (1947-48), 343-5.

14. Roy F. Nichols, "The Kansas and Nebraska Act: A Century of Historiography," *Miss. Vall. Hist. Rev.*, 43 (1956-57), 196-7.

15. See reviews in *Miss. Vall. Hist. Rev.*, 35 (1948-49), 128-9 and *South Atlantic Quarterly*, 47 (1948), 387-92.

16. Avery Craven on *The Emergence of Lincoln* in *Yale Review*, 40 (1950-51), 722-5.

17. S. E. Morison, "History as a Literary Art," *By Land and By Sea* (Knopf, 1953), 289-98.

Index